D1121640

Progress in Psychobiology and Physiological Psychology

Volume 10

Contributors to This Volume

Gregory A. Clark

Brian Y. Cooper

Ove Franzén

I. Gormezano

Joel D. Greenspan

Takuji Kasamatsu

E. James Kehoe

Ronald E. Kettner

David G. Lavond

David A. McCormick

Beverly S. Marshall

Michael D. Mauk

Louis A. Ritz

Richard F. Thompson

Charles J. Vierck, Jr.

Progress in PSYCHOBIOLOGY AND PHYSIOLOGICAL PSYCHOLOGY

Edited by JAMES M. SPRAGUE
Department of Anatomy
The School of Medicine
University of Pennsylvania
Philadelphia, Pennsylvania

ALAN N. EPSTEIN
Leidy Laboratory
Department of Biology
University of Pennsylvania
Philadelphia, Pennsylvania

Volume 10

1983

ACADEMIC PRESS
A Subsidiary of Harcourt Brace Jovanovich, Publishers
New York • London
Paris • San Diego • San Francisco • São Paulo • Sydney • Tokyo • Toronto

ACADEMIC PRESS, INC.
111 Fifth Avenue, New York, New York 10003

United Kingdom Edition published by
ACADEMIC PRESS, INC. (LONDON) LTD.
24/28 Oval Road, London NW1 7DX

LIBRARY OF CONGRESS CATALOG CARD NUMBER: 66–29640

ISBN 0-12-542110-9

PRINTED IN THE UNITED STATES OF AMERICA

83 84 85 86 9 8 7 6 5 4 3 2 1

Contents

The Engram Found? Initial Localization of the Memory Trace for a Basic Form of Associative Learning

Richard F. Thompson
In collaboration with *David A. McCormick, David G. Lavond, Greagory A. Clark, Ronald E. Kettner, and Michael D. Mauk*

Twenty Years of Classical Conditioning Research with the Rabbit

I. Gormezano, E. James Kehoe, and Beverly S. Marshall

List of Contributors

Numbers in parentheses indicate the pages on which the authors' contributions begin.

Gregory A. Clark, Department of Psychology, Stanford University, Stanford, California 94305 (167)

Brian Y. Cooper, Department of Neuroscience and Center for Neurobiological Sciences, University of Florida, College of Medicine, Gainesville, Florida 32610 (113)

Ove Franzén, Department of Psychology, University of Uppsala, Uppsala, Sweden (113)

I. Gormezano, Department of Psychology, University of Iowa, Iowa City, Iowa 52242 (197)

Joel D. Greenspan, Department of Physiology, School of Medicine, University of North Carolina, Chapel Hill, North Carolina 27514 (113)

Takuji Kasamatsu, Division of Biology, California Institute of Technology, Pasadena, California 91125 (1)

E. James Kehoe, Department of Psychology, University of New South Wales, Kensington, New South Wales, Australia (197)

Ronald E. Kettner, Department of Psychology, Stanford University, Stanford, California 94305 (167)

David G. Lavond, Department of Psychology, Stanford University, Stanford, California 94305 (167)

David M. McCormick, Department of Psychology, Stanford University, Stanford, California 94305 (167)

Beverly S. Marshall, Department of Psychology, University of Iowa, Iowa City, Iowa 52242 (197)

Michael D. Mauk, Department of Psychology, Stanford University, Stanford, California 94305 (167)

Louis A. Ritz, Department of Psychology, School of Medicine, University of North Carolina, Chapel Hill, North Carolina 27514 (113)

Richard F. Thompson, Department of Psychology, Stanford University, Stanford, California 94305 (167)

Charles J. Vierck, Jr., Department of Neuroscience and Center for Neurobiological Sciences, University of Florida, College of Medicine, Gainesville, Florida 32610 (113)

Preface

This volume, like its predecessors in this series, attempts to provide contemporary and stimulating reviews and syntheses of selected areas of research relating brain mechanisms and behavior. The selection necessarily reflects the biases and limitations of the editors and therefore is not representative of all major and important developments in this field. We believe, however, that this volume of *Progress in Psychobiology and Physiological Psychology* presents articles of high quality and value to student and expert alike.

Volume 10 is composed of four chapters, two of which are closely related. Gormezano and colleagues give us an extensive and scholarly review of the principles and methods of classical conditioning, centered on the nictitating membrane response (NMR) in the rabbit. Their chapter attempts to place conditioning in this preparation in a broad experimental and theoretical context. Thompson and co-workers have beautifully analyzed the neural basis of the NMR electrophysiologically, recording from a number of brain sites. Their conclusion that the memory trace for this conditioned response is localized in the cerebellum is extremely challenging and thought provoking.

The other two chapters are unrelated to one another but cover research fields that are very active today. Vierck and his colleagues have written a critical and insightful analysis of pain sensations and responses in monkeys and humans, the effect of morphine on them, and the neural pathways in the spinal cord mediating them. The contribution of Kasamatsu synthesizes and critically reviews the elegant body of research originating in his laboratory relating the norepinephrine system of the brain and plasticity in the developing visual cortex.

As in the previous volumes of this series, we have asked the authors to discuss the anatomy and function of the brain in terms of behavior expressed by the organism. We have attempted to keep highly visible the importance of behavior in understanding how the brain works. Our authors have, in every case, taken advantage of the opportunity to do this, and we are very grateful to them.

We wish to thank Mary Jack for help in handling manuscripts and correspondence and keeping our records.

James M. Sprague
Alan N. Epstein

Contents of Previous Volumes

PROGRESS IN PSYCHOBIOLOGY AND PHYSIOLOGICAL PSYCHOLOGY, VOL. 10

Neuronal Plasticity Maintained by the Central Norepinephrine System in the Cat Visual Cortex

Takuji Kasamatsu
Division of Biology
California Institute of Technology
Pasadena, California

I. Postnatal Plasticity: An Answer to Selection Pressure in Evolution

In the long history of evolution, animals have acquired various mechanisms and developed different strategies by which to maximize their chances of survival. The nervous system, which includes various neurotransmitter subsystems and neurohormones, provides us with a good example of these strategies. As such, then, those structures and functions of the nervous

ISBN 0-12-542110-9

system which control an animal's behavior have to be the result of the selection pressures of evolution.

We may consider two distinctive aspects of animal behavior which are complementary to each other. One is innately determined, and the other is learned in response to the particular environments in which the individuals are placed. The former is supposed to be controlled by a type of nervous system whose structure and function are rigidly determined by genetic codes. The latter is supposed to be maintained by a group of neurons which can modify their connectivity, within the grand framework of genetics, when necessary. As an intermediate between these two extremes, a particular type of synaptic plasticity has developed in various creatures. This special type of synaptic plasticity preferentially operates, usefully or hazardously, only in the early stages of individual life (critical period). It is in studying this third type of animal behavior that our catecholamine (CA) hypothesis for synaptic plasticity has emerged and matured, as will be detailed below. Our CA hypothesis proclaims the importance of the central CA system as a morphological or chemical substrate for synaptic plasticity, especially in the immature mammalian neocortex.

Genetically determined behavior has been primarily studied in invertebrates. The analysis of spontaneous patterned motor action led to the discovery of inherited motor program tapes in the central nervous system (CNS) (e.g., Hoyle, 1970). Ikeda and Wiersma (1964) and Wiersma and Ikeda (1964), in studying the motion of the swimmerets of crayfish, derived the concept of the command interneuron that produces triggering signals to play back the programmed motor tapes. The fruit fly has also become a favorite subject in studying the genetic control of a wide variety of behavior, such as circadian activity (e.g., Konopka, 1980), courtship (Hotta and Benzer, 1976), and even a lack of learning (Dudai *et al.,* 1976; for reviews, see Benzer, 1973; Hall and Greenspan, 1979). In a temperature-sensitive mutant *Shibire,* a single gene mutation causes, at 29°C, a blockade of the neuromuscular transmission which leads, in turn, to reversible paralysis of mesothoracic flight muscles (Ikeda *et al.,* 1976).

Needless to say, learned behaviors are widely recognizable in the animal kingdom; a set of modifiable or plastic synapses (Hebb, 1949) is needed to make this second type of control possible. The neuronal circuitry which is responsible for associative learning has been studied intensively in various paradigms, from the presumably simple systems in invertebrates (e.g., *Aplysia,* Kandel, 1979; crayfish, Krasne, 1978) to the complex behavior patterns of mammals (e.g., Thompson *et al.,* 1978; also Thompson *et al.* in this volume). Furthermore, hippocampal slices from mammalian brain (rats, guinea pigs) have also been used as a model system for long-term enhancement of synaptic efficacy (Lynch *et al.,* 1977; Andersen *et al.,* 1977; Browning *et al.,* 1979; Andersen and Wigström, 1980).

To study the neuronal basis for the third type of behavior control (critical period plasticity), the neuromuscular junction and the peripheral sympathetic ganglion in frogs, newts, rats, and rabbits have provided us with useful models. Well-known examples of this type of modifiable behavior include the filial imprinting of Lorenz, which is observed in chickens and ducklings only within 15 hours or so after hatching (Hess, 1959; Bateson, 1966), the sexual imprinting in zebra finches (Immelmann, 1972), and the learning of species-specific songs by male song birds (Konishi, 1978; Nottebohm, 1980). Moreover, by exposing owlets to an abnormal visual experience, Pettigrew and Konishi (1976) observed age-dependent changes in the neuronal connectivity in the owlet visual Wulst like those seen in the visual cortex of cats and monkeys (see below). Even at the level of insects, a similar phenomenon of critical period plasticity has been described: The threshold of giant interneurons in the cricket lumbar ganglion to sound stimuli is determined by the use of cerci during the critical period after hatching (Murphy and Matsumoto, 1976; Matsumoto and Murphy, 1977).

Although by no means simple systems, single cells in the immature visual cortex of young cats and monkeys have also received particular attention in the last 2 decades as a unique animal model in examining synaptic plasticity. There are three advantages to studying a system as intricate as the mammalian brain. First, the susceptibility of immature neurons to alterations in their sensory afferents (critical period plasticity) usually lasts much longer in higher mammals than in lower ones, so that in dealing with higher mammals, it may be more feasible to intervene in the natural processes by imposing various experimental manipulations. Second, the higher mammals provide us, because of the complexity of their brain organization, with an opportunity to establish the "multiplicity" of the critical period in the same neurons depending on the number of subsystems which involve the same sets of neurons. For example, in the cat visual cortex, the start and the duration of the period for modifying binocularity differ from those defined for directionality of visual cortical cells (e.g., Daw and Wyatt, 1976), and the two sublaminae in layer IVc of the monkey visual cortex apparently provide the different durations in sensitivity for the reexpansion of the ocular dominance column following reverse suture of the eyelid (e.g., Le Vay *et al.,* 1979, 1980). Third, and most importantly, the results from higher mammal models may provide us with direct cues to understanding similar clinical problems in humans. For example, a significant proportion of the population (4% in the United States) is reported to suffer from the lack of stereopsis or depth perception (Julesz, 1971). Psychophysical studies in humans suggest not only that some types of visual deficits may be due to abnormal visual experiences in infancy but also that the critical period for the correction of the central effects of a squint lasts only up to 3 years of age (Banks *et al.*, 1975; Hohmann and Creutzfeldt, 1975). Neurophysiological and morphological studies in cats and monkeys have provided insight into the neural mechanisms underlying such abnormalities by producing essentially similar changes in these animals, although the duration of the critical period for normal maturation of their binocular vision is presumably far shorter. A clinical study showed that covering one eye of an infant (for therapeutic purposes) by an eyepatch for only 1 week caused a severe decrease in visual acuity later in adulthood (Awaya *et al.*, 1974). It is also reported that uncorrected astigmatism in childhood causes poor stereoscopic vision as well as a decrease in the sensitivity to a certain orientation in the affected eye in adulthood (Freeman *et al.*, 1972; Mitchell *et al.*, 1973).

In the following section, I review briefly some topics on synaptic plasticity in the developing visual cortex, including a discussion of several factors which are suggested as possible mechanisms underlying cortical plasticity. This will serve as a general introduction to our CA hypothesis, which strongly suggests the importance of a central catecholaminergic system, especially the norepinephrine (NE)-containing one, for enhancing synaptic plasticity in the mammalian neocortex.

Readers who want to know more about synaptic plasticity in the central visual system may refer to several reviews by other authors (Barlow, 1975; Grobstein and Chow, 1975; Daniels and Pettigrew, 1976; Pettigrew, 1978; Blakemore, 1978). Likewise, good review articles are available for the central catecholamine system and the locus coeruleus (LC) (Amaral and Sinnamon, 1977; Coyle, 1977; Maeda and Shimizu, 1978; Bloom, 1978; Moore and Bloom, 1979; Björklund and Stenevi, 1979; Emson and Lindvall, 1979).

II. Visual Cortical Plasticity in Higher Mammals

A. Experimental Amblyopia ex Anopsia: Changes in Binocularity

1. *A Basic Finding*

In the early sixties, Wiesel and Hubel (1963b) introduced a simple animal model to study amblyopia ex anopsia (malfunction in vision due to nonretinal neuronal factors in the central visual pathways). They closed one eye of young kittens by either surgical lid suture or the use of a black eyepatch before the natural opening of the eye (7–10 days of age). Single-unit recordings, made when the animal reached adulthood, demonstrated a lack of binocularly driven cells in the visual cortex of such animals. They were unable to drive cells in the visual cortex by stimulation of the occluded eye. This finding was in sharp contrast to that seen in the normal visual cortex, in which more than 80% of cells are driven through both eyes (Hubel and Wiesel, 1962). Soon they found that the receptive fields of single cells in the lateral geniculate nucleus (LGN) were functionally quite normal in animals which had been monocularly deprived (Wiesel and Hubel, 1963a). They then concluded that the changes in the ocular dominance distribution following monocular lid suture take place at the geniculo-cortical synapses in the visual cortex. These changes occur quickly: Within 3 days of monocular lid suture, the visual cortex can be totally dominated by monocular cells that respond to stimulation of the nondeprived eye (Hubel and Wiesel, 1970; Olson and Freeman, 1975). Other paradigms, such as artificial squinting caused by cutting a lateral rectus muscle of one eye or alternating monocular occlusion, resulted in the disappearance of normal binocular cells, and all cells in the cortex responded to stimulation of either eye, but not of both eyes at the same time (Hubel and Wiesel, 1965). These initial results evoked strong interest and expectation among neuroscientists and established the study of synaptic modifiability in the immature visual cortex as a new frontier in developmental neurobiology.

2. *Various Paradigms*

To study the correlation between the physical characteristics of objects in a particular visual environment to which an animal is exposed and the receptive field properties of individual cells in its visual cortex, it is important to control physically the visual environment which defines the actual experience an animal undergoes. Many new experimental designs have been invented to serve this purpose. For example, (*a*) binocular deprivation of visual inputs by rearing animals in total darkness (Pettigrew, 1974; Blakemore and Van Sluyters, 1975; Buisseret and Imbert, 1976; Leventhal and Hirsch, 1977; Frégnac and Imbert, 1978); (*b*) rearing animals in complete darkness except for intermittent exposure to small spots of light coming through many pinholes in a dark box (Pettigrew and Freeman, 1973; Van Sluyters and Blakemore, 1973); (*c*) rearing animals in a room with low-frequency flickering light (Cynader *et al.*, 1973; Olson and Pettigrew, 1974); (*d*) exposing animals (otherwise kept in a dark room) to stationary or slowly moving, high-contrast black and white stripes, the stripes being oriented in one of three directions: horizontal, vertical, or oblique (Blakemore and Cooper, 1970; Blakemore and Mitchell, 1973; Hirsch and Spinelli, 1970, 1971; Leventhal and Hirsch, 1975; Stryker and Sherk, 1975; Blasdel *et al.*, 1977; Stryker *et al.*, 1978); and (*e*) intermittent exposure to unidirectionally moving, high-contrast gratings (Cynader *et al.*, 1975; Tretter *et al.*, 1975; Daw and Wyatt, 1976). Besides these manipulations of the external physical environment, alterations of visual inputs were accomplished by simple surgery or application of particular optical instruments to the animals themselves. These include (*a*) binocular deprivation by bilateral lid suture (Wiesel and Hubel, 1965; Watkins *et al.*, 1978); (*b*) reversal of the sutured eyelid (reverse suture) (Blakemore and Van Sluyters, 1974; Movshon and Blakemore, 1974; Movshon, 1976; Blakemore *et al.*, 1976, 1978; LeVay *et al.*, 1980); (*c*) frequent alteration of monocular occlusion by a black eyepatch (Hubel and Wiesel, 1965) or other means (Blasdel and Pettigrew, 1979); (*d*) squint introduced by cutting either a lateral or a medial rectus muscle of one or both eyes (Hubel and Wiesel, 1965; Baker *et al*, 1974); (*e*) squint introduced by fitting a goggle with a prism to one eye (Van Sluyters and Levitt, 1980); (*f*) changes in binocular disparity introduced by fitting a prism to one eye (Shlaer, 1971); and (*g*) fitting a goggle with a cylinder lens to blur visual images only in a particular orientation (Cynader and Mitchell, 1977; Rauschecker and Singer, 1979, 1981). Moreover (*h*) the effects of eyeball rotation (Yinon, 1975, 1976; Blakemore *et al.*, 1975; Crewther *et al.*, 1980), monocular eye rotation combined with monocular lid suture (Singer *et al.*, 1979), and surgical immobilization of eyeballs (Fiorentini and Maffei, 1974; Maffei and Fiorentini, 1976b) have also been studied.

3. The Susceptible Term: Critical Period

The alteration of receptive field properties of single cells in the visual cortex and the superior colliculus (SC) has already been documented in great detail following each of these forms of interference (whether applied alone or in combinations) with normal visual experience during the early postnatal maturation. Monocular lid suture for only 3 days was sufficient, if the operation was done during a particular time in early postnatal life, to force virtually all cortical cells to change their preferred ocularity to the non-deprived eye (Hubel and Wiesel, 1970; Olson and Freeman, 1975). If lid suture was done either too early or too late, no obvious changes took place in ocular dominance. From these observations, Hubel and Wiesel (1970) defined the term of susceptibility to monocular occlusion as weeks 4–13 of postnatal life in kittens.

Later, applying a much more stringent procedure, namely reverse suture, Blakemore and Van Sluyters (1974) obtained similar results. There is, however, a certain difference between the results obtained by these two arrangements in that, when tested with monocular lid suture, the cortical susceptibility remained high through 6–8 weeks of age and started to decline gradually around 13 weeks. In the reverse-suture situation, however, the susceptibility dropped exponentially and showed almost no reversibility after 12 weeks of age.

Any conclusions must be amended further by at least two recent findings, both of which show the persistence of synaptic plasticity throughout adulthood, provided that the animals have been treated by one of the following two conditions: (*a*) dark-rearing from the time before normal eye opening (Mower *et al.*, 1979; Cynader and Mitchell, 1980; Timney *et al.*, 1980; Kuppermann and Ramachandran, 1981), or (*b*) a high level of intracortical catecholamines. The latter issue will be discussed later in detail (section IV, B, 4, *12*).

4. Multiple Critical Periods

Another important development in this area occurred when Daw and Wyatt (1976) showed the presence of a critical period for modification of the direction selectivity in kitten visual cortex. It starts a week earlier than the critical period for the modification of binocularity and ends abruptly after 5 weeks of age. Daw and Wyatt suggested the presence in the brain of many critical periods, each depending on the particular experimental emphasis of the investigators. This concept has been further explored by examining changes in the width of the ocular dominance column in autoradiograms after reverse suture. In rhesus monkey visual cortex, the reversibility of effects of monocular lid suture seems to end earlier in layer IVc_{α}, which receives magnocellular afferents, than in layer IVc_{β}, in which parvocellular afferents terminate (LeVay *et al.*, 1979, 1980). This may be related to another recent morphological finding in macaque striate cortex which showed the wider spread (700 μm) of magnocellular afferents in layer IVcα than parvocellular afferents in layer IVc_{β} (200 μm) (Blasdel *et al.*, 1981). It has been shown that in cats the lateral spread of the terminal arborization of presumably Y geniculate axons in the upper subdivision of layer IV is larger than that of X axons in the lower part of layer IV (Ferster and LeVay, 1978).

B. Nature vs. nurture: is the orientation specificity modifiable?

As mentioned above, it has been established that the binocularity and direction selectivity of single cortical cells are subject to possible modification by the quality as well as the quantity of visual experiences received by individuals in their early postnatal life. Orientation selectivity is by far the most important parameter for a given cortical cell, since it unequivocally emerges only at the level of the cerebral cortex, not at the thalamus or the retina, at least in higher mammals such as cats and monkeys. The question of whether orientation selectivity is modifiable has stirred a very stimulating and productive debate. Let us briefly review this long-standing controversy.

1. An Original Proposal and Challenges

Recording from a few cells which had normal, adult-type orientation tuning in very young, visually inexperienced kittens, Hubel and Wiesel (1963) proposed an innate determination of orientation selectivity in visual cortical cells. A similar study was later carried out in monkeys to confirm their thesis (Wiesel and Hubel, 1974). Their original thesis, however, was challenged later by two groups of investigators working independently.

First, Hirsch and Spinelli (1970, 1971) raised kittens fitted with a specially designed goggle that had three black stripes oriented either horizontally or vertically in frosted glass. When the visual cortex of these animals was physiologically studied later, many cells were found whose preferred orientation seemed to match that of the stripes in a given goggle. Using a different method to expose animals preferentially to either a vertical or a horizontal grating, Blakemore and Cooper (1970) also obtained essentially similar results. These early results strongly suggested that orientation specificity of single visual cortical cells could also be modified by exposing kittens to a restricted visual environment with a uniform orientation component. Barlow and Pettigrew (1971), and Pettigrew and his associates (Pettigrew and Freeman, 1973; Pettigrew, 1974; Olson and Pettigrew, 1974; Blasdel *et al.,* 1977), intensively studied receptive field properties of visual cortical cells in normally maturing kittens as well as in cats which had been raised in various abnormal visual environments. They concluded that visual experience finely tunes the specificity of synapse formation in the visual cortex within the framework of genetic control. Exhaustive studies by other investigators describe not only the rapidly decreasing proportion of visually unresponsive, sluggish, and nonselective cells during normal maturation with binocular experience but also the reverse trend in animals without normal vision (Blakemore and Van Sluyters, 1975; Singer and Tretter, 1976; Imbert and Buisseret, 1975; Buisseret and Imbert, 1976; Leventhal and Hirsch, 1977; Bond, 1978; Frégnac and Imbert, 1978). However, other studies revealed the presence of a type of cell which innately (at least, right after birth) was tuned in orientation (see also Barlow, 1975; Blakemore and Van Sluyters, 1975; Buisseret and Imbert, 1976; Sherk and Stryker, 1976; Leventhal and Hirsch, 1977; Frégnac and Imbert, 1978). This type of cell was found in deep layers of the visual cortex, especially in layer IV of very young kittens. A different study has since shown that cells in layer IV are less modifiable than those in other layers (Shatz and Stryker, 1978). These oriented cells are thought to belong to the category of simple cells and to be driven monocularly (Blakemore and Van Sluyters, 1975; Leventhal and Hirsch, 1977).

2. *Reexamination*

Stryker and Sherk (1975), and Stryker and others (1978), have reexamined this long-standing debate about the modifiability of orientation specificity of visual cortical cells. They sampled each cell at regular intervals along an electrode track and studied its orientation tuning by means of a computerized sytem. They failed to confirm the findings of Blakemore and Cooper, but did report, however, that in a group of kittens raised with a Hirsch-type technique, more than half of the cells they recorded showed the orientation specificity that corresponded with the individual animal's visual experience. Stryker (1977) then argued that orientation specificity is acquired innately by cortical cells, but that without the proper visual experience those cells cannot maintain their innately acquired specificity.

The reverse-suture paradigm seems to give us an opportunity to clarify this point. Blakemore and his associates were impressed by the orderly, nonrandom reappearance of clusters of cells which responded to the previously deprived eye at the initial change following reverse suture (Blakemore and Van Sluyters, 1974; Blakemore *et al.,* 1976). Apparently, no silent area was noted along the electrode tracks in such visual cortices. These observations by themselves do not seem to guarantee the return of original connectivity between the now monocular cortical cells and the afferents from the previously deprived eye, as these authors apparently believe. In some cases, however, binocular cortical cells in the reverse-sutured cats showed a clear suggestion of independent orientation sequences for the two eyes (Movshon, 1976). Furthermore, the broader than normal interocular difference of preferred orientation for the two eyes was consistently found in the binocular cells, although a minority in number, for the reverse-sutured kitten (Blakemore and Van Sluyters, 1974; Blakemore *et al.,* 1976; Movshon, 1976). These last two findings seem to favor the interpretation of respecification of the orientation specificity rather than reactivation of the synapses once silenced by the initial monocular deprivation. In fact, the distribution of the interocular difference was as narrow as the normal distribution if the kittens had experienced binocular vision prior to brief monocular lid suture followed by reverse suture (a case of reactivation) (Blakemore *et al.,* 1976; Van Sluyters, 1978). Blakemore and his associates thus strongly argued that immature cortical cells can respecify their orientation specificity according to their visual experience.

Blasdel and others (1977) joined the debate by exposing kittens to far better controlled visual stimuli than any previous investigators had used. Using a computerized system to measure the orientation tuning of each cell in the visual cortex, they confirmed that two-thirds of the cortical cells they recorded at regular intervals responded to the stimulus orientations to which they had been conditioned. Taking into account the results obtained by psychophysical tests in the same animals that had been used for single-unit physiological study, they concluded that the orientation specificity of single visual cortical cells can be modified postnatally. In a more recent study, kittens' visual experiences were restricted to either horizontal or vertical contours by means of cylindrical lenses with high refractive power in only one orientation (Rauschecker, 1979; Rauschecker and Singer, 1979, 1981). Their findings constituted further evidence for the theory of modifiable orientation specificity.

3. *A Basic Difficulty and Summary*

Such a review of these debates on the modifiability of receptive field properties emphasizes a basic difficulty here: We do not know exactly how receptive field properties of individual cells normally mature in the visual cortex. As argued by Pettigrew (1978) and others, if specific visual stimuli used during a recording session can, by and large, affect the properties of individual cells that are maturing moment by moment, the currently available techniques themselves then impose serious limitations on gaining a definitive answer to the question. This consideration seems to deserve more attention than before as a consequence of a recent discovery that NE enhances synaptic plasticity. Changes in ocular dominance of single cortical cells, for example, may take place in a matter of hours if cortical synapses are exposed to sufficient amounts of NE (Heggelund and Kasamatsu, 1981; Kasamatsu and Heggelund, 1981). Tsumoto and Freeman (1981) also reported briefly that ocular dominance of single cortical cells can be changed quickly during physiological recordings if monocular stimulation is combined with periodic conjugated eye movements induced by electrical stimulation of the internal medullary lamina in the thalamus. We have not, however, seen a definitive study that demonstrates changes in receptive field properties of given cells during manipulation of visual afferents. At any rate, a direct demonstration of changes in receptive field properties of individual cells, rather than comparisons between various populations of recorded cells, is obviously needed to give us a far more satisfactory understanding of the modifiability of receptive fields (see also section III, A, C).

In summary, the current understanding about the modifiability of properties of single visual cortical cells is as follows:

1. The majority of area 17 cells in immature animals, especially cats, does not have the adult-type receptive fields with a sharply tuned orientation. Visual experience in a normal environment is needed for their maturation.

2. The receptive field properties of these maturing cortical cells can be modified by the actual visual experience of individuals during the postnatal susceptible period.

3. A group of cells in layer IV of the visual cortex has innately the adultlike receptive fields. Thus, general consensus holds that the final details of receptive field properties of visual cortical cells are tuned according to the quality as well as the quantity of the individual's visual experiences during the postnatal critical period.

C. Morphological correlates

1. Changes in the Ocular Dominance Column

Besides the physiological changes that follow monocular deprivation in the visual cortex, changes in the width of the ocular dominance column have been observed in monocularly deprived animals (cats and monkeys) by a transneuronal transport autoradiographic method (Wiesel *et al.*, 1974; Shatz *et al.*, 1977). Hubel, Wiesel, and LeVay (1976, 1977), first in the monkey visual cortex, demonstrated an increased width of the ocular dominance column that corresponded with the used, open eye at the expense of the closed eye. Later, similar findings were reported in the cat visual cortex (Shatz and Stryker, 1978).

Applying a new method of [^{14}C]2-deoxyglucose (2-DG) introduced by Sokoloff and his associates (Kennedy *et al.*, 1976; Sokoloff *et al.*, 1977), Des Rosiers and others (1978) observed a total disappearance of ocular dominance columns or bands in the visual cortex of monkeys which had been subjected to monocular occlusion for 3 months from the day of birth. It has been known that in newborn (Old World) monkeys, one can visualize the ocular dominance column by the transneuronal transport autoradiography (Rakic, 1976, 1977). The ocular dominance column, however, does not exist in newborn kittens. Its segregation starts at 3 weeks of age, and at least 3 more weeks are required before it reaches its adult form (LeVay *et al.*, 1978). Stryker (1980) reported suppression of this segregation of ocular dominance columns in cats which had received repeated injections of tetrodotoxin (TTX) into the two eyes before 3 weeks of age. Stryker and his associates, however, noted the formation of ocular dominance columns in the control, dark-reared kittens. Recently, however, Swindale (1981) has claimed that ocular dominance columns disappear in dark-reared kittens. Rakic (1981) showed the total disappearance of ocular dominance columns, along with the lack of lamination in the LGN, from the visual cortex of an adult monkey whose one eye had been enucleated in early fetal life (the monkey was delivered normally). These results in the mammalian visual cortex seem to be consistent with the thesis which has been put forward by a beautiful demonstration of regularly spaced band formations in the optic tectum of three-eyed frogs (Constantine-Paton and Law, 1978) or in the remaining tectum of frogs after ablation of the other tectum (Law and Constantine-Paton, 1980). In short, these recent advances, taken together with a previous proposal (Kasamatsu, 1976b), strongly suggest an important role of tonic retinal discharges for maintaining binocular competition among active optic terminals, which in turn seems to dictate the formation of eye preference bands in the visual center.

Recently, using a reverse-suture paradigm, changes in the width of ocular dominance columns were autoradiographically demonstrated in layer IVc_{β} in monkey visual cortex, although no change was seen in layer IVc_{α} of the same animals (LeVay *et al.*, 1979, 1980).

2. *Orientation Columns*

The presence of orientation columns was first demonstrated in the macaque striate cortex by the [^{14}C]2-DG method (Hubel *et al.*, 1978). Singer and his associates (1981) later applied this method, along with physiological recordings, to visualize the expansion of orientation columns in the nongranular layers of the visual cortex which were preferentially stimulated by prior exposure of kittens to a single orientation. This expansion was seen, as expected, at the expense of the orientation columns which corresponded to the orthogonal (inadequately stimulated) orientation. Flood and Coleman (1979) and Albus (1979) also briefly reported a similar result (see section IV, B, *11* for further discussion of the [^{14}C]2-DG method). A recent result by Schoppmann and Stryker (1981) has provided further evidence for the usefulness of this anatomical method in visualizing orientation columns in cats.

3. *Changes in Geniculate Cell Size*

At the beginning of their studies in monocularly deprived cats, Wiesel and Hubel (1963a) described obvious changes in Nissl-stained sections of the lateral geniculate nucleus. This was confirmed by Kupfer and Palmer (1964). They noted that geniculate cells in laminae which corresponded to the deprived eye stained paler in appearance and smaller in size than cells in the normal laminae. As will be mentioned in section III, A, this finding was fully explored later by Guillery and his associates.

4. *Morphometry in the Altered Visual Cortex*

Although less easy to interpret, several quantitative changes have occurred in the morphology of the visual cortex of animals which are exposed to certain abnormal visual experience. For example, the number of synapses per neuron decreases in the cat visual cortex that has been binocularly lid-sutured before normal eye opening (30% decrease at 45 days of age; Cragg, 1975b) or in the visual cortex of monocularly deprived rats (Fifkova, 1970). Furthermore, the number of dendritic spines of pyramidal cells in deep cortical layers decreases following dark rearing (Globus and Scheibel, 1967; Valverde, 1967; Valverde and Marcos, 1967). Reduction in both the size and the degree of dendritic branching was noted in layer IV stellate cells, but not in layer V pyramidal cells, in the striate cortex of cats which were raised in the dark from birth to adulthood (Coleman and Riesen, 1968). The orientation of dendrites in stellate cells is also reported to change in dark-reared rats (Borges and Berry, 1976). The overall effects of visual deprivation on the maturation of visual cortical synapses seem to be more profound in binocular than in monocular lid suture in first 110 days of the kitten's postnatal life (Winfield, 1981). This appears especially true for asymmetric axospinous (and, to a lesser degree, axodendritic) synapses. In addition, the temporal suppression (for the first 4 months) of cell size growth has been cited as an effect of dark rearing (up to 16 weeks of age) in cat LGN (Kalil, 1978).

In summary, these changes in the number of spines and the dendritic morphology in dark-reared animals may be understood as a result of the arrest of neuronal maturation due to the lack of some trophic influence of visual afferents on immature neurons (Kupfer and Palmer, 1964). It should also be noted that during ontogeny the total number of dendritic spines in the normal visual cortex may decrease spontaneously after peaking at a certain age (mouse, rat, and monkey) (Ruiz-Marcos and Valverde, 1969; Feldman and Dowd, 1975; Lund *et al.*, 1977).

D. Changes in Geniculate Cell Physiology

Despite the obvious changes in cell morphology mentioned in the next section, the receptive field organization of LGN cells in the deprived lamina seems to be essentially unchanged in the visually deprived cats, although the sampling rate of so-called Y cells (e.g., Rowe and Stone, 1977) in the monocularly deprived LGN is conspicuously reduced (Sherman *et al.*, 1972; Hoffmann and Cynader, 1977). Moreover, there is some evidence which suggests the existence of abnormal X cells in monocularly deprived LGNs. Specifically, deprived LGN cells are less sensitive to stimulation by a grating with high spatial frequency (Maffei and Fiorentini, 1976a; Ikeda *et al.*, 1978; Lehmkuhle *et al.*, 1980). Applying an intracellular injection of horseradish peroxidase (HRP) into the LGN cells, Friedlander and associates (1980) obtained a new result which may explain this reduced frequency of physiologically defined Y cells in the deprived LGN: They found not only many LGN cells which appeared to be X cells in function but were more like Y cells in their dendritic morphology, but also a few deprived Y cells which had unusual physiological properties and different dendritic patterns not known in Y cells.

E. Retinal ganglion cells

No obvious changes have been generally reported in morphology and physiology of retinal ganglion cells in animals exposed to varying visual environments (Sherman and Stone, 1973; Hendrickson and Boothe, 1976; Cleland *et al.,* 1980). There is, however, a report which claimed a reduced resolution in spatial frequency by ganglion cells in the deviated eye of strabismic cats (Ikeda and Tremain, 1979). Another early report described extensive degeneration of retinal ganglion cells in dark-reared chimpanzees (Chow *et al.,* 1957). They also reported a significant reduction in the thickness of the inner plexiform layer, as well as a lowering not only of the cytoplasmic and nucleolar RNA (ribonucleic acid) content but also of the amount of cellular protein in nonganglion cells in the retina of dark-reared (~ 3 years) cats and rats (Rasch *et al.,* 1961). A monocular lid suture 2 years in duration led to a significant decrease in both cell density and cell size in ganglion cells in the parafoveal retina of nine monkeys (von Noorden *et al.,* 1977). A recent histochemical study found that in rats raised in total darkness, the natural maturation of their dopamine (DA)-containing amacrine cells had ceased, as measured by the increase in their fluorescent intensities (Kato *et al.,* 1980).

F. Behavioral changes and recovery

Numerous studies have described not only the concomitant changes in physiology and morphology at the cellular level, as mentioned above, but also the severe impairment, to the point of apparent blindness, in the vision of animals exposed to various forms of abnormal visual experience during the critical period. (Ganz and Fitch, 1968; Dews and Wiesel, 1970; Sherman, 1973, 1974a; Cynader *et al.,* 1976; Kalil, 1978). Although these animals require more trials than normal animals to learn such complex visual tasks as pattern discrimination, they nevertheless apparently maintain the capability to do so (Rizzolatti and Tradardi, 1971; Chow and Stewart, 1972; Ganz *et al.,* 1972; Ganz and Haffner, 1974; Spear and Ganz, 1975; Van Hof-Van Duin, 1976) but cannot accomplish those tasks which require visuomotor control (Van Hof-Van Duin, 1976). After extensive and long-term (over a year) use of the deprived eye under the reverse-suture paradigm, monocularly deprived animals also demonstrated fairly good visual acuity when tested for the previously deprived eye. The extent of such restoration in visual functions, however, has varied largely, ranging from considerable recovery (Chow and Stewart, 1972; Mitchell *et al.*, 1977; Giffin and Mitchell, 1978) to little reversal of the deficit (Wiesel and Hubel, 1965; Hubel and Wiesel, 1970; Dews and Wiesel, 1970; Sherman, 1974a).

These very different results are likely the product of differences in the parameters used in the different studies; it is important to note that this functional recovery in visual behavior is not accompanied by a similar effect in either the cortical physiology or morphology in the LGN (Wiesel and Hubel, 1965; Dews and Wiesel, 1970; Garey and Dürsteler, 1975; Cragg *et al.*, 1976; Hoffmann and Holländer, 1978). Global recovery, however, was most likely to occur when the initial impairment was light and limited, probably due to either the late start or the short (a few weeks rather than several months) duration of deprivation, or both (Blakemore and Van Sluyters, 1974; Movshon and Blakemore, 1974; Movshon, 1976; Van Sluyters, 1978; Blasdel and Pettigrew, 1978; Olson and Freeman, 1978; Mitchell *et al.*, 1978). Mitchell and his associates have sought to explain this discrepancy among the behavioral, physiological, and morphological deficits as a psychophysical threshold mechanism possessed by only a set of the most sensitive neurons rather than by the total number of neurons involved in executing a behavior (Giffin and Mitchell, 1978). A recent study showed that the morphological changes in the LGN usually seemed to be preceded by physiological changes in cortical plasticity (Spear and Hickey, 1979). Another group of investigators, however, has maintained an opposite view, in which the equally quick, large changes in both cortical physiology and LGN cell size are reported following reverse suture (Dürsteler *et al.*, 1976). The relationship among morphology, physiology, and behavior obviously needs further study.

III. Proposed Mechanisms for Plastic Changes in Binocularity of Visual Cortical Cells

In this section, I consider the likely neuronal mechanisms underlying the obvious changes induced not only physiologically in the visual cortex but also morphologically in the LGN cells, as well as their intracortical terminals, following one of the simplest procedures used to modify normal visual experience, the monocular lid suture. Despite many studies and colorful debates, reviewed above, unfortunately not much work has been undertaken to reveal the underlying mechanisms responsible for cortical plasticity. First, I will review the following three topics: binocular competition, GABA (gamma aminobutyric acid) ergic inhibition, and intracortical inhibition maintained through tonic retinal discharges. Then I shall introduce our CA hypothesis in greater detail.

A. Binocular competition

In 1965 Wiesel and Hubel found more binocularly driven cells in the visual cortex of cats that had been subjected to binocular lid suture since their birth than in animals that had been monocularly deprived postnatally for an equal amount of time. They also noted that the incidence of cortical cells which did not respond to visual stimulation or cells which did not show orientation selectivity was far larger in binocularly deprived than in normal or even monocularly deprived animals. Accordingly, they proposed that in the deprived visual cortex, the two sets of comparable visual afferents from both eyes are competing with each other for the available postsynaptic sites, which are presumably limited in number.

Guillery and his associates later expanded this idea of binocular competition and applied it to test the maturation of dorsal geniculate neurons in cats. They reported that in monocularly deprived cats, the cell size became smaller only in the binocular segment of the deprived lamina as compared with that at the corresponding site (in terms of retinotopy) in the nondeprived lamina (Guillery and Stelzner, 1970; Guillery, 1973; Sherman *et al.,* 1974). They noted no changes in the geniculate cells of the monocular segment of lamina A, which normally does not have a corresponding part in lamina A1. Guillery further pursued this question by experimentally producing a monocular segment (critical segment) in the middle of the binocular segment of lamina A (Guillery, 1972). He made a small lesion on the surface of one temporal retina with a laser beam to produce a patch of transneuronal degeneration in lamina A1. Then he found that cells in deprived lamina A contralateral to the monocular lid suture became smaller, as expected, but not those in the part of lamina A which corresponded to the patch of degeneration in lamina A1. The cell shrinkage following monocular lid suture was far less in this critical segment than in the rest of the binocular segment of lamina A. Sherman and others, using a perimetry method in behaving animals, obtained behavioral results that seemed to be consistent with these results in geniculate morphology (Sherman *et al.,* 1974; Sherman and Guillery, 1976). Under some circumstances, an increase in cell size was also reported in dorsal geniculate cells in the nondeprived lamina (Sherman and Wilson, 1975; Hickey *et al.,* 1977).

Later studies showed that besides binocular competition between cells in the corresponding laminae of the LGN, the diameter of cell soma seemed to be affected by the number of visual afferents from the eyes (Hickey *et al.,* 1977). Continuous bombardment by tonic retinal discharges (dark discharge) may work directly, as a trophic factor, on the maturing geniculate cells. Consistent with this suggestion, we recently observed a very strong, quick shrinkage of geniculate cells after monocular injections of TTX to silence reversibly the total retinal output from one eye. The cell shrinkage was observed equally well in both binocular and monocular segments (Kuppermann and Kasamatsu, 1980).

I have long been interested in studying binocular competition in the immature visual cortex. I reasoned that if, as proposed by Wiesel and Hubel, binocular inputs from the two eyes compete with each other for the limited number of postsynaptic sites, any imbalance between the two sets of visual afferents might change the binocularity of single visual cortical cells. Then, by direct application of a small amount of local anesthetic to one optic nerve before the optic chiasm, I created in young kittens a drastic but reversible imbalance in the total output from the retina. In 60% of the cells studied for at least 1 hour under acute recording conditions (the animals were anesthetized and immobilized), the blockade of tonic retinal input from one eye caused cortical cells to respond better to stimulation of the other eye (Kasamatsu, 1976b). No such changes were observed in the adult cortex treated similarly. I then interpreted the results to suggest the existence of constant binocular competition between the two sets of visual afferents on single cells in the developing visual cortex. This observation has been extended by Tsumoto and Suda (1979), who observed that conditioning tetanic stimulation of one optic nerve of the normal kitten enhanced visual cortex evoked potentials in response to stimulation of the conditioned optic nerve, whereas similar potentials induced by stimulation of the other optic nerve were concurrently suppressed. The effect lasted up to 9 hours after the tetanic stimulation. However, the question of whether the two sets of retinal tonic discharges themselves can compete with each other without reference to light-evoked activity remains unanswered. As will be discussed in detail in section IV, B, 7, we now have a tool with which to study this question.

As a variation on binocular competition in the maturing visual cortex, Cynader and his associates (1981) recently introduced a new scheme of interhemispheric competition in kittens subjected to surgical sagittal section of the optic chiasm in addition to concurrent monocular lid suture. In this preparation, in which the binocular convergence was still possible via the callosal connection, the dominance of inputs from the nondeprived eye (temporal retina) over similar inputs from the deprived eye is proven, independent of which hemisphere was recorded. However, since the indirect callosal afferents are weaker than the direct ipsilateral geniculate afferents in activating cortical cells, the effects of monocular deprivation were stronger when recorded from the visual cortex ipsilateral to the nondeprived eye in comparison to those in the other hemisphere.

Blasdel and Pettigrew (1978), who were studying the recovery of visual cortical cells from the effects of monocular lid suture, realized the importance of normal binocular experience before the animals were subjected to monocular lid suture. Kittens which had more binocular experience prior to monocular lid suture showed faster as well as better recovery of normal binocularly driven cells following reopening of the closed eyelid. A similar observation was made by Van Sluyters (1978). They interpreted this finding to suggest that besides the better alignment of visual axes, there might exist more mature and thus less vulnerable neuropils for binocular input in animals with more prior binocular experience than in ones with only a little binocular exposure. Their interpretation *a priori* seems to depend on the hypothesis that cortical synapses receiving input from a nonused, deprived eye are functionally suppressed, although they appear to be morphologically intact (synaptic suppression), or eliminated through retraction of their terminals (synaptic elimination). A similar hypothesis was originally advanced to explain not only the disappearance of multiple innervation at the neuromuscular junctions of maturing mammalian skeletal muscle (Brown *et al.*, 1976; Korneliussen and Jansen, 1976; Riley, 1977) but also the segregation of geniculate axon terminals in the visual cortex to form the adult-type ocular dominance column (Rakic, 1976, 1977; Hubel *et al.*, 1977; LeVay *et al.*, 1978). Although some morphological evidence (i.e., a decrease in the width of the ocular dominance column for the deprived eye; see also Thorpe and Blakemore, 1975; Singer, 1977) is consistent with the synaptic elimination hypothesis, the two lines of evidence in physiology seem to favor the synaptic suppression hypothesis. This will be discussed in section III, B and C.

At any rate, anatomical and physiological studies on the plasticity of ocular dominance columns seem to provide a profitable working basis for the search for a unified principle which explains visual cortical plasticity. Normal segregation of ocular dominance columns in ontogeny and its changes following various experimental manipulations in the eye have already been examined extensively within the context of binocular competition (see section II, C).

B. GABAergic inhibition

Previously, Duffy and his associates briefly reported an interesting result which suggests an involvement of GABA-mediated mechanisms in neural plasticity in visual cortical cells (Duffy *et al.*, 1976b). By intravenous injection of a subconvulsive dose of bicuculline (a GABA antagonist), they were able to recover the lost receptive fields in the visual cortex of adult cats that had been monocularly deprived since birth. They maintained that 60% (N = 33) of the receptive fields thus recovered for the deprived eye had quite normal properties as compared with those for the nondeprived eye.

In his series of iontophoretic studies, Sillito (1977) has shown that some of the receptive field properties of visual cortical cells, e.g., directional selectivity of complex cells, can be modified by iontophoresis of bicuculline. By using bicuculline methiodide (N-methyl bicuculline) in place of bicuculline, he further reported the temporary disappearance of orientation selectivity from normal cortical cells (including both complex and simple cells) which were narrowly tuned to certain orientations (Sillito, 1979, 1980). Tsumoto and others (1979) also demonstrated changes in orientation selectivity by iontophoresis of a GABA antagonist. In consideration of the roles played by GABA-dependent inputs in the receptive field organization, it seems quite reasonable to expect an involvement of GABA mechanisms in controlling changes in ocular dominance as well. The fact that the initial results of Duffy and his associates were obtained in locally anesthetized and immobilized cats may have hampered efforts by other investigators to duplicate their results. The same group of investigators, however, reported later in an abstract that ammonium salt in place of bicuculline produced similar results (Duffy *et al.*, 1976a). To support their original observation, Burchfiel and Duffy (1981) recently showed recovery of receptive fields for the monocularly deprived eye by iontophoresis of bicuculline methiodide. The report was based on 31 cells recorded from the visual cortex of 5-month-old cats whose one eyelid was closed since birth. As an aside, if the involvement of GABA-mediated synapses is likely in this phenomenon, it seems reasonable to test the effects of another type of GABA antagonist, such as picrotoxin; to date, this has not yet been done.

Recently, Sillito and his associates have demonstrated, by iontophoresis of bicuculline methiodide, a significant change in ocular dominance grouping for 50% of the cells studied ($N = 42$) in the normal cat visual cortex (1980). Sillito and his associates (1981) further reported the reappearance of a response to stimulation of the deprived eye during iontophoresis of *N*-methyl-bicuculline in the visual cortex of monocularly deprived cats. One-third of the 51 cells that were initially monocular showed this change, but none of them was ever dominated by the previously deprived eye. Thus, the results of Sillito and his associates do not necessarily support the hypothesis originally presented by Duffy and his associates. Rather, the former group believes that the redistribution of excitatory LGN terminals may play much more important roles in the shift of ocular dominance following monocular deprivation than those attributed to the GABAergic inhibition by the latter group.

C. Tonic inhibition due to afferents from the normal eye

In the early fifties, Chang reported a unique phenomenon in visual physiology that has since been referred to as "Chang's effect" (Chang, 1952): The amplitude of cortical-evoked potentials in response to electrical stimulation of the LGN becomes larger when the animal's eyes have had light shone upon them for a while. Arduini and Hirao (1959, 1960) and Posternak and others (1959), who carried out experiments complementary to Chang's study by either inducing artificial glaucoma or sectioning the optic nerve to block reversibly or irreversibly the total retinal outputs, have established that visual cortical cells are under the control of tonic inhibition maintained by tonic retinal discharges. A similar study with single-unit recordings was successfully carried out in the LGN (Suzuki, 1967; Suzuki and Ichijo, 1967) which also confirmed the reversibility of the artificial glaucoma. The same type of experiment by previous authors in pretrigeminal or anesthetized cats was later extended to animals chronically blinded by eye enucleation. The results in the latter study suggested that an essentially similar mechanism of intracortical inhibition is continuously in operation in freely behaving animals (Kasamatsu *et al.*, 1967).

Following monocular lid suture, most cells in the cat SC lose binocularity and become unresponsive to stimulation of the deprived eye due to the impairment of layer V complex cells driven through the Y-indirect pathway. More characteristically, the sampling frequency of directionally selective cells dramatically decreases in such a colliculus (Wickelgren and Sterling, 1969; Hoffmann and Sherman, 1974). Removing most of the visual cortex contralateral to the previously lid-sutured eye, Wickelgren and Sterling (1969) and Berman and Sterling (1974, 1976) found that many collicular cells in the cortex-ablated side became responsive only to stimulation of the previously deprived contralateral eye. However, these cells were nonselective in their orientation tuning. Similarly, by placing large lesions in the visual cortex contralateral to the deprived eye, Sherman (1974b) observed improved visual behaviors in the monocularly deprived cats. This result was interpreted as suggesting that a certain amount of recovery of vision occurs through the previously deprived eye.

Spear and his associates removed the normal eye of 4 ~ 5-month-old cats that had been subjected to monocular lid suture before natural eye opening (Kratz *et al.*, 1976). Within 30 minutes after eye enucleation, they recorded visual cortical cells that responded to stimulation of the previously deprived eye. On average, 40% of cells encountered in their recordings had receptive fields for the previously deprived eye. The majority (61%) of such receptive fields, however, were abnormal and did not have normal selective properties. They interpreted this finding as suggesting that the intracortical inhibition which was maintained by retinal afferents from the normal eye, including retinal tonic discharges, was removed by enucleation of the normal eye. This group and others (Hoffmann and Cynader, 1977; Spear and Hickey, 1979) have since presented morphological data on changes in dorsal geniculate cell size which are consistent with this interpretation of the initial physiological findings.

In support of the above interpretation, Tsumoto and Suda (1978) were able to record short-latency excitatory synaptic responses in the cat visual cortex by electric stimulation of the optic nerve which corresponded to the previously monocularly deprived eye. This result, however, is not fully consistent with that by Singer (1977) on the same subject. There seem to be still other inconsistencies in the interpretation of the results of eye enucleation studies by other investigators as well: Harris and Stryker (1977) and Hawken and others (1978) could not duplicate the original findings by Kratz and others. Crewther and others (1978) did obtain results similar to those reported first by Kratz and others, but only under the condition that they recovered the lost receptive fields for the previously deprived eye after a combined treatment of retrobulbar anesthesia with a local anesthetic and artificial glaucoma in the normal, nondeprived eye. They thus proposed a role for the proprioceptive afferents from eye muscles, in addition to the visual afferents, in modulating visual cortical plasticity, as had already been suggested by Maffei and Bisti (1976) and Maffei and Fiorentini (1976b).

There is yet another twist to this story, however: Van Sluyters and Levitt (1980) recently argued against the interpretation favored by Maffei and his associates as to the reason for changes in ocular dominance induced by an artificial squint after cutting eye muscles. Van Sluyters and Levitt obtained the expected changes in ocular dominance in kittens through optically induced strabismus, without disturbing the putative proprioceptive afferents from eye muscles to the visual cortex.

D. CA Hypothesis

I have briefly reviewed the developmental studies in synaptic plasticity in the central visual system. Attention was focused on a simple but most fruitful experimental paradigm, that of the monocular lid suture. I then discussed some proposed mechanisms that seem to underlie the changes in ocular dominance following monocular deprivation.

In 1976, in collaboration with J. D. Pettigrew, I introduced a new approach to the study of the mechanisms underlying synaptic plasticity in the maturing visual cortex (Kasamatsu and Pettigrew, 1976). Before we began our exploration of the central CA system as it relates to cortical plasticity, Kety and Crow had already proposed a CA hypothesis to explain the function of the neocortex in learning and memory as well as in the control of emotion. Kety (1970) suggested a possible involvement of NE secreted in the forebrain, as a reinforcement, in the enhancement of learning. In the late sixties and early seventies, thanks to massive efforts by a Swedish group (Fuxe, 1965; Fuxe *et al.*, 1968; Ungerstedt, 1968, 1971a) and others in Japan (Maeda and Shimizu, 1972), the complexity of the central CA system was revealed step by step. Crow (1968, 1973) developed the CA hypothesis further and proposed that those neurons which originate in the LC and its ascending CA bundles with NE-containing terminals in the neocortex may be a morphological substrate for reinforcement as well as for learning and memory. A series of initial studies produced results substantiating Crow's proposal (Randt *et al.,* 1971; Stein *et al.,* 1975; Crow and Wendlandt, 1976; Meligeni *et al.,* 1978), although not all of the recent reports are in harmony with one another. For example, Mason and Iversen (1975) and Mason and Fibiger (1979b) concluded, after a series of well-planned analyses of rat behavior, that the ascending NE fiber pathways play a role in neither the acquisition nor the retrieval of learned behaviors. The only behavioral change they noted in rats which had received localized lesions in the ascending NE pathway was the persistence of learned behaviors during the extinction process. Crow and his associates (Crow *et al.,* 1977) have also arrived at similar conclusions. Researchers in the field now have second thoughts about a role for the DA system in these behaviors, so that the connection between the supposed function of the LC and prominent behaviors such as instrumental learning and the intracranial self-stimulation of J. Olds seems to have become indistinct again. It is not my intention to mention further the possible roles played by CA systems in controlling reward and motivation; interested readers are referred instead to other reviews (Olds, 1976; Wise, 1978; see also Kornetsky, 1979).

IV. Catecholaminergic Control of Visual Cortical Plasticity

A. Background: projections of private thoughts

1. Nonvisual Inputs to the Visual Cortex

I have been impressed by the fact that neuronal activity in the central visual pathway is controlled not only by light-evoked afferent activity from the retina but also by inputs from nonvisual sources (Kasamatsu and Iwama, 1966; Kasamatsu, 1970, 1976a,b; Kasamatsu and Adey, 1973, 1974). A well-documented example is that the spontaneous activity as well as the firing probability of single cells in the LGN, SC, visual cortex, and other brain areas is modulated by the same neuronal mechanisms which control the alternation of sleep with waking. This long-forgotten simple fact about the global change in neuronal excitability deserves a second look in connection with the functional mapping of active cortical cells by either ^{14}C or $[^3H]$2-DG autoradiography (Livingston and Hubel, 1981) or $[^3H]$glycine (Rojik and Fehér, 1980).

An especially interesting example of nonvisual afferents is the impulses which appear in the central visual as well as the oculomotor systems synchronous with saccades in both waking and rapid eye movement (REM) sleep. This impulse is generated at the midbrain oculomotor center and eventually reaches the visual system through the ascending bundles, but is not secondary to REMs which themselves change the temporal pattern of visually evoked afferent volleys. This impulse, which is believed to be a case of Helmholz's Efferenzkopien (von Holst and Mittelstaedt, 1950) or corollary discharges (Sperry, 1950), can be easily recorded either as PGO (ponto-geniculo-occipital) waves in REM sleep (Jouvet and Michel, 1959; Mikiten *et al.*, 1961; Mouret *et al.*, 1963; Bizzi and Brooks, 1963; Brooks, 1968; Brooks and Gershon, 1971; Brooks *et al.*, 1972) or as eye movement potentials in waking (Brooks, 1968; Brooks and Gershon, 1971; Jeannerod and Sakai, 1970; Sakai, 1973; Sakai *et al.*, 1976) by gross wire electrodes placed in the LGN or the visual cortex.

Reserpine blocks the uptake by aminergic terminals of monoamines into the synaptic vesicles and thus effectively empties these vesicles. It has been known for the last 15 years that PGO waves can easily be induced in waking cats if they are pretreated with reserpine (Delorme *et al.*, 1965; Brooks and Gershon, 1971; Brooks *et al.*, 1972). A paper by Laurent and others (1974) is particularly significant: They systematically studied the effects of the partial destruction of the brainstem on the frequency and pattern of PGO waves in sleeping cats. They concluded that PGO waves are generated at an area in the pontine brainstem including the LC and the nucleus subcoeruleus (NSC). They also suggested, with some caution, that the ascending pathways of PGO waves are largely overlapped with the ascending CA bundles as visualized by a histofluorescence method (Maeda *et al.*, 1973). A later study showed that a group of non-CA (most likely cholinoceptive) cells in the areas "X" (or nucleus brachiorum conjunctivorum), nucleus parabrachialis lateralis, and nucleus laterodorsalis tegmenti may be the true source for the production of PGO waves since these cells showed burst firing at (or before) the onset of PGO waves recorded in the LGN and were invaded antidromically (mean latency, 5.5 msec) following electrical stimulation of the LGN (Sakai and Jouvet, 1980; Sakai, 1980). It is also known that a CA-related neurotoxin, 6-hydroxydopamine (6-OHDA) (Bloom *et al.*, 1969; Ungerstedt, 1968, 1971b; Breese and Traylor, 1970; Uretsky and Iversen, 1970), injected either locally into the pontine tegmentum or intraventricularly, suppresses the production of PGO waves on a long-term basis (Buguet *et al.*, 1970; Laguzzi *et al.*, 1972; Kasamatsu and Pettigrew, 1976).

When one talks about the correlation between PGO waves and the ascending CA bundles, one has to evaluate the following three points.

First, independent of the possible catecholaminergic nature of signals conveyed by PGO waves or the strong anatomical similarity between the ascending CA bundles and the projection pathway of PGO waves whose chemical nature has not yet been fully determined, the production of PGO waves is tonically inhibited by inputs from serotonin (5-HT)-containing cells in the raphe complex (Brooks *et al.*, 1972; Jacobs *et al.*, 1972; Jalfre *et al.*, 1973; Dement *et al.*, 1973; Simon *et al.*, 1973). Furthermore, several lines of pharmacological evidence strongly suggest that cholinergic inputs, which are blocked by atropine, are responsible for triggering the production of PGO waves, especially those in bursts (Matsuzaki *et al.*, 1968; Magherini *et al.*, 1971; Henriksen *et al.*, 1972; Stern and Morgane, 1974).

Second, one has to explain why PGO waves, if the CA pathway is involved in their propagation, have not been recorded in the central visual pathways of rats (Stern *et al.*, 1974), the most intensively studied animals in CA research. This may not be crucial, however, for our thesis. The gross potential changes recorded as PGO waves are in fact an aggregation of single-unit discharges which take place at a given recording site following the all-or-none law of events (Malcolm *et al.*, 1970). Therefore, the manner of summation of all-or-none events in the rat visual pathway may be such as not to register PGO waves altogether. We may similarly explain another puzzle: why we usually do not record PGO waves in the cat brain outside of the central visual and oculomotor systems. Using a particular arrangement of recording electrodes, Calvet and others (1965) have indeed recorded gross potential changes similar to PGO waves throughout the neocortex of cats. Furthermore, recently the presence of PGO waves in the rat pons was demonstrated by electrophysiological recordings from the discrete area of the dorsolateral pons which included the LC (Farber *et al.*, 1981).

Third, a brief review of the ontogeny of PGO waves in cats is required. PGO waves are not observed in the kitten LGN during REM sleep before 2 weeks of postnatal age, although kittens at this age still spend a significant amount of time daily in REM sleep (Bowe-Anders *et al.*, 1974). Following the third postnatal week, both the frequency and amplitude of PGO waves increase dramatically, reaching the level seen in adult cats. The general appearance of this maturation curve of PGO waves is quite similar to that described for an increase in the monoamine content in the cat brainstem with age (Himwich, 1972; Bourgoin *et al.*, 1979). In both cases the curves show a peak, or an obvious deflection point, at 3–5 weeks of age. It is instructive that some aspects of the maturation curve of the CA system coincide well with the onset of the susceptible period of binocular cortical cells to monocular experience (Hubel and Wiesel, 1970; Blakemore and Van Sluyters, 1974).

Recently, I studied the ontogeny of endogenous monoamines, β-adrenergic receptors, and 5-HT receptors in the kitten visual cortex. Endogenous NE increased more or less continuously with age. The number of specific binding sites for [^{3}H]dihydroalprenolol increased rapidly, reached the plateau at 7 ~ 9 weeks of age, and decreased rapidly again toward the adult value, which was about 60% of the maximum (Jonsson and Kasamatsu, submitted). A small peak at 3 ~ 5 weeks of age was also noted. Thus, our biochemical studies showed that the maturation curve of β-adrenergic receptor binding sites in the kitten visual cortex seemed to correlate better with the time course of cortical susceptibility to monocular deprivation than with changes in endogenous CAs. The segregation of ocular dominance columns in the visual cortex also starts at 3 weeks of age in cats (LeVay *et al.*, 1978). These considerations lead us to the following question: What does the CA system do during the maturation of neocortex?

2. *Presence of Monoaminergic Terminals and Their Receptors in the Neocortex*

a. Ascending Catecholaminergic Bundles. Paraformaldehyde gas-induced fluorescence histochemistry clearly has shown that CA (most of them NE) neurons are found primarily in the dorsolateral part of the pontine tegmentum including the LC and the NSC, whereas serotonergic neurons are almost exclusively located in the midline structure of the raphe nuclei (Falck *et al.*, 1962; Fuxe, 1965; Andén *et al.*, 1966). More recent studies, however, have demonstrated a small number of serotonin-containing cell bodies also located in the LC complex of the primate (Sladek and Walker, 1977) and the cat (Léger *et al.*, 1979). Such discoveries spurred the development of techniques using the monoamine neurotoxins 6-OHDA and 6-hydroxydopa, as well as other substances [such as FLA-63, a dopamine-β-hydroxylase (DBH) inhibitor] to locate exactly the cell body of NE-containing neurons and to trace the extension of their axons by inducing in them specific chemical lesions (Ungerstedt, 1968, 1971a,b; Bloom *et al.*, 1969; Breese and Traylor, 1970; Corrodi *et al.*, 1970; Uretsky and Iversen, 1970; Olson and Fuxe, 1971; Jacobowitz and Kostrzewa, 1971; Sachs *et al.*, 1973).

Two types of CA-containing neurons were described in the lateral pontine tegmentum in rats (Maeda and Shimizu, 1972) and cats (Maeda *et al.*, 1973). They are distinguishable from each other on the basis of their fluorescence intensity as well as their individual cell morphology. Medium-size oval cells with weak fluorescence are packed in the dorsal caudal portion of the LC (in rats) and send axons to the ascending *dorsal* CA bundle. On the other hand, large multipolar cells with strong green fluorescence are found mainly in the ventral portion of the LC and the NSC. They are sparsely distributed in cats, invading into the dorsoanterior portion of the LC. Their axons consist of the *intermediate* CA ascending bundle, which is widespread just ventral to the brachium conjunctivum and gives dense collaterals in the mesencephalic reticular formation. This bundle crosses the midline in the supraoptic decussation, reaching mainly the posterior hypothalamus and probably the LGN. There are also noncrossing fibers which contribute to the innervation of the cerebral cortex together with fibers in the ascending dorsal CA bundle. However, Jones and Moore (1974) found no morphological basis for such a subdivision of the cat LC into two groups in either the Falck-Hillarp material or Nissl-stained tissue.

Immunocytochemical methods have been applied to map NE-containing cells and their axons using an antibody against DBH (Swanson and Hartman, 1975; Pickel *et al.,* 1976; Morrison *et al.,* 1978; Grzanna *et al.,* 1978; Grzanna and Molliver, 1980). In the rat LC complex, Grzanna and Molliver (1980) suggested the presence of four contiguous but cytologically distinct subdivisions. This point will be further discussed in connection with the possible topographical projection of NE-containing cells.

b. The Coerulo-Cortical Pathway. Using the newly developed glyoxylic acid fluorescence method, Lindvall and associates (1974b) demonstrated NE innervation of both specific and nonspecific thalamic nuclei in rats. This was confirmed by a more recent degeneration study in cats (McBride and Sutin, 1976). More directly, Léger and associates (1975) later showed retrograde transport of HRP from the LGN to the LC complex in the cat pons. The glyoxylic acid histofluorescence method also demonstrated ascending NE-containing axons in the cerebral cortex (Andén *et al.,* 1966), and their course from the pons to the neocortex has been studied in detail (Fuxe, 1965; Ungerstedt, 1971a; Maeda and Shimizu, 1972; Levitt and Moore, 1978; Lidov *et al.,* 1978a). The existence of coerulo-cortical projections was also proved by autoradiographic techniques by Segal and others (1973), Pickel and others (1974), and Jones and Moore (1977). Furthermore, by means of Nauta's method, Suárez and Llamas (1968) traced degenerated fibers to the cerebral cortex after gross destruction of the oral pontine tegmentum.

Previous studies also showed a variety of pathways by which NE fibers enter the neocortex. In rats, Ungerstedt (1971a) used 6-OHDA and electrical lesion methods to determine that the main entry course is through the medial forebrain bundle and then the septum. Using 6-hydroxydopa, Jacobowitz and Kostrezwa (1971) suggested that the ascending NE tract enters the neocortex through both the septum and the internal capsule. Later, Segal and others (1973) and Pickel and others (1974) confirmed the cortical entry through the septum and the cingulum by autoradiography. Sachs and others (1973) mapped out NE fibers entering the neocortex through the internal capsule. Shimizu and associates (1974), by a modified Fink-Heimer method, defined the whole course of degenerating fibers in the coerulo-cortical projections in rats. Using 6-hydroxydopa as a marker, a later study detailed in rats the three main regions through which the ascending NE bundles enter the cerebral cortex: the internal capsule, the external capsule, and the anterior septal region (Tohyama *et al.,* 1974b).

Despite such pioneer work, our knowledge of the coerulo-cortical pathway is far from complete, especially in the cat and kitten visual cortex, where we wish to study neuronal plasticity. For example, we do not know whether the three different pathways revealed by Tohyama and others (1974b) are composed of collaterals originating from the same cells or axons in the LC. Only the outline of the ascending NE bundles, dorsal and intermediate, was presented in cats by Maeda and associates (1973). In cats, McBride and Sutin (1976) followed degenerating fibers from the dorsolateral tegmentum, including the LC, mainly to the nucleus centrum mediarum parafascicular complex, with few axons branching to the pretectal area, the medial nuclei, and the LGNs, but they failed to trace any fibers up to the neocortex. In the squirrel monkey, Freedman and others (1975) demonstrated labeled neurons in the LC after injections of HRP into the temporal, frontal, and occipital cortices. They also found heavily labeled fibers ascending in the midbrain following direct injection of [^{3}H]proline into the entire LC, portions of the brachium conjunctivum, and adjacent areas. These labeled fibers finally reached the superior temporal gyrus through the internal capsule. Dense labeling was seen in all layers of neocortex, and clusters of grains involved all types of cells. Using an HRP tracing method, Gatter and Powell (1977) studied the neocortical projection of the LC in macaque monkeys. Taking advantage of an autoradiographic method, Jones and Moore (1977) presented, again in rats, very detailed descriptions of ascending projections from the LC.

Since the distribution of NE-containing cells in the pons is so widespread, especially in cats (Maeda *et al.,* 1973; Chu and Bloom, 1974; Jones and Moore, 1974; Poitras and Parent, 1978), it may not be unreasonable to expect some sort of topographical organization in the axon trajectory of NE cells. For example, Jouvet (1974) suggested a possible functional differentiation of the dorsal and intermediate CA ascending bundles. The former, projecting to the cerebral cortex through the mesencephalon, may be responsible mainly for cortical arousal, whereas the latter, originating from large cells in the NSC, is most likely responsible for tonic as well as phasic events in REM sleep. Chu and Bloom (1974) in fact noted that CA cells in the anterior pons send their axons to form the dorsal ascending CA bundles and also give off axon collaterals to innervate the cerebellum. On the other hand, in the posterior pons, CA cells seem to innervate the cerebellum directly, without contributing to the ascending CA bundles. They also noted some differential innervation of the raphe complex by different CA cell groups. Sakai and associates (1977b) noted the rather restricted afferent projections of the dorsal raphe nucleus to the dorsomedial part of the LC. This contrasted to their finding in the same study that the ventrolateral part of the LC received rather widespread afferents from the diencephalons and rhombencephalons which included the nucleus substantia nigra, the central gray, the hypothalamus, the preoptic areas, the nuclei raphe pontis and magnus, and the cerebellar nuclei. Snider (1975) found degenerating terminals mainly in the medial dorsal part of the LC and the dorsal part of the nucleus parabrachialis lateralis after placing unilateral electrolytic lesions in the nucleus fastigii of the cat's cerebellum. Employing multiple but small injections of HRP into different areas in the cat visual cortex, Törk and associates (1979) traced back the labeled cells in various monoaminergic nuclei in the brainstem. By comparing the numbers of labeled cells, they claimed that area 18 might receive more afferents from the LC than either area 17 or area 19 did. The question of topographical organization in the LC complex and its afferent and efferent projections has received renewed interest (Lidov *et al.,* 1978a; Mason and Fibiger, 1979a; Loughlin *et al.,* 1979; Ader *et al.,* 1979; Grzanna and Molliver, 1980; Morrison *et al.,* 1981). In this regard, the presence of the two types of antidromically identified LC cells (C and T types), which have different cortical projection patterns as well as intranuclear connectivities, deserves particular attention (Nakamura, 1977; Nakamura and Iwama, 1980).

c. CA Terminals in the Kitten Visual Cortex. The intracortical distribution of NE fibers and terminals has been intensively studied in rats using various fine morphological techniques such as autoradiography (Descarries *et al.,* 1977), histofluorescence (Lidov *et al.,* 1978a,b; Levitt and Moore, 1978), and immunohistochemistry based on the localization of DBH (Swanson and Hartman, 1975; Morrison *et al.,* 1978; Grzanna *et al.,* 1978).

Several investigators have studied CA cell bodies in the pontine tegmentum as well as their ascending bundles in adult cats (Maeda *et al.,* 1973; Chu and Bloom, 1974; Jones and Moore, 1974; McBride and Sutin, 1976; Poitras and Parent, 1978). Nevertheless, no detailed study has been made in the occipital area of the neocortex, the most remote area for the NE fibers to reach in the brain.

We have been studying the nature of NE fibers and terminals in the kitten visual cortex by two approaches (Itakura *et al.,* 1978, 1979, 1981). One is CA fluorescence histochemistry to visualize the distribution pattern of CA fibers and terminals throughout all six cortical layers. The other is electron microscopy of individual CA terminal boutons to clarify the likely neural elements with which these boutons maintain intimate contact. We find that there is a rich CA innervation throughout the visual cortex, particularly in layers II and III (Fig. 1), in contrast to the dense plexus formation found by Levitt and Moore (1978) in layer I of the rat's neocortex.

In the kitten visual cortex, we found that only 20% of the terminals iden-

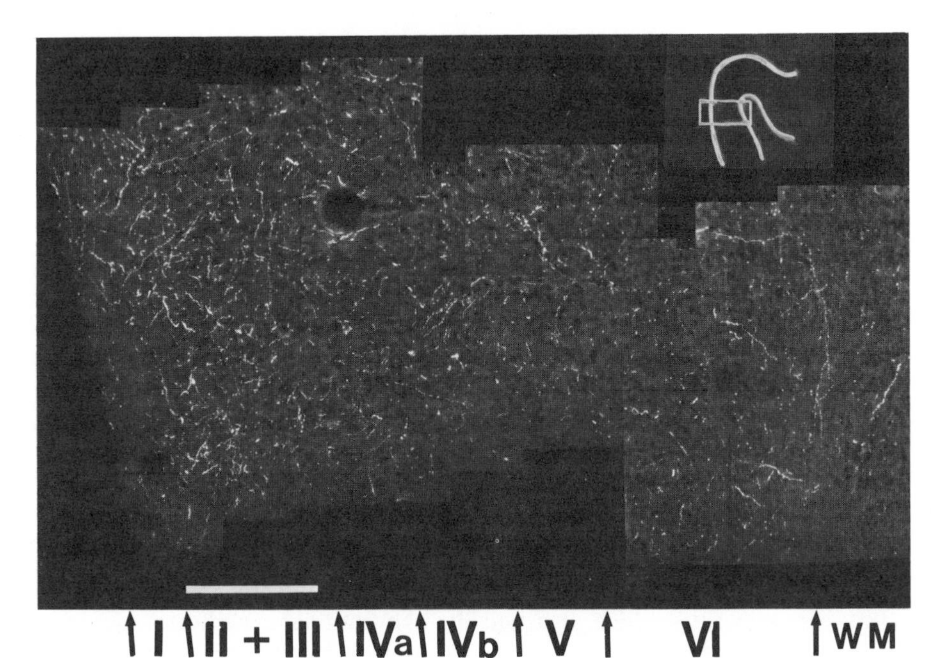

FIG. 1. A dark-field fluorescence photomicrograph (coronal section, 16 μm thick) which shows CA-containing fibers and terminals in the visual cortex of a normal 6-week-old kitten. An inset indicates the part of the visual cortex (area 17 in the medial bank of the postlateral gyrus) from which this montage picture was taken. Roman numerals I–VI represent the six cortical layers; their approximate boundaries are indicated by arrows.

Intensely fluorescent CA fibers, most of which are thought to originate from the LC complex in the pontine tegmentum, approach the cerebral cortex through the white matter (WM) and then enter layer VI by sharply changing their course. The stem fibers further proceed toward the cortical surface, having many terminal fibers with varicosities (1–3 μm in diameter) running in all directions. In the superficial layer, the fine terminal fibers tend to run primarily parallel to the surface. In layers II and III, we found the dense plexus of CA fibers. Circumstantial evidence strongly suggests that these CA terminals in fact contain NE rather than DA and 5-HT (for further details, see Itakura *et al.*, 1981). The scale bar is 300 μm. (Modified and reproduced with permission from Itakura *et al.*, 1981, *Neuroscience* **6**, 159–175).

tified as monoamine-containing by fixation with potassium permanganate showed some sign of synaptic formation, including the accumulation of cytoplasmic materials (synaptic membrane thickening), widening of the associated membrane space, and aggregation of small, dense cored vesicles adjacent to the presynaptic membrane (Itakura *et al.*, 1981). This is consistent with the previous findings in the rat brain, in which only a fraction of CA terminals (5–20%) had the typical synaptic contact with surrounding neural elements (Maeda *et al.*, 1975; Descarries *et al.*, 1977; Koda and

Bloom, 1977). The fact that a large proportion of NE terminals fail to make typical synapses, but are in close proximity to other neural elements in the cortex, supports the possibility raised by others that released NE may work as a neurohormone (extrajunctional release) as well as a neurotransmitter (junctional release). This view has been recently challenged by Molliver and his assoicates, who observed by electron microscopy that more than half of the DBH antibody-positive varicosities in the known NE terminal fields (along with a few samples in the neocortex) formed conventional axodendritic synapses (Olschowka *et al.,* 1981). It is usually assumed that since each specialized synaptic site occupies such a small fraction of the total surface area of a single varicosity, many synaptic sites may be missed in any one randomly cut, ultrathin section through the NE varicosities. Molliver and his associates thus proposed that virtually all NE terminals in the brain make conventional synapses. There are, however, two problems with their proposal. First, as a usual technical requirement for electron microscopic immunocytology, the sections in their study were treated with detergent. This procedure may significantly alter the specificity of recognition of DBH-containing sites, resulting in an unusually high rate of DBH-antibody positive varicosities which also had the conventional synapse formation. Second, the sampling frequency of the usual synaptic sites reported by Molliver and his associates (58%) in the identified DBH-containing varicosities does exceed the probability of having the specialized synaptic zone in any single ultrathin section cut randomly, as calculated by Beaudet and Sotelo (1981) to be 34% from the consideration that the diameter of a spherical synaptic bouton is 0.6 μm and the area occupied by the specialized synaptic zone is 0.2 μm across.

d. Effects of Iontophoretically Injected NE in the Cortex. Single cortical cells are known to be sensitive to iontophoretically applied NE, and the response can be either excitatory (Johnson *et al.,* 1969a,b; Stone, 1973; Szabadi *et al.,* 1977; Sharma, 1977; Bevan *et al.,* 1977) or inhibitory (Krnjević and Phillis, 1963; Frederickson *et al.,* 1971, 1972; Lake *et al.,* 1972, 1973; Stone, 1973; Foote *et al.,* 1975; Bunney and Aghajanian, 1976b; Szabadi *et al.,* 1977; Reader, 1978; Reader *et al.,* 1979). Thus, there is some controversy over the primary effect of NE in the CNS. Bloom has written that the response to NE of identified cells is inhibitory in many brain regions, with several exceptions (1975, 1978). In the mammalian cerebral cortex, however, the modes of response to NE seem to depend on various experimental conditions, such as the type of anesthesia used (Johnson *et al.,* 1969b), the pH of the NE solution (Frederickson *et al.,* 1971; Stone, 1972), and the level of ongoing spontaneous activity when NE is iontophoresed (Szabadi *et al.,* 1977). In a recent study, Bevan *et al.* (1977) presented evidence for the involvement of two basic receptor types (excitatory α and inhibitory β receptors) in explaining the two responses to NE in rat cerebral cortex. Histofluorescence (Andén *et al.*, 1966; Fuxe *et al.*, 1968; Maeda and Shimizu, 1972, Ungerstedt, 1971a; Freedman *et al.*, 1975; Zecevc and Molliver, 1978), and immunofluorescence (Swanson and Hartman, 1975; Morrison *et al.*, 1978; Grzanna *et al.*, 1978; Grzanna and Molliver, 1980) studies have established that the LC complex (LC and NSC, the Kölliker-Fuse nucleus, and the nucleus parabrachialis in the case of cats) is the primary location of NE-containing cell bodies in the mammalian brain. Therefore, it is critical to compare the effects of electrical or chemical stimulation of the LC complex with those of iontophoresis of NE onto the same single cells in a given terminal field, although few studies have used this careful twofold analytical approach.

Single cells in the visual system are among the best-characterized cells in the brain, both morphologically and physiologically. Stimulation of the LC usually results in an increase in NE turnover and NE metabolites; the elevated release of NE in the rat cerebral cortex thus decrases the intracortical NE content (Korf *et al.*, 1973a,b; Walter and Eccleston, 1973; Tanaka *et al.*, 1976). Nevertheless, because of the heterogeneity of the organization of the LC complex, especially in cats, it is crucuial to study the responses of these identified cells (with respect to, for example, their receptive field properties) to both iontophoresis of NE and direct stimulation of the LC. In the cat LGN, previous authors have observed an excitatory response to LC stimulation, which can be abolished by prior treatment with 6-OHDA (Nakai and Takaori, 1974). This effect seems to be mediated by postsynaptic α receptors (Rogawski and Aghajanian, 1980a; Kayama *et al.*, 1982). Unfortunately, these investigators did not use a receptive field analysis to identify the individual geniculate cells.

Recently, we haved studied in the cat how the responsiveness of visual cortical cells changes during NE iontophoresis, when individual receptive fields are stimulated with an appropriate visual stimulus (Kasamatsu and Heggelund, 1982). We found the three populations of cortical cells, occurring with about equal frequency, which either increased, decreased, or did not change their responsiveness during NE iontophoresis. We also noted a differential sensitivity to exogenous NE in the two distinctive cell types defined physiologically in the visual cortex. The simple cells (Hubel and Wiesel, 1962) were more sensitive to NE in changing their responsiveness to proper visual stimulation than were the complex cells. Independently of whether a spontaneously active cell in the visual cortex increased or decreased its absolute excitability to an appropriate visual stimulus during NE iontophoresis, NE seem to modulate neuronal activity in the visual cortex by enhancing the cell's responsiveness to specific afferents relative to their background spontaneous activity. Similar observations were made previously regarding different areas of the brain (Foote *et al.*, 1975; Freedman *et al.*, 1975; Moises *et al.*, 1979; Waterhouse and Woodward, 1980).

e. β-Adrenergic Receptors in the Cerebral Cortex. By iontophoresis of various CA agonists and anatagonists, as mentioned above, previous studies have suggested the presence of β-adrenergic receptors in the mammalian neocortex. More direct evidence for the presence of these β-adrenergic receptors has been obtained by quantifying receptor binding sites using radioligands such as [^{125}I]iodohydroxybenzylpindolol (Sporn and Molinoff, 1976), (−) [^{3}H]dihydroalprenolol (Alexander *et al.*, 1975; Davis and Lefkowitz, 1976; Bylund and Snyder, 1976), and [^{3}H]propranolol (Atlas *et al.*, 1974; Nahorski, 1976; Levitzki, 1976). The ontogeny of β-adrenergic receptors and CA-sensitive adenylate cyclase systems has been intensively studied in the rat brain (Schmidt *et al.*, 1970; Coyle and Campochiaro, 1976; Spano *et al.*, 1976), including the cerebral cortex (Perkins and Moore, 1973; von Hungen *et al.*, 1975; Harden *et al.*, 1977a; Walton *et al.*, 1979). The radioligand binding method was also used to demonstrate an increase in binding sites in the rat cerebral cortex due to postdenervation supersensitivity following 6-OHDA treatment (Harden *et al.*, 1977b). This finding has been confirmed in a similar study in the rat brain after neonatal 6-OHDA treatment (Jonsson and Hallman, 1978).

A pharmacological work suggests that there are two kinds of β receptors in the neocortex: one confined largely to blood vessels and glial cells and unaffected by manipulation of NE afferents (β2 type), the other associated with neurons and exhibiting denervation supersensitivity after NE denervation (β1 type) (Minneman *et al.*, 1979a). β2 Receptors have a very low affinity for NE but a correspondingly higher affinity for epinephrine. Most β adrenoreceptors in the cerebral cortex are the β1 type, whereas those in the cerebellar cortex are the β2 type (Minneman *et al.*, 1979b; Pittman *et al.*, 1980).

f. Presynaptic α-Adrenergic Receptors. Several radioligand binding studies with [^{3}H]WB4101 (an α-adrenergic antagonist of the benzodioxane family) have produced direct evidence for the presence of α-adrenergic receptors in the cerebral cortex (Greenberg *et al.*, 1976; U'prichard *et al.*, 1977; Davis *et al.*, 1978). Previous iontophoretic studies have also suggested their presence in the mammalian cerebral cortex (Johnson *et al.*, 1969a; Bevan *et al.*, 1977).

In the rat hypothalamus, an antagonistic relationship between α- and β-adrenergic receptors has been postulated to control hunger and satiety centers, respectively (Leibowitz, 1971). More importantly, the presence of α-adrenergic receptors on dendrites of the LC cells in the brainstem has been proposed as a possible mechanism of self-control of the NE system (Carlsson's autoreceptors) (Svensson *et al.*, 1975; Cedarbaum and Aghajanian, 1977; Svensson and Usdin, 1978). This thesis seems to have evolved from the biochemical studies of DA release in the neostriatum and its modification by neuroleptics (Farnebo and Hamberger, 1971; Carlsson *et al.*, 1972; Kehr *et al.*, 1972; Plotsky *et al.*, 1978; Starke *et al.*, 1978). More recently, DA autoreceptors have been intensively studied, pharmacologically as well as electrophysiologically, in the DA cells in the substantia nigra (Bunney and Aghajanian, 1976a; Korf *et al.*, 1976; Geffen *et al.*, 1976; Aghajanian and Bunney, 1977).

Furthermore, in the peripheral CA system both α- and β-adrenergic receptors are known to occur on both presynaptic and postsynaptic membranes. Presynaptic α- and β-adrenergic receptors are believed to play opposite roles in the release of NE in that α adrenoreceptors may exert a negative feedback by restricting the available calcium, and β adrenoreceptors may provide positive feedback by elevating cyclic AMP (adenosine cyclic 3′, 5′-monophosphate) levels in the nerve terminals (e.g., Langer, 1977).

Pharmacological and biochemical studies indicate that there are two subtypes of α-adrenergic receptors in the peripheral nervous system (Doxey *et al.*, 1977; see a review by Langer, 1977) as well as in the CNS (Starke and Montel, 1973; U'prichard *et al.*, 1977; Miach *et al.*, 1978; Glossmann and Presek, 1979). $\alpha 1$ Receptors are thought to be located on the postsynaptic membrane and to be preferably recognized by α antagonists such as prazosin and phenoxybenzamine, $\alpha 2$ Receptors are located on the presynaptic membrane, are stimulated by α agonists such as clonidine and α-methyl noradrenaline, and are blocked by yohimbine and piperoxan. In contrast to the two types of β-adrenergic receptors, the $\alpha 1$ and $\alpha 2$ adrenoreceptors seem to mature concurrently in the rat brain, attaining a maximum number of binding sites at 3 weeks of age, which thereafter declines to the adult value (Morris *et al.*, 1980). There is even a suggestion of heterosynaptic interaction among different neurotransmitter or neurohormone systems through a mosaic of various presynpatic receptors (e.g., Langer, 1978).

One pharmacological study has suggested that contraction of middle cerebral arteries in the cat's brain is mediated through α receptors (Edvinsson and Owman, 1974). In this study, dilatation was also achieved by activation of β receptors ($\beta 1$ type), but only in the arteries which had been tonically contracted by serotonin.

g. DA and Its Receptors in the Neocortex. In early studies of the rat cerebral cortex, DA was detected primarily in the frontal, cingulate, and entorhinal but not the occipital region (Thierry *et al.*, 1973; Berger *et al.*, 1974; Lindvall *et al.*, 1974a). It seems more likely now, however, that DA is in fact found in all parts of the neocortex, including the occipital area, when assays of higher sensitivity are used. In our preliminary studies using a radioenzymatic assay (carried out in collaboration with W. Shoemaker and

F. Bloom), the DA content in the kitten visual cortex was about half the NE content in the same area (Kasamatsu and Pettigrew, 1979). A CA assay with liquid chromatography (Keller *et al.*, 1976) in the kitten visual cortex has also produced a similar result (Kasamatsu *et al.*, 1981b). In addition, there is now evidence for a projection from the dopaminergic nucleus (nucleus linearis rostralis) to the visual cortex in cats (Törk *et al.*, 1979).

Reader and others (1976) have demonstrated, under various conditions, that DA is released along with NE into the perfusate of the cat occipital cortex. Iontophoretically injected DA and NE modulated the firing of single cells in the cat visual cortex (Reader, 1978). No radioligand binding studies are known for DA receptors in the mammalian neocortex, although many [^{3}H]haloperidol binding studies have been made in DA-rich subcortical structures (Creese *et al.*, 1975; Seeman *et al.*, 1975; Burt *et al.*, 1976b). Radiolabeled spiroperidol (Creese *et al.*, 1977), dihydroergocryptine (Tittler *et al.*, 1977; Caron *et al.*, 1978), and DA (Creese *et al.*, 1975; Calabro and MacLeod, 1978) have also been used to search in the striatum and the anterior pituitary for DA receptors. There are, however, other results which suggest that the DA receptors in the nigro-striatum system can behave like α-adrenergic receptors under various conditions (McLennan and York, 1967; Connor, 1970; York, 1972; see also Libet, 1979).

Based on differences in the threshold concentrations of agonists and antagonists required to induce various physiological responses and the multiple binding sites identified with different radioligands, at least two types of DA receptors have been classified in the peripheral nervous system and the CNS (see a review by Kebabian and Calne, 1979). The occurrence of the first type, D1 receptor, is directly related to adenylate cyclase in the same region, and DA in micromolar concentrations is needed to stimulate it. On the other hand, the second type, D2 receptor, functions independently of adenylate cyclase, and DA in nanomolar amounts is enough to activate it. DA autoreceptors in the substantia nigra, for example, are the presynaptic D2 type and are therefore not assoicated with cyclase.

h. Serotonin in the Neocortex. An early histofluorescence study first demonstrated the presence of 5-HT-containing terminals in rat cerebral cortex (Fuxe, 1965). It was reported that they were primarily located in layer I and that this distribution pattern was the same throughout different areas of the neocortex. This early result has been confirmed and was later extended by biochemical, histofluorescence, and autoradiographic studies (Kuhar *et al.*, 1972; Descarries *et al.*, 1975; Azmitta and Segal, 1978; Moore *et al.*, 1978). A recent immunohistochemical study (Lidov *et al.*, 1980) refined these earlier descriptions with the discovery that whereas the serotoninergic fibers and their terminals form a dense, relatively uniform innervation across all six cortical layers in the lateral and anterior cingulate cortices, in the posterior cingulate cortex the 5-HT fibers were primarily found only in layers I and III. They further maintained that this restricted laminar arrangement was shared by the hippocampus as well (see also Steinbusch, 1981).

A biochemical study also suggested a similar gradient of endogenous 5-HT content in the monkey cerebral cortex, with higher concentrations in the occipital area than in the frontal and pariental areas (Brown *et al.*, 1979). This distribution pattern of 5-HT is the opposite of that known for CA, at least in the rat's neocortex. In cats, however, frontal cortices such as the olfactory and piriform regions showed much higher 5-HT values than did the parietal and occipital cortices (Gaudin-Chazal *et al.*, 1979). This biochemical finding in the cat cortex seems to be in harmony with the result of an intensive autoradiographic study which concerned a topographic map of efferent projections from various raphe nuclei in the cat (Bobillier *et al.*, 1976).

The existence of a reciprocal innervation between the NE neurons in the LC complex and the 5-HT neurons in the raphe system has been confirmed by means of morphological methods such as autoradiography (Conrad *et al.*, 1974; Bobillier *et al.*, 1976; Descarries and Leger, 1978), immunohistofluorescence (Swanson and Hartman, 1975; Pickel *et al.*, 1977), and retrograde tracing with HRP (Sakai *et al.*, 1977a,b). It is generally suggested that this reciprocal innervation between the NE and 5-HT systems is inhibitory. A more recent phsyiological study (Segal, 1979) has added further support to this general belief.

The presence of negative feedback loops, such as the one well known for the nigro-striatal DA system, has been postulated to explain decreased discharges of 5-HT-containing cells in the raphe when the synaptic availability of 5-HT is increased by administration of various 5-HT- related drugs (Aghajanian, 1972). This hypothesis, however, has been challenged by Moske and Jacobs (1977), who presented physiological evidence which suggests a possibility of the direct action of increased 5-HT at 5-HT receptors on raphe cells in brainstem-transected rats.

Relatively few 5-HT receptor binding studies have been carried out in the brain (Bennett and Snyder, 1975, 1976; Lovell and Freedman, 1976; Fillion *et al.*, 1978; Leysen *et al.*, 1978; Creese and Snyder, 1978), although a recent popular view maintains that the serotonin system also includes the multiple receptors as recognized for other monoamine systems. One receptor binding study suggested the presence of two distinct subtypes of serotonin receptors in the rat cerebral cortex: One type is preferentially bound by serotonin (5-HT1), and the other is identified by its binding to spiroperidol (5-HT2) (Peroutka and Snyder, 1979). Furthermore, the claim has since been made that drug potencies in blocking hydroxytryptophan-induced head twitches in mice closely correlate with binding affinities of those drugs for the 5-HT2 receptors (at the nanomolar level) but not for the 5-HT1 receptors (Peroutka *et al.*, 1981). Serotonin-induced excitation, both in behavior and in neuronal firing after iontophoresis, seems to be mediated by the 5-HT2 receptors which are specifically antagonized by cryproheptadine. Although a good correlation was noted, at the micromolar range, between the inhibition of 5–HT-sensitive cyclase (von Hungen *et al.*, 1975) and the inhibition of 5-HT1 binding, a correlation with serotonin-induced changes in neuronal firing has not yet been clearly demonstrated due to the lack of high-affinity antagonists.

Following acute (6–24-hour) depletion of 5-HT, either with reserpine or para-chlorophenylalanine (an inhibitor of 5-HT biosynthetic enzyme) or by raphe lesions, an apparent increase in the affinity of 5-HT binding but not in the total number of binding sites was reported in various brain regions, including the cerebral cortex (Bennett and Snyder, 1976). Furthermore, a recent 5-HT binding study failed to observe changes in the 5-HT receptor sensitivity, as measured by the total number of binding sites, following chronic (3 ~ 4 weeks) application of either an 5-HT antagonist such as metergoline, an uptake inhibitor such as chlorimipramine, or an 5-HT precursor, 5-hydroxytryptophan, which increases 5-HT turnover (Wirz-Justice *et al.*, 1978).

LSD (lysergic acid diethylamide) binding is thought to involve both 5-HT and DA receptors (Burt *et al.*, 1976a). The effects of LSD, which behaves primarily as an agonist of 5-HT receptors (5-HT1 and 5-HT2), are inhibitory to the firing of single cells in various brain sites, including the raphe nuclei and target areas such as the amygdala and the ventral LGN (see the review by Haigler and Aghajanian, 1977). LSD does appear, however, to be a 5-HT antagonist in the hippocampus (Segal, 1976). Although 5-HT itself seems to inhibit equally the presynaptic (in the raphe nuclei) and postsynaptic receptors (in the target areas), LSD is more potent in inhibiting the raphe neurons than the target cells. Despite these many physiological as well as biochemical studies in the 5-HT system, we remain still quite ignorant of the function of 5-HT in the neocortex (see also IV, D, 3).

3. *Possible Role for NE Terminals in the Maturation of the Neocortex*

Monoaminergic inputs seem to be the earliest afferents which invade the neocortex during the late stage of embryogenesis. In the rat, CA fibers reach the frontal cortex at about embryonic day 16 (Seiger and Olson, 1973; Schlumpf *et al.*, 1980). The presence of monoaminergic terminals at birth has been demonstrated either by various biochemical assays for endogenous monoamines, their synthesizing enzymes (Coyle and Axelrod, 1972a,b; Breese and Traylor, 1972; Porcher and Heller, 1972; Nomura *et al.*, 1976;

Coyle, 1977; Levitt and Moore, 1979; Daszuta *et al.,* 1979) and uptake mechanisms (Coyle and Axelrod, 1971; Kellogg and Lundborg, 1972, Nomura *et al.,* 1976, Coyle and Molliver, 1977; Kirksey *et al.,* 1978), or by such morphological methods as fluorescence histochemistry (Loizou, 1972; Levitt and Moore, 1978). Further maturation of the intracortical monoamine-containing machinery continues throughout postnatal development. As most previous biochemical studies have shown, the content of endogenous monoamines increases gradually toward the adult level, attaining either an obvious change in the slope or a plateau at 1–2 weeks of postnatal age (in the rat). This trend has been noted for endogenous monoamines not only in the whole brain (Karki *et al.,* 1962; Agrawal *et al.,* 1968; Breese and Traylor, 1972) but in various parts of the brain as well (Loizou and Salt, 1970; Loizou, 1972; Bourgoin *et al.,* 1977, 1979), including the cerebral cortex (Harden *et al.,* 1977a). A slightly different maturation curve was reported in another study, in which an early peak of endogenous NE was observed in the neocortex a few days after birth, followed by a drop at around 1 week of age (Levitt and Moore, 1979) before it increased gradually toward the adult level.

By applying a factor of 2.6–3.0, figured by adjusting the difference between rats and cats in terms of their gestational periods and start of breeding age, the maturation stage at 1–2 weeks of age in rats may correspond to that at 3–5 weeks of age in cats. Thus, we may expect certain changes in maturation curves of monoamine contents in the cat brain at 3–5 weeks in postnatal life. In fact, those few studies already carried out in developing kittens have shown such changes in various parts of the brain at this age (Bourgoin *et al.,* 1979). Our own biochemical assays in the kitten cortex, using high-pressure liquid chromatography combined with electrochemical recordings developed by Adams and his associates (Keller *et al.,* 1976), have also produced maturation curves for cortical monoamines which fit this expectation quite well (Jonsson and Kasamatsu, submitted). We have noted small but significant plateaus in the endogenous NE and DA levels, superimposed on their gradual increase, at 3–5 and 9–13 weeks of age in both the frontal and occipital cortices. The behavior of the 5-HT content was similar, although the early peak at 3–5 weeks was much more prominent and was followed by a sharp drop later on. This result for 5-HT in the cat neocortex is at variance with that in the rat forebrain, in which a relatively montonous increase with or without a small plateau at 4 weeks of age was observed (Loizou and Salt, 1970; Bourgoin *et al.,* 1977).

Another recent observation generated by CA fluorescence histochemistry in developing kitten cortices suggests that at 6 weeks of age the distribution pattern of CA fibers and terminals becomes rather similar to that seen in the adult cortex, although the density and intensity of fibers with CA fluorescence continue to increase further with age (Itakura and Kasamatsu, unpublished). Furthermore, the correspondence between the maturation of the CA system and that of the visual cortical cells seems to become more related in consideration of the ontogeny of β-adrenergic receptor binding sites as an index of the development of the CA system (Harden *et al.*, 1977a; Pittman *et al.*, 1980; Jonsson and Kasamatsu, submitted).

At 3–5 weeks of age, when the CA system within the cerebral cortex undergoes significant changes, as mentioned above, the majority of individual cells in the kitten visual cortex already express receptive field properties specific for each cell (Hubel and Wiesel, 1963; Pettigrew, 1974; Blakemore and Van Sluyters, 1975; Buisseret and Imbert, 1976, Frégnac and Imbert, 1978). Nevertheless, most of the developing cells in young animals are not by any means irreversibly committed to a particular set of receptive field properties obtained thus postnatally. These properties can easily be modified experimentally by exposing young animals to restricted visual environments, as described in the section II, A, B. The quality as well as the quantity of visual experience received by individuals during the postnatal critical period in fact permanently determines the synaptic connections committed to certain receptive field properties. We may say that the critical period is like a term of engagement between the physical nature of various objects in the visual space and individual cells in the visual cortex. Throughout this engagement, certain selection processes seem to occur, suggested by the gradual decline to the adult level in the synaptic density and the average number of synapses per cortical cell, as studied by Cragg (1975a) in the kitten visual cortex, from a peak density at 5 weeks of age (or 10 weeks; Winfield, 1981). This a normal process of rearrangement of tentative, functionally established synaptic contacts between afferent terminals and postsynaptic sites on the cortical cell surface. Certain synapses which have failed to strengthen the functional and morphological ties between the presynaptic and postsynaptic membranes seem subsequently to disappear, although the presence of degenerating terminal boutons has never been established morphologically in the normally maturing cortex. The initial overproduction and later reduction of synapses (synapse elimination) are one of the consistent observations in developing synapses in various nervous systems, such as the neuromuscular junction and the autonomic ganglia (Brown *et al.*, 1976; Korneliussen and Jansen, 1976; Riley, 1977; Lichtman, 1977; Betz *et al.*, 1980; Lichtman and Purves, 1980; see also a review by Purves and Lichtman, 1980). In certain systems, such as the frog and chicken spinal motoneurons and the chicken isthmo-optic tract nucleus, the reduction in the total number of cells in a given structure is also an important factor in the development of the normal axon–target cell connections during ontogeny (programmed cell death) (Prestige, 1970, 1974; Cowan, 1973; Clarke and Cowan, 1975, 1976; Landmesser and Pilar, 1976; Oppenheim, 1981).

The similarity in the developmental time course of the intracortical CA system and the synaptogenesis in the visual cortex suggests that the two processes may be related. Although Jouvet (1975a) has expressed some doubt about this possibility, another group of authors had proposed that *patterned* activity, like the PGO waves and the silent period which follows in REM sleep, may play an important role as an organizing force in brain maturation, especially in early postnatal days when the central target cells do not receive enough primary sensory afferents (Roffwarg *et al.*, 1966). Below, I will review some evidence which suggests the occurrence of abnormal cell morphology in animals whose CA systems have been neonatally destroyed.

Maeda and associates (1974) found that the maturation of layer VI pyramidal cells was suppressed in the rat somatosensory cortex ipsilateral to the LC region which had been electrolytically destroyed immediately after birth. These abnormal pyramidal cells stretched their apical dendrites all the way up to layer I, and fewer than normal branches were observed along their course. A similar finding was reported in pyramidal cells in the hippocampus of rats which had been neonatally subjected to subcutaneous injection of 6-OHDA (Amaral *et al.*, 1975), although this procedure did not induce the abnormal morphology of pyramidal cells in the neocortex, as reported by Maeda and others (Lidov and Molliver, 1979). Systemic injection of 6-OHDA in neonate rats, however, brought about many subtle changes in neuron morphology, such as an increase in the dendritic branching of pyramidal cells in the neocortex and the hippocampus (Wendlandt *et al.*, 1977), an increased contribution of a number of apical dendrites which form a columnar bundle in the neocortex (Hicks and D'Amato, 1975), a decrease in length as well as branching of basal dendrites of layers III and V pyramidal cells in the frontal and cingulate cortices, and the premature termination in layer III of apical dendrites of layer V pyramidal cells in the cingulate cortex (Felten *et al.*, 1982). Furthermore, a cluster of ectopic cells appears in such 6-OHDA-treated rats just beneath the pia mater on the surface of layer I of the neocortex (Lidov and Molliver, 1979). Parnavelas and associates even described a transient increase in the total number of synapses, during the first postnatal week, in the visual cortex of rats which received 6-OHDA neonatally (Blue *et al.*, 1980; Blue and Parnavelas, 1982). The specificity and significance of these changes are left unexplored.

The cyclic AMP–protein kinase system in the cell appears to be responsible for a variety of phenomena related to neuronal development and plasticity, such as mitosis (Raff *et al.*, 1978), axogenesis (Roisen *et al.*, 1972), selection of transmitter synthesizing enzymes (Schrier and Shapiro, 1973; Prasad, *et al.*, 1973), activation of tyrosine hydroxylase (Harris *et al.*, 1974), and phosphorylation of a microtubule-associated protein (Sloboda *et al.*, 1975). In connection with these divergent functions of cyclic AMP, it is intriguing to speculate on the possible role played by NE terminals in the migration of various types of cortical cells, their lamination, and their synapse formation. In 1975 Molliver and Kristt made an interesting observation in the parietal cortex of 6-day-old rat pups. They noted that, although synapse formation occurred rarely in the young cortex, 70% of all synapses sampled in the cortical zone (which later becomes layer IV) were made by monoaminergic terminals. Although the systemic injection of 5-OHDA as a nontoxic false transmitter for labeling monoaminergic terminals is problematical due to the questionable specificity of 5-OHDA uptake by CA nerve terminals. This finding sharply contrasts to repeated observations in the adult cortex that only a very small proportion (5–20%) of identified monoaminergic terminals maintains the usual synaptic contact with target cells in the mature cortex (Fuxe *et al.*, 1968; Maeda *et al.*, 1975; Descarries *et al.*, 1977; Itakura *et al.*, 1981). Other differences, such as the varying degrees of maturation of the cortex in question, and methodological variations in such procedures as electron microscopic autoradiography with [^{3}H]NE in glutaraldehyde-fixed tissue, 5-OHDA labeling, and visualization of endogenous CA by $KMnO_4$, may also contribute to this discrepancy. Using a DBH antibody as a probe, Olschowka and others (1981) in fact reported that 58% of all DBH-positive terminal boutons form axodendritic synapses in various NE terminal fields of the rat brain. As discussed above (Sections IV, A, 2, and IV, C), this crucial issue concerning the mode of action of monoamines in the brain has not yet been settled.

Synaptic plasticity in the immature visual cortex has been described in detail. Only a few studies, however, have tried to elucidate the possible mechanisms by which visual cortical cells can maintain their plasticity (see the preceding section). By superimposing the question of visual cortical plasticity on the recent development in CA studies, we have formulated a novel working hypothesis as follows: Synaptic plasticity in the visual cortex is maintained by the presence of a central NE system in the brain. In the next section, I will describe the maturation of our NE hypothesis by reviewing the results in each series of experiments carried out in our laboratory for the past 6 years.

B. Various tests of the NE hypothesis

I will now talk about the results of various experiments which we have devised to establish the basic correlation between cortical plasticity and the presence of NE-containing nerve terminals in the visual cortex. I will not describe the techniques used in our studies, except to mention a few specific aspects. Readers may refer for details to the original articles (Kasamatsu and Pettigrew, 1976, 1979; Pettigrew and Kasamatsu, 1978; Kasamatsu *et al.*, 1979, 1981a,b; Itakura *et al.*, 1981). Although our studies have been carried out in binocular cells in the feline visual cortex as a model system, I expect that a similar relationship exists in other parts of the feline brain, as well as the central visual system of other mammals—monkeys, for example—provided the CA innervation and the critical period plasticity occur. In fact, Daw and associates (Daw and Rader, 1981; and also Daw *et al.*, submitted) have recently shown that the modifiability of directional selectivity by single cells in the kitten visual cortex is reduced significantly if young kittens have been depleted of CA terminals in the visual cortex. They utilized a technique of 6-OHDA perfusion similar to the one used in our previous studies (described below) to place chemical lesions in the intracortical CA terminals.

1. Loss of Synaptic Plasticity Following Intraventricular Injections of 6-OHDA

We first noted a lack of neuronal plasticity in the visual cortex of kittens in which CA-containing nerve terminals in the brain had been chemically destroyed. We made chemical lesions of CA-containing fibers and terminals in the brain of 4 ~ 6-week-old kittens by repeated injections into the lateral ventricle of a CA-related neurotoxin, 6-OHDA, dissolved in saline and 0.1% in ascorbate to lower the pH of the solution in order to suppress auto-oxidation of 6-OHDA (pH 6). Daily injections were made through a chronically implanted cannula and were continued until the total amount of injected 6-OHDA reached 10 mg or more over 10 days. A few days after the start of the 6-OHDA injection, we closed one eye surgically by lid suture for 1 week. Paired control kittens from the same litters were injected with saline which contained 0.1% ascorbate.

The results of the first recordings, which took place in the summer of 1975, were very impressive. We found many binocularly driven cells in the visual cortex of the 6-OHDA-treated kittens which had been subjected to brief monocular deprivation. This finding contrasted strongly to the results in the control kittens from the same litters: The overwhelming majority of cells in their visual cortex, as expected following monocular deprivation, responded exclusively to stimulation of the nondeprived eye. It should be noted that in the 6-OHDA-treated and monocularly deprived kittens, all receptive field properties, such as orientation specificity, direction selectivity, and velocity sensitivity, were essentially normal, and the proportion of binocularly driven cells (binocularity), which was the parameter we wanted to modify by monocular lid suture, also remained high as compared to the control. We further noted the dose-response relationship between the total amount of 6-OHDA injected intraventricularly and the extent of binocularity preserved. The results of the initial tests of the CA hypothesis thus seemed

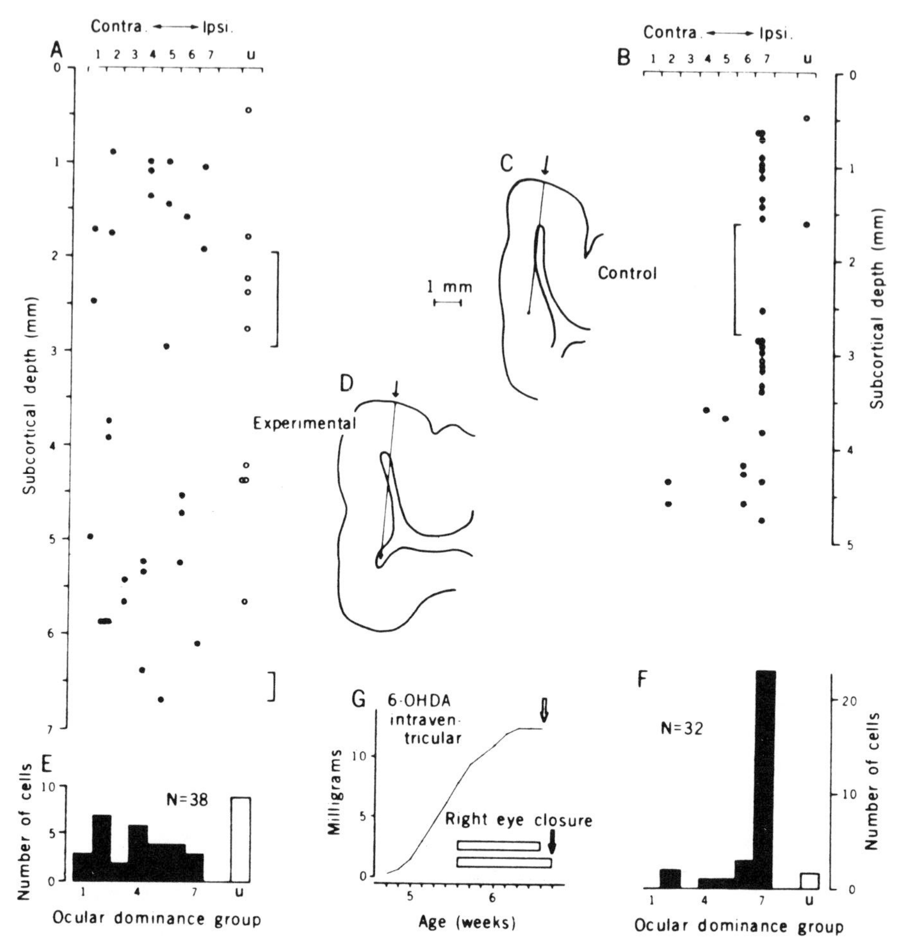

FIG. 2. Failure of the ocular dominance shift to occur, as observed after monocular lid suture in the kitten treated with a CA neurotoxin, 6-OHDA. (A, B) The location of single cortical cells recorded along a single electrode track is plotted in millimeters in the ordinate (filled circles, visually responsive; open circles, unresponsive). (A) represents a 6-OHDA-treated kitten and (B) a paired control kitten. The extent of binocular convergence of visual inputs on single cortical cells was semiquantitatively estimated, and each visually responding cell was accordingly classed into one of seven ocular dominance groups (Hubel and Wiesel, 1962). Briefly, group 4 cells receive well-balanced excitatory inputs from the two eyes. Groups 1 and 7 cells respond exclusively to stimulation of the contralateral or the ipsilateral eye, respectively. Cells in remaining groups, except group 4, fall between these two extremes. U stands for visually unresponsive cells. (C,D) Reconstruction of long, oblique electrode tracks for an experimental kitten (D) and a paired control kitten (C). They are projected in coronal sections which contain the microlesion made at the end of the tracks. In the brain, actual tracks were angled 5 degrees medially and anteriorly from the vertical. (E,F) Results in (A) and (B) are shown in ocular dominance histograms (38 and 32 cells, respectively). (G) The daily dose (in milligrams) of

to be encouraging and were interpreted as suggesting the necessity of intact CA-containing fibers and terminals in the brain, most likely within the visual cortex, for maintaining visual cortical plasticity. The results are summarized in Fig. 2.

Let us consider several practical problems involved in this paradigm of intraventricular injection of 6-OHDA. First, the amount of 6-OHDA used in this study (>10 mg) was quite large compared with the usual dose of 6-OHDA used to place chemical lesions in the CA system of rodents. The total amount of 6-OHDA could have been much smaller if we had used the acidic vehicle solution with 0.4% ascorbate (pH 3), as was used in later studies, rather than the 0.1% ascorbate which reduced the pH of the 6-OHDA solution to only 6. In 6-OHDA-treated kittens, a few days after the start of the treatment we began to observe certain behavioral changes, such as irregular pupil size and signs of epileptic fits, which conceivably might challenge our preferred interpretation of the physiological results. However, there was no consistent relationship between these adverse behavioral effects and the extent of binocularity preserved in monocularly deprived and 6-OHDA-treated animals. Furthermore, we did not make lesions to eliminate directly the LC, which contains CA-rich cell bodies, because the CA-containing cell bodies in the cat brainstem do not make the same sort of compact structure as occurs in the brains of rats and monkeys (German and Bowden, 1975; Demirjian *et al.*, 1976): In the cat pontine tegmentum, the CA cells are scattered even within the LC and NSC areas (see section IV, A,

(Figure 2 continued)

6-OHDA injected into the lateral ventricle of the experimental kitten is shown by a cumulative dose curve (solid line) against the postnatal days. The daily injection started with 200 μg and was doubled every day until it reached some upper limit (1.6 mg) determined behaviorally at the fourth injection. The total dose for 2 weeks was 12.4 mg. The control kitten received an equal volume of the acidic vehicle solution (dashed line). The timing and duration of monocular lid suture are indicated by open bars for both kittens. Single-unit recordings took place on postnatal day 46 for the experimental kitten (open arrow) and day 47 for the control one (filled arrow). The difference in the proportion of binocularly driven cells between the experimental (0.79) and the control (0.23) kittens is obvious. This failure of shift in ocular dominance does not seem to be explained well by a certain difference in the sampling efficiency of single cells between the experimental [(A), 180 μm per cell, track length 7mm] and control [(B) 118 μm per cell, track length 5mm] animals. In the four pairs of kittens used in this study series, including the pair exemplified here, the mean distance per visually responding cell was 112 μm for both control and experimental animals. The less than average sampling efficiency in the experimental kitten (A) exemplified here may be explained by the smaller exposed tip of microelectrode used (7.5 μm in length) in comparison to the usual tip size (10–15 μm) (see Fig. 6 in Kasamatsu and Pettigrew, 1979). Ten days after the start of 6-OHDA injection, the experimental kitten showed signs of localized seizure activity, which sometimes developed into a grand mal attack (for details, see Fig. 3A in Kasamatsu and Pettigrew, 1979). (Modified and reproduced with permission from Kasamatsu and Pettigrew, 1976, *Science* **194**, 206–209.)

2,a–c); there is also a relatively large group of CA cells in the nucleus parabrachialis. A further difficulty arose from our ignorance, especially in kittens, about which group of CA cells in the LC complex sends axons all the way up to the visual area of the neocortex. Recent studies, in fact, have suggested some sort of topographical organization of ascending CA pathways which originate from the LC complex (Mason and Fibiger, 1979a; Morrison *et al.*, 1981). Even so, the organization of this CA network is thought to be relatively loose compared with that of the DA (Moore and Bloom, 1978). It may yet be possible, however, to place chemical lesions with a small amount of 6-OHDA at small areas along the ascending CA bundles in the central gray region and the lateral hypothalamus.

Later, we studied histologically the visual cortex of 6-OHDA-treated kittens by means of CA histofluorescence. We, in fact, found remaining CA terminals, although fragmented and far less densely distributed, in layers II and III (Kasamatsu *et al.*, 1981b), where we usually observed the highest density of CA innervation among the six layers in the normal visual cortex (Itakura *et al.*, 1981). Biochemical assays of endogenous CAs also indicated their partial depletion in the visual cortex in kittens which received a total intraventricular injection of >10 mg 6-OHDA (Kasamatsu and Pettigrew, 1979). The susceptibility of CA terminals to 6-OHDA apparently varies largely from species to species.

2. *Localized and Continuous Microperfusion of the Visual Cortex with 6-OHDA: A Technical Improvement and a Conceptual Leap*

Next, we continued our research using a more sophisticated and less laborious method than that of daily injections for making chemical lesions of CA terminals in the visual cortex. In place of repeated intraventricular injections, I developed a method for direct and continuous microperfusion of the visual cortex with the 6-OHDA solution. This newly designed method of continuous microperfusion utilizes an osmotic minipump (Alza Corp.) which became commercially available a short time ago. The 6-OHDA solution (in 0.4% ascorbate saline, pH 3) is led through a polyethylene tubing (PE 60) from the minipump to a cannula (made of 26-G hypodermic needle) which is directly implanted in the cortical tissue. An osmotic minipump is placed subcutaneously at the neck. When the minipump is soaked with tissue fluid, it builds up an osmotic pressure and starts to compress the solution (which is kept in a reservoir) at a precalibrated constant rate of 1 μl/hour. An obvious advantage of this new method is the higher efficiency in placing specific chemical lesions with a small amount of 6-OHDA so that we can *localize* the effects of 6-OHDA primarily within a small area in the visual cortex. Another advantage is, then, that one can use the opposite hemisphere of the same animal as the nonperfused internal control. We soon learned that the area of the general tissue damage caused by a combination of direct placement of the cannula and continuous perfusion of the acidic 6-OHDA solution for 1 week was surprisingly small (1–2 mm in diameter), far smaller than originally believed (Kasamatsu *et al.,* 1979). The results in physiological recordings matched this histological finding in that we consistently recorded completely normal cells with the usual receptive field properties in an area only 1.5 mm away from the center of perfusion. When an electrode track was placed too close to the damaged region, we could not plot receptive fields at all, or could plot only nonselective fields, even if the cells were discharging spontaneously. The extent of tissue damage may actually be much smaller if we use a 30-G cannula in place of a 26-G cannula. Later, we also proved by CA fluorescence histochemistry that the dimension of the CA terminal depleted area, beyond the nonspecific lesion area mentioned above, was large enough to carry out single unit recordings (ca. 5 mm in radius for 4 m*M* 6-OHDA in 1 week) (Fig. 3; see also Kasamatsu *et al.,* 1979, 1981b). As will be seen below, direct perfusion with a minipump has resolved several doubts about the specificity of 6-OHDA treatment and has thus provided a great leap forward in our methodology.

With continuous perfusion of the visual cortex with 6-OHDA, we repeated the question: Can one prevent the shift of ocular dominance which usually follows brief monocular lid suture if one depletes specifically the CA-containing nerve terminals in the visual cortex? The answer was yes. We were delighted when we duplicated the initial results of blocking ocular dominance shift by this new method of continous and localized microperfusion of 6-OHDA. The right eyelid of kittens several weeks old was sutured for a week. Simultaneously with lid suture, a cannula was implanted into the left visual cortex. A cannula–minipump system was filled with 4 m*M* 6-OHDA. Thus, throughout a week of monocular experience, an area in the left visual cortex was perfused continuously with 6-OHDA to ensure the total destruction of intracortical CA terminals in the affected cortical area. In this experiment, a total of about 170 μg 6-OHDA was injected into the cortex (4 m*M*, 1 μg/μl/hour for 1 week). We then penetrated the cortex with microelectrodes, usually 2 mm away from the perfusion site, and found many binocular cells. Thus, the usual shift of ocular dominance after monocular deprivation was prevented. By placing other recording electrodes in an area farther away from the perfusion site, we noted that this effect of 6-OHDA perfusion could reach an area as far as 6 mm anterior to the perfusion site (Kasamatsu *et al.,* 1979). In contrast, ocular dominance in the opposite hemisphere of the same kitten showed a strong bias toward the nondeprived left eye. These results are summarized in Fig. 4. In biochemical studies, we later found that 4 m*M* 6-OHDA itself could reach an area max-

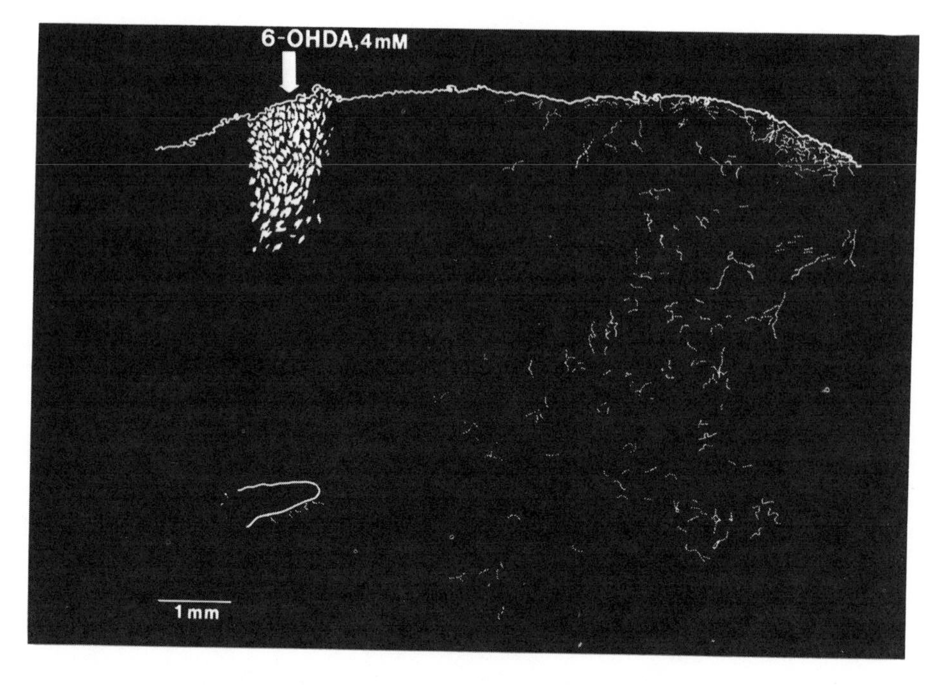

FIG. 3. Disappearance of CA-containing nerve fibers and terminals in the visual cortex of a 6-week-old kitten. The local area in the visual cortex was continuously perfused with 4m*M* 6-OHDA for a period of 1 week. A parasagittal section, treated with glyoxylic acid, was observed under a dark-field fluorescence microscope fitted with a drawing tube. The dense plexus of CA fibers and terminals totally disappeared in the vicinity of the perfusion site, which is indicated by a cluster of white markings. The radius of direct, nonspecific tissue damage due primarily to the chronic placement of 26-G hypodermic needle as a cannula was about 1 mm (usually <1.5mm; see Fig. 11 in Kasamatsu *et al.*, 1979). Remaining CA fibers are shown by dotted lines, which tended to be fragmented and short. Thus, the radius of the primary CA-specific lesion appears to be about 5 mm in the parasagittal plane (including the nonspecific lesion at the perfusion site, as mentioned above). (Reproduced with permission from Kasamatsu *et al.*, 1981b, *Journal of Pharmacology and Experimental Therapeutics* **217**, 841–850.)

imally 10 mm from the perfusion site in the same cortex (see also Fig. 3). Below, I will discuss further the maximal spread of 6-OHDA perfused locally, as well as its actual concentration at the recording site (Section IV, B, *10*).

3. Restoration of Plasticity with Microperfusion of Exogenous NE

The results of the two series of experiments described above strongly suggested that the loss of CA-containing terminals in the visual cortex was related to the lack of neuronal plasticity in such cortex. To reemphasize, the overwhelming majority of cells recorded from the 6-OHDA treatment and

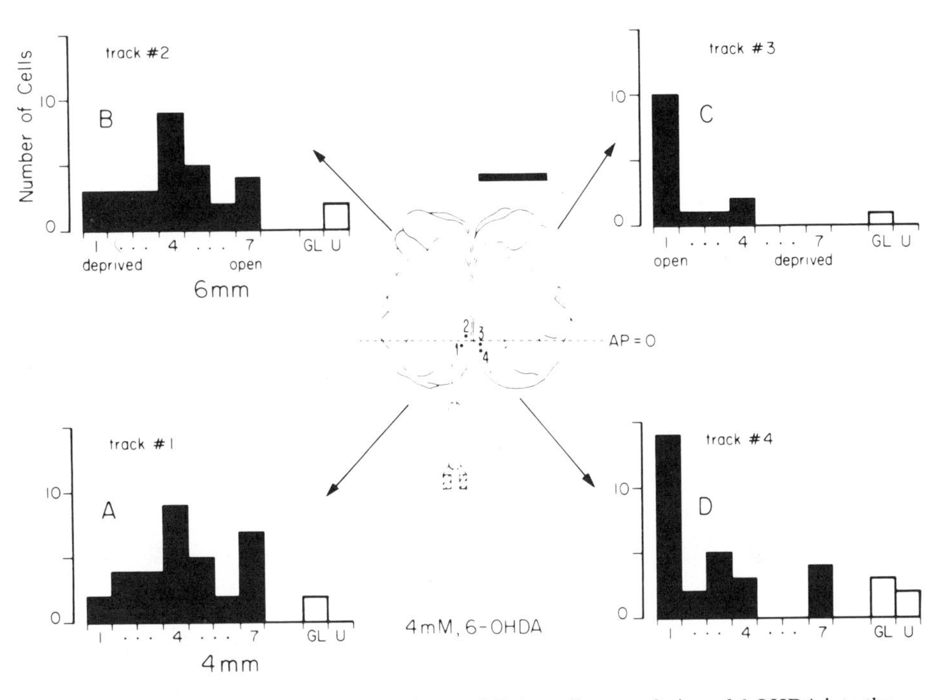

FIG. 4. Blockade of the ocular dominance shift by a direct perfusion of 6-OHDA into the visual cortex. (A,B) The expected shift of ocular dominance did not occur following monocular lid suture if the kitten's visual cortex had been continuously perfused with 4m*M* 6-OHDA throughout the period of monocular deprivation, which had lasted for 1 week. (C,D) The ocular dominance distribution in the other, unperfused hemisphere of the same kitten was dominated, as expected, by monocular cells which exclusively responded to stimulation of the nondeprived left eye, suggesting that this animal certainly had had an abnormal visual experience. The inset shows the approximate location of an implanted cannula, which was connected to an osmotic minipump (Alzet) and filled with 4m*M* 6-OHDA in 0.4% ascorbate and normal saline (pH 3). Concurrently, the right eyelid was surgically sutured shut. The entry points of four electrode tracks (1–4) are marked on the surface of the visual cortices. Ocular dominance histograms were prepared following the scheme of Hubel and Wiesel (1962). GL is for presumed genicualte axons within the cortex and U for visually unresponsive cells. See the legend for Fig. 2 for further details. The blocking effect of 6-OHDA on the shift of ocular dominance could be traced up to an area at least 6 mm away from the perfusion site. (Modified and reproduced with permission from Kasamatsu *et al.*, 1979, *Journal of Comparative Neurology* **185**, 163–182, and Fig. 1 in *Trends in Neurosciences* **3**, V.)

monocularly deprived cortex was quite normal in terms of the receptive field properties, including binocularity. As already mentioned, from the beginning of the project until now, we had strongly suspected that among the three major monoamines in the brain, it was the nerve fibers and terminals containing NE which were primarily, if not soley, responsible for the modulation of synaptic plasticity. These NE fibers in the neocortex uniquely originate from the NE-containing cells in the LC complex in the pons.

We then became interested in inceasing plasticity rather than decreasing it, as we had done in our previous studies, by determining whether synaptic plasticity can be restored by the continuous administration of NE to the visual cortex which had lost its plasticity due to prior lesions of intracortical CA terminals. In retrospect, we were naive, and the method we used to answer this question was bold. In the cholinergic system, for example, excess acetylcholine (ACh) or ACh agonists readily desensitize cholinoceptive receptors on target cells. A similar phenomenon has been reported for adrenergic receptors *in vitro* (Kebabian *et al.*, 1975; Mukherjee *et al.*, 1975; Strittmatter *et al.*, 1977). Nevertheless, the answer to the above question was again yes. We demonstrated the restoration of plasticity by direct perfusion of exogenous NE into the cortex which had been depleted of its CA terminals by prior 6-OHDA treatment. The design of the experiments was as follows: First, the visual cortex of 5 ~ 6-week-old kittens was depleted of its CA terminals by either intraventricular injections or direct localized perfusion of 6-OHDA into both hemispheres. Either approach was found equally valid as a pretreatment. Then, usually 10 days after the beginning of intraventricular 6-OHDA administration (or 1 week after implantation of a 6-OHDA-containing cannula–minipump), microperfusion of NE was started in the left hemisphere, and the right hemisphere was treated similarly with the vehicle solution alone (0.4% ascorbate in saline). The right eyelid was sutured simultaneously with the implantation of the NE cannula-minipump system and was kept closed until the day of single-unit recordings, which were carried out 1 week later. We expected not only to obtain many binocular cells in the right visual cortex perfused with the vehicle solution alone, since plasticity had been once lost equally in both hemispheres, but also to find that the majority of cells in the left cortex perfused with exogenous NE had become monocular again, responding exclusively to stimulation of the nondeprived left eye.

A few examples from this replacement study are shown in Fig. 5. In the NE-perfused cortex, in an area 2 mm away from the perfusion site, we found mostly monocular cells which responded only to stimulation of the nondeprived ipsilateral eye. In the control hemispheres of the same kittens, we obtained a nearly normal distribution of ocular dominance. We interpreted these findings as suggesting that the modifiability of neuronal connectivity is restored by exogenous NE given to the visual cortex which had lost its CA terminals due to prior 6-OHDA treatment. In an extreme example (Fig. 5, bottom), which is one of my favorites, we were able to demonstrate the presence of two quite different ocular dominance distributions in the same hemisphere generated by localized perfusion of 6-OHDA and NE at two distant sites in the visual cortex of a monocularly deprived kitten.

By changing the concentration ($5 \times 10^{-3} \sim 5$ mg/ml) of NE stored in the

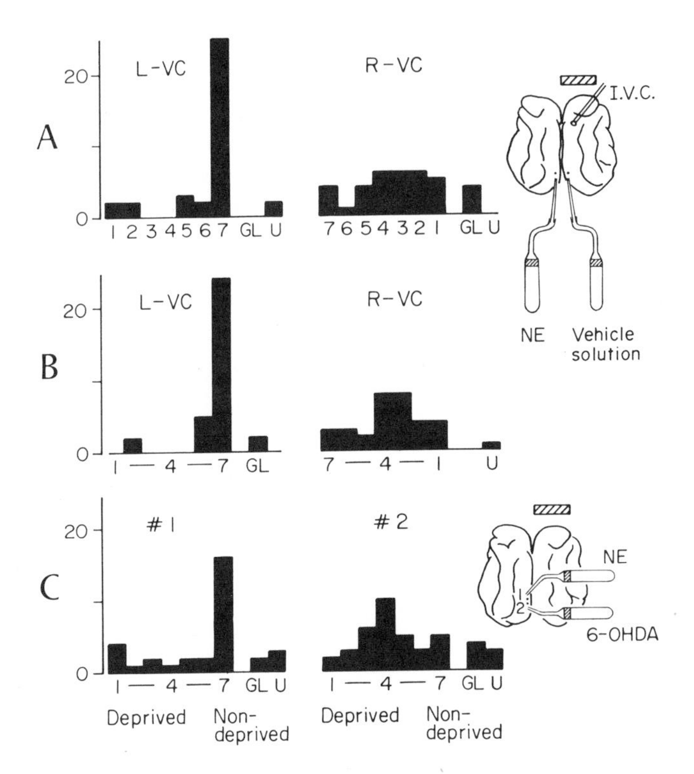

FIG. 5. Restoration of cortical sensitivity to cells subjected to monocular lid suture was demonstrated by localized continuous perfusion of the visual cortex with exogenous NE. (A,B) The brain of 6-week-old kittens had been first depleted of their CA-containing fibers by repeated injections of 6-OHDA (a total dose of > 10 mg) into the lateral ventricle (I.V.C. at the upper inset) over a period of 10 days. The right eyelid was then sutured closed simultaneously with the implantation of a pair of cannula-minipumps which contained either NE (50 μM or 0.5 mM, left hemisphere) or an acidic vehicle solution (pH 3, right hemisphere). The ocular dominance distribution was studied for both hemispheres at the end of NE perfusion and monocular deprivation, both of which concurrently lasted for 1 week. NE-perfused hemispheres were dominated by monocular cells which responded exclusively to stimulation of the nondeprived left eye, suggesting that a high level of neuronal plasticity was present in the left hemisphere. On the other hand, we found many binocularly driven cells in the control right hemisphere, and the ocular dominance distribution seemed to be unchanged even after monocular experience. This latter finding ensured that the CA terminals in both hemispheres had once been destroyed by prior administration of intraventricular 6-OHDA. (C) In an extreme case, we successfully created two cortical areas with quite different properties in the same hemisphere of one 7-week-old monoculary deprived kitten. One area (no.1) near the site of localized perfusion with 5 mM NE was dominated by group 7 monocular cells, suggesting a high level of plasticity. In contrast, the other area (no.2) was dominated by normal binocular cells, showing the lack of cortical sensitivity to monocular deprivation. This was found in the CA terminal-depleted area which was produced by the local perfusion with 4 mM 6-OHDA. The start of 6-OHDA perfusion preceded that of NE by 4 days, and both types of cortical perfusion lasted for 7 days. These two electrode tracks were comparable and had similar orientations as well as about equal length. Their entry points, marked by no. 1 and no. 2 in the lower inset, were in fact only 2 mm apart. (Modified and reproduced with permission from Pettigrew and Kasamatsu, 1978, *Nature (London)* **271**, 761–763.

cannula- minipump, we repeated the experiments, and soon noted the usual concentration–effect relationship in restoring plasticity. This is shown in Fig. 6. The proportion of cells whose plasticity revived (i.e., the proportion of monocular cells which responded exclusively to stimulation of the nondeprived ipsilateral eye) increased quickly when the concentration of NE became higher than the threshold level of 50 μM, even though the lowest effective concentration at the recording site had to be much lower (this matter will be discussed in detail in Section IV, B, *10*). Furthermore, when the con-

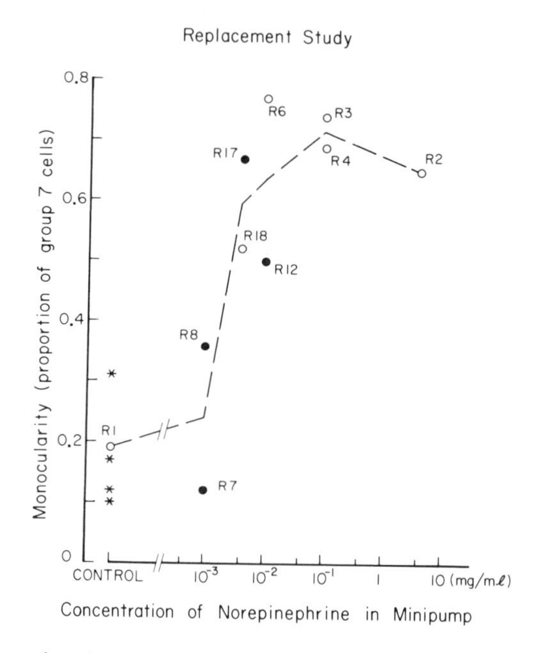

FIG. 6. In the series of replacement studies exemplified in Fig. 5 (A,B) the causal dose–effect relationship was established by changing the concentration of exogenous NE stored in the cannula-minipump. Here, the proportion of group 7 cells which responded exclusively to stimulation of the ipsilateral nondeprived eye is plotted in the ordinate against the log concentration of NE (in milligrams per milliliter) in the abscissa. Each symbol with an identification number represents an ocular dominance histogram from a single animal. Open circles: kittens used in the paradigm in which the local perfusion of NE was started before the end of intraventricular 6-OHDA injection. Filled circles: kittens used in the paradigm in which there was no temporal overlap between the two treatments. The start and duration of monocular lid suture always coincided with those of NE perfusion. Five control values, including the four (asterisks) borrowed from our previous study in the 6-OHDA-treated cortex (Kasamatsu and Pettigrew 1979), are plotted at the left end of the abscissa. The threshold concentration of NE (stored in minipumps) for the restoration of plasticity seemed to be between 10^{-3} and 5×10^{-3} mg/ml (5–25 μM). As was discussed in the text, the actual effective concentration at the recording site should be much lower than these values. (Modified and reproduced with permission from Kasamatsu *et al.*, 1979, *Journal of Comparative Neurology* **185**, 163–182).)

centration of NE in the minipump exceeded 10^{-1} mg/ml, the effect of NE perfusion appeared to spread from one hemisphere to the other since the control, nonperfused hemisphere also started to lose binocular cells, resulting in a W- or U-shaped distribution of ocular dominance. With much higher concentrations of NE, this trend became obvious, and both hemispheres showed a clear shift in ocular dominance to the nondeprived ipsilateral eye.

In this series of experiments, NE perfusion was started 3–4 days before the end of daily injections of 6-OHDA into the ventricle. Because of this temporal overlap of the two chemical treatments, it is possible that exogenous NE competed with 6-OHDA molecules for the uptake sites at CA terminals, resulting in a weakening of the lesion effect of 6-OHDA. However, since the uptake of 6-OHDA is a fast process, occurring in less than 1 hour (Jonsson, 1976), and since the intraventricular injections of 6-OHDA preceded the NE perfusion by at least 3–4 days, this possibility would seem to play a minor role, if any. To clarify this matter, nevertheless, we studied another group of kittens which received the local perfusion of NE after the cessation of 6-OHDA treatment. The results were essentially the same as seen previously, with a slight shift of the concentration–effect curve toward the left, suggesting a higher sensitivity of cortical cells to exogenous NE in this paradigm compared to the previous one. This subtle difference may deserve further clarification in connection with the postdenervation supersensitivity of NE-related receptors (see below).

At any rate, we happily concluded that exogenous NE compensated for the lack of endogenous NE due to chemical lesions of CA-conatining terminals in the visual cortex and thus restored its synaptic plasticity. Unexpectedly, at the same time, this result suggests a neurohumoral function for NE. In our study, exogenous NE necessarily acts directly on the adrenergic receptors in the visual cortex since CA terminals were lost in the localized cortical area due to the 6-OHDA pretreatment. For the sake of simplicity, however, in the current discussion we ignored the denervation supersensitivity which was supposed to be activated in the 6-OHDA pretreated cortex at the time when recordings were made (Palmer, 1972; Kalisker *et al.,* 1973; Huang *et al.,* 1973; Harden *et al.,* 1977b), but recognized that the actual situation in replacement studies such as these seems to be much more complicated than the picture given above implies (see section IV,C). Furthermore, it is worthwhile to note that CA fluorescence histochemistry cannot clearly differentiate between depletion of the CA content from vesicles at the terminals and fibers and complete morphological disappearance of CA terminals due to lesions. This matter has been fully discussed elswhere (Kasamatsu *et al.,* 1981b) (see also Section IV, B, *10*). Although it is unlikely that only the CA content has been depleted from the vesicles instead of lesions of CA terminals because of the dose and duration of the 6-OHDA treatment, an uptake study of NE, which is the most sensitive way to measure the number of active terminals, is desirable to clarify this point.

4. Demonstration of Synaptic Plasticity in the Adult Cortex by Continuous Perfusion with NE

As has been repeatedly observed by many authors, the adult visual cortex is not sensitive to the effects of monocular lid suture at all, even if it lasts for over a year, under normal circumstances. We have demonstrated, however, that the adult cortex becomes susceptible to the effects of monocular lid suture if enough exogenous NE is applied.

A visually normal adult cat was first implanted in the left visual cortex with a cannula–minipump which contained 4.86 m*M* (1mg/ml) NE, and the right eye was sutured for 1 week. Despite even such a brief term of monocular deprivation, binocularly driven cells disappeared dramatically from the cortex due to the NE perfusion, and the ocular dominance histogram became U- or W-shaped. These results persisted through several such experiments despite changes in the concentration of NE or in the duration of the perfusion term (Fig. 7). The ocular dominance distribution in the control, nonperfused hemisphere stayed normal if the concentration of NE was not too high. Similar experiments in older kittens which had outgrown their susceptible period (9 ~ 13 weeks of age) again generated U-shaped ocular dominance distributions.

In this study, it was quite important to show not only that the restoration (or significant increase) of neuronal plasticity, although partial, was due to the continuous perfusion with NE but also that this occurred in the normal mature cortex. Since the pretreatment of the cortex with 6-OHDA was not involved in this paradigm, there could be no question of pathology to confuse the conclusions. Furthermore, despite the longer term of NE perfusion (up to 3 weeks), we were not able to force all cortical cells to change their eye preference toward the nondeprived ipsilateral eye, i.e., we did not observe the shift of ocular dominance in these NE-perfused adult cats and older kittens. One of the following two explanations, or a combination of the two, is possible: Either (a) separate factors are involved in the two successive changes which usually follow monocular deprivation to induce the ocular dominance shift, with NE playing a more important role in the initial loss of binocularity and other unknown factors playing a major role in the later reduction of synaptic efficacy of the closed eye's inputs, or (b) because of receptor desensitization triggered by excess NE, the total efficiency of the NE perfusion in increasing plasticity may reach its maximum soon after its initiation. At the moment, we cannot tell why and how the matured brain is

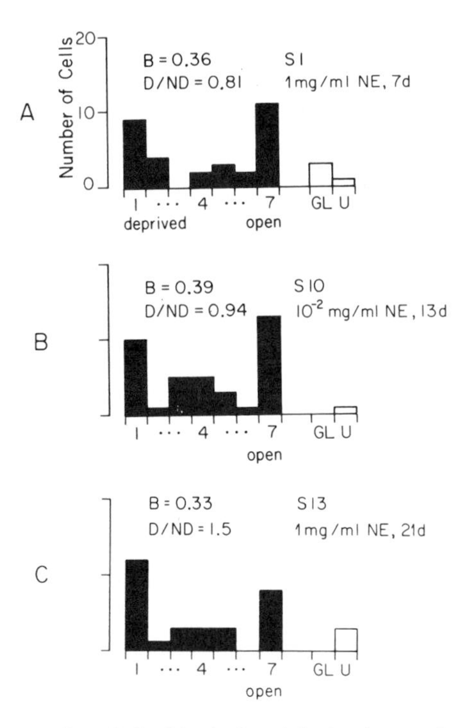

FIG. 7. Partial restoration of plasticity in the adult visual cortex by exogenous NE. Three adult cats were subjected to monocular lid suture for 1, 2, and 3 weeks. Local perfusion of the cortex with NE was started at the beginning of monocular deprivation, and perfusion was maintained throughout the period of monocular deprivation. The concentration of NE (in the cannula–minipump) was either 1 or 10^{-2} mg/ml (5 m*M* or 50 μ*M*). The significant reduction in the proportion of binocularly driven cells (B, binocularity) was observed in the NE-perfused hemisphere, whereas the other hemisphere stayed essentially unchanged (not shown here), as expected, after monocular deprivation. Nevertheless, the shift of ocular dominance did not take place. Accordingly, the ratio of the number of cells dominated by the deprived eye to that dominated by the nondeprived eye (D/ND) did not change. (Reproduced with permission from Kasamatsu *et al.*, 1979, *Journal of Comparative Neurology* **185**, 163–182.

different from the immature one. As will be explained later, however, my most recent study with cyclic nucleotides may shed some light on this subject (see section IV, B, *12*).

An important question left unanswered is how long the high level of plasticity lasts in the adult cortex once it is restored by NE perfusion. Since the methodology using NE perfusion into the normal adult cortex does not presume a possible morphological recovery of the CA-containing terminals within the lesion area, as might be the case in the 6-OHDA-treated cortex (Nakai *et al.*, 1981), the current paradigm is suitable, because of its simplicity, for following the time course of NE-induced changes in cortical plasticity.

5. *Recovery from the Effects of Monocular Deprivation: Its Acceleration with NE and Its Suppression with 6-OHDA*

Up to now, I have described the results of physiological tests of our CA hypothesis in which we were able to correlate the high level of synaptic modifiability induced by exogenous NE with a decrease in binocular cells or an increase of monocular cells in the visual cortex, using monocularly deprived kittens and cats as model systems to evaluate the extent of synaptic plasticity.

As is well known, a brief monocular lid suture causes a complete shift of the ocular dominance distribution in favor of the nondeprived eye, and the closed eye becomes behaviorally blind. Thus, the kitten loses normal binocular vision. If the closed eyelid is reopened again, however, especially while the kitten is still young, its binocular vision may quickly revive. Following reopening of the previously sutured eyelid, the monocularly deprived eye, which once appeared to have lost its central connections, starts to regain control over cortical cells. Thus, normal receptive fields are gradually restored for the previously deprived eye (Hubel and Wiesel, 1970; Olson and Freeman, 1978; Mitchell *et al.,* 1978; Blasdel and Pettigrew, 1978; Van Sluyters, 1978).

Using this paradigm of physiological recovery from the prior monocular deprivation (Hubel and Wiesel, 1970) in place of monocular deprivation itself, we asked whether the proportion of normal binocular cells is quickly restored when the level of synaptic plasticity is maintained at a high level with NE perfusion. We expected to find that cortical recovery is accelerated in the cortex concomitantly perfused with NE (i.e., more binocular cells), and largely suppressed (i.e., fewer binocular cells) in the visual cortex in which CA terminals have been destroyed by 6-OHDA perfusion. That this is indeed the case is demonstrated by the clear separation of recovery curves for the three conditions (NE, control, and 6-OHDA) when the extent of recovery was plotted against the days after reopening of the closed eye (Kasamatsu *et al.,* 1981a). This is shown by two summary diagrams in Fig. 8. In the NE-perfused hemisphere, recovery of binocularity was certainly accelerated by at least 1 week when compared with that in the control hemisphere of the same kitten. In the CA terminal-depleted cortical area, on the contrary, the recovery trend was suppressed for a long time; binocularity stayed at about half that of the control even 30 days after reopening. If this very slow recovery trend is sustained at the same rate, 6-OHDA-treated kittens may again obtain normal binocularity within 11 weeks at the earliest after reopening. However, this result is not guaranteed due to the increasing

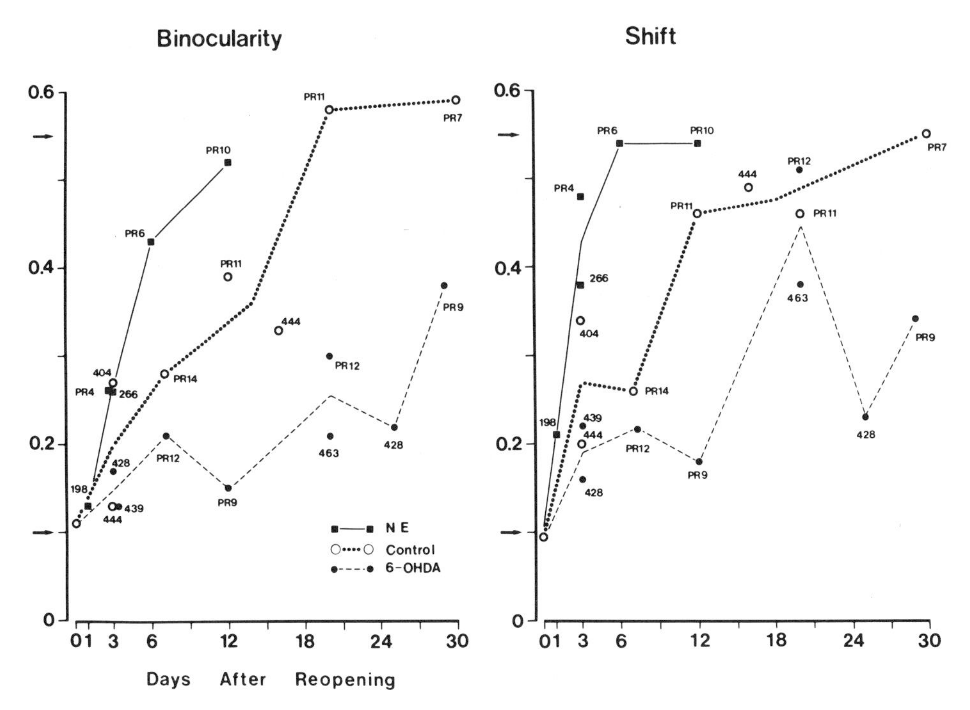

FIG. 8. The shifted ocular dominance distribution in monocularly deprived kittens may return to normal in time with reopening of the closed eyelid, if this operation is done while the kittens are still young. This recovery of binocular cortical cells from the effects of the prior monocualr lid suture was accelerated by concomitant and continuous perfusion of the visual cortex with exogenous NE. The recovery was largely delayed in the visual cortex which had been depleted of its CA terminals by 6-OHDA perfusion. In order to describe numerically the sequential changes in the shape of ocular dominance distribution, we calculated the two weighted indices as follows: *Weighted binocularity* was defined as the proportion of binocularly driven cells after the number of cells in each ocular dominance group is multiplied by weighting factors calculated in the following fashion. Based on an assumption of linear progression in the degree of binocular convergence on single cortical cells from monocular cells (group 1 or 7) to group 4 binocular cells, a weighting factor of 1 is assigned to group 4 cells (maximum), 2/3 to cells in groups 3 and 5, 1/3 to cells in groups 2 and 6, and 0 to cells in groups 1 and 7 (minimum). The weighted binocularity, then, is 1 if all cells in a given histogram fall in group 4. *Weighted shift* was introduced to assess the shift of ocular dominance from the normal pattern to the distribution dominated by group 7 monocular cells after monocular lid suture of the contralateral eye. The weighting factor here was assumed to fluctuate linearly between 0 (monocular cells responding exclusively to the deprived contralateral eye) and 1 (monocular cells responding exclusively to the nondeprived ipsilateral eye). Thus, the weighting factor is 0 for group 1 cells, 1/6 for group 2 cells, 2/6 for group 3 cells, 3/6 for group 4 cells, 4/6 for group 5 cells, 5/6 for group 6 cells, and 1 for group 7 cells. Then, if all visually responsive cells are obtained only by stimulating the nondeprived ipsilateral eye, the weighting shift is 1 in such an ocular dominance distribution. Since we are interested in tracing an increasing trend of binocular cells which is initiated by reopening of the closed eyelid (shift back), the order of weighting factors assigned to

(*continued on p. 56*)

age of the animals: The kitten in this experiment was already 9 weeks old when he showed only a 50% recovery 30 days after the eye was reopened (the initial monocular lid suture had been started at 4 weeks of age).

Another interesting observation made in this series of studies characterizes the initial stage of the recovery process, independent of the three experimental conditions considered here, by the early appearance of a group of monocular cells which exclusively respond to stimulation of the previously deprived contralateral eye. Thus, before binocularity fully recovers, the ocular dominance distribution under all three experimental conditions always shows a W-shaped histogram which appears earliest (3 days after reopening) in the NE-perfused cortex, followed by the control cortex (12 days), and again is most delayed in the 6-OHDA-perfused cortex (20 days). These findings, taken together with the well-known fact that the W-shaped ocular dominance distribution (loss of binocular cells) is the first change to appear following monocular deprivation, suggests that a mutually inhibitory mechanism operates between the two sets (contralateral vs. ipsilateral) of visual afferents as a first step in binocular competition.

In summary, the local availability of NE is a determining factor in the level of neuronal plasticity operating in the immature visual cortex, a correlation independent of an increase or a decrease in binocularity.

6. A Problem with the Reverse Suture Paradigm

It is obvious to wonder whether the neuronal processes in visual cortical cells affected by the reverse suture method are also subject to the availability of NE. The procedure used to check this possibility was as follows: After a brief (usually 1 week) monocular lid suture started at 4~5 weeks of age, the side of the suture was switched, and this reverse suture was maintained for another week or so until the day of single-unit recordings. Continuous perfusion of the cortex with either NE or 6–OHDA was maintained, starting at the

(Figure 8 continued)

all ocular dominance groups was so arranged as to give a larger number for a better recovery. The weighted shift (right) and weighted binocularity (left) are plotted in the ordinates against days after reopening of the closed eyelid. In both diagrams the separation among the three curves is obvious. Each symbol, with the animal's code (filled squares for NE, open circles for control, and filled circles for 6-OHDA), represents a single ocular dominance histogram which comprises 30 visually active cells. The upper (0.55) and lower (0.1) limits for both weighted indices, which are shown by arrows in the ordinates, were calculated respectively from the previously published ocular dominance histograms in normal adult cats (Hubel and Wiesel, 1962; Blakemore and Pettigrew, 1970) and 224 cells in eight monocularly deprived kittens in our own studies (see Fig. 5A in Kasamatsu *et al.*, 1981a). (Reproduced with permission from Kasamatsu *et al.*, 1981a, *Journal of Neurophysiology* **45**, 254–266.)

time of suture reversal, and continued throughout the period of reverse suture. In other cases, 6-OHDA was also applied via intraventricular injections. Insofar as these preliminary studies were concerned, we observed rather small changes in modifying the extent of recapture of cortical cells by the previously deprived eye (Ary *et al.*, 1979).

The parameters involved in the reverse suture paradigm are not well understood at this time. Thus, it would be difficult to ascertain why the neuronal processes involved in the procedure are indifferent to the presence or absence of NE-containing terminals. However, a tentative conclusion is that neuronal plasticity maintained by the NE system works only for synaptic changes due to competition.

7. Exogenous NE Accentuates the Binocular Competition in the Normal Visual Cortex

I have been describing how we evolved the concept of NE modulation of cortical sensitivity to alterations in visual inputs. A skeptical soul, a valuable asset in research in such an eye-catching phenomenon as synaptic plasticity, might still wonder whether our results may merely reflect some sort of direct chemical effect due to the drugs used rather than the genuine changes in neuronal connectivity induced by an altered visual experience. Such a consideration has in fact opened up other interesting paths of research.

The simplest way to control for the direct chemical effects of perfused drugs is to study the visually normal cortex which has received only the perfusion of the drug in question. If our interpretation of our previous findings was correct, we should see quite a normal distribution of ocular dominance in such animals. First, when we recorded from the visual cortex of visually normal kittens which had been subjected to a local perfusion of 6-OHDA, we did not observe any obvious changes in ocular dominance (Kasamatsu *et al.*, 1981a). We obtained a similar result in animals which received 6-OHDA intraventricularly (Kasamatsu and Pettigrew, 1979). Thus, our thesis seemed to survive the test. When we studied the NE-perfused visual cortex of normal cats and kittens, however, we did encounter a puzzling finding: There was a conspicuous lack of cells dominated by inputs from the ipsilateral eye, although the binocularity stayed close to the normal range (70%) (Kasamatsu *et al.*, 1979). The trend was more obvious in kittens than in adult cats. After being annoyed by this observation, I was struck by an attractive and plausible explanation for this apparent challenge to our main theory: The naturally occurring dominance of contralateral over ipsilateral inputs is expressed maximally because of the enhanced synaptic plasticity due to exogenous NE. This enhancement of subtle binocular competition may result in a skew distribution of ocular dominance, determined primarily by inputs from the contralateral eye. A crucial test for this interpretation was carried out satisfactorily when I recorded from kittens which had received NE perfusion for 1 week while being kept in the dark. As I had predicted, the visual cortex of these kittens that did not receive visual experience and therefore did not use their visual pathways during the NE perfusion stayed quite normal (Kuppermann and Kasamatsu, 1979). This is shown in Fig. 9. This study unmistakably indicates how powerful the NE system is in modulating cortical sensitivity to the imbalance of binocular afferents. I am sure that this paradigm will serve as another useful model system in future studies.

The above story is not yet complete, however. By placing animals in the dark, we effectively eliminated visually evoked impulses, but we did not disrupt retinal tonic discharges (random noise) which actually become more active in the dark than in the light. Referring back to my previous study, in which changes in ocular dominance were demonstrated in the visual cortex of normal young kittens following unilateral silencing of retinal tonic

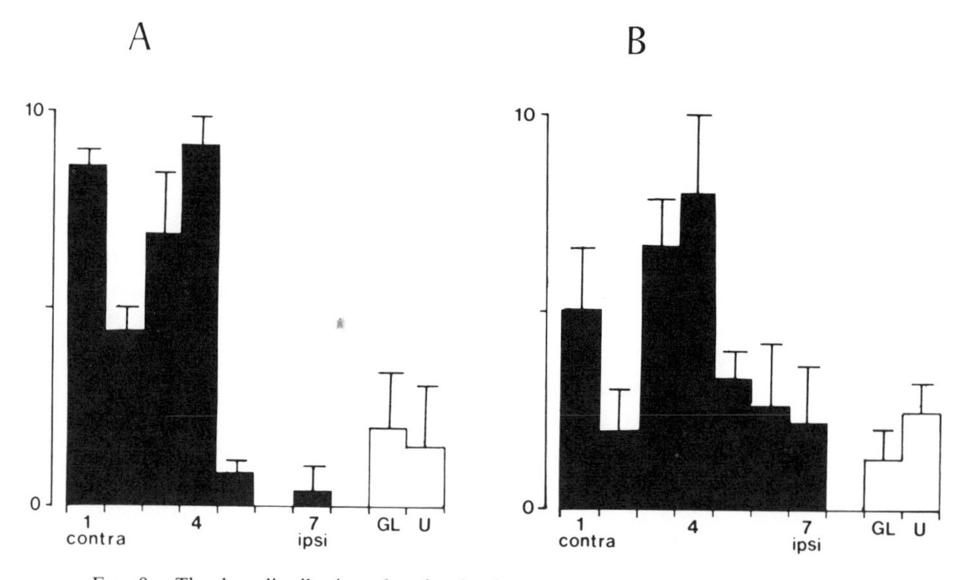

FIG. 9. The skew distribution of ocular dominance in the normal visual cortex is a result of enhanced binocular competition by exogenous NE. (A) A conspicuous lack of cells dominated by the ipsilateral eye (groups 5–7) in the visual cortex of normal kittens (5–6 weeks of age) which was directly perfused with 50 μM NE for a week. This enhancement in binocular competition was not detected before 7 days of NE perfusion. Three kittens in this study were kept in the normal laboratory environment, in which the light-dark cycle alternated. (B) Results from littermates which were treated similarly with NE but were kept in the dark during NE perfusion. The ocular dominance distribution thus stayed essentially normal due to the lack of effective binocular competition. (Unpublished illustration. See also Kuppermann and Kasamatsu, 1979.) The ordinate, number of cells. A vertical bar at the top of each column shows a standard deviation.

discharges in one optic nerve (Kasamatsu, 1976b), I wondered whether there is any active competition between the two sets of tonic discharges in the contralateral and ipsilateral visual pathways. This question is now under study; our paradigm is as follows: A sodium channel blocker, TTX, is injected into the vitreus of one eyeball to silence *reversibly* the total retinal output. Animals are to be kept in the dark during the entire process except for the eye injection, which usually takes several minutes to accomplish. A few days before the recovery of the pupillary reflex from the TTX-injected eye, we will start perfusion with exogneous NE of the visual hemisphere which is contralateral to the TTX-injected eye. By changing the duration of the NE perfusion, we will study the time course for the recovery of the normal ocular dominance distribution from the apparently shifted distribution in both the NE perfused and nonperfused control hemispheres of the same animals. If we see a significant acceleration in recovery of normal binocular cells in the NE-perfused side, we may conclude that the two sets of tonic retinal discharges, intact and once-silenced, also compete with each other for restoring binocularity to single cortical cells. We may also compare the time saving of recovery in this paradigm with that seen in light-reared animals which were once monocularly deprived and then subjected to pure recovery by the reopening of the one closed eye. (In the present paradigm, we cannot differentiate the process of inducing strong binocular imbalance from that of blinding one eye, which in effect produces the apparently shifted ocular dominance distribution in favor of the noninjected eye. Accordingly, we are not able to study the cortical affects of the former process *per se* in terms of changes in ocular dominance.).

Using TTX injections into the eyeball as a handy tool, we have furthermore been led to an interesting observation in LGN morphology. We found a significant cell size shrinkage in the LGN layers which receive input from the injected eye (Kuppermann and Kasamatsu, 1980). Since we had already noted an equally marked shrinkage of cell size in the monocular segment, this observation has to be interpreted as suggesting an involvement of factors other than binocular competition in determining cell size in the LGN. A further study is in progress to determine the initial locus of this *pure* deprivation (trophic) effect.

8. How Quickly Can the Ocular Dominance Shift Take Place?

In a previous study with a recovery protocol (Section IV, B, 5), we started to detect within 3 days an obvious difference in the ocular dominance distribution between the NE-perfused and control cortices. In those studies, 1 day after reopening there was only a slight indication of accelerated recovery in the NE-perfused cortex. It recently became clear, however, that even 1 day after NE perfusion, a kitten can develop an unusual visual cortex in which the ocular dominance distribution in the two hemispheres is quite different. A simple trick in this study was to use NE concentrated 10 times (i.e., 0.5 mM or a total of 2.4 μg/24 μl for 24 hours) more than the concentration used routinely in the previous studies. In order to avoid unnecessary misunderstanding, I want to reemphasize that this was the concentration of NE stored in the cannula–minipump system. As will be discussed in detail later, the actual concentration at the recording site was, at most, $< 1/100$ of 0.5 mM. Quick changes in plasticity were thus tested with a perfusion of highly concentrated NE in the following two paradigms: monocular lid suture alone and monocular deprivation followed by reopening of the closed eyelid to induce cortical recovery. We concluded that a high level of exogenous NE can very quickly facilitate (<24 hours) the plastic changes in ocular dominance in some paradigms which lead to either an increase or a decrease in the number of normal binocularly driven cells (Heggelund and Kasamatsu, 1981).

During iontophoresis of NE in the cat visual cortex, we also encountered a unique situation which confirmed this conclusion. We studied, under N_2O anesthesia and Flaxedil paralysis, a normal adult cat and several kittens whose CA terminals in the visual cortex had been previously destroyed by localized 6-OHDA perfusion. After the repeated iontophoretic applications of NE (0.4 M NE•bitartrate in saline, pH 4–5) in these visual cortices, we encountered, to our surprise, more monocular cells than usual, indiciating an obvious loss of binocular cells throughout the striate cortex. We found, however, the normal distribution of ocular dominance in a control animal which was subjected for about 24 hours to repeated current injections but not to NE iontophoresis (Kasamatsu and Heggelund, 1981). It is most likely, then, that the changes in ocular dominance took place during the recording sessions (<24 hours) due to excess NE combined with the lack of normal convergence of the two visual axes in the anesthetized and paralyzed animals. We therefore assume that the effects of *squinting* found by Hubel and Wiesel (1965) were acutely induced in the visual cortex in which the cortical synapses were highly plastic due to the intermittent supply of highly concentrated exogenous NE, resulting in disruption of the normal binocularity. Further studies have been made to verify this paralysis squint hypothesis (Heggelund and Kasamatsu, in preparation).

9. *Involvement of β-Adrenergic Receptors in Cortical Plasticity*

Thus, the intracortical NE terminals play an important role in maintaining visual cortical plasticity. An apparent question, then, was, what types of receptors mediate the effects of NE in enhancing synaptic plasticity in the cerebral cortex? Are they α- or β-adrenergic receptors? Previous authors have demonstrated the presence of β-adrenergic receptors in rat cerebral cortex

(Davis and Lefkowitz, 1976; Sporn and Molinoff, 1976), and some of the behaviors of these receptors, such as increased binding sites in the deafferented cortex, have also been thoroughly described (Palmer, 1972; Kalisker *et al.*, 1973; Huang *et al.*, 1973; Harden *et al.*, 1977b). We have been studying the ontogeny of β-adrenergic receptors, using [^{3}H]dihydroalprenolol as a probe, in the kitten visual cortex (Jonsson and Kasamatsu, submitted), a subject to which I will return again later.

Using the same paradigm of localized microperfusion of the visual cortex with a β-adrenergic blocker, propranolol, I have been able to duplicate the blockade of ocular dominance shift in monocularly deprived kittens (Kasamatsu, 1979). By varying the concentration of propranolol stored in the cannula–minipump, I have also studied the concentration–effect relationship: A half-maximal effect was obtained at a concentration of 10^{-4} *M*. At the moment, I still do not know whether this concentration was sufficiently low to ensure the specific blockade of β-adrenergic receptors. Needless to say, however, 10^{-4} *M* (Kasamatsu, in preparation) refers to the concentration in the minipump; the actual value at the recording site was probably far lower (see below).

Since I observed quite normal receptive fields for the overwhelming majority of cells recorded, even the highest concentration used in this study (10^{-2} *M* in the minipump) was still low enough to avoid the so-called local anesthetic effect. When we use the *l*-isomer in place of the *d, l*-propranolol used in this study, the efficiency may be increased further (illustrated as a leftward shift of the concentration–effect curve). It is desirable, at any rate, to carry out a similar study using a cleaner β blocker, such as sotalol, which does not have any local anesthetic effect. Although this series of studies has not yet been completed, I may say that β-adrenergic receptors are most likely to mediate changes in cortical plasticity. As will be mentioned below (Section IV, B, *12*), the involvement of cyclic nucleotides in cortical plasticity seems to provide further strong support for this suggestion.

10. Intracortical Spread of 6-OHDA and Exogenous NE

As mentioned briefly earlier, the size of specific chemical lesions with continuous microperfusion of 6-OHDA and the maximal reach of exogenous NE are crucial variables to consider in analyzing the effects of localized perfusion. In addition to physiological recordings at various sites increasingly distant from the perfusion site, we carried out the following four studies to assess the lowest but still effective concentration of 6-OHDA and exogenous NE in suppressing or enhancing the modifiability of cortical synapses:

1. CA fluorescence histochemistry in the 6-OHDA-perfused cortex (4 m*M*, 1 week).

2. Biochemical assays of endogenous NE, DA, and 5-HT in the 6-OHDA-perfused cortex (4 m*M*, 1 week). High-pressure liquid chromatography was used in combination with electrochemical detection methods to isolate the specific monoamines.

3. Evaluation of the spatial distribution of tritium counts in the visual cortex perfused with either [^{3}H]6-OHDA or [^{3}H]NE. The radioactivity was measured in samples of cortical tissue taken at regular intervals (1 mm) from the perfusion site.

4. Paper electrophoresis of tissues obtained from the [^{3}H]NE-perfused cortices to isolate unchanged NE from NE metabolites and oxidation products.

The results of these rather tedious but still very important studies are summarized as follows (see also Kasamatsu *et al.*, 1979, 1981b). Fluorescence histochemistry in the visual cortex locally perfused with 4 m*M* 6-OHDA revealed, under a fluorescence microscope, the presence of a localized area (radius 4–5 mm) in which no trace of CA fibers and terminals was found (Fig. 3). With 100 times less concentrated 6-OHDA, the radius was considerably reduced, to a radius as small as 2 mm. A single injection of the rat striatum with 1–2 μl (1–2 μg/μl) 6-OHDA produced a CA-specific lesion with a diameter of 1.5–2.0 mm (Ungerstedt, 1971b).

In the visual cortex perfused with [^{3}H]6-OHDA for 1 week, the radioactivity dropped exponentially with increasing distance and leveled off at about 10 mm from the perfusion site. The spatial distribution of endogenous NE in the similarly treated cortex correlated quite well with this distribution pattern of radioactivity, but in a complementary fashion. As mentioned previously (Fig. 4), physiological recordings have also shown that the effects of 6-OHDA reached to an area at least 6 mm away from the perfusion site. By comparing the profile of endogenous NE in the cortex and the montage photomicrograph in CA histochemistry, we estimated that the threshold of endogenous NE for detection by our glyoxylic acid–perfusion histofluorescence method is 20% of the control. Since our recording microelectrodes were usually placed 2 mm away from the center of perfusion, we are quite sure that cortical cells studied in our physiological assays were free from the influences of NE terminals.

The spread of [^{3}H]NE seemed about the same as that of [^{3}H]6-OHDA. This result is shown in Fig. 10. Although the front plane of equilibrium of radioactivity appeared to move back and forth at 1, 3, and 7 days after the start of perfusion, the general profile stayed the same: That is, the counts dropped exponentially with increasing distance and leveled off into the background at an area as far as 10 mm away from the perfusion site.

We then carried out a simple calculation to obtain an estimate of *dilution factors* for perfused NE at a given site and time. Since we knew the specific

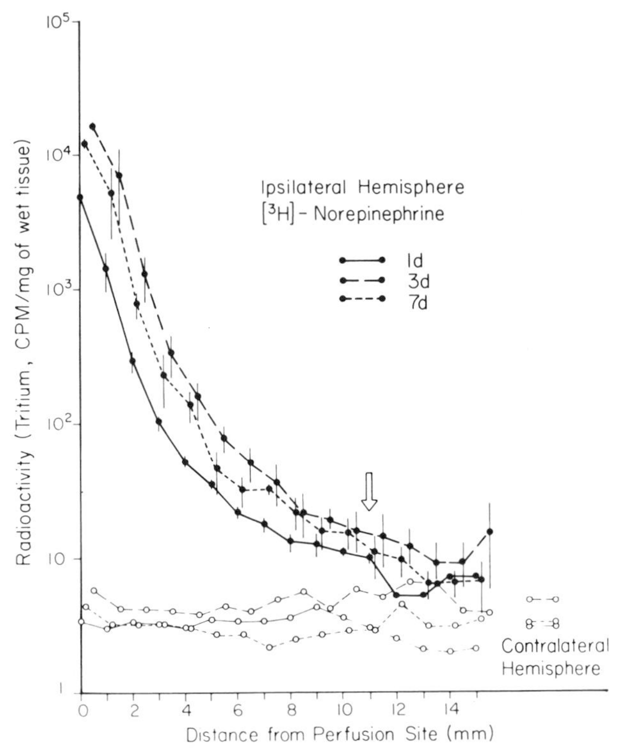

FIG. 10. The spatial distribution of tritium counts in cat visual cortex which was locally perfused with [^{3}H]NE (specific activity, 2.0 Ci/mmole; 43.2 μM). The cortical slab (15 mm long × 5 mm wide × 2–3 mm thick) which contained the perfusion site was first dissected out horizontally, and then cortex samples were taken from this slab at 1-mm intervals from the perfusion site. The corresponding samples were also taken from the opposite hemisphere. The radioactivity in each sample was measured, after the tissue was solubilized, by a conventional liquid scintillation spectrophotometer. The total radioactivity (CPM counts per minute per milligram of wet tissue) was plotted (in the log scale) in the ordinate against the distance (in millimeters) from the perfusion site in the abscissa. The perfusion term varied from 1 day (solid lines), 3 days (broken lines), to 7 days (dotted lines). Each filled circle represents the average of two measures in the perfused cortex of two animals. Similarly, each open circle represents the value in the opposite nonperfused cortex. A thin vertical bar at each filled circle indicates a double standard deviation (range of the two measures). For the sake of illustration, a set of points for three different perfusion terms were dislocated laterally from each other. The average radioactivity throughout the whole slab in the opposite hemisphere is given by three lines for the three perfusion terms at the right end. The radioactivity decreased exponentially with increased distance in the perfused hemisphere. Although the radioactivity at a given site changed with time, the maximal extent of its spread stayed the same at 10–11 mm from the perfusion site, as marked by an open arrow. Note the low radioactivity profile throughout the other hemisphere, suggesting the lack of effective spread of activity via the callosum. (Reproduced with permission from Kasamatsu *et al.*, 1981b, *Journal of Pharmacology and Experimental Therapeutics* **217,** 841–850.

activity of [^{3}H]NE stored in the minipump, the amount of cortical tissue used for each measure, and the tritium counts recovered at a given distance and moment, we could estimate the dilution factor of NE in this continous perfusion paradigm. It was 1/124 at an area 2 mm away from the perfusion site 3 days after the start of perfusion when the count was maximal. In order to obtain this approximation of a dilution factor, we took into account the proportion of tritium counts which were derived from unchanged NE (an average of 66% within a 5-mm radius) rather than either NE metabolites or oxidation products. Taking this dilution factor together with the results obtained in our previous physiological recordings, we finally obtained estimates of the lowest effective concentration of 6-OHDA for depletion, and NE for restoration, of synaptic plasticity. It was about 3 μM (at 7 days after application, at a radius of 6 mm) for 6-OHDA and 0.3 μM (at 3 days, at a radius of 2 mm) for NE. These values are certainly low enough to ensure the specific uptake of these drugs at the CA-containing nerve terminals in the cat visual cortex. (See Kasamatsu *et al.*, 1979; 1981b for further discussions.)

11. Morphological Changes

Now we are ready to ask one of the toughest questions about synaptic plasticity: Do any changes in morphology follow these clear-cut alterations in cortical physiological observed in the CA-manipulated brain, and if so, how do they occur?

As already reviewed in the earlier sections, changes in the width of ocular dominance columns and cell shrinkage in the LGN are at the moment the most popular morphological correlates studied in monocularly deprived animals. Changes in the size of ocular dominance columns may be examined in autoradiograms prepared either by the transneuronal transport of tritiated amino acids injected into the eyeball (Grafstein and Laureno, 1973; Wiesel *et al.*, 1974; Shatz, *et al.*, 1977) or by the [^{14}C]2-DG method (Sharp, 1976; Kennedy *et al.*, 1976; Sokoloff *et al.*, 1977; Des Rosiers *et al.*, 1978). It has become alarmingly clear, however, that neither of these methods is free from technical complication. For example, the problem of "spillover" at the LGN and the irregularity of columnar organization in layer IV of the cat visual cortex (Le Vay *et al.*, 1978; Shatz and Stryker, 1978) may hamper a straightforward application of transneuronal transport autoradiography to our system. The [^{14}C]2-DG method seems to have some advantages for our purpose, since it allows us to map out the columns of metabolically active cells above and below layer IV, which is packed with cells least susceptible to monocular deprivation (Shatz and Stryker, 1978). In recent reports, however, [^{14}C]2-DG autoradiography revealed regular repeats of radial zones at about 500-μm intervals, especially in layers II and III of the striate cortex of squirrel and macaque monkeys which viewed the normal environment through one eye (Kennedy *et al.*, 1976; Hendrickson and Wilson, 1979) or which were binocularly stimulated with stripes having all orientations (Humphrey and Hendrickson, 1980). It was observed that the pattern made of these patches of high glucose uptake was virtually identical to that demonstrated by cytochrome oxidase staining (Wong-Riley, 1976, 1979) in layers II and III (Humphrey and Hendrickson, 1980). Similar patches of high metabolic activity stained for cytochrome oxidase were independently shown in the striate cortex of normal macaque monkeys (Horton and Hubel, 1980). The latter authors demonstrated further that these regular patches stained for cytochrome oxidase in layers II and III were in fact aligned with and located in the center of the ocular dominance columns visualized in layer IVC by transneuronal transport autoradiography or in layers II and III by the 2-DG method in animals exposed to all orientatons (Horton and Hubel, 1981). They also noted unexpectedly that in monkeys which had been stimulated by spatial gratings with a single orientation, either vertical or horizontal, cytochrome oxidase patches fell along the lattice of strips formed by 2-DG-labeling in layers II and III. They concluded, therefore, that the pattern visualized by the [^{14}C]2-DG method occupied the same site in the striate cortex as cytochrome oxidase patches, but that the former extended beyond the individual boundary of the latter. Hendrickson and her associates further showed that this patchy pattern stained for cytochrome oxidase was in fact identical to that visualized by antisera against γ-amino acid decarboxylase in layers II and III of the normal macaque striate cortex (Hendrickson *et al.*, 1981). It should be remembered that in a carefully designed study, Schoppmann and Stryker (1981) demonstrated a strong correlation between orientation columns revealed by physiological recordings and those revealed by [^{14}C]2-DG autoradiography. The lack of cytochrome oxidase patches in the normal cat visual cortex (Horton and Hubel, 1981) may contribute to their results. At any rate, it is obvious that for the moment, the [^{14}C]2-DG method applied to the visual cortex can register elevated cell activity which is not necessarily induced by direct visual inputs. Thus, we are still largely ignorant about the resolution power of these autoradiographic techniques when applied to such a quantitative study, especially outside of layer IV, that concerns the effects of *brief* monocular deprivation, as in our experiments.

A cell size measurement in the LGN of monocularly deprived animals may also suffer from a shortcoming similar to that of the autoradiographic method in its resolution power when applied to brief monocular deprivation. Another practical problem results from relatively large animal-to-animal variation in the extent of cell shrinkage in the deprived LGN (6–38% in lamina A) (Hickey, 1980). Nevertheless, an attempt was made recently, using the LGNs of kittens which had been physiologically recorded in our previous studies (see Section IV, B, *3*), to determine whether the dramatic changes observed in cortical physiology following monocular deprivation primed with manipulation of the NE system may be reflected as well in geniculate morphology. The result we obtained so far is suggestive, although still preliminary and subject to an alternative interpretation (see below). We carried out measurements of LGN cell size in monocularly deprived kittens which had been first injected with 6-OHDA into the lateral ventrical to destroy CA-containing terminals in the brain and then, concurrently with monocular lid suture, had been continuously perfused with NE only in the left visual cortex for 1 week. In addition, LGNs from three control kittens were studied to estimate the degree of cell shrinkage following brief monocular deprivation which lasted for only 1 week. We first established that after a week-long monocular deprivation, the average cell size in the deprived lamina became significantly smaller (10% in A1,$p<0.05$; 14% in A, $p<0.01$) than the corresponding nondeprived lamina of the same kittens. A small increase in cell size also seemed to occur in the binocular segment of the nondeprived laminae (Sherman and Wilson, 1975; Hickey, *et al.*, 1977). Thus, when we calculated the relative cross-sectional area in deprived vs. nondeprived laminae, the ratio A/A1 tended to increase in the LGN ipsilateral to lid suture and the ratio in the contralateral LGN to decrease. Thus, the two A/A1 values were significantly different from one another.

Using this A/A1 ratio as an index, we then compared the effect of brief monocular deprivation in the right (ipsilateral to the closed eye) LGN of the 6-OHDA-pretreated kittens with those in the control monocular kittens. In fact, these experimental kittens were first intraventricularly injected with 6-OHDA; then, only their left visual cortices were locally perfused with various concentrations of the NE solution. Since we wanted to compare the changes in cortical physiology and those in geniculate morphology, I believed that it was necessary to include or exclude a particular animal from the present statistical treatment, depending on the results already obtained in cortical physiology. Thus, for the present calculation, 3 of 10 kittens were excluded from the 6-OHDA group because the presumed control hemisphere of these three animals also showed the shifted ocular dominance due to the interhemispheric spread of concentrated NE (see also Section IV, B, *3*). Although we obtained the substantially smaller A/A1 ratio for the 6-OHDA-pretreated animals (0.96 ± 0.08) than the control animals (1.07 ± 0.06), the difference did not reach the significant level (Pr. $\{F>4.18\}>5\%$), probably due to the small sample size (control group, $N = 3$; 6-OHDA group, $N = 7$). This result may suggest, however, that intraventricular 6-OHDA prevents, at least in part, the expected extent of cell shrinkage in the deprived lamina and cell hypertrophy in the nondeprived lamina of kitten LGNs. Carrying out a similar comparison of A/A1 ratios for the left LGNs, we noted that the A/A1 ratio was about the same (Pr. $\{F>0.013\} \gg 5\%$) for both the control kittens (0.83 ± 0.03) and animals which had been first treated with 6-OHDA and then perfused with NE only in the left visual cortex (0.84 ± 1.0). The extent of cell shrinkage in the deprived A lamina of the left LGN, ipsilateral to the localized perfusion of NE in the visual cortex, was as extensive as that seen in the counterpart of the control kittens. This last result may suggest the *reappearance* of the expected cell shrinkage in the left LGN of the monocularly deprived kittens due to the restoration of binocular competition in the NE-perfused visual cortex.

It has to be pointed out, however, that there are some arguments against the authenticity of the above grouping of experimental animals depending on the results of cortical physiology (Hitchcock and Hickey, 1982). Grouping together all right LGNs from the 6-OHDA-injected kittens which had also been perfused with NE in the left visual cortex, irrespective of the results in cortical physiology, these authors reached the following conclusion: Intraventricular injection of 6-OHDA did not appear to prevent deprivation-induced changes in geniculate cell size, and there was no evidence to suggest that the local perfusion of NE enhanced deprivation-induced changes in geniculate cell size. Thus, the three investigators involved in the above project have derived different conclusions from the same set of measurements in geniculate cell size. It is my belief that we should refrain, at the moment, from making a strong negative statement such as the above because these experiments were primarily designed for cortical physiology, not LGN morphology.

Further studies are needed to settle the issue without any ambiguity. The best and simplest test is to compare the A/A1 ratios obtained from monocularly deprived kittens which receive no drug treatment with those derived from animals which have been monocularly deprived for the same period as the control and simultaneously treated only by 6-OHDA. In this paradigm there is no argument about inclusion or exclusion of particular individuals, and one can reach a clear conclusion if chemical lesions of CA terminals in the visual cortex caused by 6-OHDA block the expected cell size changes in the LGN of monocularly deprived kittens. Only such a study will provide baseline data with which the replacement effects of NE perfusion may be adequately compared.

12. Cyclic Nucleotides

Knowing that NE and β-adrenergic receptors are involved in maintaining and enhancing visual cortical plasticity, I wondered whether the search for factors underlying synaptic plasticity can be extended into the second messenger system (Kasamatsu, 1980). I hypothesized that the high level of cyclic nucleotides in the visual cortex is correlated with an increase in the modifiability of neuronal connectivity. The paradigm was as follows: Since I wanted to test the hypothesis that cyclic nucleotides *enhance* neuronal plasticity, I first created brain regions, at corresponding sites in both hemispheres of the kitten visual cortex, which had lost their plasticity due to continuous localized perfusion with 6-OHDA. After 1 week of this pretreatment, when the 6-OHDA-containing minipump became empty, the discharged minipump in the left visual cortex was replaced by a new one filled with dibutyryl adenosine cyclic monophosphate (dbc AMP), leaving the implanted cannula at the same site in the cortex. The other discharged minipump in the right hemisphere was replaced with a new one which contained the vehicle solution alone. At the same time as the start of cortical perfusion with dbc AMP, the right eyelid was surgically sutured and kept closed until the day of single-unit recordings, another week later. By changing the concentration of dbc AMP stored in the minipump, I have obtained a family of ocular dominance histograms from both left (experimental) and right (control) hemispheres in the same animals. The concentration step of dbc AMP in the minipump from 10^{-2} *M* to 10^{-9} *M* allowed for the determination of concentration–effect relationships. At a concentration of 10^{-6} *M,* I still found a clear shift of ocular dominance in favor of the nondeprived ipsilateral eye. This trend was also the case, although less obviously so, for the control right hemisphere, suggesting that the effects of dbc AMP spread to the other hemisphere when its concentration was still high. A similar situation occurred in the replacement study with NE (see Section IV, B, *3*). The fact that in the control hemisphere the nondeprived eye served contralateral (dominant) inputs to the cortex may also help to explain why the monocular cells which receive inputs only from the contralateral eye predominate in the control hemisphere. When dbc AMP 10 times more dilute was used, the ocular dominance distribution finally became U-shaped, suggesting that this concentration (10^{-7} *M*) was near the threshold for the shift of ocular dominance. In fact, ocular dominance in the control hemisphere of the same kitten stayed for the first time rather close to normal. Reference to the phsyiological and histochemical studies ensured the integrity of the initial chemical lesions of the intracortical CA system by pretreatment with 6-OHDA (see Section IV, B, *10*).

These results, therefore, strongly suggest that dbc AMP perfused directly into the extracellular space of the CA-depleted visual cortex genuinely compensated for the lack of NE. Another piece of evidence, which is a strong and potentially more interesting support for this thesis, came from a similar study in the adult cat cortex. Since the normal adult brain is supposed to be no longer sensitive to monocular deprivation, I asked straightaway whether cortical perfusion with dbc AMP without preceding pretreatment with 6-OHDA made the adult cortex plastic again. The results I have obtained so far are remarkable, although they have to be considered preliminary findings (Kasamatsu, 1980). I found a shifted ocular dominance in the dbc AMP-perfused hemisphere of the adult cortex following monocular deprivation which lasted only for 1 week, leaving the other hemisphere of the same animal almost unchanged. This is a very suggestive finding which, if it holds, sharply contrasts to our previous *partial* success by NE perfusion in which ocular dominance in the adult cortex became W-shaped but did not shift in favor of the nondeprived eye following brief monocular deprivation (Kasamatsu *et al.*, 1979). Further studies are in progress in my laboratory to establish roles played by cyclic nucleotides in cortical plasticity.

C. Comments on alternative interpretations

I have described above the results of various tests which have been imposed on our NE hypothesis. It is worthwhile to look back again on the path we took before considering our future plans. There are basically two types of challenges to our interpretations of the last 6 years' work: One is the question of the specificity of the chemicals used in our experiments to manipulate the function of the monoamine systems, including the total amount of drugs used, and the duration as well as the method of their administration. The other concerns the possibility that the very presence of these chemicals directly interferes with neuronal processes, which are currently unknown, underlying the changes in ocular dominance. As the reader may have already realized, all previous studies, except for the very first experiment with intraventricular injections of 6-OHDA, were designed to answer specific questions raised in interpreting the data from the preceding studies. Thus, all results have been interpreted uniquely with reference to the NE systems, although not all findings were necessarily positive.

1. The Specificity of 6-OHDA

One of the major criticisms of our first report in the series (Kasamatsu and Pettigrew, 1976) was derived from doubts about the specificity of 6-OHDA treatment. This skepticism was quite understandable since we had injected a total of 10 mg or more of 6-OHDA into the lateral ventricle of young kittens. However, in addition to the early preliminary biochemical results obtained in collaboration with W. Shoemaker and F. Bloom, which indicated about a 50% reduction of endogenous CAs in the visual cortex of such kittens (Kasamatsu and Pettigrew, 1979), we later demonstrated by histofluorescence that even 10 mg 6-OHDA, when injected into the lateral ventricle over

10 days, in fact produced only an incomplete lesion of CA terminals in the kitten's visual cortex (Kasamatsu *et al.*, 1981b). In comparing these results to those obtained later in the cortex locally perfused with 6-OHDA, we have concluded that the efficiency of intraventricular injection of 6-OHDA was far lower than that of direct perfusion in placing chemical lesions of the CA-containing terminals in the visual cortex.

In the localized perfusion paradigm, in contrast to intraventricular injections, the extent of spread of perfused chemicals in the cortex becomes a crucial issue. In the latter situation, however, CA fluorescence histochemistry showed no obvious gradient of depletion of CA terminals with 6-OHDA when examined along the anterior-posterior plane in the visual cortex. The equally strong lesions, except for layers II and III, were also seen in the two hemispheres (Fig. 2 in Kasamatsu *et al.*, 1981b). Utilizing a few methods, such as CA fluorescence histochemistry, biochemical assays for endogenous CAs, and evaluation of the spatial distribution of tritium counts after perfusing the cortex with either [^{3}H]6-OHDA or [^{3}H]NE, we estimated how far exogenous CAs can extend from the site of perfusion in the visual cortex. It was maximally about 10 mm, provided that the concentration of CAs in the perfusion solution was not too high. Next, by taking this result together with those in both multiple physiological recordings and fluorescence histochemistry, we obtained an approximate estimate, at a given site and time after the start of perfusion, of the lowest effective concentration of 6-OHDA and NE required to cause lesions in the intracortical CA terminals and to restore the neuronal plasticity in such visual cortex (Kasamatsu *et al.*, 1981b). The threshold concentration for 6-OHDA (3×10^{-6} *M*) and NE (3×10^{-7} *M*) turned out to be reasonably low for their specific uptake by CA terminals (see Section IV, B, *10*). I believe that we have thus answered the question of specificity properly. It is, of course, desirable to carry out similar assays for the other chemicals, such as propranolol and dbc AMP, used in later studies.

2. *Effects of Binocular Deprivation*

The second major objection concerns our choice of changes in binocularity as a physiological measure of the extent of cortical plasticity in action: Specificially, it is crucial to clarify whether 6-OHDA administered to the monocularly deprived kitten can produce the effects of either binocular deprivation or strabismus in terms of changes in ocular dominance. Since we still do not know the cellular mechanisms responsible for the changes in ocular dominance, hundreds of peculiar situations might possilby be imagined to cause such effects which are typical of binocular deprivation. The nonspecific effect of 6-OHDA may fit one such situation. For example, the nonspecific cytotoxicity of 6-OHDA may affect visual cortical synapses directly to reduce their efficiency, equally for both types of synapses on those cells which receive afferents from both the deprived and nondeprived eyes. To complicate this possibility, since 6-OHDA was injected into the lateral ventrical and the LGN receives a rich projection of NE fibers, 6-OHDA might reach the LGN and demolish the facilitory effect of NE on the firing of the geniculate cells (Nakai and Takaori, 1974; Rogawski and Aghajanian, 1980b). Thus, the imbalance between the two sets of afferent activity from the two eyes, one being in use and the other lid-sutured, becomes small enough to reduce the effects of monocular deprivation, resulting in little change in the ocular dominance distribution. The final effect of 6-OHDA, then, as known for binocular deprivation, might be to produce many visually unresponsive cells and cells without orientation as well as direction selectivity, although the ocular dominance distribution stays close to normal. However, since the proportion of visually unresponsive cells was no different between the 6-OHDA-treated (5.5%) and control animals (4.3%) in our study, and since both orientation and direction selectivity also did not differ in the two types of animals (Kasamatsu and Pettigrew, 1979), it is difficult to argue, on the basis of receptive field properties alone, that for the majority of cells in the visual cortex, 6-OHDA produced effects on ocularity similar to binocular deprivation.

Even the specific action of 6-OHDA within the visual cortex, as maintained by some critics, may first abolish the excitatory or inhibitory action of NE in the spontaeous as well as the visually evoked activity of individual visual cortical cells, and thus reduce the effects of imbalance of visual afferents from the two eyes on the binocularity of cortical cells in the monocularly deprived animal. Such a possibility, however, may be ruled out since we found rather subtle changes by NE iontophoresis in the visual responsiveness of visual cortical cells when their receptive fields were stimulated by an appropriate visual stimulus. In this study (Kasamatsu and Heggelund, 1982), visual cortical cells either increased, decreased or did not change their visual responsiveness. Furthermore, the effects of NE were seen only in the minority of complex cells, although most simple cells clearly change their responsiveness during NE iontophoresis, and the effects of NE, if any, were weak on complex cells as compared to those on neighboring simple cells. These results led us to suggest that NE may have at least two roles in the visual cortex, one being to modulate the neuronal responsiveness and the other to enhance plasticity. These two functions of NE are apparently independent of each other, since neuronal plasticity necessarily includes all classes of neurons in the kitten visual cortex.

It is also important to point out that the continuous presence of 6-OHDA is not only unnecessary for our purpose, once chemical lesions of CA terminals are formed, but also may possibly cause a nonspecific adverse effect. In this sense, our study in preventing the ocular dominance shift in monocularly deprived kittens is quite different from the previous demonstration of recovery of lost receptive fields for the previously deprived eye by Duffy *et al.* (1976a,b) and Sillito *et al.* (1981), in which such an effect was observed only in the presence of the GABA antagonist, bicuculline.

The argument may be extended to include possible changes in the function of various neurohormones secreted from the hypothalamus–hypophysis system following the production of chemical lesions by intraventricular 6-OHDA. Since it was hard to provide an unequivocal control for each of the above arguments, in later studies we avoided injecting 6-OHDA into the ventricle by switching to the new method of localized microperfusion in the visual cortex. Microperfusion of 6-OHDA proved equally or more effective in blocking the shift of ocular dominance in monocularly deprived kittens, if recordings were made in an area close enough to be affected by 6-OHDA above the threshold concentration (Kasamatsu *et al.*, 1979). In retrospect, we were lucky enough not to be totally discouraged by the strong antagonisms we encountered. Instead, we were able to design new types of experiments each time to provide us with reasonable answers to these rather "unspecified" criticisms.

3. Cerebral Blood Supply

There is a strong correlation between neuronal activity and the amount of glucose consumption measured by a method such as 2-DG analysis, as evidenced by its successful autoradiographic application in visualizing ocular dominance or orientation columns (see Section II, C). This may suggest an increase in energy demand in that brain area where a high level of synaptic plasticity is occurring. If so, we have to face the following problem of the NE control of blood circulation in the brain.

The cerebral blood vessels receive projections of NE-containing fibers from two distinct soucres: The large vessels in the pia mater and the superficial part of layer I are innervated by peripheral sympathetic fibers from the superior cervical ganglion (Falck *et al.*, 1965; Nelson and Rennels, 1970; Harper *et al.*, 1972), whereas the small intracortical vessels, including capillaries, in the rest of the cortical layers receive central NE fibers from the LC complex (Hartman *et al.*, 1972; Edvinsson *et al.*, 1973; Itakura *et al.*, 1977). Accordingly, the hypothesis has been put forward as a collective effort that the central NE system plays a role in regulating blood circulation in the brain (Molnar and Seylaz, 1965; Csillik *et al.*, 1971; Hartman *et al.*, 1972; Edvinsson *et al.*, 1973; Maeda *et al.*, 1973; Raichle *et al.*, 1975; Itakura *et al.*, 1977; see also a review by Edvinsson and MacKenzie, 1977). Chemical and electrical stimulation of the LC results in either a prompt reduction in cerebral blood flow, accompanied by an increase in the vascular permeability of water, in the hemisphere ipsilateral to the stimulation (Raichle *et al.*, 1975; De la Torre 1976), or a small (8%) but significant decrease in 2-DG uptake in the ipsilateral cerebral cortex, but not in subcortical regions, of mice (Abraham *et al.*, 1979). A unilateral lesion in the LC was reported as significantly increasing 2-DG uptake by the granule but not the Purkinje cells in both sides of the cerebellum (Schwartz, 1978). A quick summary of these results may suggest that activation of the LC system, which certainly leads to release of NE in the cerebral cortex (Korf *et al.*, 1973b; Tanaka *et al.*, 1976), cannot also function to enhance neuronal plasticity, which may require a higher blood supply as well as an increased cortical cell metabolism.

However, intraventricularly administered NE has apparently the opposite effects: an increase in glucose uptake, oxygen consumption, and regional cerebral blood flow in the cat parietal cortex (MacKenzie *et al.*, 1976). Bates *et al.* (1977) carried out a careful study in physiological responses of cerebral blood flow (for the whole brain) by measuring ^{133}Xe washout in the normal cat and compared the results with those obtained from cats in which the LC neurons had been bilaterally destroyed. They examined the dynamic range of changes in cerebral blood flow in response to alterations of blood CO_2 and mean arterial blood pressure. An essence of their results was as follows: Although the direction of changes in cerebral blood flow in LC lesion cats was the same as in the control, when challenged first by hypercapnia and then by hypocapnia (both in ~50% change), the response magnitude became significantly smaller in LC lesion animals as compared with the control. They also noted that in LC lesion animals the resting level during normocapnia was significantly higher than in the control. Among the two groups of animals, however, no change was seen in the autoregulatory response of cerebral blood flow to 30% changes in blood pressure.

By means of simultaneous recording of single-unit firing and local cerebral blood flow (hydrogen clearance method) from the nucleus ventralis posterolateralis, the somatosensory cortex, and the visual cortex of cats, Tsubokawa *et al.* (1980) examined the possibility that an increase in local cerebral blood flow might be *secondary* to an increase in neuronal firing. They demonstrated the concomitant increase in the two parameters in the somatosensory cortex and the nucleus ventralis posterolateralis, but not in the visual cortex, when the sciatic nerve was electrically stimulated by a train of pulses. Interestingly, in cats pretreated with 6-OHDA intraventricularly, no concurrent increase in local blood flow was observed despite an increase in neuronal firing in response to stimulation of the sciatic nerve. They further reported that in cat frontal cortex, suppression of unit firing which followed LC stimulation in 55% of cells studied always recovered 0.5–1.5

minutes before the return of concomitantly decreased local cerebral blood flow (Katayama *et al.,* 1981).

In summary, at the moment one cannot decide which event comes first, changes in neuronal activity or local cerebral flow, after activation of the central NE system. Even we are not quite sure whether the activation of the central NE system leads to an increase or a decrease, under the physiological condition, in local cerebral blood flow only in an area of interest, or whether this change must always be global. In this regard, the ways in which the central NE system is activated seem to be critical. At any rate, it has been established that the central NE system is necessary to maintain changes in local cerebral blood flow induced primarily by either neuronal or non-neuronal factors. Thus, it is likely that the high level of neuronal plasticity is supported by an accompanying elevation in local cerebral blood flow, at least secondary to a still unknown neuronal change. In addition, a recent discovery of the wide distribution of vasoactive intestinal polypeptide in the mammalian brain suggests that this neuron-cerebral blood flow interaction may be in reality much more complicated than discussed above. (Lorén *et al.,* 1979; Sims *et al.,* 1980).

Furthermore, it has been reported that the primary effects of NE on the cerebral vessels are mediated through α-adrenergic receptors, resulting in their contraction, and that activation of β-adrenergic receptors leads to their dilatation only when they are contracted (Edvinsson and Owman, 1974). Under certain conditions, therefore, an increase in synaptic plasticity by activation of β receptors in the visual cortex, as suggested in our studies, may be accompanied by a concurrent increase in the local blood supply. It will be interesting to determine if a pure β agonist such as isoproterenol is in fact less effective than NE in enhancing plasticity because of this differential control of cerebral blood flow by the two types of adrenergic receptor (see also Section IV, A, *2, e*).

4. Regrowth of CA Fibers

Next, I would like to discuss the problem of the gradual disappearance of those changes induced by the 6-OHDA treatment, whether given either intraventricularly or locally into the visual cortex. The 6-OHDA-induced blockade of the ocular dominance shift in monocularly deprived animals did not last forever, but started to wane 3–6 weeks after the discontinuation of intraventricular injections of 6-OHDA (Kasamatsu and Pettigrew, 1979). In another paradigm of cortical recovery from the effects of monocular deprivation (Kasamatsu *et al.,* 1981a), the suppression of a return of binocluar cells to the visual cortex was neither complete with localized perfusion of the cortex with 6-OHDA nor did it last forever, as might be expected in a visual cortex in which NE-containing terminals had been morphologically removed. The binocluar cells reappeared slowly but steadily, a pattern which became evident 12 days after the reopening of the closed eyelid. At 30 days after, the maximal duration of our observation term in this study, binocularity had returned to about 50% of that of the age-matched control kittens, although we did not expect further quick recovery beyond this level because of the maturity of the kittens (9 weeks of age at the last recording). How can we explain this retrogression without any complicated assumptions?

Because the initial lesions produced by intraventricular 6-OHDA were quite incomplete in the visual cortex (Kasamatsu *et al.*, 1981b), collateral sprouting was possibly induced (e.g., Moore *et al.*, 1974). Even in the case of localized perfusion of 6-OHDA, convincing evidence from CA fluorescence histochemistry as well as from biochemical assays for endogenous CAs strongly indicated the remarkably quick regrowth of CA terminal fibers in the area surrounding the perfusion site (Nakai *et al.*, 1981). Even 2 weeks after 6-OHDA perfusion was stopped, the CA terminal-depleted area reduced significantly (a radius 2–3 mm from the center of perfusion). Within 4 weeks after the end of perfusion, CA fibers with varicosities were seen virtually everywhere in the visual cortex, including the gliosis region due to the previous cannulation, although the intensity of the CA fluorescence had not yet returned to the control level. Thus, the effects of CA terminal depletion by 6-OHDA appear to wane with time. Due to this well-acknowledged nature of CA fibers to regrow, especially when the initial damage is partial and limited to the distal end of axons, sparing the proximal end as well as the somatas, I would suggest that in our paradigm of local microperfusion, both degeneration and regeneration of the distal ends of CA fibers occur simultaneously only under the influence of a gradient of opposite polarity from the center of perfusion.

5. *Receptor Supersensitivity*

The final point of this discussion concerns the denervation supersensitivity of the CA-related receptors in the 6-OHDA-treated cortex and their desensitization when a high level of exogenous NE is maintained beyond a certain time limit. Since both sensitization and desensitization of receptors were demonstrated in the central CA system both biochemically and behaviorally (e.g., Kalisker *et al.*, 1973; Mukherjee *et al.*, 1975; Kebabian *et al.*, 1975; Harden *et al.*, 1977b; see also Ungerstedt, 1974), changes in the receptor sensitivity due to 6-OHDA application must account reasonably well for some of the previous observations which appeared to be inconsistent with the CA hypothesis. For example, in some ocular dominance histograms appearing in our first publication in the series, the dominance of ipsilateral nondeprived eye over the contralateral deprived eye was noted in 6-OHDA-treated and monocularly deprived kittens, although the majority of cells in such histograms were binocular (see Figs. 2, 4, and 8 of Kasamatsu and Pettigrew, 1979). Since these cells were seen mostly in animals which were recorded at least a few days after the cessation of the 6-OHDA injections into the ventricle (~ 10 mg), this ipsilateral, open eye dominance may be explained by the extent of regrowth of CA terminals toward the outside of layers II and III, where the remaining CA fibers and terminals are usually seen immediately after the end of 6-OHDA injections. The expected blockade of ocular dominance in these monocularly deprived animals may also be counteracted by the higher sensitivity of those CA-related receptors which make up the loss of normal levels of afferents in the CA system. In this regard, it is intriguing to remember the earlier speculation by Kety (1970) that biogenic amines circulating through cerebrospinal fluid (CSF) may affect wide areas of the brain, modifying such various forebrain functions as emotion and learning. Morphological studies in the 5-HT system in fact suggest that some 5-HT-containing terminals from the raphe nuclei may terminate on the surface of ependymal cells in the ventricle (Aghajanian and Gallager, 1975; Chan-Palay, 1976). Although there is still no direct evidence to indicate a morphological arrangement similar to this in the central CA system, a small increase in circulating NE in the CSF, possibly due to an increased production of NE in the LC after partial lesions at the terminal fields in the neocortex, could be significantly effective, if β-adrenergic receptors have been sensitized, to induce visible changes in the overall cortical phsyiology.

D. Possible roles for other monoamines in visual cortical plasticity

1. DA

We have considered the roles played by the central CA system, especially the ascending NE pathways which originate in the LC complex, in affecting visual cortical plasticity. Although previous reports in the rat brain have suggested a lack of DA in the occipital cortex (Section IV, A, *2, g*), we have found a substantial amount of endogenous DA (about half the NE content) in the kitten visual cortex using two different biochemical methods (enzymatic assay and liquid chromatography with electrochemical detection) (Kasamatsu *et al.*, 1981b). These results in our biochemical assays are in harmony with those of Reader and others (1976) in their perfusion study of the cat occipital cortex, wherein they measured a significant amount of DA in the perfusate which was collected under various conditions of sleep and waking, and during sensory stimulation. Other investigators have shown the presence of single units in the cat occipital cortex which were sensitive to iontophoretically ejected DA (Krnjević and Phillis, 1963; Reader, 1978).

What is the role, then, that these intracortical DA-containing terminals play in controlling visual cortical plasticity? Since 6-OHDA cannot differentiate NE terminals from DA terminals, we have to look for other means of manipulating only the DA system. Although we have not yet done any serious tests to evaluate a possible contribution of the DA system in enhancing cortical plasticity, the basic strategy seems to be already available. As indicated by preliminary success in the studies with a β-adrenergic blocker, manipulating the DA receptors directly appears to be more sensible than manipulating the DA-containing nerve terminals. Nevertheless, it is possible, by combining various monoamine-related chemicals, to make a special preparation in which only the central DA system but not the NE system is preferentially activated. For example, in order to maintain the high level of DA in the brain, a large quantity of L-dopa (dihydroxyphenylalanine) may be systemically delivered in combination with a dopa decarboxylase inhibitor in the periphery (Carbidopa) with or without the simultaneous administration of a DBH inhibitor. These approaches, although not particularly attractive in experimental design, still have certain clinical interest, should DA also prove to enhance neuronal plasticity.

2. α Adrenoreceptor

Since NE activates not only β adrenoreceptors but also α adrenoreceptors, and since contraction of cerebral arteries in the cat's brain is mediated through α adrenoreceptors (Edvinsson and Owman, 1974), as mentioned previously (Section IV, A, 2, *f*), it is quite important to determine whether the same α receptors are also involved in the enhancement of cortical plasticity. As a first step in answering this question, I have started to test the effects of two types of α-adrenergic antagonists (phentolamine and phenoxybenzamine) in the same monocular deprivation paradigm as for β antagonists. So far, I have found the usual shift of ocular dominance in the α antagonist-perfused as well as the nonperfused control cortices of the same kittens which had been monocularly deprived for a week, although the proportion of binocular cells was slightly higher in the former than in the latter (Kasamatsu, unpublished observation). Thus, the tentative conclusion at the moment is that the contribution of α adrenoreceptors in cortical plasticity seems to be minimal, if it exists at all.

3. Serotonin

At the beginning of this project, we studied the kitten cortex which had been treated with a serotonergic neurotoxin, 5,7-dihydroxytryptamine

(5,7-DHT) in place of 6-OHDA. Despite the lower specificity of 5,7-DHT uptake by 5-HT terminals relative to 6-OHDA uptake by CA terminals, we obtained a result which might suggest an increased neuronal plasticity in the serotonin-terminal depleted visual cortex (Kasamatsu and Pettigrew, 1976). Furthermore, it was reported that intraventricular injections of a 5-HT partial antagonist, LSD, partially restored neural plasticity in the adult cat visual cortex (McCall *et al.,* 1979).

In addition to the classic antagonism between the catecholaminergic and serotonergic systems in alternations of sleep–waking cycles, as proposed by Jouvet and his associates, there are many phenomena which suggest the mutually inhibitory interaction between these two monoamine systems. For example, one report has described interesting changes in rat social behavior due to such drug manipulations (Ellison, 1976): In an open field rat colony, rats which were subjected to lesions of the CA system by 6-OHDA dropped dramatically in the social scale, whereas those which received 5,6-dihydroxytryptamine (like 5,7-DHT, a serotonergic toxin) improved their social status.

Morphological studies with various new methods indicate a reciprocal innervation between the LC and the raphe complexes (see Section IV, A, *2, h*). Serotonin-containing nerve terminals and fibers in the LC have been demonstrated by means of autoradiography (Conrad *et al.,* 1974; Bobillier *et al.,* 1976; Descarries and Léger, 1978), immunofluorescence (Pickel *et al.,* 1977), and retrograde tracing with HRP (Sakai *et al.,* 1977b). Conversely, endings of LC fibers in the raphe complex have been shown by CA histofluorescence (Fuxe, 1965; Loizou, 1969), HRP tracing (Sakai *et al.,* 1977a), and immunofluorescence with DBH antibody (Swanson and Hartman, 1975). Furthermore, various pharmacological and biochemical interactions are known to exist between these two morphologically discrete monoamine systems in the mammalian brain (Pujol *et al.,* 1973; Kostowski *et al.,* 1974; Renaud *et al.,* 1975; Lewis *et al.,* 1976).

The presence of 5-HT-containing nerve terminals in the rat neocortex has been shown by various techniques, such as histofluorescence (Fuxe, 1965), biochemical assay (Kuhar *et al.,* 1972), autoradiography (Descarries *et al.,* 1975), and immunohistochemistry (Lidov *et al.,* 1980). It is very tempting to imagine that serotonergic nerve terminals in the neocortex also play a role in controlling synaptic plasticity. If so, can it be the reverse of the role played by the NE system, as our preliminary results have suggested? At the moment, all these questions are still unanswered. We have made, however, an interesting observation while studying the ontogeny of monoaminergic receptor binding sites in the early postnatal life of kittens. In the kitten neocortex, the number of 5-HT receptor binding sites attains a peak density with a sharply rising phase at least 4 weeks before the peaking of the β-adrenergic receptor binding site concentration (Jonsson and Kasamatsu, submitted). The profile of increasing binding sites in β-adrenergic receptors appears to fit the susceptibility curves of visual cortical cells to monocular experience during the criticial period better than changes in endogenous NE alone might indicate. If this preliminary result holds, the expected role for the 5-HT system cannot simply be to terminate the critical period sensitivity of the cortex to changes in visual experience. It may well be, then, a signal for the start rather than the end of the critical period. Alternatively, as implied in other systems, the 5-HT system is involved in other functions, such as controlling cell differentiation (Lauder and Krebs, 1978) and cell migration (Yamamoto *et al.*, 1980). These are certainly much earlier events in the life of neurons in the brain than is their need of plasticity to adjust the synaptic function for the proper neuronal connectivity.

V. Perspective of the NE Hypothesis

What is the implication of our NE hypothesis in synaptic plasticity in general? We are looking for mechanisms which underlie neuronal plasticity in the mammalian neocortex, and the roles played by the various monoamine systems may be just such mechanisms. Comparative studies by Tohyama (1976) and Tohyama and others (1974a, 1976) suggest that the number of CA-containing cells in the pontine tegmentum which are thought to belong to the LC complex increases along with the advancing levels of evolution attained by various animals, from bullfrog to human. Thus, there may be a parallel between encephalization and the evoltuion NE systems which innervate the neocortex as their ultimate target.

Advances in monoamine research have revealed that by constructing mutually inhibitory networks, the three major monoamine subsystems in the brain seem to modulate the input–output transactions in any specific system. For example, Lidov and others (1978b) found a rich innervation by NE terminals in the whisker barrel field, especially in its hollow, which is located in layer IV of the mouse somatosensory cortex; it is interesting that this same layer IV is also the site where the thalamic afferents terminate. This finding may be related to our own observation in the kitten visual cortex, in that a dense plexus is formed by CA terminals and fibers in layers II and III, where the impulse transaction between visual afferents and cortical efferents takes place (Itakura *et al.*, 1981). In general, NE terminals may not be distributed at random in the neocortex, as has been proposed previously. A recent light autoradiographic study has suggested a preferential distribution (in layers I–III) of β-adrenergic receptors in the cerebral cortex of rats (Palacios and Kuhar, 1980) and cats (Nakai, Jonsson, and Kasamatsu, submitted). It is hard to believe, however, the function of a given NE-containing terminal bouton in the visual cortex, or even that of an LC neuron, which has an average of 19×10^3 NE varicosities in the neocortex (rat, Descarries, 1974), is critically affected by which type of cortical cell it contacts or where a sensory receptive field or a motor field for that cell is located. This notion may be consistent with Nakamura's results, in which the wide distribution of NE axons from a single LC cell was elegantly demonstrated by means of antidromic invasion (1977).

The point to be emphasized, then, is that if NE terminals have a specific function, this specificity has to derive from the target cells in a particular system, for example, layer III pyramidal cells in area 17 which are output cells with complex cell properties, on which NE terminals place their influence. I have already pointed out that the blood circulation in the brain is under the control of NE terminals which originate in the LC (Raichle *et al.*, 1975; Itakura *et al.*, 1977; Abraham *et al.*, 1979) (Section IV, C, *3*). The type of β adrenoceptor ($\beta 2$) in the vascular system seems to differ from that ($\beta 1$) on neurons (Minneman *et al.*, 1979a,b). Another pharmacological study has suggested that contraction and dilatation of feline cerebral arteries are mediated through α- and $\beta 1$-adrenergic receptors, respectively (Edvinsson and Owman, 1974). The NE system thus is not a crucial relay station in the main pathway of information transaction but may work as a mediator to amplify ongoing events without reference to their sign (excitatory or inhibitiory). The modulatory roles for monoamine-containing nerve terminals, which may or may not form the conventional synapse with surrounding neural elements, have been proposed in various regions of the mammalian brain (Kety, 1970; Bloom, 1974; Descarries *et al.*,1975, 1977; Chan-Palay, 1977; Maeda and Shimizu, 1978; Moore and Bloom, 1979). It is thus quite important for prospective research on the monoamine system to pursue its interaction with such well-understood specific systems as the central visual pathway. In this sense, I believe that our study of the NE system has provided a good example from which future neuropeptide research may also benefit.

How general is the role of the NE system in controlling synaptic plasticity outside the visual cortex? We do not have enough data to answer this question sensibly. I would like to point out, however, that there may be various types of neuronal plasticity. In other words, there may exist different neuronal events which derive from different underlying mechanisms, all described by the word "plasticity." Three such examples in the different brain regions will be mentioned below.

1. As was first demonstrated by Raisman (1969), synapse formation on septal cells in the adult rat brain may exhibit plasticity, which implies the replacement of deafferented terminals on the surface of septal cells by other types of active terminals in the neighborhood. (The septum is known for its

innervation by monoamine terminal fields.) The presence of degenerating terminals seems to be crucial for this reorganization of connectivity. It is important to point out that this rearrangement is carried out at the expense of the specificity of the original connectivity. An electron microscopic observation (Lund and Lund, 1971) in the rat SC has also shown that the characteristics of the reformed synapses resemble those of the intact ones but are not identical with them.

2. The hippocampus, especially in the hilus of area dentata, receives a dense innervation by LC projections. Physiology also demonstrates clearly that the hippocampal pyramidal cells are sensitive to exogenous NE and receive inputs from the LC (Segal and Bloom, 1976; Nakamura, 1977; Segal, 1981). Long-lasting potentiation of postsynaptic potentials is a unique feature in pyramidal cells in the dorsal hippocampus. Expansion of one type of terminal field has been shown by autoradiography in the granule cell layer in the rat dentate gyrus following denervation of the other type of afferent. Thus, the dentate gyrus provides us with another beautiful system in which to study neuronal plasticity. Yet, an attempt to block this type of plasticity by application of 6-OHDA was recently reported to be unsuccessful (Amaral *et al.,* 1980). Interestingly enough, however, the magnitude of long-term potentiation in the hilus of the dentate gyrus became significantly reduced in NE-depleted rats which had received bilaterally an intracerebral injection of 6-OHDA into the dorsal NE bundles (Goddard *et al.,* 1980; Bliss *et al.,* 1981).

3. The red nucleus in adult cats normally receives two types of exictatory inputs: one from the somatosensory cortex and the other from the nucleus interpositus of the cerebellum. By using intracellular recordings, Tsukahara and his associates have presented a beautiful example of plasticity between these two types of nerve endings (for a review, see Tsukahara, 1981). Interestingly, the red nucleus is a unique site in the brain because it is the one least innervated by LC projections.

As the reader may have realized already, one of the differences between synaptic plasticity we have been studying in the immature visual cortex and the type in the above-cited studies in the adult brain is the apparent lack of degenerative processes by afferent fibers in the young cortex. In an extensive study with electron microscopy in the lateral vestibular nucleus of the normal adult rat, Sotelo and Palay (1971) described in detail various forms of unusual ultrastructural profiles in axons and axon terminals which had then been interpreted as suggesting degenerative or regenrative changes in the fine morphology of individual nerve endings. Furthermore, as evidenced, for example, by Cragg's study (1975a), which examined postnatal changes in the average number of synapses per neuron and synaptic density in the developing kitten visual cortex, a substantial proportion (30–40%) of cortical synapses is supposed to disappear during the normal maturation of the visual cortex (see also Section IV, A, *3*). Nevertheless, no such extensive terminal degeneration that may correspond to the substantial loss of cortical synapses has ever been visualized in either the normal or the visually deprived young visual cortex. As has been known for some time (e.g., Liu and Chambers, 1958), degenerating terminals in fact help to induce intense sprouting of active terminals to occupy the emptied postsynaptic sites. Sprouting has been observed, however, without the preceding degeneration under some conditions, such as colchicine treatment in the salamander's skin (Aguilar *et al.,* 1973) and TTX-induced paralysis of the sciatic nerve of adult mice (Brown and Ironton, 1977). Furthermore, evidence exists that collaterals may sprout from nondegenerating terminals even in the CNS (Tsukahara and Fujito, 1976; Freeman, 1977). Thus, it has to be determined if the collateral sprouting from active visual terminals is a crucial step in the cascade of biochemical and morphological events following monocular lid suture which eventually leads to the shift of ocular dominance in the visual cortex.

VI. Conclusion

I have described the birth of our NE hypothesis for visual cortical plasticity and its maturation during the last 6 years. Our main thesis, that the central NE system is necessary for maintaining neuronal plasticity in cat viusal cortex, seems to have survived the various challenges we presented. Accordingly, then, NE molecules released from terminals within the neocortex work as modulators to imprint the summary of incoming sensory afferents due to the animal's experience into the brain via still unknown cellular mechanisms which change the mode of synaptic connectivity in the brain area involved. Our success in the formation of the NE hypothesis by no means excludes possible roles played in synaptic plasticity by other neurotransmitters, neurohormones, and neuropeptides. Furthermore, as was stressed often, the presence of NE terminals and the ready availability of NE for the NE-related receptors are necessary but not sufficient conditions by themselves to induce changes in synaptic connectivity. The role of NE, whatever its mechanisms may be, seems to be submissive to neuronal events due to changes in specific afferent activity. We do not know yet, for example, what the crucial event is in the cascade of changes which follow monocular lid suture. But our studies in binocular cortical cells have clearly shown that the NE system enhances the impact of the imbalance in the two sets of related but discrete afferents in the central visual pathway in both normal and experimentally created conditions. Despite the limitations of the NE story at its current stage of development, I am convinced that we are correct to turn our attention to the second messenger system in the cortical cells. Roles for cyclic AMP in controlling another type of synaptic plasticity in fact have been suggested in presumably much simpler nervous systems than the cat visual cortex (e.g., synaptic facilitation and sensitization in the abdominal ganglion of *Aplysia:* Cedar and Schwartz, 1972; Brunelli *et al.*, 1976; Kandel *et al.*, 1975; Shimahara and Tauc, 1977; Klein and Kandel, 1978; also heterosynaptic facilitation in the rabbit superior cervical ganglion: Libet, 1979). This consideration thus may lead us in the near future to the discovery of biochemical as well as morphological changes in synaptic plasticity in the neocortex which may be mediated by cyclic AMP-dependent protein phosphorylation and phospholipid methylation in the cell organelles.

Acknowledgments

I thank Dr. John D. Pettigrew, with whom I have enjoyed a fruitful collaboration for the last 6 years at Caltech. Without his collaboration, the outcome of this project could have been quite different. I am grateful to Dr. Jeremy P. Brockes, who has shared our confidence in the CA hypothesis and has always provided stimulating discussions. I also express my gratitude to Drs. Toru Itakura, Gösta Jonsson, Paul Heggelund, and Kunio Naki, who have made essential and indispensable contributions to the morphological, biochemical and physiological studies of the central CA system. Finally, I would like to dedicate this review to Dr. Kitsuya Iwama, on his 63rd birthday, who introduced me to neurophysiology some years ago, and from whom I have received unfailing encouragement in pursuing my career as a researcher. The secretarial service was provided by Mrs. P. Brown, Ms. S. Canada, and Mrs. C. Katz. This work was supported by the following grants: USPHS EY-03409 (TK), USPHS EY-03291 (JDP), the Whitehall Foundation (JDP) and the Pew Memorial Trust (JDP).

References

Abraham, W. C., Delanoy, R. L., Dunn, A. J., and Zorentzer, S. F. (1979). Locus coeruleus stimulation decreases deoxyglucose uptake in ipsilateral mouse cerebral cortex. *Brain Research* **172,** 387–392.

Ader, J.-P., Postrema, F., and Korf, J. (1979). Contribution of the locus coeruleus to the adrenergic innervation of the rat spinal cord: A biochemical study. *Journal of Neural Transmission* **44,** 159–173.

Aghajanian, G. K. (1972). Chemical feedback regulation of serotonin-containing neurons in brain. *Annals of the New York Academy of Sciences* **193,** 86–94.

Aghajanian, G. K., and Bunney, B. S. (1977). Dopamine "autoreceptors": Pharmacological characterization by microiontophoretic single cell recording studies. *Naunyn-Schmiedebergs Archives of Pharmacology* **297,** 1–7.

Aghajanian, G. K., and Gallager, D. W. (1975). Raphe origin of serotonergic nerves terminating in the cerebral ventricles. *Brain Research* **88,** 221–231.

Agrawal, H. C., Glisson, S. N., and Himwich, W. A. (1968). Developmental changes in monoamines of mouse brains. *International Journal of Neuropharmacology* **7**, 97–101.

Aguilar, C. E., Bisby, M. A., Cooper, E., and Diamond, J. (1973). Evidence that axoplasmic transport of trophic factors is involved in the regulation of peripheral nerve fields in salamanders *Journal of Physiology (London)* **234**, 449–464.

Albus, K. (1979). ^{14}C-deoxyglucose mapping of orientation subunits in the cat visual cortical areas. *Experimental Brain Research* **37**, 609–613.

Alexander, R. W., Davis, J. N., and Lefkowitz, R. J. (1975). Direct identification and characterization of β-adrenergic receptors in rat brain. *Nature (London)* **258**, 437–440.

Amaral, D. G., and Sinnamon, H. M. (1977). The locus coeruleus: Neurobiology of a central noradrenergic nucleus. *Progress in Neurobiology* **9**, 147–196.

Amaral, D. G., Foss, J. A., Kellogg, C., and Woodward, D. J. (1975). Effects of subcutaneous administration of 6-hydroxydopamine (6-OHDA) in neonatal rats on dendritic morphology in the hippocampus. *Society for Neurosceince Abstracts* **1**, 789.

Amaral, D. G., Avendaño, C., and Cowan, W. M. (1980).The effects of neonatal 6-hydroxydopamine treatment on morphological plasticity in the dentate gyrus of the rat following entorhinal lesions. *Journal of Comparative Neurology* **194**, 171–191.

Andén, N. E., Dahlström, A., Fuxe, K., Larsson, K., Olson, L., and Ungerstedt, U. (1966) Ascending monoamine neurons to the telencephalon and diencephalon. *Acta Physiologica Scanadinavica* **67**, 313–326.

Andersen, P., and Wigström, H. (1980). Possible mechanism for long-lasting potentiation of hippocampal synaptic transmission. *In Neurobiological Basis of Learning and Memory* (Y. Tsukada and B. W. Agranoff, eds.), pp. 37–47. Wiley, New York.

Andersen, P., Sundberg, S. H., Sveen, O., and Wigström, H. (1977) Specific long-lasting potentiation of synaptic transmission in hippocampal slices. *Nature (London)* **266**, 736–737.

Arduini, A., and Hirao, T. (1959). On the mechanism of the EEG sleep patterns elicited by acute visual deafferentation. *Archives Italiennes de Biologie* **97**, 140–155.

Arduini, A., and Hirao, T. (1960) Enhancement of evoked responses in the visual system during reversible retinal inactivation. *Archives Italiennes de Biologie* **98**, 182–205.

Ary, M., Pettigrew, J. D., and Kasamatsu, T. (1979). Manipulations of cortical catecholamines fail to affect suppression of deprived eye response after reverse suture. *ARVO Abstract (Supplement to Investigative Ophthalmology and Visual Science), 18,* 136.

Atlas, D., Steer, M. L., and Levitzki, A. (1974). Stereospecific binding of propranolol and catecholamines to the β-adrenergic receptor. *Proceedings of the National Academy of Sciences of the U.S.A.* **71**, 4246–4248.

Awaya, S., Miyake, Y., Kanda, T., and Shiose, Y. (1974). Further studies on cases of suspected stimulus deprivation amblyopia. *Folia Ophthalamologica Japonica* **25**, 270–281.

Azmitta, E. C., and Segal, M. (1978). An autoradiographic analysis of the differential ascending projections of the dorsal and median raphe nuclei in the rat. *Journal of Comparative Neurology* **179**, 641–668.

Baker, F. H., Grigg, P., and von Noorden, G. K. (1974). Effects of visual deprivation and strabismus on the responses of neurons in the visual cortex of the monkey, including studies on the striate and prestriate cortex in the normal animal. *Brain Research* **66**, 185–208.

Banks, M. S., Aslin, R. N., and Letson, R. D. (1975) Sensitive period for the development of human binocular vision. *Science* **190**, 675–677.

Barlow, H. B. (1975) Visual experience and cortical development. *Nature (London)* **258**, 199–204.

Barlow, H. B., and Pettigrew, J. D. (1971). Lack of specificity of neurones in the visual cortex of young kittens. *Journal of Physiology (London)* **281**, 98P–100P.

Bates, D., Weinshilboum, R. M., Campbell, R. J., and Sundt, T. M., Jr. (1977). The effects of lesions in the locus coeruleus on the physiological responses of the cerebral blood vessels in cats. *Brain Research* **136**, 431–443.

Bateson, P. P. G. (1966). The characteristics and context of imprinting. *Biological Reviews* **41,** 177–220.
Beaudet, A., and Sotelo, C. (1981). Synaptic remodeling of serotonin axon terminals in rat agranular cerebellum. *Brain Research* **206,** 305–329.
Bennett, J.-P., Jr., and Snyder, S. H. (1975). Stereospecific binding of d-lysergic acid diethylamide (LSD) to brain membranes: relationship to serotonin receptors. *Brain Research* **94,** 523–544.
Bennett, J.-P., Jr., and Snyder, S. H. (1976). Serotonin and lysergic acid diethylamide binding in rat brain membranes: Relationship to postsynaptic serotonin receptors. *Molecular Pharmacology* **12,** 373–389.
Benzer, S. (1973). Genetic dissection of behavior. *Scientific American* **229,** 24–37.
Berger, B., Tassin, J. P., Blanc, G., Moyne, M. A., and Thierry, A. M. (1974). Histochemical confirmation for dopaminergic innvervation of the rat cerebral cortex after destruction of the noradrenergic ascending pathways. *Brain Research* **81,** 332–337.
Berman, N., and Sterling, P. (1974). Immediate reversal of eye dominance in the superior colliculus of the monocularly deprived cat following cortical removal. *Anatomical Record* **178,** 310.
Berman, N., and Sterling, P. (1976). Cortical suppression of the retinocollicular pathway in the monocularly deprived cat. *Journal of Physiology (London)* **255,** 263–273.
Betz, W. J., Caldwell, J. H., and Ribchester, R. R. (1980) The effects of partial denervation at birth on the development of muscle fibres and motor units in rat lumbrical muscle. *Journal of Physiology (London)* **303,** 265–279.
Bevan, P., Bradshaw, C. M., and Szabadi, E. (1977). The pharmacology of adrenergic neuronal responses in the cerebral cortex: Evidence for excitatory α- and inhibitory β-receptors. *British Journal of Pharmacology* **59,** 635–641.
Bizzi, E., and Brooks, D. C. (1963). Functional connections between the pontine reticular formation and lateral geniculate nucleus during deep sleep. *Archives Italiennes de Biologie* **101,** 666–680
Björklund, A., and Stenevi, U. (1979). Regeneration of monaminergic and cholinergic neurons in the mammalian central nervous system. *Physiological Reviews* **59,** 62–100.
Blakemore, C. (1978). Maturation and modification in the developing visual system. In R. Held, H. W. Leibowitz, and H. L. Teuber (Eds.), *Handbook of Sensory Physiology, Perception.* vol. VIII, pp. 377–436. Springer, Berlin, Heidelberg, New York.
Blakemore, C., and Cooper, G. F. (1970). Development of the brain depends on visual envrionment. *Nature (London)* **228,** 477–478.
Blakemore, C., and Mitchell, D. E. (1973). Environment modification of the visual cortex and the neural basis of learning and memory. *Nature (London)* **241,** 467–468.
Blakemore, C., and Pettigrew, J. D. (1970). Eye dominance and the visual cortex. *Nature (London)* **225,** 426–429.
Blakemore, C., and Van Sluyters, R. C. (1974). Reversal of the physiological effects of monocular deprivation in kittens: Further evidence for a sensitive period. *Journal of Physiology (London)* **237,** 195–216.
Blakemore, C., and Van Sluyters, R. C. (1975). Innate and environmental factors in the development of the kitten's visual cortex. *Journal of Physiology (London)* **248,** 663–716.
Blakemore, C., Van Sluyters, R. C., Peck, C. K., and Hein, A. (1975). Development of cat visual cortex following rotation of one eye. *Nature (London)* **257,** 584–586.
Blakemore, C., Van Sluyters, R. C., and Movshon, J. A. (1976). Synaptic competition in the kitten's visual cortex. *Cold Spring Harbor Symposia on Quantitative Biology* **40,** 601–609.
Blakemore, C., Garey, L. J., and Vital-Durand, F. (1978). The physiological effects of monocular deprivation and their reversal in the monkey's visual cortex. *Journal of Physiology (London)* **283,** 223–262.
Blasdel, G. G., and Pettigrew, J. D. (1978) The effect of prior visual experience on recovery from monocular deprivation. *Journal of Physiology (London)* **274,** 601–619.

Blasdel, G. G., and Pettigrew, J. D. (1979). Degree of interocular synchrony required for maintenance of binocularity in kitten's visual cortex. *Journal of Neurophysiology* **42,** 1692–1710.

Blasdel, G. G., Mitchell, D. E., Muir, D. W., and Pettigrew, J. D. (1977) A physiological and behavioral study in cats of the effect of early visual experience with contours of a single orientation. *Journal of Physiology (London)* **265,** 615–636.

Blasdel, G. G., Lund, J. S., and Mates, S. L. (1981) Afferent axon arborizations in layer 4C of macaque striate cortex. *ARVO Abstract (Supplement to Investigative Ophthalmology and Visual Science)* **20,** 175.

Bliss, T. V. P., Goddard, G. V., Robertson, H. A., and Sutherland, R. J. (1981). Noradrenaline depletion reduces long term potentiation in the rat hippocampus. *In "Advances in Physiological Sciences"* (O. Fehér and F. Joó, eds.), Vol. 36: "Cellular Analogues of Conditioning and Neural Plasticity," pp. 175–185. Akadémiai Kiadó, Budapest; Pergamon, Oxford.

Bloom, F. E. (1974). Dynamics of synaptic modulation: Perspectives for the future. *In "The Neurosciences, Third Study Program"* (F. O. Schmitt and F. G. Warden, eds.), MIT Press, pp. 989–999. Cambridge, Massachusetts.

Bloom, F. E. (1975). Amine receptors in CNS. I. Norepinephrine. *In "Handbook of Psychopharmacology"* (L. L. Iversen, S. D. Iversen, and S. H. Snyder, eds.), Vol. 6: "Biogenic Amine Receptors," pp. 1–22. Plenum, New York.

Bloom, F. E. (1978). Central noradrenergic systems: Physiology and pharmacology. *In "Psychopharmacology—A 20 Year Progress Report"* (M. E. Lipton, K. C. Killam, and A. Di Mascio, eds.) pp. 131–142. Raven, New York.

Bloom, F. E., Algeri, S., Groppetti, A., Ruvuelta, A., and Costa, E. (1969). Lesions of central norepinephrine terminals with 6-OH-dopamine: Biochemistry and fine structure. *Science* **166,** 1284–1286.

Blue, M. E., and Parnavelas, J. G. (1982). The effect of neonatal 6-hydroxydopamine treatment on synaptogenesis in the visual cortex of the rat. *Journal of Comparative Neurology 205,* 199–205.

Blue, M. E., Parnavelas, J. G., and Liberman, A. R. (1980). Synaptogenesis in the visual cortex of normal and 6-OHDA-treated rats. *Society for Neurosecience Abstracts* **6,** 567.

Bobillier, P., Seguin, S., Petitjean, F., Salvert, D., Touret, M., and Jouvet, M. (1976). The raphe nuclei of the cat brain stem: A topographical atlas of their efferent projections as revealed by autoradiography. *Brain Research* **113,** 449–486.

Bond, A. B. (1978). Development of orientation tuning in the visual cortex of kittens. *In "Developmental Neurobiology of Vision"* (R. D. Freeman, ed.), pp. 31–41.Plenum, New York.

Borges, S., and Berry, M. (1976). Preferential orientation of stellate cell dendrites in the visual cortex of the dark-reared rat. *Brain Research* **112,** 141–147.

Bourgoin, S., Artaud, F., Adrien, J., Hery, F., Glowinski, J., and Hamon, M. (1977) 5-Hydroxytryptamine catabolism in the rat brain during ontogenesis. *Journal of Neurochemistry* **28,** 415–422.

Bourgoin, S., Adrien, J., Laguzzi, R. F., Dorphin, A., Bockaert, J., Hery, F., and Hamon, M. (1979). Effects of intraventricular injection of 6-hydroxydopamine in the developing kitten. II. On the central monaminergic innvervation. *Brain Research* **160,** 461–478.

Bowe-Anders, C., Adrien, J., and Roffwarg, H. P. (1974). Ontogenesis of ponto-geniculo-occipital activity in the lateral geniculate nucleus of the kitten. *Experimental Neurology* **43,** 242–260.

Breese, G. R., and Traylor, T. D. (1970). Effect of 6-hydroxydopamine on brain norepinephrine and dopamine: Evidence for selective degeneration of catecholamine neurons. *Journal of Pharmacology and Experimental Therapeutics* **174,** 413–420.

Breese, G. R., and Traylor, T. D. (1972). Developmental characteristics of brain catecholamines and tyrosine hydroxylase in the rat: Effects of 6-hydroxydopamine. *British Journal of Pharmacology* **44**, 210–222.
Brooks, D. C. (1968). Waves associated with eye movement in the awake and sleeping cat. *Electroencephalography and Clinical Neurophysiology* **24**, 532–541.
Brooks, D. C., and Gershon, M. D. (1971). Eye movement potentials in the oculomotor and visual systems of the cat: A comparison of reserpine induced waves with those present during wakefulness and rapid eye movement sleep. *Brain Research* **27**, 223–239.
Brooks, D. C., Gershon, M. D., and Simon, R. P. (1972). Brain stem serotonin depletion and ponto-geniculo-occipital wave activity in the cat treated with reserpine. *Neuropharmacology* **11**, 511–520.
Brown, M. C., and Ironton, R. (1977). Motor neurone sprouting induced by prolonged tetrodotoxin block of nerve action potentials. *Nautre (London)* **265**, 459–461.
Brown, M. C., Jansen, J. K. S., and Van Essen, D. (1976). Polyneuronal innervation of skeletal muscle in new-born rats and its elimination during maturation. *Journal of Physiology (London)* **261**, 387–422.
Brown, R. M., Crane, A. M., and Goldman, P. S. (1979). Regional distribution of monoamines in the cerebral cortex and subcortical structures of the rhesus monkey: Concentrations and *in vivo* synthesis rates. *Brain Research* **168**, 133–150.
Browning, M., Dunwiddie, T., Bennett, W., Gispen, W., and Lynch, G. (1979). Synaptic phosphoproteins: Specific changes after repetitive stimulation of the hippocampal slice. *Science* **203**, 60–62.
Brunelli, M., Castellucci, V., and Kandel, E. R. (1976). Synaptic facilitation and behavioral sensitization in Aplysia: Possible role of serotonin and cyclic AMP. *Science* **194**, 1178–1181.
Buguet, A., Petitjean, F., and Jouvet, M. (1970). Suppression des pointes ponto-géniculo-occipitales du sommeil par lésion ou injection in situ de 6-hydroxydopamine au niveau du tegmentum pontique. *Comptes Rendus des Séances de la Société de Biologie* **164**, 2293–2298.
Buisseret, P., and Imbert, M. (1976). Visual cortical cells: Their development properties in normal and dark-reared kittens. *Journal of Physiology (London)* **255**, 511–525.
Bunney, B. S., and Aghajanian, G. K. (1976a). d-Amphetamine-induced inhibition of central dopaminergic neurons: Mediation by a striato-nigral feedback pathway. *Science* **192**, 391–393.
Bunney, B. S., and Aghajanian, G. K. (1976b). Dopamine and norepinephrine innervated cells in the rat prefrontal cortex: Pharmacological differentiation using microiontophoretic techniques. *Life Sciences* **19**, 1783–1792.
Burchfiel, J. L., and Duffy, F. H. (1981). Role of intracortical inhibition in deprivation amblyopia: reversal by microiontophoretic bicuculline. *Brain Research* **206**, 479–484.
Burt, D. R., Creese, I., and Snyder, S. H. (1976a). Binding interactions of lysergic acid diethylamine and related agents with dopamine receptors in the brain. *Molecular Pharmacology* **12**, 631–638.
Burt, D. R., Creese, I., and Snyder, S. H. (1976b). Properties of [^{3}H]haloperidol and [^{3}H]dopamine binding associated with dopamine receptors in calf brain membrane. *Molecular Pharmacology* **12**, 800–812.
Bylund, D. B., and Snyder, S. H. (1976). Beta adrenergic binding in membrane preparations from mammalian brain. *Molecular Pharmacology* **12**, 568–580.
Calabro, M. A., and MacLeod, R. M. (1978). Binding of dopamine to bovine anterior pituitary gland membranes. *Neuroendocrinology* **25**, 32–46.
Calvet, J., Calvet, M.-C., and Langloise, J. M. (1965). Diffuse cortical activation waves during so-called desynchronized EEG patterns. *Journal of Neurophysiology* **28**, 893–907.

Carew, T. J., Walters, E. T., and Kandel, E. R. (1981). Associative learning in *Aplysia:* Cellular correlated supporting a conditioned fear hypothesis. *Science* **211,** 501–504.

Carlsson, A., Kehr, W., Lindqvist, M., Magnusson, T., and Atack, C. V. (1972). Regulation of monamine metabolism in the central nervous system. *Pharmacological Reviews* **24,** 371–84.

Caron, M. G., Beaulieu, M., Raymond, V., Gagné, B., Drouin, J., Lefkowitz, R. J., and Labrie, F. (1978). Dopaminergic receptors in the anterior pituitary gland. *Journal of Biological Chemistry* **253,** 2244–2253.

Cedar, H., and Schwartz, J. H. (1972). Cyclic adenosine monophosphate in the nervous system of *Aplysia californica.* II. Effect of serotonin and dopamine. *Journal of General Physiology* **60,** 570–587.

Cedarbaum, J. M., and Aghajanian, G. K. (1977). Catecholamine receptors on locus coeruleus neurons: Pharmacological characterization. *European Journal of Pharmacology* **44,** 375–385.

Chang, H. T. (1952). Cortical response to stimulation of lateral geniculate body and the potentiation thereof by continuous illumination of retina. *Journal of Neurophysiology* **15,** 5–26.

Chan-Palay, V. (1976). Serotonin axons in the supra-and subependymal plexuses and in the leptomeninges: Their roles in local alterations of cerebrospinal fluid and vasomotor activity. *Brain Research* **102,** 103–130.

Chan-Palay, V. (1977). "Cerebellar Dentate Nucleus," Springer-Verlag, Berlin and New York.

Chow, K. L., and Stewart, D. L. (1972). Reversal of structural and functional effects of long-term visual deprivation in cats. *Experimental Neurology* **34,** 409–433.

Chow, K. L., Riesen, A. H., and Newell, F. W. (1957). Degeneration of retinal ganglion cells in infant chimpanzees reared in darkness. *Journal of Comparative Neurology* **107,** 27–42.

Chu, N.-S. and Bloom, F. E. (1974). The catecholamine-containing neurons in the cat dorsolateral pontine tegmentum: Distribution of the cell bodies and some axonal projections. *Brain Research* **66,** 1–21.

Clarke, P. G. H., and Cowan, W. M. (1975). Ectopic neurons and aberrant connections during neural development. *Proceedings of the National Academy of Sciences of the U.S.A.* **72,** 4455–4458.

Clarke, P. G. H., and Cowan, W. M. (1976). The development of the isthmo-optic tract in the chick, with special reference to the occurrence and correction of developmental errors in the location and connections of isthomo-optic neurons. *Journal of Comparative Neurology* **167,** 143–164.

Cleland, B. B., Mitchell, D. E., Gillard-Crewther, S., and Crewther, D. P. (1980). Visual resolution of retinal ganglion cells in monocularly deprived cats. *Brain Research* **192,** 261–266.

Coleman, P. D., and Riesen, A. H. (1968). Envrionmental effects on cortical dendritic fields. *Journal of Anatomy* **102,** 363–374.

Connor, J. D. (1970). Caudate nucleus neurones: Correlation of the effects of substantia nigra stimulation with iontophoretic dopamine. *Journal of Physiology (London)* **208,** 691–703.

Conrad, L. C. A., Leonard, C. M., and Pfaff, D. W. (1974). Connections of the median and dorsal raphe nucleus in the rat: An autoradiographic and degeneration study. *Journal of Comparative Neurology* **156,** 179–206.

Constantine-Paton, M., and Law, M. I. (1978). Eye-specific termination bands in tecta of three-eyed frogs. *Science* **202,** 639–641.

Corrodi, H., Fuxe, K., Hamberger, B., and Ljungdahl, Å. (1970). Studies on central and peripheral noradrenaline neurons using a new dopamine-β-hydroxylase inhibitor. *European Journal of Pharmacology* **12,** 145–155.

Cowan, W. M. (1973). Neuronal death as a regulative mechanism in the control of cell number in the nervous system. *In "Development and Aging in the Nervous System"* (M. Rockstein, ed), pp. 19–41. Academic Press, New York.

Coyle, J. T. (1977). Biochemical aspects of neurotransmission in the developing brain. *International Review of Neurobiology* **20,** 65–103.

Coyle, J. T., and Axelrod, J. (1971). Development of the uptake and storage of L-[^{3}H] norepinephrine in rat brain. *Journal of Neurochemistry* **18,** 2061–2075.

Coyle, J. T., and Axelrod, J. (1972a). Dopamine-β-hydroxylase in the rat brain: Developmental characteristics. *Journal of Neurochemistry* **19,** 449–459.

Coyle, J. T., and Axelrod, J. (1972b). Tyrosine hydroxylase in rat brain: Developmental characteristics. *Journal of Neurochemistry* **19,** 1117–1123.

Coyle, J. T., and Campochiaro, P. (1976). Ontogenesis of dopaminergic-cholinergic interactions in the rat striatum: A neurochemical study. *Journal of Neurochemistry* **27,** 673–678.

Coyle, J. T., and Molliver, M. E. (1977). Major innervation of newborn rat cortex by monoaminergic neurons. *Science* **196,** 444–447.

Cragg, B. G. (1967). Changes in visual cortex on first experience of rats to light. *Nature (London)* **215,** 251–253.

Cragg, B. G. (1975a). The development of synapses in the visual system of the cat. *Journal of Comparative Neurology* **160,** 147–166.

Cragg, B. G. (1975b). The development of synapses in kitten visual cortex during visual deprivation. *Experimental Neurology* **46,** 445–451.

Cragg, B., Anker, R., and Wan, Y. K. (1976). The effect of age on the reversibility of cellular atrophy in the LGN of the cat following monocular deprivation: A test of two hypotheses about cell growth. *Journal of Comparative Neurology* **168,** 345–354.

Creese, I., and Snyder, S. H. (1978). ^{3}H-Spiroperidol labels serotonin receptors in rat cerebral cortex and hippocampus. *European Journal of Pharmacology* **49,** 201–202.

Creese, I., Burt, D. R., and Snyder, S. H. (1975). Dopamine receptor binding: Differentiation of agonist and antagonist states with ^{3}H-dopamine and ^{3}H-haloperidol. *Life Sciences* **17,** 993–1002.

Creese, I., Schneider, R., and Snyder, S. H. (1977). ^{3}H-Sprioperidol labels dopamine receptors in pituitary and brain. *European Journal of Pharmacology* **46,** 377–381.

Crewther, D. P., Gillard-Crewther, S., and Pettigrew, J. D. (1978). A role for extraocular afferents in postcritical period of monocular deprivation. *Journal of Physiology (London)* **282,** 181–195.

Crow, T. J. (1968). Cortical synapses and reinforcement: A hypothesis. *Nature (London)* **219,** 736–737.

Crow, T. J. (1973). Catecholamine-containing neurones and electrical self-stimulation: 2. A theoretical interpretation and some psychiatric implications. *Psychological Medicine* **3,** 66–73.

Crow, T. J., and Wendlandt, S. (1976). Impaired acquistion of a passive avoidance response after lesions induced in the locus coeruleus by 6-OH-dopamine. *Nature (London)* **259,** 42–44.

Crow, T. J., Longden, A., Smith, A., and Wendlandt, S. (1977). Pontine tegmental lesions, monoamine neurons, and varieties of learning. *Behavioral Biology* **20,** 184–196.

Csillik, A., Jancso, G., Toth, L., Kozma, M., Kalman, G., and Karcsu, S. (1971). Adrenergic innervation of hypothalamic blood vessels. A contribution to the problem of central thermo-detectors. *Acta Anatomica* **80,** 142–151.

Cynader, M., and Mitchell, D. E. (1977). Monocular astigmatism effects on kitten visual cortex development. *Nature (London)* **270,** 177–178.

Cynader, M., and Mitchell, D. E. (1980). Prolonged sensitivity to monocular deprivation in dark reared cats. *Journal of Neurophysiology* **43,** 1026–1040

Cynader, M., Berman, N., and Hein, A. (1973). Cats reared in stroboscopic illumination: Effects on receptive fields in visual cortex. *Proceedings of the National Academy of Sciences of the U.S.A.* **70,** 1353–1354.

Cynader, M., Berman, N., and Hein, A. (1975). Cats raised in a one-directional world: Ef-

fects on receptive fields in visual cortex and superior colliculus. *Experimental Brain Research* **22,** 267–280.
Cynader, M., Berman, N., and Hein, A. (1976). Recovery of function in cat visual cortex following prolonged deprivation. *Experimental Brain Research* **25,** 139–156.
Cynader, M., Lepore, F., and Guillemot, J.-P. (1981) Inter-hemispheric competition during postnatal development. *Nature (London)* **290,** 139–140.
Daniels, J. D., and Pettigrew, J. D. (1976). Development of neuronal respones in the visual system of cats. *In* "Neural and Behavioral Specificity. Studies on the Development of Behavior and the Nervous System" Vol. 3, (G. Gottlieb, ed.), pp. 195–232. Academic Press, New York.
Daszuta, A., Gaudin-Chazal, G., Faudon, M., Barrit, M. C., and Ternaux, J. P. (1979). Endogenous levels of tryptophan, serotonin and 5-hydroxyindole acetic acid in the developing brain of the cat. *Neuroscience Letters* **11,** 187–192.
Davis, J. N., and Lefkowitz, R. J. (1976). β-Adrenergic receptor binding: Synaptic localization in rat brain. *Brain Research* **113,** 214–218.
Davis, J. N., Arnett, C. D., Hoyler, E., Stalvey, L. P., Daly, J. W., and Skolnick, P. (1978). Brain α-adrenergic receptors: Comparison of [^{3}H] WB4101 binding with norepinephrine-stimulated cyclic AMP accumulation in rat cerebral cortex. *Brain Research* **159,** 125–135.
Daw, N. W., and Rader, R. K. (1981). Effects of intracortical infusion of 6-hydroxydopamine on monocular and direction deprivation. *ARVO Abstract (Supplement to Investigative Ophthalmology and Visual Science)* **20,** 72.
Daw, N. W., and Wyatt, H. J. (1976). Kittens reared in a unidirectional envrionment: Evidence for a critical period. *Journal of Physiology (London)* **257,** 155–170.
Daw, N. W., Rader, R. K., Robertson, T. W., and Ariel, M. (1982). Effects of 6-hydroxydopamine on visual deprivation in the kitten visual cortex. *Journal of Neuroscience* (submitted).
De la Torre, J. C. (1976) Evidence for central innvervation of intracerebral blood vessels: local cerebral blood flow measurements and histofluorescence analysis by the sucrose-phosphate-glyoxylic acid (SPG) method. *Neuroscience* **1,** 455–457.
Delorme, F., Jeannerod, M., and Jouvet, M. (1965). Effets remarquables de la reserpine sur l'activité EEG phasique ponto-géniculo-occipitale. *Comptes Rendus Des Séances de la Société de Biologie, Paris* **159,** 900–903.
Dement, W. C., Henriksen, S., and Fergunson, J. (1973). The effect of the chronic administration of para-chloro-phenylalanine (PCPA) on sleep-parameters in the cat. *In* "Serotonin and Behavior" (J. Barchas and E. Usdin, eds.), pp. 419–424. Academic Press, New York.
Demirjian, C., Grassman, R., Meyer, R., and Katzman, R. (1976). The catecholamine pontine cellular groups locus coeruleus, A4, subcoeruleus in the primate *Cebus apella. Brain Research* **115,** 395–411.
Descarries, L. (1974). High resolution radioautography of noradrenergic axon terminals in the neocortex. *In* "Vision in Fishes" (M. A. Ali, ed.), pp. 211–232. Plenum, New York.
Descarries, L., and Léger, L. (1978). Serotonin nerve terminals in the locus coeruleus of the adult rat. *In* "Interaction between Neurotransmitters in the Brain" (S. Garattini, J. F. Pujol, and Samanin, eds.), pp. 355–367. Raven, New York.
Descarries, L., Beaudet, A., and Watkins, K. C. (1975). Serotonin nerve terminals in adult rat neocortex. *Brain Research* **100,** 563–588.
Descarries, L., Watkins, K. C., and Lapierre, Y. (1977). Noradrenergic axon terminals in the cerebral cortex of rat. III. Topometeric ultrastructural analysis. *Brain Research* **133,** 197–222.
Des Rosiers, M. H., Sakurada, O., Jehle, J., Shinohara, M., Kennedy, C., and Sokoloff, L. (1978). Functional plasticity in the immature striate cortex of the monkey shown by the [^{14}C] deoxyglucose method. *Science* **200,** 447–449.

Dews, P. B., and Wiesel, T. N. (1970). Consequences of monocular deprivation on visual behavior in kittens. *Journal of Physiology (London)* **206,** 437–455.

Doxey, J. C., Smith, C. F. C., and Walker, J. M. (1977). Selectivity of blocking agents for pre-and postsynaptic α-adrenoceptors. *British Journal of Pharmacology* **60,** 91–96.

Dudai, Y., Jan, J.-N., Byers, D., Quinn, W. C., and Benzer, S. (1976). *Dunce,* a mutant of *Drosophila* deficient in learning. *Proceedings of the National Academy of Sciences of the U.S.A.* **73,** 1684–1688.

Duffy, F. H., Burchfiel, J. L., and Snodgrass, S. R. (1976a). Ammonium acetate reversal of experimental amblyopia. *Society for Neuroscience Abstracts* **2,** 1109.

Duffy, F. H., Snodgrass, S. R., Burchfiel, J. L., and Conway, J. L. (1976b). Bicuculline reversal of deprivation amblyopia in the cat. *Nature (London)* **260,** 256–257.

Dürsteler, M. R., Garey, L. J., and Movshon, J. A. (1976). Reversal of the morphological effects of monocular deprivation in the kitten's lateral geniculate nucleus. *Journal of Physiology (London)* **261,** 189–210.

Edvinsson, L., and MacKenzie, E. T. (1977) Amine mechanisms in the cerebral circulation. *Pharmacological Review* **28,** 275–348.

Edvinsson, L., and Owman, C. (1974). Pharmacological characterization of adrenergic alpha and beta receptors mediating the vasomotor responses of cerebral arteries in vitro. *Circulation Research* **35,** 935–849.

Edvinsson, L., Lindvall, M., Nielsen, K. C., and Owman, C. (1973). Are brain vessels innervated also by central (non-sympathetic) adrenergic neuron? *Brain Research* **63,** 496–499.

Ellison, G. (1976). Monoamine neurotoxins: Selective and delayed effects on behavior in colonies of laboratory rats. *Brain Research* **103,** 81–92.

Emson, P. C., and Lindvall, O. (1979). Distribution of putative neurotransmitters in the neocortex. *Neuroscience* **4,** 1–30.

Falck, B., Hillarp, N.-A., Thieme, G., and Torp, A. (1962). Fluorescence of catecholamines and related compounds condensed with formaldehyde. *Journal of Histochemistry and Cytochemistry* **10,** 348–354.

Falck, B., Mchedlishivili, G. I., and Owman, C. (1965). Histochemical demonstration of adrenergic nerves in the cortex-pia of rabbit. *Acta Pharmacologica et Toxicologica* **23,** 133–142.

Farber, J., Marks, G. A., and Roffwarg, H. P. (1981). Rapid eye movement sleep PGO-type waves are present in the dorsal pons of the albino rat. *Science* **209,** 615–617.

Farnebo, L. O., and Hamberger, B. (1971). Drug-induced changes in the release of ^{3}H-monoamines from field stimulated rat brain slices. *Acta Physiological Scandinavica* **84** (Suppl. 371), 35–44.

Feldman, M. L., and Dowd, C. (1975). Loss of dendritic spines in aging cerebral cortex. *Anatomy and Embryology* **148,** 279–301.

Felten, D. L., Hallman, H., and Jonsson, G. (1982). Evidence for a neurotrophic role of noradrenaline neurons for the postnatal development of rat cerebral cortex. *Journal of Neurocytology 11,* 119–135.

Ferster, D., and LeVay, S. (1978). The axonal arborization of lateral geniculate neurons in the striate cortex of the cat. *Journal of Comparative Neurology* **182,** 923–944.

Fifkova, E. (1970). The effect of monocular deprivation on the synaptic contacts of the visual cortex. *Journal of Neurobiology* **1,** 285–294.

Fillion, G. M. B., Rousselle, J. C., Fillion, M. P., Beaudoin, D. M., Goiny, M. R., Denian, J. M., and Jacob, J. J. (1978). High affinity binding of [^{3}H] 5-hydroxytryptamine to brain synaptosomal membranes: Comparison with [^{3}H] lysergic acid diethylamide binding. *Molecular Pharmacology* **14,** 50–59.

Fiorentini, A., and Maffei, L. (1974). Changes of binocular properties of the simple cells of the cortex in adult cats following immobilization of one eye. *Vision Research* **14,** 217–218.

Flood, D. G., and Coleman, P. D. (1979). Demonstration of orientation columns with [^{14}C]2-deoxyglucose in a cat reared in a striped environment. *Brain Research* **173,** 538–542.

Foote, S. L., Freedman, R., and Oliver, P. (1975). Effects of putative neurotransmitters on neuronal activity in monkey auditory cortex. *Brain Research* **86,** 229–242.

Frederickson, R. C. A., Jordan, L. M., and Phillis, J. W., (1971). The action of noradrenaline on cortical neurons: Effects of pH. *Brain Research* **35,** 556–560.

Frederickson, R. C. A., Jordan, L. M., and Phillis, J. W. (1972). A reappraisal of the actions of noradrenaline and 5-hydroxytryptamine on cerebral cortical neurons. *Comparative General Pharmacology* **3,** 443–456.

Freedman, R., Foote, S. L., and Bloom, F. E. (1975). Histochemical characterization of a neocortical projection of the nucleus locus coeruleus in the squirrel monkey. *Journal of Comparative Neurology* **164,** 209–232.

Freeman, J. A. (1977). Possible regulatory function of acetylcholine receptor in maintenance of retinotectal synapses. *Nature (London)* **269,** 218–222.

Freeman, R. D., Mitchell, D. E., and Millodot, M. (1972). A neural effect of partial visual deprivation in humans. *Science* **175,** 1384–1386.

Frégnac, Y., and Imbert, M. (1978). Early development of visual cortical cells in normal and dark-reared kittens: Evidence for a relationship between orientation selectivity and ocular dominance. *Journal of Physiology (London)* **278,** 27–44.

Friedlander, M. J., Stanford, L. R., and Sherman, S. M. (1980). Effects of monocular eyelid suture on the structure of physiologically identified neurons in the dorsal lateral geniculate nucleus. *Society for Neuroscience Abstracts* **6,** 789.

Fuxe, K. (1965). Evidence for the existence of monoamine neurons in the central nervous system. IV. Distribution of monoamine terminals in the central nervous system. *Acta Physiologica Scandinavica* **64,** (Suppl. 247), 38–120.

Fuxe, K., Hamberger, B., and Hökfelt, T. (1968). Distribution of noradrenaline nerve terminals in cortical areas of the rat. *Brain Research* **8,** 125–131.

Ganz, L., and Fitch, M. (1968). The effect of visual deprivation on perceptual behavior. *Experimental Neurology* **22,** 638–660.

Ganz, L., and Haffner, M. E. (1974). Permanent perceptual and neurophysiological effects of visual deprivation in the cat. *Experimental Brain Research* **20,** 67–87.

Ganz, L., Hirsch, H. V. B., and Tieman, S. B. (1972). The nature of perceptual deficits in visually deprived cat. *Brain Research* **44,** 547–568.

Garey, L. J., and Dürsteler, M. R. (1975). Reversal of deprivation effects in the lateral geniculate nucleus of the cat. *Neuroscience Letters* **1,** 19–23.

Gatter, K. C., and Powell, T. P. S. (1977). The projection of the locus coeruleus upon the neocortex in the macaque monkey. *Neuroscience* **2,** 441–445.

Gaudin-Chazal, G., Daszuta, A., Faudon, M., and Ternaux, J. P. (1979). 5-HT-concentration in cats brain. *Brain Research* **160,** 281–293

Geffen, L. B., Jessell, T. M., Cuello, A. C., and Iversen, L. L. (1976). Release of dopamine from dendrites in rat substantia nigra. *Nature, (London)* **260,** 258–260.

German, D. C., and Bowden, D. M. (1975). Locus coeruleus in rhesus monkey *(Macaca mulatta):* A combined histochemical fluorescence, Nissl and silver study. *Journal of Comparative Neurology* **161,** 19–30

Giffin, F., and Mitchell, D. E. (1978). The rate of recovery of vision after early monocular deprivation in kittens. *Journal of Physiology (London)* **274,** 511–537.

Gillard-Crewther, S., Crewther, D. P., Peck, C. K., and Pettigrew, J. D. (1980). Visual cortical effects of rearing cats with monocular or binocular cyclotorsion. *Journal of Neurophysiology* **44,** 97–118.

Globus, A., and Scheibel, A. B. (1967). The effect of visual deprivation on cortical neurons: A Golgi study. *Experimental Neurology* **19,** 331–345.

Glossman, H., and Presek, P. (1979). Alpha noradrenergic receptors in brain membranes: Sodium, magnesium and guanyl nucleotides modulate agonist binding. *Naunyn-Schmiedebergs Archives of Pharmacology* **306,** 67–73.

Goddard, G. V., Bliss, T. V. P., Robertson, H. A., and Sutherland, R. S. (1980). Noradrenaline levels affect long-term potentiation in the hippocampus. *Society for Neuroscience Abstracts* **6,** 89.

Grafstein, B., and Laureno, R. (1973). Transport of radioactivity from eye to visual cortex in the mouse. *Experimental Neurology* **39,** 44–47.

Greenberg, D. A., U'prichard, D. C., and Snyder, S. H. (1976). α-Noradrenergic receptor binding in mammalian brain: Differential labeling of agonist and antagonist states. *Life Sciences* **19,** 69–76.

Grobstein, P., and Chow, K. L. (1975). Receptive field development and individual experience. *Science* **190,** 352–358.

Grzanna, R., and Molliver, M. E. (1980). The locus coeruleus in the rat: An immunohistochemical delineation. *Neuroscience* **5,** 21–40.

Grzanna, R., Molliver, M. E., and Coyle, J. T. (1978). Visualization of central noradrenergic neurons in thick sections by the unlabeled antibody method: A transmitter specific Golgi image. *Proceedings of the National Academy of Sciences of the U.S.A.* **75,** 2502–2506.

Guillery, R. W. (1972). Binocular competition in the control of geniculate cell growth. *Journal of Comparative Neurology* **144,** 117–130.

Guillery, R. W. (1973). The effect of lid suture upon the growth of cells in the dorsal lateral geniculate nucleus of kittens. *Journal of Comparative Neurology* **148,** 417–422.

Guillery, R. W., and Stelzner, D. J. (1970). The differential effects of unilateral lid closure upon the monocular and binocular segments of the dorsal lateral geniculate nucleus of the cat. *Journal of Comparative Neurology* **139,** 413–422.

Haigler, H. J., and Aghajanian, G. K. (1977). Serotonin receptors in the brain. *Federation Proceedings* **36,** 2159–2164.

Hall, J. C., and Greenspan, R. J. (1979). Genetic analysis of Drosophila neurobiology. *Annual Review of Genetics* **13,** 127–195.

Harden, T. K., Wolfe, B. B., Sporn, J. R., Perkins, J. P., and Molinoff, P. B. (1977a). Ontogeny of β-adrenergic receptors in rat cerebral cortex. *Brain Research* **125,** 99–108.

Harden, T. K., Wolfe, B. B., Sporn, J. R., Poulos, B. K. , and Molinoff, P. B. (1977b). Effects of 6-hydroxydopamine on the development of the *beta* adrenergic receptor/adenylate cyclase system in rat cerebral cortex. *Journal of Pharmacology and Experimental Therapeutics* **203,** 132–143.

Harper, A. M., Deshmukh, V. D., Rowan, J. O., and Jennett, W. B. (1972). The influence of sympathetic nervous activity on cerebral blood flow. *Archives of Neurology* **27,** 1–6.

Harris, J. E., Baldessarini, R. J., Morgenroth, V. H., III, and Roth, R. H. (1974). Activation by cyclic 3′,5′-adenosine monophosphate of tyrosine hydroxylase in the rat brain. *Proceedings of the National Academy of Sciences of the U.S.A.* **72,** 789–793.

Harris, W. A., and Stryker, M. P. (1977). Attempts to reverse the effects of monocular deprivation in the adult cat's cortex. *Society for Neuroscience Abstracts* **3,** 562.

Hartman, B. K., Zide, D., and Udenfriend, S. (1972). The use of dopamine-β-hydroxylase as a marker for the central noradrenergic nervous system in rat brain. *Proceedings of the National Academy of Sciences of the U.S.A.* **69,** 2722–2726.

Hawken, M., Mark, R., and Blakemore, C. (1978). The effects of pressure blinding in monocularly deprived kittens. *Archives Italiennes de Biologie* **116,** 448–451.

Hebb, D. O. (1949). "The Organization of Behavior" Wiley, New York.

Heggelund, P., and Kasamatsu,T. (1981). Exogenous noradrenaline increases the neuronal plasticity in cat visual cortex: Localized, continuous microperfusion and iontophoresis. *In*

"Advances in Physiological Sciences" Vol. 36, "Cellular Analogues of Conditioning and Neural Plasticity" (O. Fehér and F. Jóo eds.), pp. 233–242. Akadémiai Kiadó, Budapest; Pergamon, Oxford.

Hendrickson, A. E., and Boothe, R. (1976). Morphology of the retina and dorsal lateral geniculate nucleus in dark-reared monkeys *(Macaca nemestrina). Vision Research* **16**, 517–521.

Hendrickson, A. E., and Wilson, J. R. (1979). A difference in [^{14}C] deoxyglucose autoradiographic patterns in striate cortex between Macaca and Saimiri monkeys following monocular stimualtion. *Brain Research* **170**, 353–358.

Hendrickson, A. E., Hunt, S. P., and Wu, J.-Y. (1981). Immunocytochemical localization of glutamic acid decarboxylase in monkey striate cortex. *Nature (London)* **292**, 605–607.

Henriksen, S. J., Jacobs, B. L., and Dement, W. C. (1972). Dependence of REM sleep PGO waves on cholinergic mechanisms. *Brain Research* **48**, 412–416.

Hess, E. H. (1959). Imprinting. An effect of early experience, imprinting determines later social behavior in animals. *Science* **130**, 133–141.

Hickey, T. L. (1980). Development of the dorsal lateral geniculate nucleus in normal and visually deprived cats. *Journal of Comparative Neurology* **189**, 467–481.

Hickey, T. L., Spear, P. D., and Kratz, K. E. (1977). Quantitative studies of cell size in the cat's dorsal lateral geniculate nucleus following visual deprivation. *Journal of Comparative Neurology* **172**, 265–282.

Hicks, S. P., and D'Amato, C. J. (1975). Six-hydroxydopamine (6-OHDA) alters developing cortex and locomotion in rats. *Society for Neuroscience Abstracts* **1**, 788.

Himwich, W. A. (1972). Developmental changes in neurochemistry during the maturation of sleep behavior. *In* "Sleep and the Maturing Nervous System" (C. D. Clemente, D. P. Purpura, and F. E. Mayer, eds.), pp. 125–140. Academic Press, New York.

Hirsch, H. V. B., and Spinelli, D. N. (1970) Visual experience modifies distribution of horizontally and vertically oriented receptive fields in cats. *Science* **168**, 869–871.

Hirsch, H. V. B., and Spinelli, D. N. (1971). Modification of the distribution of receptive field orientation in cats by selective visual exposure during development. *Experimental Brain Research* **12**, 509–527.

Hitchcock, P. F., and Hickey, T. L. (1982). Cell size changes in the lateral geniculate nuclei of normal and monocularly deprived cats treated with 6-hydroxydopamine and/or norepinephrine. *Journal of Neuroscience* **2**, 681–686.

Hoffmann, K.-P., and Cynader, M. (1977). Functional aspects of plasticity in the visual system of adult cats after early monocular deprivation. *Philosophical Transactions of the Royal Society, London, Series B* **278**, 411–424.

Hoffmann, K.-P., and Holländer, H. (1978). Physiological and morphological changes in cells of the lateral geniculate nucleus in monocularly-deprived and reverse-sutured cats. *Journal of Comparative Neurology* **177**, 145–158.

Hoffmann, K.-P., and Sherman, S. M. (1974). Effect of early monocular deprivation on visual input to cat superior colliculus. *Journal of Neurophysiology* **37**, 1276–1286.

Hohmann, A., and Creutzfeldt, O. D. (1975). Squint and the development of binocularity in humans. *Nature* (London) **254**, 613–614.

Horton, J. C., and Hubel, D. H. (1980). Cytochrome oxidase stain preferentially labels intersection of ocular dominance and vertical orientation columns in macaque striate cortex. *Society for Neuroscience Abstracts* **6**, 315.

Horton, J. C., and Hubel, D. H. (1981). Regular patchy distribution of cytochrome oxidase staining in primary visual cortex of macaque monkey. *Nature (London)* **292**, 762–764.

Hotta, Y., and Benzer, S. (1976). Courtship in Drosophila mosaics: Sex-specific foci for sequential action pattern. *Proceedings of the National Academy of Sciences of the U.S.A.* **73**, 4154–4158.

Hoyle, G. (1970). Cellular mechanisms underlying behavior—Neuroethology. *Advances in Insect Physiology* **7**, 349–444.

Huang, M., Ho, A. K. S., and Daly, J. W. (1973). Accumulation of adenosine cyclic 3′, 5′-monophosphate in rat cerebral cortical slices. Stimulatory effect of *alpha* and *beta* adrenergic agents after treatment with 6-hydroxydopamline, 2,3,5,-trihydroxyphenethylamine, and dihydroxytryptamines. *Molecular Pharmacology* **9,** 711–717.

Hubel, D. H., and Wiesel, T. N. (1962). Receptive fields, binocular interaction and functional architecture in the cat's visual cortex. *Journal of Physiology* (London) **160,** 106–154.

Hubel, D. H., and Wiesel, T. N. (1963). Receptive fields of cells in striate cortex of very young visually inexperienced kittens. *Journal of Neurophsiology* **26,** 994–1002.

Hubel, D. H., and Wiesel, T. N. (1965). Binocular interaction in striate cortex of kittens reared with artificial squint. *Journal of Neurophysiology* **28,** 1041–1059.

Hubel, D. H., and Wiesel, T. N. (1970). The period of susceptibility to the physiological effects of unilateral eye closure in kittens. *Journal of Physiology (London)* **206,** 419–436.

Hubel, D. H., Wiesel, T. N., and LeVay, S. (1976). Functional architecture of area 17 in normal and monocularly deprived macaque monkeys. *Cold Spring Harbor Symposia on Quantitative Biology* **40,** 581–589.

Hubel, D. H., Wiesel, T. N., and LeVay, S. (1977). Plasticity of ocular dominance columns in monkey striate cortex. *Philosophical Transactions of the Royal Society, London, Series B* **278,** 377–409.

Hubel, D. H., Wiesel, T. N., and Stryker, M. P. (1978). Anatomical demonstration of orientation columns in macaque monkey. *Journal of Comparative Neurology* **177,** 361–380.

Humphrey, A. L., and Hendrickson, A. E. (1980). Radial zones of high metabolic activity in squirrel monkey striate cortex. *Society for Neuroscience Abstracts* **6,** 315.

Ikeda, H., and Tremain, K. E. (1979). Amblyopia occurs in retinal gangloin cells in cats reared with convergent squint without alternating fixation. *Experimental Brain Research* **35,** 559–582.

Ikeda, H., Tremain, K. E., and Einon, G. (1978). Loss of spatial resolution of lateral geniculate nucleus neurones in kittens raised with convergent squint produced at different stages in development. *Experimental Brain Research* **31,** 207–220.

Ikeda, K., and Wiersma, C. A. G. (1964). Autogenic rhythmicity in the abdominal ganglia of the crayfish: The control of swimmeret movement. *Comparative Biochemistry and Physiology* **12,** 107–115.

Ikeda, K., Ozawa, S., and Hagiwara, S. (1976). Synaptic transmission reversibly conditioned by single-gene mutation in *Drosophila melanogaster. Nature (London)* **259,** 489–491.

Imbert, M., and Buisseret, P. (1975). Receptive field characteristics and plastic properties of visual cortical cells in kittens reared with or without visual experience. *Experimental Brain Research* **22,** 25–36.

Immelmann, K. (1972). Sexual and other long-term aspects of imprinting in birds and other species. *In "Advances in the Study of Behavior"* (D. S. Lehrman, R. A. Hinde and E. Shaw, eds.). vol. 4, pp. 147–174, Academic Press, New York.

Itakura, T., Tohyama, M., and Nakai, K. (1977). Experimental and morphological study of the innervation of cerebral blood vessels. *Acta Histochemica et Cytochemia* **10,** 52–65.

Itakura, T., Kasamatsu, T., and Pettigrew, J. D. (1978). Catecholaminergic terminals in kitten visual cortex: The normal distribution and its changes following the local perfusion of 6-OHDA. *Society for Neuroscience Abstracts* **4,** 475.

Itakura, T., Kasamatsu, T., and Pettigrew, J. D. (1979). Morphology of catecholamine-containing terminals in kitten visual cortex. *ARVO Abstract (Supplement to Investigative Ophthalmology and Visual Science)* **18,** 158.

Itakura, T., Kasamatsu, T., and Pettigrew, J. D. (1981). Norepinephrine-containing terminals in kitten visual cortex: Laminar distribution and ultrastructure. *Neuroscience* **6,** 159–175.

Jacobowitz, D. M., and Kostrzewa, R. (1971). Selective action of 6-hydroxydopa on nonadrenergic terminals: Mapping of preterminal axons of the brain. *Life Sciences* **10,** 1329–1342.

Jacobs, B. L., Henriksen, S. J., and Dement, W. C. (1972). Neurochemical basis of the PGO waves. *Brain Research* **48**, 406–411.

Jalfre, M., Monachon, M.-A., and Haefely, W. (1973). Drug and PGO waves in the cat. *In* "First Canadian International Symposium on Sleep" (D. T. McClure, ed.), pp. 155–185. Roche Scientific Service, Montreal.

Jeannerod, M., and Sakai, K. (1970). Occipital and geniculate potentials related to eye movements in the unanesthetized cat. *Brain Research* **19**, 361–377.

Johnson, E. S., Roberts, M. H. T., Sobieszek, A., and Straughan, D. W. (1969a). Noradrenaline sensitive cells in cat cerebral cortex. *International Journal of Neuropharmacology* **8**, 549–566.

Johnson, E. S., Roberts, M. H. T., and Straughan, D. W. (1969b). The responses of cortical neurones to monoamines under differing anesthetic conditions. *Journal of Physiology (London)* **203**, 261–280.

Jones, B. E., and Moore, R. Y. (1974). Catecholamine-containing neurons of the nucleus locus coeruleus in the cat. *Journal of Comparative Neurology* **157**, 43–52.

Jones, B. E., and Moore, R. Y. (1977). Ascending projections of the locus coeruleus in the rat. II. Autoradiographic study. *Brain Research* **127**, 23–53.

Jonsson, G. (1976). Studies on the mechanisms of 6-hydroxydopamine cytotoxicity. *Medical Biology* **54**, 406–420.

Jonsson, G., and Hallman, H. (1978). Changes in β-receptor binding sites in rat brain after neonatal 6-hydroxydopamine treatment. *Neuroscience Letters* **9**, 27–32.

Jonsson, G., and Kasamatsu, T. (1982). Maturation of monoamine neurotransmitters and receptors in cat occipital cortex during postnatal critical period. *Experimental Brain Research* (submitted).

Jouvet, M. (1974). Monoaminergic regulation of the sleep-waking cycle in the cat. *In "The Neurosciences, Third Study Program"*. (F. O. Schmitt, and F. G. Worden, eds.), pp. 499–508, The MIT Press, Cambridge, Massachusetts, and London, England.

Jouvet, M. (1975a). The function of dreaming: A neurophysiologist's point of view. *In* "Handbook of Psychobiology" (M. S. Gazzaiza and C. Blakemore, eds.) pp. 499–527. Academic Press, New York.

Jouvet, M. (1975b). Cholinergic mechanisms and sleep. *In* "Cholinergic Mechanisms" (P. G. Waser, ed.), pp. 455–476. Raven, New York.

Jouvet, M., and Michel, F. (1959). Correlations electromyographiques du sommeil chez le chat décortique et mesencéphalique chronique. *Comptes Rendus des Séances de la Société de Biologie, Paris* **153**, 422–425.

Julesz, B. (1971). "Foundations of Cyclopean Perception." University of Chicago Press, Chicago, Illinois.

Kalil, R. (1978). Dark rearing in the cat. Effects on visuomotor behavior and cell growth in the dorsal lateral geniculate nucleus. *Journal of Comparative Neurology* **178**, 451–468.

Kalisker, A., Rutledge, C. O., and Perkins, J. P. (1973). Effect of nerve degeneration by 6-hydroxydopamine on catecholamine-stimulated adenosine 3′,5′-monophosphate formation in rat cerebral cortex. *Molecular Pharmacology* **9**, 619–629.

Kandel, E. R. (1979). Small system of neurons. *Scientific American* **241**, 66–76.

Kandel, E. R., Brunelli, M., Byrne, J., and Castellucci, V. (1975). A common presynaptic locus for the synaptic changes underlying short-term habituation and sensitization of the gill-withdrawal reflex in *Aplysia*. *Cold Spring Harbor Symposia on Quantitative Biology* **40**, 465–482.

Karki, N., Kuntzman, R., and Brodie, B. B. (1962). Storage, synthesis, and metabolism of monoamines in the developing brain. *Journal of Neurochemistry* **9**, 53–58.

Kasamatsu, T. (1970). Maintained and evoked unit activity in the mesencephalic reticular formation of the freely behaving cat. *Experimental Neurology* **28**, 450–470.

Kasamatsu, T. (1976a). Visual cortical neurons influenced by the oculomotor input: Characterization of their receptive field properties. *Brain Research* **113**, 271–292.

Kasamatsu, T. (1976b). A long-lasting change in ocular dominance of kitten striate neurons induced by reversible unilateral blockade of tonic retinal discharges. *Experimental Brain Research* **26,** 487–494.

Kasamatsu, T. (1979). Involvement of the β-adrenergic receptor in cortical plasticity. *ARVO Abstract (Supplement to Investigative Ophthalmology and Visual Science)* **18,** 135.

Kasamatsu, T. (1980). A possible role for cyclic nucleotides in plasticity of visual cortex. *Society for Neuroscience Abstracts* **6,** 494.

Kasamatsu, T., and Adey, W. R. (1973). Visual cortical units associated with phasic activity in REM sleep and wakefulness. *Brain Research* **55,** 323–331.

Kasamatsu, T., and Adey, W. R. (1974). Excitability changes in various types of visual cortical units in freely behaving cats. *Physiology and Behavior* **13,** 101–112.

Kasamatsu, T., and Heggelund, P. (1981). Norepinephrine iontophoresis in cat visual cortex: A quick change in ocular dominance. *Society for Neuroscience Abstracts* **7,** 142.

Kasamatsu, T., and Heggelund, P. (1982). Single cell responses in cat visual cortex to visual stimulation during iontophoresis of noradrenaline. *Experimental Brain Research* **45,** 317–327.

Kasamatsu, T., and Iwama, K. (1966). Two types of light sleep and central visual function in cats. *Tohoku Journal of Experimental Medicine* **88,** 289–303.

Kasamatsu, T., and Pettigrew, J. D. (1976). Depletion of brain catecholamines: Failure of ocular dominance shift after monocular occulsion in kittens. *Science* **194,** 206–209.

Kasamatsu, T., Kiyono, S., and Iwama, K. (1967). Electrical activities of the visual cortex in vation in the striate cortex of kittens treated with 6-hydroxydopamine. *Journal of Comparative Neurology* **185,** 139–162.

Kasamatsu, T., Kiyono, S., and Iwama, K. (1967). Electrical activities of the visual cortex in chronically blinded cats. *Tohoku Journal of Experimental Medicine* **93,** 139–152.

Kasamatsu, T., Pettigrew, J. D., and Ary, M. (1979). Restoration of visual cortical plasticity by local microperfusion of norepinephrine. *Journal of Comparative Neurology* **185,** 163–182.

Kasamatsu, T., Pettigrew, J. D., and Ary, M. (1981a). Recovery from effects of monocular deprivation: Acceleration with norepinephrine and suppression with 6-hydroxydopamine. *Journal of Neurophysiology* **45,** 254–266.

Kasamatsu, T., Itakura, T., and Jonsson, G. (1981b). Intracortical spread of exogenous catecholamines: Effective concentration for modifying cortical plasticity. *Journal of Pharmacology and Experimental Therapeutics* **217,** 841–850.

Katayama, Y., Ueno, Y., Tsukiyama, T., and Tsubokawa, T. (1981). Long lasting suppression of firing of cortical neurons and decrease in cortical blood flow following train pulse stimulation of the locus coerulus in the cat. *Brain Research* **216,** 173–179.

Kato, S., Nakamura, T., and Negishi, K. (1980). Postnatal development of dopaminergic cells in the rat retina. *Journal of Comparative Neurology* **191,** 227–236.

Kayama, Y., Negi, T., Sugitani, M., and Iwama, K. (1982). Effects of locus coeruleus stimulation on neuronal activities of dorsal lateral geniculate nucleus and perigeniculate reticular nucleus of the rat. *Neuroscience* **7,** 655–666.

Kebabian, J. W., and Calne, D. B. (1979). Multiple receptors for dopamine. *Nature (London)* **277,** 93–96.

Kebabian, J. W., Zatz, M., Romero, J. A., and Axelrod, J. (1975). Rapid changes in rat pineal β-adrenergic receptor: Alterations in 1-[^{3}H] alprenolol binding and adenylate cyclase. *Proceedings of the National Academy of Sciences of the U.S.A.* **72,** 3735–3739.

Kehr, W., Carlsson, A., Lindqvist, M., Magnusson, T., and Atack, C. V. (1972). Evidence for a receptor-mediated feedback control of striatal tyrosine hydroxylase activity. *Journal of Pharmacy and Pharmacology* **24,** 744–747.

Keller, R., Oke, A., Mefford, I., and Adams, R. N. (1976). Liquid chromatographic analysis of catecholamines. Routine assay for regional brain mapping. *Life Sciences* **19,** 995–1004.

Kellogg, C., and Lundborg, P. (1972). Production of [^{3}H] catecholamines in the brain following the peripheral administration of ^{3}H-DOPA during pre- and postnatal development. *Brain Research* **36,** 333–342.

Kennedy, C., Des Rosiers, M. H., Sakurada, O., Shinohara, M., Reivich, M., Jehle, J. W., and Sokoloff, L. (1976). Metabolic mapping of the primary visual system of the monkey by means of the autoradiographic [^{14}C] deoxyglucose technique. *Proceedings of the National Academy of Sciences of the U.S.A.* **73,** 4230–4234.

Kety, S. S. (1970). The biogenic amines in the central nervous system: Their possible roles in arousal, emotion, and learning. *In* "The Neurosciences, Second Study Program" (F. O. Schmitt, ed.) pp. 324–336. Rockefeller University Press, New York.

Kirksey, D. F., Seidler, F. J., and Slotkin, T. A. (1978). Ontogeny of (−) [^{3}H] norepinephrine uptake properties of synaptic storage vesicles of rat brain. *Brain Research* **150,** 367–375.

Klein, M., and Kandel, E. R. (1978). Presynaptic modulation of voltage-dependent Ca^{2+} current: Mechanism for behavioral sensitization in *Aplysia californica. Proceedings of the National Academy of Sciences of the U.S.A.* **75,** 3512–3516.

Koda, L. T., and Bloom, F. E. (1977). A light and electron microscopic study of noradrenergic terminals in the rat dentate gyrus. *Brain Research* **120,** 327–335.

Konishi, M. (1978). Auditory environment and vocal development in birds. *In* "Perception and Experience" (R. D. Walk and H. L. Pick, Jr., eds.), pp. 105–118. Plenum, New York.

Konopka, R. J. (1980). Genetics and development of circadian rhythms in invertebrates. *In* "Handbook of Behavioral Neurobiology" Vol. 4. (J. Aschoff, ed.), pp. 173–181. Plenum, New York.

Korf, J., Aghajanian, G. K., and Roth, R. H. (1973a). Stimulation and destruction of the locus coeruleus: Opposite effects of 3-methoxy-4-hydroxyphenylglycol sulfate levels in the rat cerebral cortex. *European Journal of Pharmacology* **21,** 305–310.

Korf, J., Roth, R. H., and Aghajanian, G. K. (1973b). Alterations in turnover and endogenous levels of norepinephrine in cerebral cortex following electrical stimulation and acute axotomy of cerebral noradrenergic pathways. *European Journal of Pharmacology* **23,** 276–282.

Korf, J., Zieleman, M., and Westerink, B. H. C. (1976). Dopamine release in substantia nigra *Nature (London)* **260,** 257–258.

Korneliussen, H., and Jansen, J. K. S. (1976). Morphological aspects of the elimination of polyneuronal innervation of skeletal muscle fibers in newborn rats. *Journal of Neurocytology* **5,** 591–604.

Kornetsky, C. (1979). Functional, anatomical and pharmacological aspects of central motivational systems: A tribute to James Olds. A Symposium at the 62nd Annual Meeting of the Federation of American Society of Experimental Biology. *Federation Proceedings* **38,** 2445–2476.

Kostowski, W., Samanin, R., Bareggi, S., Marc, V., Garattini, S., and Valzelli, L. (1974). Biochemical aspects of the interaction between midbrain raphe and locus coeruleus in the rat. *Brain Research* **82,** 178–182.

Krasne, F. B. (1978). Extrinsic control of intrinsic neuronal plasticity: A hypothesis from work on simple systems. *Brain Research* **140,** 197–216.

Kratz, K. E., Spear, P. D., and Smith, D. C. (1976). Postcritical-period reversal of effects of monocular deprivation on striate cortex cells in the cat. *Journal of Neurophysiology* **39,** 501–511.

Krnjević, K. and Phillis, J. W. (1963). Actions of certain amines on cerebral cortical neurones. *British Journal of Pharmacology* **20,** 471–490.

Kuhar, M. J., Aghajanian, G. K., and Roth, R. H. (1972). Tryptophan hydroxylase activity and synaptosomal uptake of serotonin in discrete brain regions after midbrain raphe lesions: Correlations with serotonin levels and histochemical fluorescence. *Brain Research* **44,** 165–176.

Kupfer, C., and Palmer, P. (1964). Lateral geniculate nucleus: Histological and cytochemical changes following afferent denervation and visual deprivation. *Experimental Neurology* **9,** 400–409.

Kuppermann, B., and Kasamatsu, T. (1979). Binocular competition: Its enhancement by norepinephrine. *Society for Neuroscience Abstracts* **5,** 792.

Kuppermann, B., and Kasamatsu, T. (1980). Cell shrinkage in geniculate neurons following brief unilateral blockade of retinal ganglion cell activity. *Society for Neuroscience Abstracts* **6,** 790.

Kuppermann, B., and Ramachandran, V. S. (1981). Prolonging the "critical period" for plasticity in the cat visual cortex. *ARVO Abstract (Supplement to Investigative Ophtalmology and Visual Science)* **20,** 71.

Laguzzi, R., Petitjean, F., Pujol, J. F., and Jouvet, M. (1972). Effets de l'injection intraventriculaire de 6-hydroxydopamine. II. Sur le cycle veille-sommeils du chat. *Brain Research* **48,** 295–310.

Lake, N., Jordan, L. M., and Phillis, J. W. (1972). Studies on the mechanism of noradrenaline action in cat cerebral cortex. *Nature (London) New Biology* **240,** 249–250.

Lake, N., Jordan, L. M., and Phillis, J. W. (1973). Evidence against cyclic adenosine 3′,5′-monophosphate (AMP) mediation of noradrenaline depression of cerebral cortical neurones. *Brain Research* **60,** 411–421.

Landmesser, L., and Pilar, G. (1976). Fate of ganglionic synapses and ganglion cell axons during normal and induced cell death. *Journal of Cell Biology* **68,** 357–374.

Langer, S. Z. (1977). Presynaptic receptors and their role in the regulation of transmitter release. *British Journal of Pharmacology* **60,** 481–497.

Langer, S. Z. (1978). Physiological and pharmacological role of presynaptic receptor systems in neurotransmission. *In* "Presynaptic Receptors. Advances in the Biosciences" Vol. 18, (S. Z. Langer, K. Starke, and M. L. Dubocovich, eds.), pp. 13–22. Pergamon, Oxford.

Lauder, J. M., and Krebs, H. (1978). Serotonin as a differentiation signal in early neurogenesis. *Developmental Neuroscience* **1,** 15–30.

Laurent, J.-P., Cespuglio, R., and Jouvet, M. (1974). Delimitation des voies ascendantes de l'activité ponto-géniculo-occipitale chez le chat. *Brain Research* **65,** 29–52.

Law, M. I., and Constantine-Paton, M. (1980). Right and left eye bands in frogs with unilateral tectal ablations. *Proceedings of the National Academy of Sciences of the U.S.A.* **77,** 2314–2318.

Léger, L., Sakai, K., Salvert, D., Touret, M., and Jouvet, M. (1975). Delineation of dorsal lateral geniculate afferents from the cat brainstem as visualized by the horseradish peroxidase technique. *Brain Research* **93,** 490–496.

Léger, L., Wilkund, L., Descarries, L., and Persson, M. (1979). Description of an indolaminergic cell component in the cat locus coeruleus: A fluorescence histochemical and radioautographic study. *Brain Research* **168,** 54–56.

Lehmkuhle, S., Kratz, K. E., Mangel, S. C., and Sherman, S. M. (1980). Effects of early monocular lid suture on spatial and temporal sensitivity of neuorns in dorsal lateral geniculate nucleus of the cat. *Journal of Neurophysiology* **43,** 542–556.

Leibowitz, S. F. (1971). Hypothalamic alpha- and beta-adrenergic systems regulate both thirst and hunger in the rat. *Proceedings of the National Academy of Sciences of the U.S.A.* **68,** 332–334.

LeVay, S., Stryker, M. P., and Shatz, C. J. (1978). Ocular dominance columns and their development in layer IV of the cat's visual cortex: A quantitative study. *Journal of Comparative Neurology* **179,** 223–244.

LeVay, S., Wiesel, T. N., and Hubel, D. H. (1979). Effects of reverse suture on ocular dominance columns in rhesus monkey. *Society for Neuroscience Abstracts* **5,** 793.

LeVay, S., Wiesel, T. N., and Hubel, D. H. (1980). The development of ocular dominance columns in normal and visually deprived monkeys. *Journal of Comparative Neurology* **191,** 1–51.

Leventhal, A. G., and Hirsch, H. V. B. (1975). Cortical effect of early selective exposure to diagonal lines. *Science* **190,** 902–904.

Leventhal, A. G., and Hirsch, H. V. B. (1977). Effects of early experience upon orientation sensitivity and binocularity of neurons in visual cortex of cats. *Proceedings of the National Academy of Sciences of the U.S.A.* **74,** 1272–1276.

Levitt, P., and Moore, R. Y. (1978). Noradrenaline neuron innervation of the neocortex in the rat. *Brain Research* **139,** 219–231.

Levitt, P., and Moore, R. Y. (1979). Development of the noradrenergic innervation of neocortex. *Brain Research* **162,** 243–259.

Levitzki, A. (1976). Catecholamine receptors. *In* "Receptors and Recognition" (P. Cuatrecasas and M. F. Greaves, eds.), Series A, Vol. 2, pp. 200–229. Chapman & Hall, London.

Lewis, B. D., Renaud, B., Buda, M., and Pujol, J.-F. (1976). Time-course variations in tyrosine hydroxylase activity in the rat locus coeruleus after electrolytic destruction of nuclei raphe dorsalis or raphe centralis. *Brain Research* **108,** 339–349.

Leysen, J. E., Niemegers, C. J. E., Tollenaere, J. P., and Laduron, P. M. (1978). Serotonergic component of neuroleptic receptors. *Nature (London)* **272,** 163–166.

Libet, B. (1979). Which postsynaptic action of dopamine is mediated by cyclic AMP? *Life Sciences* **24,** 1043–1058.

Lichtman, J. W. (1977). The reorganization of synaptic connections in rat submandibular ganglion during postnatal development. *Journal of Physiology (London)* **273,** 155–177.

Lichtman, J. W., and Purves, D. (1980). The elimination of redundant preganglionic innverva-tion to hamster sympathetic ganglion cells in early post-natal life. *Journal of Physiology (London)* **301,** 213–228.

Lidov, H. G. W., and Molliver, M. E. (1979). Neocortical development after prenatal lesions of noradrenergic projections. *Society for Neuroscience Abstracts* **5,** 341.

Lidov, H. G. W., Molliver, M. E., and Zecevic, N. R. (1978a). Characterization of the monoaminergic innervation of immature rat neocortex: A histofluorescence analysis. *Journal of Comparative Neurology* **181,** 663–680.

Lidov, H. G. W., Rice, F. L., and Molliver, M. E. (1978b). The organization of the catecholamine innervation of somatosensory cortex: The barrel field of the mouse. *Brain Research* **153,** 577–584.

Lidov, H. G. W., Grzanna, R., and Molliver, M. E. (1980). The serotonin innervation of the cerebral cortex in the rat - An immunohistochemical analysis. *Neuroscience* **5,** 207–227.

Lindvall, O., Björklund, A., Moore, R. Y., and Stenevi, U. (1974a). Mesencephalic dopamine neurons projecting to neocortex. *Brain Research* **81,** 324–331.

Lindvall, O., Björklund, A., Nobin, A., and Stenevi, U. (1974b). The adrenergic innervation of the rat thalamus as revealed by the glyoxylic acid fluorescence method. *Journal of Comparative Neurology* **154,** 317–348.

Liu, C.-N., and Chambers, W. W. (1958). Intraspinal sprouting of dorsal root axons. *Archives of Neurology and Psychiatry* **79,** 46–61.

Livingston, M. S., and Hubel, D. H. (1981). Effects of sleep and arousal on the processing of visual information in the cat. *Nature (London)* **291,** 554–561.

Loizou, L. A. (1969). Projections of the nucleus locus coeruleus in the albino rat. *Brain Research* **15,** 563–566.

Loizou, L. A. (1972). The postnatal ontogeny of monoamine-containing neurones in the central nervous system of the albino rat. *Brain Research* **40,** 395–418.

Loizou, L. A., and Salt, P. (1970). Regional changes in monoamines of the rat brain during postnatal development. *Brain Research* **20,** 467–470.

Lorén, I., Emson, P. C., Fahrenkrug, J., Björklund, A., Alumets, J., Håkanson, R., and Sundler, F. (1979). Distribution of vasoactive intestinal polypeptide in the rat and mouse brain. *Neuroscience* **4,** 1953–1976.

Loughlin, S. E., Foote, S. L., and Bloom, F. E. (1979). Topographical organization of locus coeruleus: Efferent projections of constituent neurons. *Society for Neuroscience Abstracts* **5,** 342.

Lovell, R. A., and Freedman, D. X. (1976). Stereospecific receptor sites for d-lysergic acid diethylamide in rat brain: Effects of neurotransmitters, amine antagonists and other psychotropic drugs. *Molecular Pharamcology* **12,** 620–630.

Lund, J. S., Boothe, R. G., and Lund, R. D. (1977). Development of neurons in the visual cortex (area 17) of the monkey *(Macaca nemestrina).* A golgi study from fetal day 127 to postnatal maturity. *Journal of Comparative Neurology* **176,** 149–188.

Lund, R. D., and Lund, J. S. (1971). Synaptic adjustment after deafferentation of the superior colliculus of the rat. *Science* **171,** 804–807.

Lynch, G. , Dunwiddie, T., and Gribkoff, V. (1977). Heterosynaptic depression: A postsynaptic correlate of long-term potentiation. *Nature (London)* **266,** 737–739.

McBride, R. L., and Sutin, J. (1976). Projections of the locus coeruleus and adjacent pontine tegmentum in the cat. *Journal of Comparative Neurology* **165,** 265–284.

McCall, M. A., Tieman, D. G., and Hirsch, H. V. B. (1979). Chronic intraventricular administration of LSD affects the sensitivity of cortical cells to monocular deprivation. *Society for Neuroscience Abstracts* **5,** 631.

MacKenzie, E. T., McCulloch, J., O'Keane, M., Pickard, J. D., and Harper, A. M. (1976). Cerebral circulation and norepinephrine: Relevance of the blood-brain barrier. *American Journal of Physiology* **231,** 483–488.

McLennan, H., and York, D. H. (1967). The action of dopamine on neurones of the caudate nucleus. *Journal of Physiology (London)* **189,** 393–402.

Maeda, T., and Shimizu, N. (1972). Projections ascendantes du locus coeruleus et d'autres neurones aminergiques pontiques au niveau du prosencephale du rat. *Brain Research* **36,** 19–35.

Maeda, T., and Shimizu, N. (1978). The nucleus locus coeruleus. *Noh to Shinkei* **30,** 235–257 (in Japanese).

Maeda, T., Pin, C., Salvert, D., Ligier, M., and Jouvet, M. (1973). Les neurones contenant des catécholamines du tegmentum pontique et leurs voies de projection chez le chat. *Brain Research* **57,** 119–152.

Maeda, T., Tohyama, M., and Shimizu, N. (1974). Modification of postnatal development of neocortex in rat brain with experimental deprivation of locus coeruleus. *Brain Research* **70,** 515–520.

Maeda, T., Kashiba, A., Tohyama, M., Itakura, T., Hori, M., and Shimizu, N. (1975). Demonstration of aminergic terminals and their contacts in rat brain by perfusion fixation with potassium permanganate. *Abstracts for the 10th International Congress of Anatomy Tokyo* p. 142.

Maffei, L., and Bisti, S. (1976). Binocular interaction in strabismic kittens deprived of vision. *Science* **191,** 579–580.

Maffei, L., and Fiorentini, A. (1976a). Monocular deprivation in kittens impairs the spatial resolution of geniculate neurones. *Nature (London)* **264,** 754–755.

Maffei, L., and Fiorentini, A. (1976b). Asymmetry of motility of the eyes and change of binocular properties of cortical cells in adult cats. *Brain Research* **105,** 73–78.

Magherini, P. C., Pompeiano, O., and Thoden, U. (1971). The neurochemical basis of REM sleep: A cholinergic mechanism responsible for rhythmic activation of the vestibular oculomotor system. *Brain Research* **35,** 565–569.

Malcolm, L. J., Watson, J. A., and Burke, W. (1970). PGO waves as unitary events. *Brain Research* **24**, 130–133.

Mason, S. T., and Fibiger, H. C. (1979a). Regional topography with noradrenergic locus coeruleus as revealed by retrograde transport of horseradish peroxidase. *Journal of Comparative Neurology* **187**, 703–724.

Mason, S. T., and Fibiger, H. C. (1979b). Noradrenaline and avoidance learning in the rat. *Brain Research* **161**, 321–333.

Mason, S. T., and Iversen, S. D. (1975). Learning in the absence of forebrain noradrenaline. *Nature (London)* **258**, 422–424.

Matsumoto, S. G., and Murphy, R. K. (1977). Sensory deprivation during development decreases the responsiveness of cricket giant interneurones. *Journal of Physiology (London)* **268**, 533–548.

Matsuzaki, M., Okada, Y., and Shuto, S. (1968). Cholinergic agent related to parasleep state in acute brain stem preparations. *Brain Research* **9**, 253–267.

Melamed, E., Lahav, M., and Atlas, D. (1977). β-Adrenergic receptors in rat cerebral cortex: Histochemical localization by a fluorescent β-blocker. *Brain Research* **128**, 379–384.

Meligeni, J. A., Ledergerber, S. A., and McGaugh, J. L. (1978). Norepinephrine attenuation of amnesia produced by diethyldithiocarbamate. *Brain Research* **149**, 155–164.

Miach, P. J., and Dausse, J.-P., and Meyer, P. (1978). Direct biochemical demonstration of two types of α-adrenoceptors in rat brain. *Nature (London)* **274**, 492–494.

Mikiten, T. M., Niebyl, P. H., and Hendley, C. D. (1961). EEG desynchronization during behavioral sleep associated with spike discharges from the thalamus of the cat. *Federation Proceedings* **20**, 327.

Minneman, K. P., Dibner, M. D., Wolfe, B. B., and Molinoff, P. B. (1979a). β1- and β2-Adrenergic receptors in rat cerebral cortex are independently regulated. *Science* **204**, 866–868.

Minneman, K. P., Hegstrand, L. R., and Molinoff, P. B. (1979b). Simultaneous determination of β1- and β2-adrenergic receptors in tissues containing both receptor subtypes. *Molecular Pharmacology* **16**, 34–46.

Mitchell, D. E., Freeman, R. D., Millodot, M., and Haegerstrom, G. (1973). Meriodional amblyopia: Evidence for modification of the human visual system by early visual experience. *Vision Research* **13**, 535–558.

Mitchell, D. E., Giffin, F., and Timney, B. (1977). A behavioral technique for the rapid assessment of the visual capabilities of kittens. *Perception* **6**, 181–193.

Mitchell, D. E., Cynader, M., and Movshon, J. A. (1978). Recovery from the effects of monocular deprivation in kittens. *Journal of Comparative Neurology* **176**, 53–64.

Moises, H. C., Woodward, D. J., Hoffer, B. J., and Freedman, R. (1979). Interactions of norepinephrine with Purkinje cell responses to putative amino acid neurotransmitters applied by microiontophoresis. *Experimental Neurology* **64**, 493–515.

Molliver, M. E., and Kristt, D. A. (1975). The fine structural demonstration of monoamingeric synapses in immature rat neocortex. *Neuroscience Letters* **1**, 305–310.

Molnar, L., and Seylaz, J. (1965). Mise en evidence et interpretation des effets de la décérébration et des sinus carotidiens sur la circulation cérébrale. *Comptes Rendus des Séances de la Société de Biologie, Paris* **260**, 3164–3167.

Moore, R. Y., and Bloom, F. E. (1978). Central catecholamine neuron systems: Anatomy and physiology of the dopamine systems. *Annual Review of Neuroscience* **1**, 129–169.

Moore, R. Y., and Bloom, F. E. (1979). Central catecholamine neuron systems: Anatomy and physiology of the norepinephrine and epinephrine systems. *Annual Review of Neuroscience 2,* 113–168.

Moore, R. Y., Björklund, A., and Stenevi, U. (1974). Growth and plasticity of adrenergic neurons. *In* "The Neurosciences, Third Study Program" (F. O. Schmitt and F. G.

Worden, eds.), pp. 961-977. The MIT Press, Cambridge, Massachusetts and London, England.
Moore, R. Y., Halaris, A. I., and Jones, B. E. (1978). Serotonin neurons of the midbrain raphe ascending projections. *Journal of Comparative Neurology* **180**, 417–438.
Morris, M. J., Dausse, J.-P., Devynck , M.-A., and Meyer, P. (1980). Ontogeny of α1- and α2-adrenoceptors in rat brain. *In* "Biogenic Amines in Development" (H. Parvez and S. Parvez, eds.), pp. 241-261. Elsevier, Amsterdam.
Morrison, J. H., Grzanna, R., Molliver, M. E., and Coyle, J. T. (1978). The distribution and orientation of noradrenergic fibers in neocortex of the rat: An immuno-fluorescence study. *Journal of Comparative Neurology* **181**, 17–40.
Morrison, J. H., Molliver, M. E., Grzanna, R., and Coyle, J. T. (1981). The intra-cortical trajectory of the coerulo-cortical projection in the rat: A tangentially organized cortical afferent. *Neuroscience* **6**, 139–158.
Moske, S. S., and Jacobs, B. L. (1977). Electrophysiological evidence against negative neuronal feedback from the forebrain controlling midbrain raphe unit activity. *Brain Research* **119**, 291–303.
Mouret, J., Jeannerod, M., and Jouvet, M. (1963). L'activité electrique du système visuel au cours de la phase paradoxale du sommeil chez le chat. *Journal de Physiologie (Paris)* **55**, 305–306.
Movshon, J. A. (1976). Reversal of the phsyiological effects of monocular deprivation in the kitten's visual cortex. *Journal of Physiology (London)* **261**, 125–174.
Movshon, J. A., and Blakemore, C. (1974). Functional reinnervation in kitten visual cortex. *Nature (London)* **251**, 504–505.
Mower, G. D., Duffy, F. H., and Burchfiel, J. (1979). Dark rearing delays onset of the critical period in kitten visual cortex. *Society for Neuroscience Abstracts* **5**, 799.
Mukherjee, C., Caron, M. G., and Lefkowitz, R. J. (1975). Catecholamine-induced subsensitivity of adenylate cyclase associated with loss of β-adrenergic receptor binding sites. *Proceedings of the National Academy of Sciences of the U.S.A.* **72**, 1945–1949.
Murphy, R. K., and Matsumoto, S. G. (1976). Experience modifies the plastic properties of identified neurons. *Science* **191**, 564–566.
Nahorski, S. R. (1976). Association of high affinity stereospecific binding of [^{3}H]propranolol to cerebral membranes with β-adrenoreceptor. *Nature (London)* **259**, 488–489.
Nakai, K., Jonsson, G., and Kasamatsu, T. (1981). Regrowth of central catecholaminergic fibers in cat visual cortex following localized lesion with 6-hydroxydopamine. *Society for Neuroscience Abstracts* **7**, 675.
Nakai, K., Jonsson, G., and Kasamatsu, T. (1983). Regeneration of central norepinephrine fibers in cat visual cortex following localized lesions with 6-hydroxydopamine. *Journal of Comparative Neurology* (submitted)
Nakai, Y., and Takaori, S. (1974). Influence of norepinephrine-containing neurons derived from the locus coeruleus on lateral geniculate activities in cats. *Brain Research* **71**, 47–60.
Nakamura, S. (1977). Some electrophysiological properties of neurones of rat locus coeruleus. *Journal of Physiology (London)* **267**, 641–658.
Nakamura, S., and Iwama, K. (1980). Recurrent facilitiation of locus coeruleus neurons of the rat. *In* "The Reticular Formation Revisited" (J. A. Hobson and M. A. B. Brazier, eds.) pp. 303-315. Raven, New York.
Nelson, E., and Rennels, M. (1970). Innervation of intracranial arteries. *Brain* **93**, 475–490.
Nomura, Y., Naitoh, F., and Segawa, T. (1976). Regional changes in monoamine content and uptake of the rat brain during postnatal development. *Brain Research* **101**, 305–315.
Nottebohm, F. (1980). Brain pathways for vocal learning in birds: A review of the first 10 years. *Progress in Psychobiology and Physiological Psychology*. **9**, 85–124. Academic Press, New York.
Olds, J. (1976). Brain stimulation and the motivation of behavior. *In* "Perspectives in Brain Re-

search, Progress in Brain Research" (M. A. Corner and D. F. Swaab, eds.), Vol. 45, pp. 401–426. Elsevier, Amsterdam.

Olschowka, J. A., Molliver, M. E., Grzanna, R., Rice, F. L., and Coyle, J. T. (1981). Ultrastructural demonstration of noradrenergic synapses in the rat central nervous system by dopamine-β-hydroxylase immunocytochemistry. *Journal of Histochemistry and Cytochemistry* **29,** 271–280.

Olson, C. R., and Freeman, R. D. (1975). Progressive changes in kitten striate cortex during monocular vision. *Journal of Neurophysiology* **38,** 26–33.

Olson, C. R., and Freeman, R. D. (1978). Monocular deprivation and recovery during sensitive period in kittens. *Journal of Neurophysiology* **41,** 65–74.

Olson, C. R., and Pettigrew, J. D. (1974). Single units in visual cortrex of kittens reared in strobscopic illumination. *Brain Research* **70,** 189–204.

Olson, L., and Fuxe, K. (1971). On the projections from the locus coeruleus noradrenaline neurons: The cerebellar innervation. *Brain Research* **28,** 165–171.

Oppenheim, R. W. (1981). Cell death of motoneurons in the chick embryo spinal cord. V. Evidence on the role of cell death and neuromuscular function in the formation of specific peripheral connections. *Journal of Neuroscience* **1,** 141–151.

Palacios, J. M., and Kuhar, M. J. (1980). Beta-adrenergic receptor localization by light microscopic autoradiography. *Science* **208,** 1378–1380.

Palmer, G. C. (1972). Increased cyclic AMP response to norepinephrine in the rat brain following 6-hydroxydopamine. *Neuropharmacology* **11,** 145–149.

Perkins, J. P., and Moore, M. M. (1973). Regulation of the adenosine cyclic 3′, 5′-monophosphate content of rat cerebral cortex: Ontogenetic development of the responsiveness to catecholamines and adenosine. *Molecular Pharmacology* **9,** 774–782.

Peroutka, S. J., and Snyder, S. H. (1979). Multiple serotonin receptors: Differential binding of [^{3}H]5-hydroxytryptamine, [^{3}H]lysergic acid diethylamide and [^{3}H]spiroperidol. *Molecular Pharmacology* **16,** 687–699.

Peroutka, S. J., Lebovitz, R. M., and Snyder, S. H. (1981). Two distinct central serotonin receptors with different physiological functions. *Science* **212,** 827–829.

Pettigrew, J. D. (1974). The effect of visual experience on the development of stimulus specificity by kitten cortical neurones. *Journal of Physiology (London)* **237,** 49–74.

Pettigrew, J. D. (1978). The paradox of the critical period for striate cortex. *In* "Neural Plasticity" (C. W. Cotman, ed.), pp. 311–330. Raven, New York.

Pettigrew, J. D., and Freeman, R. D. (1973). Visual experience without lines: Effect on developing cortical neurons. *Science* **182,** 599–601.

Pettigrew, J. D., and Kasamatsu, T. (1978). Local perfusion of noradrenaline maintains visual cortical plasiticity. *Nature (London)* **271,** 761–763.

Pettigrew, J. D., and Konishi, M. (1976). Effect of monocular deprivation on binocular neurones in the owl's visual Wulst. *Nature (London)* **264,** 753–754.

Pickel, V. M., Segal, M., and Bloom, F. E. (1974). A radioautographic study of the efferent pathways of the nucleus locus coeruleus. *Journal of Comparative Neurology* **155,** 15–42.

Pickel, V. M., Joh, T. H., and Reis, D. J. (1976). Monoamine-synthesizing enzymes in central dopaminergic, noradrenergic and serotonergic neurons. Immunocytochemical localization by light and electron microscopy. *Journal of Histochemistry and Cytochemistry* **24,** 792–806.

Pickel, V. M., Joh, T. H., and Reis, D. J. (1977). A serotonergic innervation of noradrenergic neurons in nucleus locus coeruleus: Demonstration by immunocytochemical localization of the transmitter specific enzymes tyrosine and tryptophan hydroxylase. *Brain Research* **131,** 197–214.

Pittman, R. N., Minneman, K. P., and Molinoff, P. B. (1980). Ontogeny of β1-and β2-adrenergic receptors in rat cerebellum and cerebral cortex. *Brain Research* **188,** 357–368.

Plotsky, P. M., Wightman, R. M., Chey, W., and Adams, R. N. (1978). Liquid chromatographic analysis of endogenous catecholamine released from brain slices. *Science* **197,** 904–906.

Poitras, D., and Parent, A. (1978). Atlas of the distribution of monoamine-containing nerve cell bodies in the brain stem of the cat. *Journal of Comparative Neurology* **179,** 699–718.

Porcher, W., and Heller, A. (1972). Regional development of catecholamine biosynthesis in the rat brain. *Journal of Neurochemistry* **19,** 1917–1930.

Posternak, J. M., Fleming, T. C., and Evarts, E. V. (1959). Effects of interruption of the visual pathway on the response to geniculate stimulation. *Science* **129,** 39–40.

Prasad, K. N., Kumar, S., Gilmer, K., and Vernadakis, A. (1973). Cyclic AMP-induced differentiated neuroblastoma cells: Changes in total nucleic acid and protein contents. *Biochemical and Biophysical Research Communication* **50,** 973–977.

Prestige, M. C. (1970). Differentiation, degeneration and the role of the periphery: Quantitative considerations. *In* "The Neurosciences. Second Study Program" (F. O. Schmitt, ed.), pp. 73–82. Rockefeller University Press, New York.

Prestige, M. C. (1974). Axon and cell numbers in the developing nervous system. *British Medical Bulletin* **30,** 107–111.

Pujol, J.-F., Stein, D., Blondaux, C., Petitjean, F., Froment, J. L., and Jouvet, M. (1973) Biochemical evidences for interaction phenomena between noradrenergic and serotonergic systems in the cat brain. *In* "Frontiers in Catecholamine Research" (E. Usdin and S H. Snyder, eds.), pp. 771–772. Pergamon, Oxford.

Purves, D., and Lichtman, J. W. (1980). Elimination of synapses in the developing nervous system. *Science* **210,** 153–157.

Raff, M. C., Hornby-Smith, A., and Brockes, J. P. (1978). Cyclic AMP as a mitogenic signal for cultured rat Schwann cells. *Nature (London)* **273,** 672–673.

Raichle, M. E., Hartman, B. K., Eichling, J. O., and Sharpe, L. G. (1975). Central noradrenergic regulation of cerebral blood flow and vascular permeability. *Proceedings of the National Academy of Sciences of the U.S.A.* **72,** 3726–3730.

Raiseman, G. (1969). Neuronal plasticity in the septal nuclei of the rat. *Brain Research* **14,** 25–48.

Rakic, P. (1976). Prenatal genesis of connections subserving ocular dominance in the rhesus monkey. *Nature (London)* **261,** 467–471.

Rakic, P. (1977). Prenatal developmental of the visual system in rhesus monkey. *Philosophical Transactions of the Royal Society, London, Series B* **278,** 245–260.

Rakic, P. (1981). Development of visual centers in the primate brain depends on binocular competition before birth. *Science* **214,** 928–931.

Randt, C. T., Quartermain, D., Goldstein, M., and Anagnoste, B. (1971). Norepinephrine biosynthesis inhibition: Effects on memory in mice. *Science* **172,** 498–499.

Rasch, E., Swift, H., Riesen, A. H., and Chow, K. L. (1961). Altered structure and composition of retinal cells in dark-reared mammals. *Experimental Cell Research* **25,** 348–363.

Rauschecker, J. P. (1979). Orientation-dependent changes in response properties of neurons in kitten's visual cortex. *In* "Development Neurobiology of Vision" (R. Freeman, ed.) pp. 121–133. Plenum, New York.

Rauschecker, J. P., and Singer, W. (1979). Changes in the circuitry of the kitten's visual cortex are gated by postsynaptic activity. *Nature (London)* **280,** 58–60.

Rauschecker, J. P., and Singer, W. (1981). The effects of early visual experience on the cat's visual cortex and their possible explanation by Hebb synapses. *Journal of Physiology (London)* **310,** 215–239.

Reader, T. A. (1978). The effects of dopamine, noradrenaline and serotonin in the visual cortex of the cat. *Experientia* **34,** 1586–1587.

Reader, T. A., De Champlain, J., and Jasper, H. H. (1976). Catecholamines released from cerebral cortex in the cat: Decrease during sensory stimulation. *Brain Research* **111,** 95–108.

Reader, T. A., Ferron, A., Descarries, L., and Jasper, H. H. (1979). Modulatory role for biogenic amines in the cerebral cortex. Microiontophoretic studies. *Brain Research* **160,** 217–229.

Renaud, B., Buda, M., Lewis, B. D., and Pujol, J.-F. (1975). Effects of 5, 6-dihydroxytryptamine on tyrosine-hydroxylase activity in central catecholaminergic neurons of the rat. *Biochemical Pharmacology* **24,** 1739–1742.

Riley, D. A., (1977). Spontaneous elimination of nerve terminals from the endplates of developing skeletal myofibers. *Brain Research* **134,** 279–285.

Rizzolatti, G., and Tradardi, V. (1971). Pattern discrimination in monocularly reared cats. *Experimental Neurology* **33,** 181–194.

Roffwarg, H. P., Muzio, J. N., and Dement, W. C. (1966). Ontogenetic development of the human sleep-dream cycle. *Science* **152,** 604–619.

Rogawski, M. A., and Aghajanian, G. K. (1980a). Activation of lateral geniculate neurons by norepinephrine: Mediation by an α-adrenergic receptor. *Brain Research* **182,** 345–359.

Rogawski, M. A., and Aghajanian, G. K. (1980b). Modulation of lateral geniculate neurone excitability by noradrenaline microiontophoresis or locus coeruleus stimulation. *Nature (London)* **387,** 731–734.

Roisen, F. J., Murphy, R. A., and Braden, W. G. (1972). Dibutyryl cyclic adenosine monophosphate stimulation of colcemid-inhibited axonal elongation. *Science* **177,** 809–811.

Rojik, I., and Fehér, O. (1980). Correlations between glycine incorporation and cerebral cortical activity. *Experimental Brain Research* **39,** 321–326.

Rowe, M. H., and Stone, J. (1977). Naming of neurons. Classification and naming of cat retinal ganglion cells. *Brain, Behavior, and Evolution* **14,** 185–216.

Ruiz-Marcos, A., and Valverde, F. (1969). The temporal evolution of the distribution of dendritic spines in the visual cortex of normal and dark raised mice. *Experimental Brain Research* **8,** 284–294.

Sachs, C., Jonsson, G., and Fuxe, K. (1973). Mapping of central noradrenaline pathways with 6-hydroxydopa. *Brain Research* **63,** 249–261.

Sakai, K. (1973). Phasic electrical activity in the brain associated with eye movement in waking cats. *Brain Research* **56,** 135–150.

Sakai, K. (1980). Some anatomical and physiological properties of ponto-mesencephalic tegmental neurons with special reference to the PGO waves and postural atonia during paradoxical sleep in the cat. *In* "The Reticular Formation Revisited" (J. A. Hobson and M. A. Brazier, eds.) pp. 427–447. Raven, New York.

Sakai, K., and Jouvet, M. (1980). Brain stem PGO-on cells projecting directly to the cat dorsal lateral geniculate nucleus. *Brain Research* **194,** 500–505.

Sakai, K., Petitjean, F., and Jouvet, M. (1976). Effects of ponto-mesencephalic lesions and electrical stimulation upon PGO waves and EMPs in unanesthetized cats. *Electroencephalography and Clinical Neurophysiology* **41,** 49–63.

Sakai, K., Salvert, D., Touret, M., and Jouvet, M. (1977a). Afferent connections of the nucleus raphe dorsalis in the cat as visualized by the horseradish peroxidase technique. *Brain Research* **137,** 11–35.

Sakai, K., Touret, M., Salvert, D., Léger, L., and Jouvet, M. (1977b). Afferent projections to the cat locus coeruleus as visualized by the horseradish peroxidase technique. *Brain Research* **119,** 21–41.

Schlumpf, M., Lichtensteiger, W., Shoemaker, W. J., and Bloom, F. E. (1980). Fetal monoamine systems: Early stages and cortical projections. *In* "Biogenic Amines in Development" (H. Parvez and S. Parvez, eds.), pp. 567–590. Elsevier, Amsterdam.

Schmidt, M. J., Palmer, G. C., Dettbarn, W. D., and Robinson, G. A. (1970). Cyclic AMP and adenylate cyclase in the developing rat brain. *Developmental Psychobiology* **3,** 53–67.
Schoppmann, A., and Stryker, M. P. (1981). Physiological evidence that the 2-deoxyglucose method reveals orientation columns in cat visual cortex. *Nature (London)* **293,** 574–576.
Schrier, B. K., and Shapiro, D. L. (1973). Effects of N^6-monobutyryl-cyclic AMP on glutamate decarboxylase activity in fetal rat brain and glial tumor cells in culture. *Experimental Cell Research* **80,** 459–462.
Schwartz, W. J. (1978). 6-Hydroxydopamine lesions of rat locus coeruleus alter brain glucose consumption, as measured by the 2-deoxy-D-[^{14}C] glucose tracer technique. *Neuroscience Letters* **7,** 141–150.
Seeman, P., Chan-Wong, M., Tedesco, J., and Wong, K. (1975). Brain receptors for antipsychotic drugs and dopamine: Direct binding assay. *Proceedings of the National Academy of Sciences of the U.S.A.* **72,** 4376–4380.
Segal, M. (1976). 5-HT antagonists in rat hippocampus. *Brain Research* **103,** 161–166.
Segal, M. (1979). Serotonergic innervation of the locus coeruleus from the dorsal raphe and its action on responses to noxious stimuli. *Journal of Physiology (London)* **286,** 401–415.
Segal, M. (1981). The action of norepinephrine in the rat hippocampus: Intracellular studies in the slice preparation. *Brain Research* **206,** 107–128.
Segal, M., and Bloom, F. E. (1976). The action of norepinephrine in the rat hippocampus. IV. The effects of locus coeruleus stimulation on evoked hippocampal unit activity. *Brain Research* **107,** 513–525.
Segal, M., Pickel, V. M., and Bloom, F. E. (1973). The projections of the nucleus locus coeruleus and autoradiographic study. *Life Sciences* **13,** 817–821.
Seiger, Å., and Olson, L. (1973). Late prenatal ontogeny of central monoamine neurons in the rat: Fluorescence histochemical observations. *Zeitschrift für Anatomie und Entwicklungsgeschichte* **140,** 281–318.
Sharma, J. N. (1977). Microiontophoretic application of some monoamines and their antagonists to cortical neurones of the rat. *Neuropharmacology* **16,** 83–88.
Sharp, F. R. (1976). Relative cerebral glucose uptake of neuronal perikarya and neuropil determined with 2-deoxyglucose in resting and swimming rat. *Brain Research* **110,** 127–139.
Shatz, C. J., and Stryker, M. P. (1978). Ocular dominance in layer IV of the cat's visual cortex and the effects of monocular deprivation *Journal of Physiology (London)* **281,** 267–283.
Shatz, C. J., Lindström, S., and Wiesel, T. N. (1977). The distribution of afferents representing the right and left eyes in the cat's visual cortex. *Brain Research* **131,** 103–116.
Sherk, H., and Stryker,M. P. (1976). Quantitative study of cortical orientation selectivity in visually inexperienced kittens. *Journal of Neurophysiology* **39,** 63–70.
Sherman, S. M. (1973). Visual field defects in monocularly and binocularly deprived cats. *Brain Research* **49,** 25–45.
Sherman, S. M. (1974a). Permanence of visual perimetry deficits in monocularly and binocularly deprived cats. *Brain Research* **73,** 491–501.
Sherman, S. M. (1974b). Monocularly deprived cats: Improvement of the deprived eye's vision by visual decortication *Science* **186,** 267–269.
Sherman, S. M., and Guillery, R. W. (1976). Behavioral studies of binocular competition in cats. *Vision Research* **16,** 1479–1481.
Sherman, S. M., and Stone, J. (1973). Phsyiological normality of the retina in visually deprived cats. *Brain Research* **60,** 224–230.
Sherman, S. M., and Wilson, J. R. (1975). Behavioral and morphological evidence for binocular competition in the postnatal development of the dog's visual system. *Journal of Comparative Neurology* **161,** 183–196.
Sherman, S. M., Hoffmann, K.-P., and Stone, J. (1972). Loss of a specific cell type from

dorsal lateral geniculate nucleus in visually deprived cats. *Journal of Neurophysiology* **35,** 532–541.

Sherman, S. M., Guillery, R. W., Kaas, J. H., and Sanderson, K. J. (1974). Behavioral, electrophysiological and morphological studies of binocular competition in the development of the geniculocortical pathways of cats. *Journal of Comparative Neurology* **158,** 1–18.

Shimahara, T., and Tauc, L. (1977). Cyclic AMP induced by serotonin modulates the activity of an identified synapse in *Aplysia* by facilitating the active permeability to calcium. *Brain Research* **127,** 168–172.

Shimizu, N., Ohnishi, S., Tohyama, M., and Maeda, T. (1974). Demonstration by degeneration silver method of the ascending projection from the locus coeruleus. *Experimental Brain Research* **20,** 181–192.

Shlaer, R. (1971). Shift in binocular disparity causes compensating change in the cortical structure of kittens. *Science* **173,** 638–641.

Sillito, A. M. (1977). Inhibitory processes underlying the directional specificity of simple, complex and hypercomplex cells in the cat's visual cortex. *Journal of Physiology (London)* **271,** 699–720.

Sillito, A. M. (1979). Inhibitory mechanisms influencing complex cell orientation selectivity and their modification at high resting discharge levels. *Journal of Physiology (London)* **289,** 33–53.

Sillito, A. M. (1980). Orientation selectivity and the spatial organization of the afferent input to the striate cortex. *Experimental Brain Research* **41,** A9.

Sillito, A. M., Kemp, J. A., and Patel, H. (1980). Inhibitory interactions contributing to the ocular dominance of monocularly dominated cells in the normal cat striate cortex. *Experimental Brain Research* **41,** 1–10.

Sillito, A. M., Kemp, J. A., and Blakemore, C. (1981). The role of GABAergic inhibition in the cortical effects of monocular deprivation. *Nature (London)* **291,** 318–320.

Simon, R. P., Gershon, M. D., and Brooks, D. C. (1973). The role of the raphe nuclei in the regulation of ponto-geniculo-occipital wave activity. *Brain Research* **58,** 313–330.

Sims, K. B., Hoffman, D. L., Said, S. I., and Zimmerman, E. A. (1980). Vasoactive intestinal polypeptide (VIP) in mouse and rat brain: An immunocytochemical study. *Brain Research* **186,** 165–183.

Singer, W. (1977). Effects of monocular deprivation on excitatory and inhibitory pathways in cat striate cortex. *Experimental Brain Research* **30,** 25–41.

Singer, W., and Tretter, F. (1976). Receptive-field properties and neuronal connectivity in striate and parastriate cortex of contour-deprived cats. *Journal of Neurophysiology* **39,** 613–630.

Singer, W., Yinon, U., and Tretter, F. (1979). Inverted monocular vision prevents ocular dominance shift in kittens and impairs the functional state of visual cortex in adult cats. *Brain Research* **164,** 294–299.

Singer, W., Freeman, B., and Rauschecker, J. P. (1981). Restriction of visual experience to a single orientation affects the organization of orientation columns in cat visual cortex. *Experimental Brain Research* **41,** 199–215.

Sladek, J. R., Jr., and Walker, P. (1977). Serotonin-containing neuronal perikarya in the primate locus coeruleus and subcoeruleus. *Brain Research* **134,** 359–366.

Sloboda, R. D., Rudolph, S. A., Rosenbaum, J. L., and Greengard, P. (1975). Cyclic AMPdependent endogenous phosphorylation of a microtubule-associated protein. *Proceedings of the National Academy of Sciences of the U.S.A.* **72,** 177–181.

Snider, R. S. (1975). A cerebellar-coeruleus pathway. *Brain Research* **88,** 59–63.

Sokoloff, L., Reivich, M., Kennedy, C., Des Rosiers, M. H., Patlak, C. S., Pettigrew, K. D., Sakurada, O., and Shinohara, M. (1977). The [^{14}C] dexoyglucose method for the measurement of local cerebral glucose utilization: Theory, procedure, and normal values in the conscious and anesthetized albino rat. *Journal of Neurochemistry* **28,** 897–916.

Sotelo, C., and Palay, S. (1971). Altered axons and axon terminals in the lateral vestibular nucleus of the rat. Possible example of axon remodeling. *Laboratory Investigation* **25,** 653–671.

Spano, P. F., Kumakura, K. Govoni, S., and Trabucchi, M. (1976). Ontogenetic development of neostriatal dopamine receptors in the rat. *Journal of Neurochemistry* **27,** 621–624.

Spear, P. D., and Ganz, L. (1975). Effects of visual cortex lesions following recovery from monocular deprivation in the cat. *Experimental Brain Research* **23,** 181–201.

Spear, P. D., and Hickey, T. L. (1979). Postcritical-period reversal of effects of monocular deprivation on dorsal lateral geniculate cell size in the cat. *Journal of Comparative Neurology* **185,** 317–328.

Sperry, R. W. (1950). Neural basis of the spontaneous optokinetic response produced by visual inversion. *Journal of Comparative and Physiological Psychology* **43,** 482–489.

Sporn, J. R., and Molinoff, P. B. (1976). β-Adrenergic receptors in rat brain. *Journal of Cyclic Nucleotide Research* **2,** 149–161.

Starke, K., and Montel, H. (1973). Involvement of α-receptors in clonidine-induced inhibition of transmitter release from central monoamine neurones. *Neuropharmacology* **12,** 1073–1080.

Starke, K., Reimann, W., Zumstein, A., and Herttig, G. (1978). Effect of dopamine receptor agonists and antagonists on release of dopamine in the rabbit caudate nucleus in vitro. *Naunyn-Schmiedebergs Archives of Pharmacology* **305,** 27–36.

Stein, L., Belluzzi, J. D., and Wise, C. D. (1975). Memory enhancement by central administration of norepinephrine. *Brain Research* **84,** 329–335.

Steinbusch, H. W. M. (1981). Distribution of serotonin-immunoreactivity in the central nervous system of the rat—cell bodies and terminals. *Neuroscience* **6,** 557–618.

Stern, W. C., and Morgane, P. J. (1974). Theoretical view of REM sleep function: Maintenance of catecholamine systems in the central nervous system. *Behavioral Biology* **11,** 1–32.

Stern, W. C., Forbes, W. B., and Morgane, P. J. (1974). Absence of PGO spikes in rats. *Physiology and Behavior* **12,** 293–295.

Stone, T. W. (1972). Noradrenaline effects and pH. *Journal of Pharmacy and Pharmacology* **24,** 422–423.

Stone, T. W. (1973). Pharmacology of pyramidal tract cells in the cerebral cortex. Noradrenaline and related substances. *Naunyn-Schmiedebergs Archives of Pharmacology* **278,** 333–346.

Strittmatter, W. J., Davis, J. N., and Lefkowitz, R. J. (1977). α-Adrenergic receptors in rat parotid cells. II. Desensitization of receptor binding sites and potassuim release. *Journal of Biological Chemistry* **252,** 5478–5482.

Stryker, M. P. (1977). The role of early experience in the development and maintenance of orientation selectivity in the cat's visual cortex. *Neuroscience Research Program Bulletin* **15,** 454–462.

Stryker, M. P. (1980). Synaptic elimination in the developing visual system. *In* "Synapse Elimination in Developing Mammals" Symposium at the Annual Meeting of the Society for Neuroscience.

Stryker, M. P., and Sherk, H. (1975). Modification of cortical orientation selectivity in cat by restricted visual experience: A reexamination. *Science* **190,** 904–906.

Stryker, M. P., Sherk, H., Leventhal, A. G., and Hirsch, H. V. B. (1978). Physiological consequences for the cat's visual cortex of effectively restricting early visual experience with oriented contours. *Journal of Neurophysiology* **41,** 896–909.

Súarez, F. R., and Llamas, A. (1968). Fibras ascendentes desde tegmento pointine oral en el ratón. *Acta Neurologica Latinoamericana* **14,** 5–16.

Suzuki, H. (1967). Effects of reversible retinal blockade on population response of the lateral geniculate nucleus. *Japanese Journal of Physiology* **17,** 335–347.

Suzuki, H., and Ichijo, M. (1967). Tonic inhibition at cat lateral genicualte nucleus maintained by retinal spontaneous discharges. *Japanese Journal of Physiology* **17,** 599–612.

Svensson, T. H., and Usdin, T. (1978). Feedback inhibition of brain noradrenaline neurons by tricyclic antidepressants: α-Receptors mediation. *Science* **202,** 1089–1091.

Svensson, T. H., Bunney, B. S., and Aghajanian, G. K. (1975). Inhibition of both noradrenergic and serotonergic neurons in brain by the α-adrenergic agonist clonidine. *Brain Research* **92,** 291–306.

Swanson, L. W., and Hartman, B. K. (1975). The central adrenergic system. An immunofluorescence study of the location of cell bodies and their efferent connections in the rat utilizing dopamine-β-hydroxylase as a marker. *Journal of Comparative Neurology* **163,** 467–506.

Swindale, N. V. (1981). Absence of ocular dominance patches in dark-reared cats. *Nature (London)* **290,** 332–333.

Szabadi, E., Bradshaw, C. M., and Bevan, P. (1977). Excitatory and depressant neuronal responses to noradrenaline, 5-hydroxytryptamine and mescaline: The role of the baseline firing rate. *Brain Research* **126,** 580–583.

Tanaka, C., Inagaki, C., and Fujiwara, H. (1976). Labeled noradrenaline release from rat cerebral cortex following electrical stimulation of locus coeruleus. *Brain Research* **106,** 384–389.

Thierry, A. M., Blanc, G., Sobel, A., Stinus, L., and Glowinski, J. (1973). Dopaminergic terminals in the rat cortex. *Science* **182,** 499–501.

Thompson, R. F., Patterson, M. M., and Berger, T. W. (1978). Associative learning in the mammalian nervous system. *In* "Brain and Learning" (T. Teyler, ed.) pp. 51–90. Greylock, Stamford, Connecticut.

Thorpe, P. A., and Blakemore, C. (1975). Evidence for a loss of afferent axons in the visual cortex of monocularly deprived cats. *Neuroscience Letters* **1,** 271–276.

Timney, B., Mitchell, D. E., and Cynader, M. (1980). Behavioral evidence for prolonged sensitivity to effects of monocular deprivation in dark-reared cats. *Journal of Neurophysiology* **43,** 1041–1054.

Tittler, M., Weinreich, P., and Seeman, P. (1977). New detection of brain dopamine receptors with [^{3}H]dihydroergocryptine. *Proceedings of the National Academy of Sciences of the U.S.A.* **74,** 3750–3753.

Tohyama, M. (1976). Comparative anatomy of cerebellar catecholamine innervation from teleosts to mammals. *Journal für Hirnforschung,* **17,** 43–60.

Tohyama, M., Maeda, T., Hashimoto, J., Shrestha, G. R., Tamura, O., and Shimizu, N. (1974a). Comparative anatomy of the locus coeruleus. I. Organization and ascending projections of the catecholamine containing neurons in the pontine region of the bird, *Melopsittacus undulatus. Journal für Hirnforschung* **15,** 319–330.

Tohyama, M., Maeda, T., and Shimizu, N. (1974b). Detailed noradrenaline pathways of locus coeruleus neuron to the cerebral cortex with use of 6-hydroxydopa. *Brain Research* **79,** 139–144.

Tohyama, M., Maeda, T., and Shimizu, N. (1976). Comparative anatomy of the locus coeruleus. II. Organization and projection of the catecholamine containing neurons in the upper rhombencephalon of the frog, *Rana catesbiana. Journal für Hirnforschung* **17,** 81–89.

Törk, I., Leventhal, A. G., and Stone, J. (1979). Brain stem afferents to visual cortical areas 17, 18, and 19 in the cat, demonstrated by horseradish peroxidase. *Neuroscience Letters* **11,** 247–252.

Tretter, F., Cynader, M., and Singer, W. (1975). Modification of direction selectivity of neurons in the visual cortex of kittens. *Brain Research* **84,** 143–149.

Tsubokawa, T., Katayama, Y., Kondo, T., Ueno, Y., Hayashi, N., and Moriyasu, N. (1980). Changes in local cerebral blood flow and neuronal activity during sensory stimulation in normal and sympathectomized cats. *Brain Research* **190,** 51–65.

Tsukahara, N. (1981). Synaptic plasticity in the mammalian central nervous system. *Annual Review of Neuroscience* **4,** 351–379.

Tsukahara, N., and Fujito, Y. (1976). Physiological evidence of formation of new synapses from cerebellum in the red nucleus neurons following cross-union of forelimb nerves. *Brain Research* **106,** 184–188.

Tsumoto, T., and Freeman, R. D. (1981). Ocular dominance in kitten cortex: Induced changes of single cells while they are recorded. *Experimental Brain Research* **44,** 347–351.

Tsumoto, T., and Suda, K. (1978). Evidence for excitatory connections from the deprived eye to the visual cortex in monocularly deprived kittens. *Brain Research* **153,** 150–156.

Tsumoto, T., and Suda, K. (1979). Cross-depression: an electrophysiological manifestation of binocular competition in the developing visual cortex. *Brain Research* **168,** 190–194.

Tsumoto, T., Eckart, W., and Creutzfeldt, O. D. (1979). Modification of orientation sensitivity of cat visual cortex neurons by removal of GABA-mediated inhibition. *Experimental Brain Research* **34,** 351–363.

Ungerstedt, U. (1968). 6-Hydroxy-dopamine induced degeneration of central monoamine neurons. *European Journal of Pharmacology* **5,** 107–110.

Ungerstedt, U. (1971a). Stereotaxic mapping of the monoamine pathways in the rat brain. *Acta Physiologica Scandinavica* **82** (Suppl. 367). 1–48.

Ungerstedt, U. (1971b). Histochemical studies on the effects of intracerebral and intraventricular injection of 6-hydroxydopamine on monoamine neurons in the rat brain. *In* "6-Hydroxydopamine and Catecholamine Neurons" (T. Malmfors and H. Thoenen, eds.), pp. 101–127. North-Holland Publishers, Amsterdam.

Ungerstedt, U. (1974). Functional dynamics of central monoamine pathways. *In* "The Neurosciences, Third Study Program" (F. O. Schmitt and F. G. Worden eds.), pp. 979–988. MIT Press, Cambridge, Massachusetts.

U'prichard, D. C., Greenberg, D. A., and Snyder, S. H. (1977). Binding characteristics of a radio-labeled agonist and antagonist at central nervous system α-noradrenergic receptors. *Molecular Pharmacology* **13,** 454–473.

Uretsky, N. J., and Iversen, L. L. (1970). Effects of 6-hydroxydopamine on catecholamine containing neurons in the rat brain. *Journal of Neurochemistry* **17,** 269–278.

Valverde, F. (1967). Apical dendritic spines of the visual cortex and light deprivation in the mouse. *Experimental Brain Research* **3,** 337–352.

Valverde, F., and Marcos, A. R. (1967). Light deprivation and the spines of apical dendrites in the visual cortex of the mouse. *Anatomical Record* **157,** 392.

Van Hof-Van Duin, J. (1976). Early and permanent effects of monocular deprivation on pattern discrimination and visuomotor behavior in cats. *Brain Research* **111,** 261–276.

Van Sluyters, R. C. (1978). Reversal of the physiological effects of brief periods of monocular deprivation in the kitten. *Journal of Physiology (London)* **284,** 1–17.

Van Sluyters, R. C., and Blakemore, C. (1973). Experimental creation of unusual neuronal properties in visual cortex of kitten. *Nature (London)* **246,** 506–508.

Van Sluyters, R. C., and Levitt, F. B. (1980). Experimental strabismus in the kitten. *Journal of Neurophysiology* **43,** 686–699.

von Holst, E., and Mittelstaedt, H. (1950). Das Reafferenzprinzip (Wechselwirkungen zwischen Zentralnervensystem und Peripherie). *Naturwissenschaften* **37,** 464–476.

von Hungen, K., Roberts, S., and Hill, D. F. (1975). Serotonin-sensitive adenylate cyclase activity in immature rat brain. *Brain Research* **84,** 257–267.

von Noorden, G. K., Crawford, M. L. J., and Middleditch, P. R. (1977). Effect of lid suture on retinal ganglion cells in *Macaca mulatta*. *Brain Research* **122,** 437–444.

Walter, D. S., and Eccleston, D. (1973). Increase of noradrenaline metabolism following electrical stimulation of the *locus coeruleus* in the rat. *Journal of Neurochemistry* **21,** 281–289.

Walton, K. G., Miller, E., and Baldessarini, R. J. (1979). Prenatal and early postnatal β-adrenergic receptor-mediated increase of cyclic AMP in slices of rat. *Brain Research* **177**, 515–522.

Waterhouse, B., and Woodward, D. J. (1980). Interaction of norepinephrine with cerebrocortical activity evoked by stimulation of somatosensory afferent pathways in the rat. *Experimental Neurology* **67**, 11–34.

Watkins, D. W., Wilson, J. R., and Sherman, S. M. (1978). Receptive-field properties of neurons in binocular and monocular segments of striate cortex in cats raised with binocular lid suture. *Journal of Neurophysiology* **41**, 322–337.

Wendlandt, S., Crow, T. J., and Stirling, R. V. (1977). The involvement of the noradrenergic system arising from the locus coeruleus in the postnatal development of the cortex in rat brain. *Brain Research* **125**, 1–9.

Wickelgren, B. G., and Sterling, P. (1969). Effect on the superior colliculus of cortical removal in visually deprived cats. *Nature (London)* **224**, 1032–1033.

Wiersma, C. A. G., and Ikeda, K. (1964). Interneurons commanding swimmeret movements in the crayfish *Procambarus clarkii* (Girard). *Comparative Biochemistry and Physiology* **12**, 509–525.

Wiesel, T. N., and Hubel, D. H. (1963a). Effects of visual deprivation on morphology and physiology of cells in the cat's lateral geniculate body. *Journal of Neurophysiology* **26**, 978–993.

Wiesel, T. N., and Hubel, D. H. (1963b). Single-cell responses in striate cortex of kittens deprived of vision in one eye. *Journal of Neurophysiology* **26**, 1003–1017.

Wiesel, T. N., and Hubel, D. H. (1965). Comparison of the effects of unilateral and bilateral eye closure on cortical unit responses in kittens. *Journal of Neurophysiology* **28**, 1029–1040.

Wiesel, T. N., and Hubel, D. H. (1974). Ordered arrangement of orientation columns in monkeys lacking visual experience. *Journal of Comparative Neurology* **158**, 307–318.

Wiesel, T. N., Hubel, D. H., and Lam, D. M. K. (1974). Autoradiographic demonstration of ocular-dominance columns in the monkey striate cortex by means of trans-neuronal transport. *Brain Research* **79**, 273–279.

Winfield, D. A. (1981). The postnatal development of synapses in the visual cortex of the cat and the effects of eyelid closure. *Brain Research* **206**, 166–171.

Wirz-Justice, A., Krauchi, K., Lichtsteiner, M., and Feer, H. (1978). Is it possible to modify serotonin receptor sensitivity? *Life Sciences* **23**, 1249–2154.

Wise, R. A. (1978). Catecholamine theories of reward: A critical review. *Brain Research* **152**, 215–247.

Wong-Riley, M.T. T. (1976). Endogenous peroxidatic activity in brain stem neurons as demonstrated by their staining with diaminobenzidine in normal squirrel monkeys. *Brain Research* **108**, 257–277.

Wong-Riley, M. (1979). Changes in the visual system of monocularly sutured or enucleated cats demonstrable with cytochrome oxidase histochemistry. *Brain Research* **171**, 11–28.

Yamamoto, M., Chan-Palay, V., Steinbusch, H. W. M., and Palay, S. L. (1980). Hyperinnervation of arrested granule cells produced by the transplantation of monoamine-containing neurons into the fourth ventricle of rat. *Anatomy and Embryology* **159**, 1–15.

Yinon, U. (1975). Eye rotation in developing kittens. The effect on ocular dominance and receptive field organization of cortical cells. *Experimental Brain Research* **24**, 215–218.

Yinon, U. (1976). Eye rotation surgically induced in cats modifies properties of cortical neurons. *Experimental Neurology* **51**, 603–627.

York, D. H. (1972). Dopamine receptor blockade—A central action of chlorpromazine in striatal neurons. *Brain Research* **37**, 91–99.

Zecevic, N. R., and Molliver, M. E. (1978). The origin of the monoaminergic innervation of immature rat neocortex: An ultrastructural analysis following lesions. *Brain Research* **150**, 387–397.

PROGRESS IN PSYCHOBIOLOGY AND PHYSIOLOGICAL PSYCHOLOGY, VOL. 10

Behavioral Analysis of CNS Pathways and Transmitter Systems Involved in Conduction and Inhibition of Pain Sensations and Reactions in Primates

Charles J. Vierck, Jr.
Department of Neuroscience and Center for Neurobiological Sciences
University of Florida College of Medicine
Gainesville, Florida

Brian Y. Cooper
Department of Neuroscience and Center for Neurobiological Sciences
University of Florida College of Medicine
Gainesville, Florida

Ove Franzén
Department of Psychology
University of Uppsala
Uppsala, Sweden

Louis A. Ritz
Department of Physiology
School of Medicine
University of North Carolina
Chapel Hill, North Carolina

Joel D. Greenspan
Department of Physiology
School of Medicine
University of North Carolina
Chapel Hill, North Carolina

ISBN 0-12-542110-9

One hundred and twenty years after Fechner's proposal of a logarithmic law relating sensory intensity to stimulus intensity, the feasibility of demonstrating a universal psychophysical law of sensation magnitude is hotly debated (Marks, 1974; Warren, 1981). Regardless of the variety of methods available to measure sensory capabilities, it is not possible to know if we all have identical sensory experiences, even under identical sampling conditions. This is true, in part, because of the unique biases we have developed from different personal histories. The attempt to eliminate all biases of subjects, in search of an absolute law, is tantamount to eliminating individual differences. On the other hand, the psychophysical methods that have been developed to characterize sensory experiences are powerful tools for explicating the changes in sensory representation of a stimulus continuum that follow manipulations of the sensory coding apparatus. Although each method incorporates biases which influence the absolute determination of sensory magnitude, secure statements can be made as to whether the growth of sensation is increased or decreased, whether the sensitivity range is altered, and whether different portions of the sensory continuum are differentially affected. In addition, most of the psychophysical techniques are applicable to nonhuman subjects (Stebbins, 1970), permitting close comparison of behavioral and neurophysiological functions and allowing accurate anatomical correlations.

The purpose of this paper is to review an animal model of pain reactivity that is employed in order to reveal principles governing neural coding and modulation of pain sensations. Because we cannot know the private sensory experiences of any animal other than ourselves, the phrase "pain reactivity" is used generically to refer to behaviors produced by stimulation that normal human subjects define as aversive. These behaviors constitute operational definitions (or reflections) of pain sensations for both human and nonhuman primates. That is, pain intensity is assumed to influence the timing, frequency, and intensity of the pain reactions. It is possible that the pain reactions could be modulated by direct influences on the activity of motor systems, leaving pain sensations intact, but it is a reasonable working assumption that pain reactions are not generated in the absence of pain sensations. The validity of the operational definitions depends upon the accuracy with which we identify behavioral reactions that are elicited or affected uniquely (in a given situation) by pain.

Pain has been regarded as especially problematic, in terms of an appropriate animal model, because analysis seems to rely critically upon category rating and magnitude estimation—psychophysical techniques that cannot be applied in the same form (requiring verbal instruction and/or responses) to human and nonhuman subjects. However, by comparisons of human and monkey performances in similar circumstances, it is possible to describe patterns of behavior that indicate the presence and magnitude of pain. Recognizing that the experience is somewhat unique for each animal and that every subject may emit an individualized pattern of behavior in response to controlled stimuli, our animal model for the study of pain permits the following goals to be realized: (*a*) The test situation is adapted to the subject in such a way that real but bearable pain is evoked; that is, the test situation is tolerable, and yet truly painful stimuli are delivered. (*b*) The characteristics of pain reactions are compared with similar motor responses to nonaversive stimuli for positive reinforcers. (*c*) An individual's pain reaction profile is evaluated for consistency, once it is established, over long periods of testing. (*d*) We determine whether each response profile is sensitive to manipulations that are effective in altering human pain. (*e*) We assess whether different response measures reflect different components of the pain experience. (*f*) The animal model is evaluated for coherence of the human and nonhuman effects, to determine whether the same types of behavior are affected similarly in the different species by similar treatments.

I. Normal Sensitivity and Reactivity to Focal Electrical Stimulation

A. The Pain Stimulus

One of the most difficult choices in the development of a pain model concerns selection of the stimulus. Ordinarily, the adequate stimulus for pain is tissue destruction, to which small-diameter nociceptors are especially sensitive. Following thermal, mechanical, or chemical trauma sufficient to cause inflammation or disruption of the tissue, the pain lingers and the stimulus site becomes sensitized. The sensation does not terminate with cessation of the stimulus or shortly thereafter, and the experimenter cannot use the same stimulus site for subsequent trials. Brief thermal stimuli within a range of 45–50° C produce pain with only mild inflammation and no detectable long-term tissue damage. However, spanning the entire range of thermal pain experiences (up to maximal pain tolerance) is not feasible (Hardy *et al.,* 1952), the onset is slow by conventional methods of stimulus control, and suppression or sensitization is observed with repeated stimulation (LaMotte and Campbell, 1978; Perl *et al.,* 1976). The gradual increase of thermal stimuli from an adapting temperature is problematic in laboratory animal experiments, in which anticipatory (avoidance) responses can be misinterpreted as escape responses. Also, the gradual onset of thermal stimuli does not facilitate analysis of reflexes or neurophysiological potentials as time-locked responses to a given temperature. Nevertheless, thermal stimuli can be used effectively in some paradigms (e.g., Casey *et al.,* 1981; Hayes *et al.,* 1979), and heat-evoked pain is of interest as a model involving activation of small myelinated (A delta) and unmyelinated (C) afferents.

There are a number of advantages that accrue from the focal passage of electrical current across the skin as a stimulus for pain. The current can be regulated and maintained with precision, and the intended value can be achieved within microseconds of stimulus onset. The stimulus is equally rapid in offset, permitting the subject immediate termination of the most salient sensation elicited. With judicious choice of the duration and frequency of current pulses or oscillations, stimulus intensity can be varied from below the detection threshold, through the pain detection threshold, to the pain tolerance threshold without traumatizing or sensitizing the skin. Because the stimulus is a discrete, time-locked event, the synchronized neural activity evoked by a brief train of current pulses can be charted through the nervous system with precision, using computerized averaging techniques. Painful intensities of electrical stimulation elicit activity in both large- and small-diameter peripheral afferents, but this is not abnormal for pain stimuli in the natural environment. Pain is often produced by abrupt contact of an object with the integument, producing synchronous excitation of touch and pain receptors, and the interaction of large and small fiber inputs in the determination of pain intensity is an important issue (Melzack and Wall, 1965; Zotterman, 1939).

When 60-Hz (AC) electric shock is delivered to a subject, it is commonly presented continuously, until an escape response is emitted or until the trial terminates; maximum trial durations usually exceed 5 seconds. In a series of psychophysical experiments, we have determined that continuous shock at 60 Hz can produce significant adaptation within the first second. However, a relatively constant intensity of sensation is obtained with intermittent stimulation. This has the further advantage of minimizing the buildup of heat and the skin trauma that can result. Brief (e.g., 0.5 msec) square pulses at low frequencies or in short trains produce maximal sensory effects with minimal trauma (Gibson, 1968). After trying a variety of frequency parameters on ourselves, at different intensities within our pain sensitivity range, we have settled on the following pattern: 50-msec trains of 0.5-msec duration pulses at 200 Hz (or three cycles of 60 Hz) with an intertrain interval of 200 msec. It is our impression that temporal summation of AC or pulsed current occurs for only a brief period (approximately 50 msec), and adaptation can be minimized by a silent period. Administering a 50-msec train every quarter of a second has the following practical advantages: (*a*) A period of 200 msec or more of silence permits recording of intermediate components of cerebral-evoked potentials. (*b*) Since minimal reaction times on somatosensory detection tasks are less than 250 msec, the subject can avoid the second stimulus train in a trial, restricting the pain input to one brief event. (*c*) The possibility of motoric "freezing" during shock is minimized by intermittent stimulation. We have used up to a 1-sec intertrain interval in our paradigm (Lineberry and Vierck, 1975), but shorter intervals are preferable.

B. The Pain Sensitivity Range

Having decided on the frequency parameters of shock, it is necessary to define the pain sensitivity range of the subjects. The *pain sensitivity range* is defined by stimulus intensities between pain detection and pain tolerance thresholds (Gelfand, 1964). For our human subjects, initial exposure to the electrical stimulation is given with an ascending series by the method of limits, providing complete control by the subject of the maximal stimulus delivered. The subject can terminate the shock by pulling a Lindsley manipulandum; otherwise stimulation continues for a maximal trial duration of 5 sec. The first trial involves nonpainful stimulation (e.g., 1 mA). Subsequent trials involve shocks at higher levels (increased by 1 mA for each trial) until the subject requests that the series be terminated. The subjects are instructed to prevent presentation of an intensity above their tolerance threshold. The major advantage of the method of limits is that it allows us to plot the time course of threshold drift with high temporal resolution. The threshold estimates are biased high (because of the exclusive use of ascending series), but we are not concerned, at this point, with absolute threshold values. It is relative changes in threshold that are of interest, because substantial criterion shifts occur as a subject becomes accustomed to shock.

Mean pain tolerance thresholds for naive subjects, in the first session of approximately 30 trials and five threshold series, are bimodal, at 12 and 25 mA DC. Over a series of repeated sessions, tolerance thresholds increase beyond 42 mA DC. At 42 mA, the subjects typically terminate trials before the second stimulus train. Stimulation below 12 mA DC elicits an abrupt, tingling sensation that seems intolerable to some naive subjects but is barely painful to experienced ones. As the feeling associated with low intensity shock becomes familiar, it is recognized as a distinct, nonpainful sensation that grows with stimulus intensity along with a painful quality that is added at high current values. Experienced subjects describe the sensation evoked by 42 mA DC trains as strong to very strong, but tolerable pain. This represents the desired endpoint of our stimulus series. It is important to recognize that the intensity of the sensation depends upon current density and therefore electrode configuration (see also Gould *et al.*, 1978). Assuming that the major portion of effective current (i.e., the area of current flow eliciting sensation) is defined by the area of the cathode, our DC current densities range from 0.4 to 2.1 mA/mm^2 (using 5-mm-diameter wells of conductive paste spaced 30 mm apart).

Figure 1 presents the results of a human psychophysical evaluation of the magnitude of pain elicited by single 50-msec trains of constant current shock delivered to the lateral calf. To compare DC pulses with the more commonly used alternating current, AC and DC trains of different intensities are presented in random sequence, with 60-msec intertrial intervals. Six magnitudes of AC trains (1.5, 2.5, 5, 8, 14, and 25 mA) and an equal number of DC magnitudes (7.5, 11, 15, 21, 30, and 42 mA) are intermixed over sessions of 48 trials. The subjects attach a verbal label to each sensation, and they draw a line that is considered proportional in length to the magnitude of the sensation (free magnitude estimation). The list of verbal descriptors defines pain detection and pain tolerance thresholds as endpoints of a continuum from very, very weak to very, very strong pain.

Category rating by verbal descriptors is unique to human subjects and can serve as a valuable referent for other measures of pain reactivity. For our experienced subjects, pain detection thresholds average 6 mA Ac (0.3 mA/mm^2) and 12 mA DC (0.6 mA/mm^2). Shock intensities below the pain detection threshold are felt as a mild tingling that seems localized to a fine point. Pain at the detection threshold is a sharp, irritating, clearly localized sensation that is devoid of a thermal quality. The transition from nonpainful to painful tingling is not abrupt, and yet the discriminability of the different stimuli is excellent. This is particularly evident within a method of limits series (during preliminary testing), in which each successive trial is clearly more intense than the preceding trial, but the relative painfulness is less clear. Increases in the intensity of tingling contribute to intensity discrimination in much the same way that pressure sensations interact with pain in a series of nonnoxious and noxious pressures applied to the skin. With in-

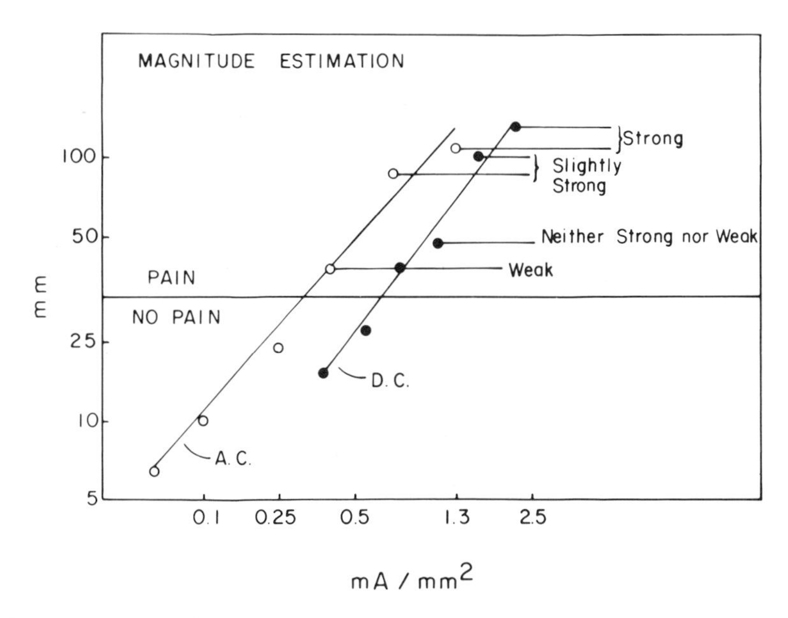

FIG. 1. Responses of two human subjects to single trains of electrocutaneous stimulation to the lateral calf. Trials were presented at 60-sec intervals and consisted of three AC cycles (50 msec) at one of six intensities or 50 msec of 0.5-msec DC pulses at 200 Hz and one of six intensities. The 12 types of trials were randomly ordered. (*a*) The subjects rated the magnitude of each stimulus by drawing a line. The length of the line was to be proportional to the intensity of the sensation. (*b*) Following each trial and line drawing, the subjects chose one of nine verbal descriptors judged to describe most closely the sensation intensity. The verbal descriptors help to locate each stimulus within the pain sensitivity range of these experienced subjects. The free magnitude estimation procedure indicates the relative growth of sensation magnitude for AC and DC stimuli.

creases of pain intensity within and above the middle portion of the pain sensitivity range, a thermal component is noticed, particularly with AC stimulation. At the highest intensities delivered, the sensation increases in apparent area but is localized clearly on the lateral calf and does not radiate up or down the leg. The sensation is startling. There is no after-sensation at low intensities of pain, but an after-sensation occurs at high stimulus levels. The highest intensities in our series generally elicit ratings of strong pain, occasionally very strong, seldom very very strong, and never intolerable (Vierck *et al.*, 1980).

Comparison of 60-Hz AC and 200-Hz DC trains reveals a greater sensitivity to the AC shock, as measured by free magnitude estimation or verbal descriptors. It is likely that this difference is related to the greater amount of current passed during 60-Hz trains and the more pronounced thermal component to the sensation evoked by the sine waves. In any case, the verbal description and magnitude estimation procedures each contribute useful and complementary definitions of the pain sensitivity range, of AC and DC currents that produce sensations of comparable intensity, and of the growth of pain magnitude within the pain sensitivity range.

The psychophysical technique of magnitude estimation cannot be utilized, in its ideal form, with nonhuman subjects, because it relies on instructing the subjects to make ratio judgments. In fact, human subjects tend to adjust their numerical values to the range of stimuli presented (Marks, 1974), and wide variability in the slopes of stimulus–response functions has been reported for different individuals, different experiments, and different psychophysical methods utilizing a given sensory continuum (Greenspan, 1980; Kruger and Kenton, 1973; Knibestol and Vallbo, 1980). Thus, from our point of view, the value of magnitude estimation does not lie in defining *the* psychophysical power function for a modality; rather, it lies in allowing assessment of relative changes in sensitivity *throughout a stimulus continuum,* following experimental manipulation. In this sense, a form of magnitude estimation (without instructions) can be applied to nonhuman subjects if they "naturally" regulate the magnitude, frequency, or latency of some response to stimuli along a continuum.

C. Pain Reactions

Identification by an observer of pain experienced by another individual is made on the basis of an array of pain reactions, including somatic reflex withdrawal, autonomic activation, overt escape and/or avoidance, and an exaggeration of relevant behaviors in proportion to the perceived intensity of pain. The observer would tend not to believe a verbal report of intense pain that is given in a calm voice, without motoric evidence of exaggerated affect. Conversely, the observer can be certain that pain has been experienced when the individual reacts strenuously, even when an overt verbal rating of the stimulus is not offered. Input to the central nervous system (CNS) from nociceptors arouses a subject much more than maximal input from non-nociceptors, and it should be possible to take advantage of this feature in a laboratory animal model of pain reactivity. However, it should be recognized that any specific pain reaction can be suppressed by a given individual in a particular situation. For example, a person may have been taught not to display discomfort, or the flexion reflex can be inhibited when it would be maladaptive, or exaggeration of one behavior may mask influences of pain on a second behavior. Hence, it is important that an operational definition of pain reactions (*a*) be based upon multiple response measures, and (*b*) allow for different profiles of responsivity on different measures by individual animals.

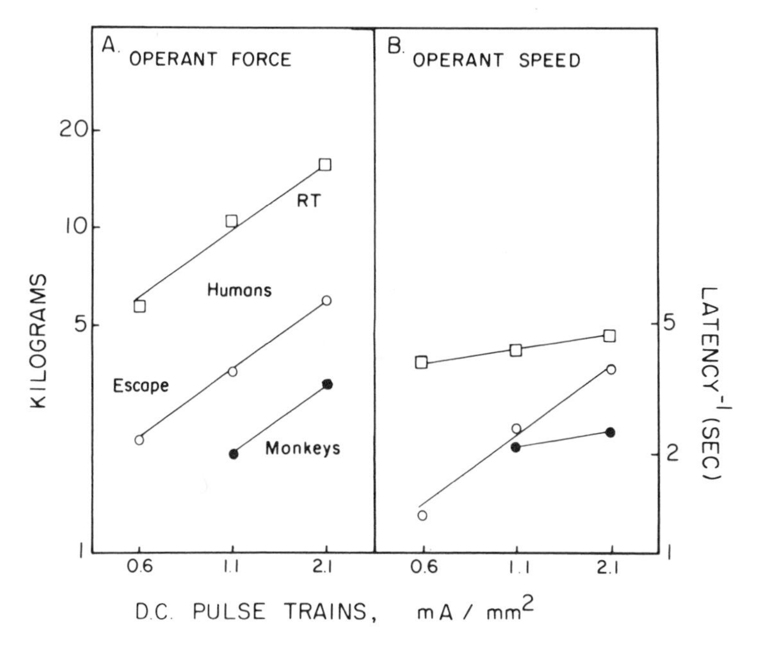

FIG. 2. Three human subjects and four *M. speciosa* monkeys pulled a lever to terminate DC trains of electrical stimulation to the lateral calf. The human subjects performed in separate sessions under two sets of instructions, labeled "RT" (reaction time; open squares; "terminate each stimulus as quickly as you can") or "escape" (open circles; "terminate the stimuli if and when you wish"). (A) The force of operant escape reactions is plotted as a function of current in milliamperes. Instructions to respond quickly increased escape force at all intensities. The slopes of the escape force vs. stimulus intensity functions are similar for monkeys (filled circles) and for humans performing under either set of instructions. These monkeys frequently did not respond to 12 mA, and therefore reliable force and latency values are not available for the low intensity of shock. (B) Operant escape "speed" (one/response latency) vs. stimulus intensity functions are influenced in magnitude and slope by instructions. The monkeys appear predisposed to respond quickly, and stimulus intensity affects response speed with a slope similar to that of humans performing under reaction time instructions.

Electrical stimulation of the skin recruits activity in peripheral fibers in inverse proportion to their diameter, and pain intensity is related to the amount of activity in the smallest somesthetic afferents (Hallin and Torebjork, 1976; Torebjork and Hallin, 1976). As the intensity of pain increases, motivation increases to terminate the stimulus quickly, and the subject becomes more strongly aroused to vigorous action. Thus, the speed and force of an operant escape reaction could be proportional to the intensity of shock in the pain sensitivity range. Figure 2 demonstrates these relationships for human and monkey subjects performing an escape response to shock trains. The human subjects are not instructed to control their responses in proportion to stimulus intensity; they are told simply to terminate a trial if and when they wish (escape paradigm) or to terminate each trial as quickly as possible (reaction time paradigm). Clearly, the approach of a subject to the task (as manipulated by instructions to humans) influences the slope of the relationship between shock intensity and escape latency.

On the reaction time paradigm, the motor systems are primed and the decision to emit an operant response is made before stimulus onset. On the escape paradigm, latencies to low-intensity stimulation include a protracted decision time for sensations that are questionably painful. The slope of operant response "speed" (1/latency) vs. stimulus intensity is relatively flat for humans on the reaction time task and for *Macaca speciosa* monkeys (stump-tailed Macaques) performing with the same manipulandum and paradigm (Fig. 2B; Vierck *et al.*, 1980). These monkeys respond somewhat digitally with respect to operant speed; that is, they respond quickly or withhold responding for the trial duration. This is apparent at near-threshold intensities (12 mA DC or 4 mA AC) when the distributions of shock duration are bimodal, at 5 sec and less than 500 msec. It should be recognized that many "latency" measurements in the literature represent a confounding of escape tendency (percentage of responses) and response latency. This combined measure should be termed "trial duration," rather than "escape latency" (Vierck and Luck, 1979). Trial durations are determined almost entirely by response percentage (Levine *et al.*, 1980), which is less sensitive than response latency to manipulations of pain sensitivity (see below).

The force of operant escape responses reflects shock intensity with high sensitivity for humans performing under either set of instructions. The slopes of the force vs. shock intensity functions are identical when subjects are given escape or reaction time instructions. The force of escape responses is increased at each stimulus intensity by telling the subjects always to respond quickly. The stump-tailed macaques produce the same slope of response force vs. shock current as human subjects, suggesting that the measurement of escape force reflects a generalizable process of motor activation that bears a predictable relationship to pain intensity. A similar correspondence of escape thresholds is obtained for monkey and human subjects. Escape thresholds (50% escape responses) for monkeys in our paradigm average 4 mA for AC trains (0.20 mA/mm^2) and 9 mA (0.46 mA/mm^2) for DC trains (see also Lineberry and Kulics, 1978). Slightly higher thresholds are obtained for humans as defined by sensory verbal descriptors (0.32 mA/mm^2 AC and 0.65 mA/mm^2 DC). The latency and force functions do not plateau at high intensities for the monkey or human subjects on the escape paradigm, suggesting that the pain sensitivity range is comparable in these primates. This relationship is predicted by similarities in the characteristics of peripheral afferents (Kumazawa and Perl, 1977; Torebjork and Hallin, 1976) and the form of psychophysical functions (LaMotte and Campbell, 1978) for monkeys and man.

D. Other Paradigms and Methods of Stimulation

In comparison to the shock parameters used and the escape threshold values reported in an extensive literature involving laboratory animal models of punishment or pain, the present results and other monkey and human psychophysical studies (Lineberry and Kulics, 1978; Tursky, 1974) define a high pain sensitivity range. This is an issue that is critical to the most fundamental interpretations of many investigations, and it raises several methodological questions that are pivotal to an understanding of the behavior of animals receiving electrical stimulation. First, the use of naive or experienced subjects is an important determinant of the pain perceived (and therefore the magnitude of the punishment effect). On our paradigm, the pain tolerance threshold for many of the naive human subjects (12 mA DC or 0.6 mA/mm^2) is comparable to the pain detection threshold of experienced subjects. If the use of a group comparison design dictates that a small number of shock trials be distributed over a single session, then administration of less than 0.6 mA/mm^2 of AC shock is advised. Stimulation below 4 mA AC with our electrodes can be interpreted as painful by a naive subject because of the abrupt, novel characteristics of the sensation, and humane considerations dictate that the minimal effective stimulus be utilized in these investigations. On the other hand, experienced subjects regard intensities below 4 mA as nonpainful. Thus, if an investigation utilizes control tests with naive subjects, followed by a series of tests with experimental treatments, the changing criteria for pain will be confounded with any treatment effects. The behavior of naive subjects is especially variable because of wide differences in interpretation of stimuli at or below pain detection thresholds of experienced subjects. The stimulus intensities appropriate for naive subjects do not elicit activity in a substantial proportion of small myelinated or unmyelinated nociceptive afferents.

Considerable interest has been focused on a demonstration of shock-maintained responding as an exception to the rule that aversive stimuli are negatively reinforcing (Kelleher and Morse, 1968). The subjects (commonly monkeys) undergo a *long period of training* that eventually leads them to self-administer brief AC shock at levels of up to 6 mA, delivered via brass electrodes in contact with approximately 200 mm^2 of the tail (0.03 mA/mm^2). The interpretation is offered that the animals learn to self-administer pain when it provides certain secondary advantages (e.g., signaling a safe period; Hendry, 1969) or because the pain defines a schedule that is capable of determining behavior (Malagodi *et al.,* 1981). However, if the sensation for experienced monkeys approximates that of humans, the monkeys should regard this sensation as a tingle, followed by adaptation and even disappearance of the sensation, if stimulation is continued beyond several hundred milliseconds. Thus, it has not been shown that the monkeys repeatedly self-administer pain. However, there are situations in which humans self-administer mild pain or subpainful dysesthesias. For example, there is a tendency to test a sore tooth by periodic manipulation with the tongue. Often it is adaptive to exercise a damaged region, both to confirm the presence of pain (and the need for caution) and to titrate motor activity to the maximally tolerable limit (e.g., when a limb is injured and should be exercised to avoid contractures).

A large number of studies have utilized "scrambled" shock to the feet of animals (commonly rodents) via metal rods that constitute the floor of an experimental chamber. A number of considerations argue against this approach. Because of the large surface area of skin in contact with the floor, current density is relatively low, and because the current is conducted throughout the body, it would be lethal to raise the stimulus intensity sufficiently to generate painful current densities at the skin–"electrode" interface. For safety, electrical stimulation should be applied focally, via adjacent bipolar leads from an isolated source to an ungrounded subject. Metal electrodes can produce irregularities in current density and, therefore, inconsistency in the sensation elicited (Gibson, 1968). Delivering stimulation through wells of electrode paste eliminates "hot spots" and stabilizes skin impedence, which influences sensation intensity (Lineberry and Kulics, 1978; Tursky, 1974). Also, the area of electrode–skin contact must be controlled in order to elicit a given sensation magnitude, and this will vary tremendously as an animal walks over electrified bars. Finally, the animal is placed in a conflict situation when grid shock is intended to elicit or reinforce activity. If the animal remains motionless and maximizes the area of skin in contact with the grid, the sensation should be minimal and should adapt, because the stimulation is continuous in most experiments. Movement, on the other hand, will deliver variable duration trains of stimulation to different locations, minimizing adaptation and occasionally delivering high-density current.

A common operant approach to the study of pain in laboratory animals has been to titrate or track thresholds for escape of shock intensities that are varied by the up-and-down or staircase method (Weiss and Laties, 1963; Yaksh, 1978). The critical assumption that these thresholds represent pain thresholds appears to be violated by this procedure, as evidenced by the low levels of current reported as liminal values. An approximate range of 0.4–2.1 mA is reported for threshold values in monkeys, using metal shoes as electrodes (up to 0.002 mA/mm^2). It is understandable that titrated shock thresholds would be held below pain threshold by the animals, because they are permitted control of the stimulus values delivered. If the subject responds to low intensities on an ascending series, then the next series (descending) begins at lower values than would occur if the animal terminated the ascending series at a high value. Similarly, continued responding on a descending series, until low levels are presented, ensures that the next (ascending) series will start low. It is to be expected that the animals would (*a*) produce titrated thresholds comparable to shock detection (i.e., tingle detection) thresholds, as low as 0.005 mA/mm^2 (100 4 A with our electrodes); (*b*) the animals could manipulate the stimuli presented within the range of intensities that support shock-maintained responding and presumably have positively reinforcing qualities.

Whether or not titrated escape thresholds can be regarded as valid estimates of pain thresholds, it is apparent that pain detection thresholds serve as highly impoverished models of pain and insensitive indicants of analgesia (Beecher, 1957; Lineberry and Vierck, 1975; Vierck *et al.*, 1971). From the applied point of view, optimal control of pain would attenuate responsivity to high levels of pain, leaving pain detection intact, to serve important protective functions. If the experimental model does not assess reactions to suprathreshold pain, a desired hypalgesia (decreased pain sensitivity) can be missed entirely, or an upward shift of the detection threshold, with increased reactivity at suprathreshold levels (hyperpathia), can be interpreted incorrectly as a global hypalgesia. Thus, it is important to span much of the pain sensitivity range in an experimental model that is tolerable to the subjects, and the method of adjusting the animal to the paradigm (and vice versa) is the key to achieving this goal.

E. Training Methods for an Escape Paradigm

Briefly, our method incorporates the following steps in a gradual shaping procedure: (*a*) After extended adaptation to the experimenter, the laboratory, and the testing apparatus, the monkeys learn to acquire food by pulling a Lindsley manipulandum (Fig. 3) during presentation of a tone, which is delivered at short and then longer intertrial intervals, up to 1 min. (*b*) After the bar response is firmly established, occurring at short latency during trials and infrequently between trials, weak shock is introduced, coincident with the tone. Both tone and shock are terminated by bar responses, and food reinforcement is continued during a long series of sessions in which the range of shock intensities is gradually increased. Each monkey is watched closely for maladaptive behavior (e.g., late responses during trials), and the shock range is adjusted down in the rare instances in which it occurs.

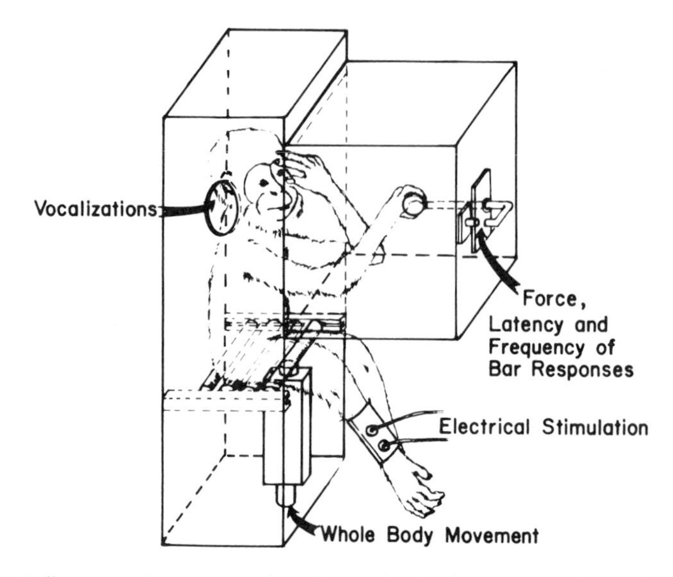

FIG. 3. A diagrammatic representation of a monkey in the testing chair, showing the location of instruments for measurement of pain reactions. Operant force is measured by a Statham gold cell transducer and a load cell assembly that serves as a stop for the bar when pulled toward the monkey. The frequency and latency of bar pulls are obtained from a switch closure that occurs before the bar contacts the load assembly. A gold cell placed under the free end of the hinged seat measures the peak force of reflex responses. A Schmitt trigger in the seat transducer circuit measures the frequency of major shifts in weight on the seat. A microphone records vocalization by the monkeys; a Schmitt trigger is set to record the occurrence of high-intensity sounds, reliably detecting vocalizations and rejecting other sounds in the chamber. Electrical stimulation is delivered via wells of conductive paste in foam pads that adhere to either lateral calf. The size of the electrodes is exaggerated in the figure, and the location shown is distal to the locus stimulated.

(*c*) When the animal is familiar with the full range of intensities, the tone and food reniforcement are faded out, and we are left with a simple escape paradigm. Important features of the training sequence are establishing the escape response before shock is introduced and providing ample experience with each successive level of stimulation in an ascending series. This ensures that the animals receive only escapable shock, in the sense that they are not in doubt concerning an adaptive response. The trials are paced at slow, regular intervals, because animals prefer predictable to unpredictable shock (Badia *et al.*, 1973), and the sessions are short (24 trials). Generally, monkeys are intolerant of punishment and will resist vigorously handlers and environments that have been associated with aversive events. However, our animals do not avoid handling or the test situation.

As observers of humans, pets, and livestock, which are subject to numerous nociceptive events in daily life, we realize that a wide variety of emotions and behaviors can be evoked by pain—e.g., fight or flight, anger, fear, or depression, dominance or submission, cursing or laughter, and barking or whining. This complexity and variability can lead to skepticism concerning the identification of reliably pain-related behaviors (Beecher, 1957). However, animals tend to adopt stereotyped behaviors in a given pain situation (Vierck and Cooper, 1980), leading to quick reactions to repetitions of pain in that particular context. There apears to be a "burning in" of each pattern of responding within a given pain context, even when the chosen response does not influence the stimulus (Hutchinson, 1977). Thus, in the development of an animal model, the particular response pattern emitted by an animal is of less concern than (*a*) differentiation of the magnitude of some response(s) with stimulus intensity, (*b*) consistency of the response pattern over time, and (*c*) sensitivity of the stimulus vs. response magnitude function to procedures known to influence pain. In practical terms, these considerations necessitate a reproducible pain context, a quantifiable stimulus, a readily available, adaptive response, and the capability of quantifying much of the behavior that is generated in the situation. When this is done, it is observed that no single behavioral measure is highly differentiated in magnitude or frequency with stimulus intensity for all animals, but that each animal differentiates one or more of the measures in a characteristic pattern that is consistent over time.

II. Effects of Direct CNS Intervention on Patterns of Pain Reactivity

A. Anterolateral Chordotomy

Anterolateral chordotomy is a surgical procedure that is known to diminish pain sensitivity contralateral to the lesion over dermatomes below the level of the lesion. Long-term quantitative evaluations of pain sensitivity in humans following chordotomy are not available, but pain detection thresholds are elevated and pain tolerance is increased for at least several months in most patients (White and Sweet, 1969). Substantial return of pain within 6 months is common, but an enduring (although partial) blunting may occur when the lesion is accurately placed (Nathan and Smith, 1979). The feasibility of daily testing and histological verification of the lesion in monkeys permits determination of the optimal lesion for long-term hypalgesia. The apparent similarity of the pain pathways in human and nonhuman primates (Kuru, 1949; Trevino and Carstens, 1975; Vierck and Luck, 1979; White and Sweet, 1969) can be tested by comparing the nature and time course of the defects in pain reactivity in monkeys and humans. Figure 4 presents the results of anterolateral chordotomy on pain reactivity measures from an *M. nemestrina* monkey (pigtailed Macaque) after right thoracic anterolateral chordotomy. The stimulus is 60-Hz AC trains at 4, 11,

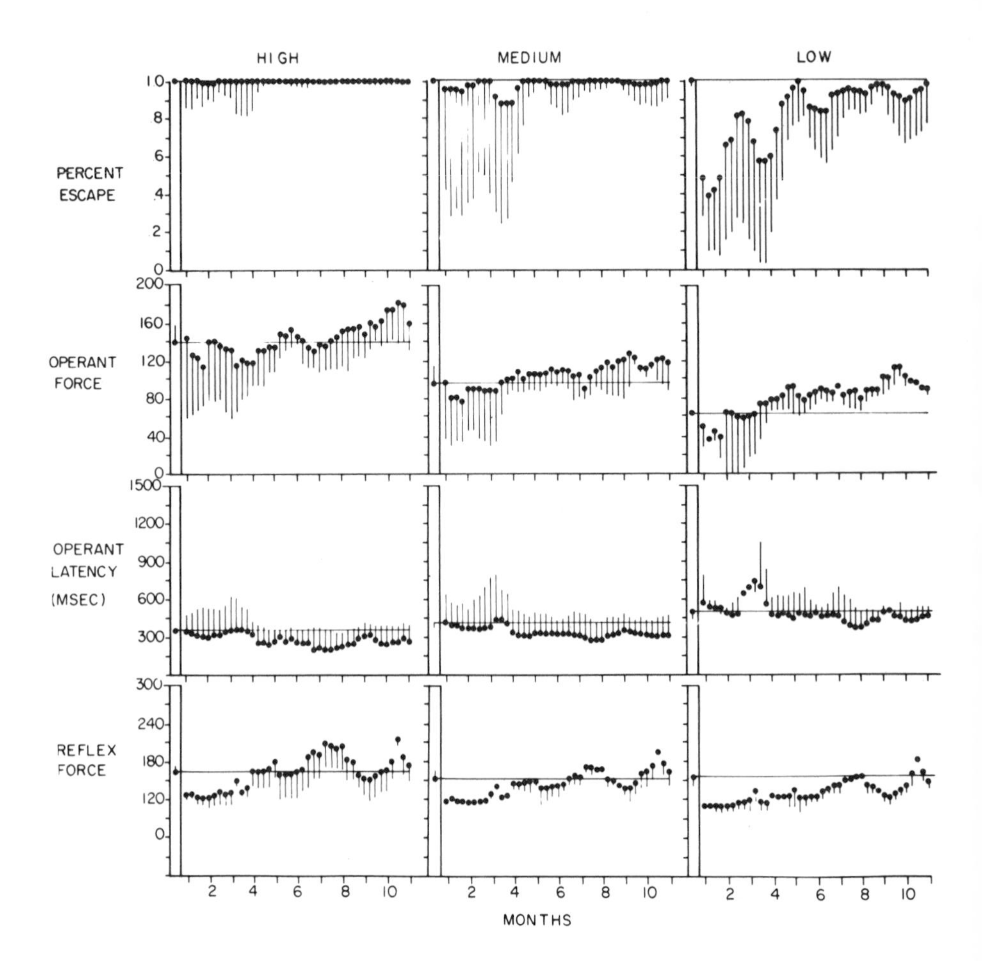

FIG. 4. The results of a thoracic spinal lesion involving one ventral quadrant are shown for four measures of pain reactivity in a single monkey. In this paradigm, AC stimulation at 4 mA (low), 11 mA (medium), and 25 mA (high) is delivered in blocks of four trials to one leg and then the other for a total of four blocks per leg per session. Each block of trials to one leg consists of the sequence 25, 11, 4, and 11 mA. Each data point on the graphs consists of the median from trials obtained over 1 month of testing; for the low and high intensities, 80 trials are obtained over a month (5 testing days per week); 160 trials at the medium intensity are obtained over the same period. In order to provide a sufficient data base for each point and to filter out high-frequency variability in the data, successive points in the postoperative period represent weekly increments of data collected over a month; that is, the first pair of points is from weeks 1–4, the second from weeks 2–5, the third from weeks 3–6, etc. Measurements from the leg ipsilateral to the lesion are plotted as dots. Data points from the contralateral leg are located at the end of the vertical lines connected to the dots; in this way, the consistency of differences between the legs over time can be appreciated readily, and the absolute values are also given. The data points to the left of the vertical line in each panel are obtained from the last month of stabilized preoperative testing; a horizontal line is carried through the postoperative period at the level on

or 25 mA, ordered in a sawtooth pattern, with alternate sequences of 25, 11, 4, and 11 mA presented to the left or right legs, for a total of 32 trials per session. The response measures for each shock intensity are percent escape responses (5-sec maximal trial duration), escape latency, escape force (measured by contact of the lever assembly with a Statham transducer and load cell), and reflex magnitude (measured as peak output, within 150 msec of trial onset, from a force transducer placed under the hinged seat of the testing chair).

The variety of changes in pain reactivity following chordotomy of the monkey shown in Fig. 4 are representative of effects observed frequently in a group of 10 chordotomized monkeys (Ritz *et al.*, 1981). All measures reveal a substantial hypalgesia contralateral to the lesion, relative to preoperative values from the same leg or as compared with postoperative measurements following ipsilateral stimulation. For both limbs, performance levels wax and wane over time to an exaggerated extent, although long periods of preoperative testing will be required to establish the relative magnitude of fluctuations in pain reactivity under normal and lesioned conditions. Oscillations of the capacity for sensory coding may represent a generalized feature of the injured spinal cord (Vierck, 1982) and may reflect cycles of synapsis and desynapsis that have been described following spinal cord injury (Bernstein and Bernstein, 1973). That is, the process of anatomical reorganization following spinal cord injury appears to involve cyclical sprouting and retraction of synaptic contacts rather than a permanent reinnervation of synaptic sites made available by the lesions. The cycles of behavioral reactivity are quite long (approximately 150 days for the monkey shown in Fig. 4), and therefore are not determined by the 4-week menstrual cycle (Tedford *et al.*, 1977).

For the animal depicted in Fig. 4, the operant measures (force, latency, and percentage of escape responses) reveal hypalgesia that is maximal up to 15 weeks following chordotomy. Chordotomy shifts the stimulus–response function to the right, as has been observed in patients with peripheral nerve lesions (Franzen and Lindblom, 1976). Pain reactions are attenuated

(Figure 4 continued)

the ordinate of the preoperative value from the ipsilateral leg. The horizontal line facilitates the determination of postoperative hyporeactivity or hyperreactivity relative to preoperative control measurements. For percentage of escape, operant force, and reflex force, hyporeactivity is indicated by down-going lines (the contralateral leg is less responsive than the ipsilateral leg) and by lower values relative to the preoperative score. For this graph, operant latency is not converted to speed, and therefore, hyporeactivity is indiciated by higher values (longer latencies). Hyporeactivity of the contralateral leg relative to the ipsilateral leg is clearly indicated by the observation that only 2 of the 492 comparisons represent a reversal from contralateral hyporeactivity. The oscillatory nature of the recovery process and the eventual development of ipsilateral hyperreactivity (relative to preoperative levels) are also apparent for this animal.

throughout the pain sensitivity range, but pain is not eliminated for strong stimuli. Beyond 5 months postoperatively, a small but consistent contralateral deficit is maintained up to at least 12 months of testing. Thus, as documented for human chordotomy patients, considerable recovery of pain sensitivity occurs (usually within 6 months; White and Sweet, 1969), but persistent hypalgesia can be present (Nathan and Smith, 1979). For each animal in our series, reactivity to near-threshold pain recovers more slowly than reactions to strong pain.

Because of the profound contralateral effects of chordotomy, it is easy to neglect the possibility that the relatively undisturbed ipsilateral side is affected by the lesion. However, a section of the ventral quadrant interrupts spinoreticular and spinothalamic fibers of ipsilateral origin and could produce hypalgesia (Fields *et al.,* 1975; Voris, 1957). Also, descending inhibition by a ventral noradrenergic pathway is diminished (Dahlström and Fuxe, 1965; Westlund and Coulter, 1980), which could produce hyperalgesia. These influences appear to cancel out in the early postoperative period, when each of our measures reveals no significant differences from control levels of reactivity, averaged across the group of chordotomized monkeys (Fig. 5).

B. Comparisons of Reflexive and Operant Pain Reactions

It is important, for the development of animal models of pain sensitivity, to determine the degree of correspondence between reflexive and nonreflexive measures of reaction to aversive stimuli. Considering the necessity for economy of neural connections in the spinal gray matter, it is conceivable that protective reflexes and rostral conduction of pain depend upon (*a*) the same population of neurons, with both local and long ascending axonal branches (Brown, 1981) or (*b*) different neurons that receive input from the same sources, in similar patterns. In either case, the preponderance of frankly reflexive or reflex-contaminated algesiometric methods (e.g., tail flick and skin twitch; Beecher, 1957; Grossman *et al.,* 1973; Yaksh, 1978) would be justified. Unfortunately, the reflexive and operant measures of reactivity to electrical stimulation have not covaried in response to any of the manipulations we have utilized to date. For example, different functions relate stimulus amplitude to (*a*) the magnitude of leg flexions occurring within 150 msec of stimulus onset and (*b*) the magnitude or latency of escape responses emitted by an unstimulated arm of the same animal more than 150 msec after the same stimulus train. Reflex responses grow more rapidly in amplitude with increases in shock strength up to the escape threshold (slope of 0.6; Cooper and Vierck, 1982) than with shock values within the pain sensitivity range (slope of 0.2; Fig. 5). In contrast, the force of the operant responses increases at the highest slope (0.5) with current levels of evoking moderate to strong pain (Fig. 5). Chordotomy reduces the force of flexion

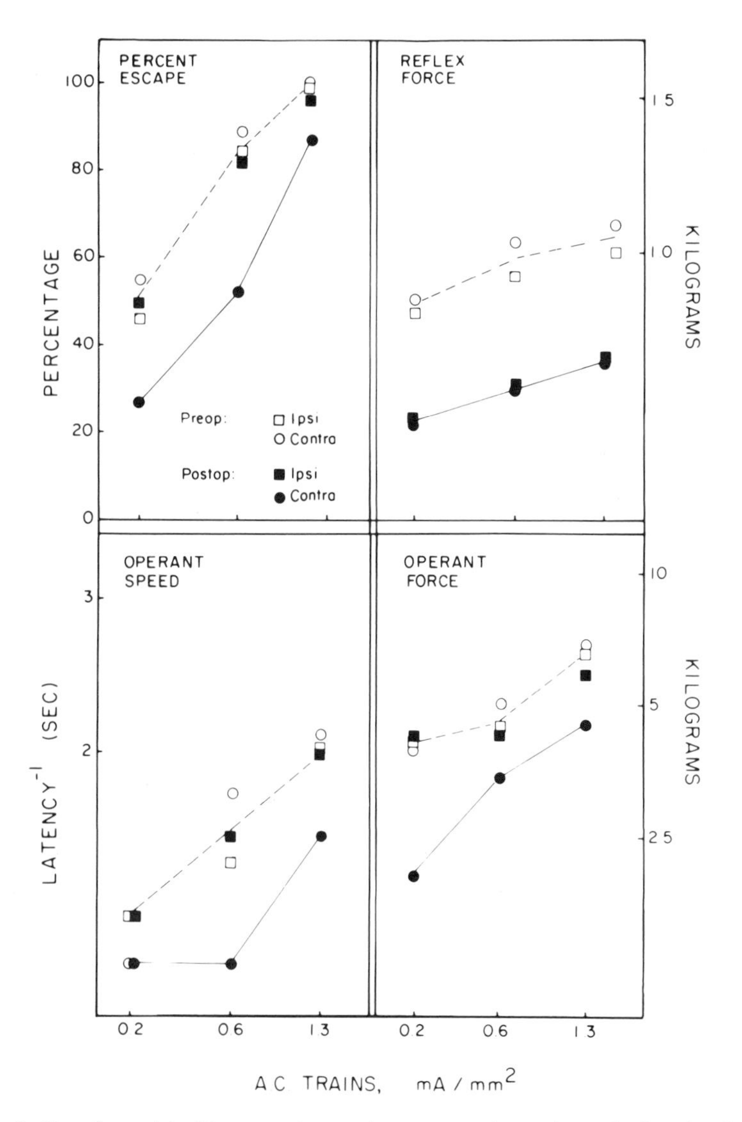

FIG. 5. Data from eight *M. nemestrina* monkeys, averaged over 1 month of testing, before (open symbols) or after (closed symbols) unilateral lesions of the anterolateral column or the ventral spinal quadrant at an upper thoracic level. For all measures, contralateral chordotomy produced hyporeactivity at all intensities of stimulation without appreciably altering the slope relating behavior to stimulus intensity. The magnitude of the averaged postoperative effect is not representative of subgroups of monkeys. Variability in the magnitude of the effect correlates with the size and locus of the lesion (fig. 7D–F). The slope of the behavior vs. stimulus functions is less characteristic of individual monkeys and correlates poorly with histological categories. For the three operant measures (percentage of escape and operant speed and force), ipsilateral reactivity was not significantly altered by the lesions, and the dashed line connects the median of the values from both legs preoperatively and the ipsilateral leg postoperatively. Reflex force was significantly diminished bilaterally by the chordotomy.

reflexes in response to near-threshold or strong, painful stimulation of either leg (Fig. 5). The incidence of ipsilateral reflex suppression (100%) contrasts sharply to a lack of strong evidence for ipsilateral hypalgesia, as indicated by the operant pain reactions. The reflex suppression is observed throughout the pain sensitivity range (Fig. 5).

The patterns of change in operant and reflexive pain reactions with extended testing following chordotomy are diagrammed in Table I. Following surgery, there is a generalized depression of reflex magnitude and a lateralized decrease in pain sensitivity. Ipsilateral operant reactions appear normal, but all other categories of early postoperative reaction are depressed for months. The long time course of functional recovery is similar to that of spatial–tactile discrimination following interruption of the dorsal spinal columns (Vierck, 1982). The postoperative period of recovery is expected to involve the following: (*a*) There is a temporary period of "shock" and trauma that depresses the activity of intact systems. These effects should be negligible within several weeks of surgery. (*b*) Anatomical reorganization is presumed to facilitate recovery by grossly redistributing information in response to synaptic losses (Goldberger and Murray, 1978) and by enhancing certain synaptic networks on the basis of repeated experience (Vrensen and Nunes Cardozo, 1981).

C. The Minimal Lesion Producing Permanent Analgesia

Following months of postchordotomy testing, the "stabilized" pattern of pain reactivity for most animals consists of ipsilateral hyperreflexia (and occasionally hyperalgesia) and contralateral hypalgesia. The contralateral attenuation of pain sensitivity is consistent with interruption of the neospinothalamic (lateral spinothalamic) tract and the contralateral component of the paleospinothalamic (sponoreticulothalamic) tract (Geisler *et al.*, 1981b; Kerr, 1975). However, the lack of permanent *analgesia* following

TABLE I
EFFECTS OF ANTEROLATERAL CHORDOTOMY

Lesion size/ measure	Early	Late
Ipsilateral		
Operant	—	↑?
Reflexive	↓↓	↑
Contralateral		
Operant	↓↓	↓
Reflexive	↓↓	—

chordotomy leaves us with the important task of determining the minimal lesion that will produce permanent and complete loss of pain—that is, to define the pain pathway(s). In addition to the contralateral spinothalamic tract, input from nociceptors is distributed to dorsal horn cells that project (*a*) bilaterally in the ventral quadrants (e.g., the spinoreticular tracts) and (*b*) ipsilaterally in the dorsal quadrant (e.g., the dorsal columns, Lissauer's tract, and the spinocervicothalamic tract).

Section of Lissauer's tract and the dorsal columns produces a significant and enduring decrease in operant vigor without changing the probablity of escaping electrical stimulation (Fig. 6; Vierck *et al.*, 1971). Because the lesion is placed between spinal levels supplying the stimulated legs and the responding arms, this effect represents attenuation of pain sensitivity and not a direct modulation of motor outflow; the response depression is observed only with ipsilateral stimulation, and the responding arm is the same with stimulation of either leg. This lasting deficit suggests the possibility that

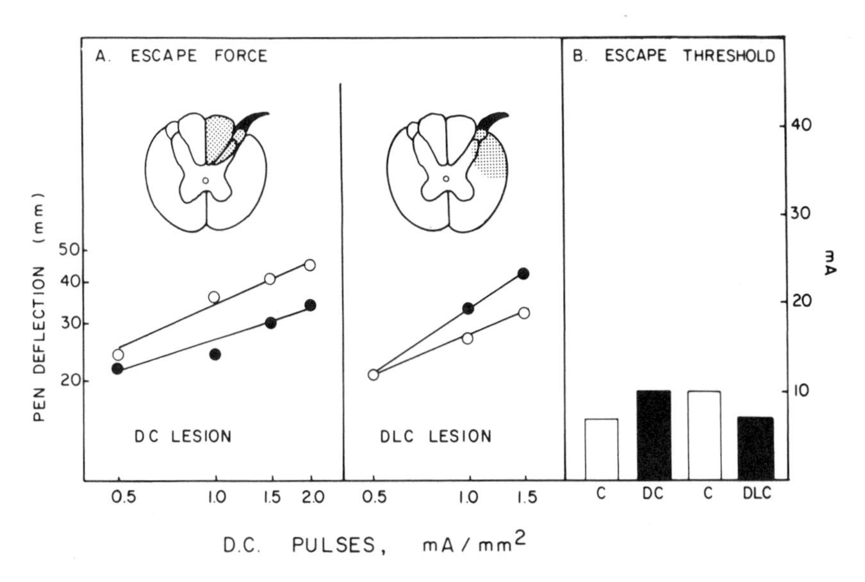

FIG. 6. Averaged data from three monkeys before and after receiving lesions of the ipsilateral dorsal column and Lissauer's tract (DC lesion) or of the ispilateral dorsolateral column and Lissauer's tract (DLC lesion). Each of the six animals showed significantly different levels of operant escape force, in the directions shown in panel A, following ipsilateral spinal lesion. Postoperative values are indicated by solid circles, and preoperative values (and/or contralateral postoperative scores) are represented by open circles. The DC plus Lissauer's lesion reliably reduced pain reactivity, as measured by operant force, but escape thresholds were unaffected by the lesion (panel B). The DLC plus Lissauer's lesion reliably increased pain reactivity, as indicated by operant force, but escape thresholds were unaffected by this lesion as well (panel B).

combining section of Lissauer's tract with chordotomy would eliminate recovery of pain, without adding unwanted deficits (Hyndman, 1942).

Bilateral section of Lissauer's tract in combination with complete contralateral chordotomy (Fig. 7B,C) does not eliminate pain reactivity. In addition, combining complete lesions of opposite dorsal and ventral quadrants (Fig. 7A) does not reduce pain reactivity permanently, indicating the nociceptive cells projecting into the ipsilateral dorsal column, dorsolateral column, and Lissauer's tract are not responsible for recovery of pain following chordotomy. Although the dorsal spinal pathways appear to contribute to the modulation of pain sensations and reactions, they are not necessary or sufficient for the rostral conduction of pain (Fig. 7A–D; Vierck and Luck,

I. LESIONS PRODUCING TEMPORARY HYPALGESIA

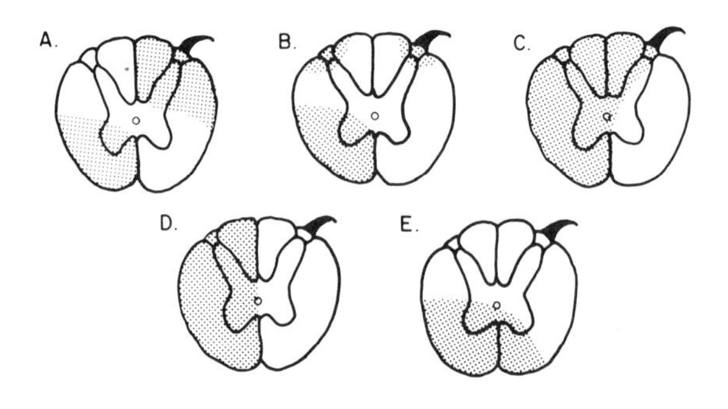

II. LESIONS PRODUCING ENDURING HYPALGESIA

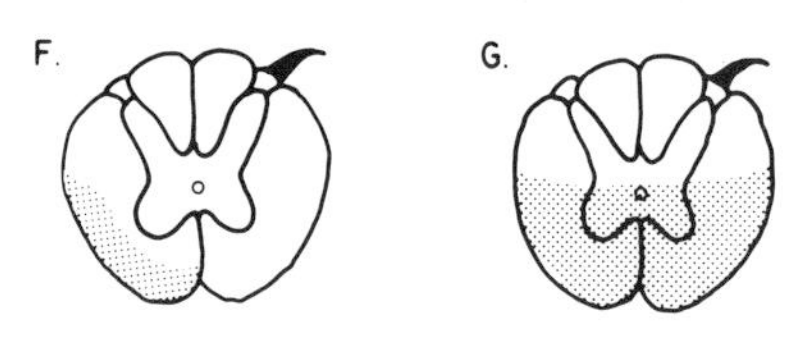

FIG. 7. Schematic diagrams of spinal lesions administered to *Cebus albifrons* monkeys trained on the pain reactivity paradigm. In each case, stimulation was delivered to the side indicated by the dorsal root on the right side of the drawing. Diagrams A, B, C, D, and G represent monkeys receiving an initial chordotomy, followed by a contralateral deficit that recovered, followed by a secondary lesion that included portions of the cord in addition to the contralateral ventral quadrant. Diagrams E and F represent primary lesions received by both *C. albifrons* and *M. nemestrina* monkeys in separate studies (88). Recovery to or near preoperative levels of pain reactivity was observed following lesions A–E. Substantial hypalgesia was sustained for a year or longer by four monkeys with lesions covering the entire border of the contralateral, anterolateral, and ventral columns (F) and by one monkey with complete ventral hemisection (G).

1979), although subtle deficits in pain reactivity are evident following dorsal lesions.

Interrupting all of the white matter unilaterally (Fig. 7D) controls for the possibility that the typical chordotomy spares some of the contralateral spinothalamic fibers, which could occur dorsally, medially, or ventrally (Applebaum *et al.,* 1975). Pain reactivity is reduced substantially and then recovers partially following such a lesion. Chordotomies that involve both ventral columns (Fig. 7E) appear to produce recovery patterns different from those of a ventral quadrant lesion (or lateral hemisection). Involvement of both ventral columns produces relatively transient hypalgesia when combined with contralateral chordotomy (Fig. 7E). The contralateral deficit can be less severe following lesion 7E than after a chordotomy. In fact, the most efficacious lesion appears to involve the lateral and ventral portions of the anterolateral and ventral columns, corresponding to the distribution shown classically for the lateral spinothalamic tract (Geisler *et al.,* 1981b; Weaver and Walker, 1941). Several monkeys receiving a lesion extending medially to the lateral edge of the ventral horn of the anterolateral and ventral columns (Fig. 7F) display a severe reduction of pain reactivity. Some recovery occurs with testing for a year postoperatively, but a consistently significant reduction of pain reactivity can exist following well-located chordotomies. The finding of relatively enduring hypalgesia following a well-placed chordotomy corroborates the supposition that the spinothalamic tract is both sufficient and necessary for normal pain perception in primates (Noordenbos and Wall, 1976; Nathan and Smith, 1979).

The relatively brief reduction of pain reactivity following involvement of both ventral columns with the anterolateral column may corroborate a recent report of hyperreactivity (of reflexive scratching) following ventral column lesions (Denny-Brown, 1979). Considering this result and the impairments of autonomic and motor functions that occur following ventral column lesions, it is important to spare this region ipsilaterally when performing chordotomy therapeutically. The most effective lesion for pain reduction should be a bilateral section of the anterolateral columns, based on the observation that ventral hemisection produces analgesia (Fig. 7G) followed by only slight recovery with extensive postoperative testing. This result implicates the ipsilateral spinoreticular tract as important for the recovery observed following unilateral chordotomy. Also, the result of ventral hemisection demonstrates an insufficiency of the spared dorsal pathways to convey impulses leading to quick and vigorous escape of normally aversive stimuli, although some of the strong stimuli are terminated. Thus, the pain pathways can be considered as ventral and bilateral in the monkey.

D. Inhibitory Spinal Pathways

A dorsolateral pathway from the raphe nuclei exerts powerful descending inhibition on cells of the ipsilateral dorsal horn; one of the transmitters for this pathway is serotonin (Fig. 8; Basbaum *et al.*, 1978; Dahlström and Fuxe, 1965; Headley *et al.*, 1978). Also, there appears to be a descending dorsolateral inhibitory pathway with noradrenaline as a transmitter within the dorsal and ventral horns (Belcher, 1977; Carlsson *et al.*, 1964; Nygren and Olson, 1977; Satoh *et al.*, 1971; Zivin *et al.*, 1975). Although we do not yet know the effects of dorsolateral tract section on caudal flexion reflexes, it is clear that operant pain reactions are exaggerated (Fig. 6). The hyperalgesia appears with resumption of testing following surgery, and remains stable over months (Vierck *et al.*, 1971). Thus, the dorsolateral tract appears to exert inhibition on the transduction of nociceptive input to long transmission cells of the dorsal horn (Willis, 1979). The inhibitory effect may be triggered by input from the pain pathways to the periaqueductal gray, the raphe nuclei, and other portions of the brainstem reticular formation (Anderson *et al.*, 1977; Basbaum *et al.*, 1977; Casey, 1969).

The ipsilateral modulation by dorsal and dorsolateral pathways of the speed and intensity of pain reactions occurs without a shifting of the pain

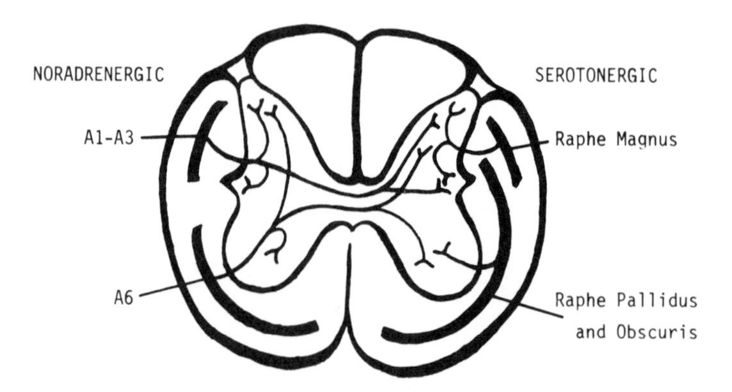

Fig. 8. A schematic diagram of the distribution of descending serotonergic and noradrenergic pathways to the dorsal and ventral horns, as worked out primarily in rats. The dorsal noradrenergic pathway originates diffusely in the reticular gray of the medullary reticular formation (areas A1–A3 of Dahlstrom and Fuxe, 1965) and is distributed bilaterally to the dorsal and intermediolateral portions of the spinal gray matter. The ventral noradrenergic pathway originates in the locus coeruleus and subcoeruleus (A6) and is distributed bilaterally to the dorsal and ventral horns. Serotonergic fibers from nucleus raphe magnus are located in the dorsolateral column and send processes to the ipsilateral dorsal and intermediolateral gray. Serotonergic fibers from raphe pallidus and obscurus nuclei are located in the lateral and ventral columns and send terminals to the ventral horn.

sensitivity range. The hyperalgesia from dorsolateral tract section and the hypalgesia from interruption of the dorsal columns and Lissauer's tract emphasize the importance of quantifying reactions to suprathreshold pain stimuli. These modulations of pain sensitivity are effective for moderate and strong pain, but measures of reactivity to stimuli near the pain threshold do not detect the facilitatory and inhibitory influences (Fig. 6; escape threshold and escape force at 10 mA). This selectivity for higher intensities is predicted by preferential inhibition of nociceptive input by the dorsolateral input to the dorsal horn (Belcher, 1977; Headly *et al.*, 1978).

Recent evidence implicates a ventral system of descending, inhibitory modulation of pain transmission within the dorsal horn (Fig. 8). A noradrenergic system projects via large and small axons that originate from neurons in the locus coeruleus and adjacent reticular formation (Dahlström and Fuxe, 1965; Westlund and Coulter, 1980). The ventral noradrenergic system terminates ipsilaterally and contralaterally in the dorsal and ventral horns (Hodge *et al.*, 1981; Karoum *et al.*, 1980). As mentioned above, a lesion of the ventral system appears to result in a late-developing ipsilateral hyperreflexia, without contralateral elevations above baseline reflex or operant response amplitude. The hyperreflexia is first observed as the positive phase of a long cycle beginning with depression and then exceeding recovery. The ipsilateral hyperreactivity endures for months once it appears.

E. Hypalgesia by Focal Stimulation of the CNS

In the search for reliable methods of pain control, it is preferable to exert reversible effects on the CNS than to destroy neural tissue. Although focal electrical stimulation of CNS tracts or nuclei is invasive and inflicts injury to minute portions of the nervous system, the electrode can be withdrawn when no longer needed, activation of the inhibitory structure can be regulated with respect to timing and intensity, and little or no functionally detectable damage can be expected from some electrode placements. Furthermore, centrally directed electrodes in laboratory animals can be valuable tools for the discovery and characterization of inhibitory circuits that can then be accessed by alternative means. For example, there is excellent correspondence between CNS sites that appear to generate inhibition of pain-related behaviors and areas that are rich in opiate receptors (Yaksh and Rudy, 1978). Investigations of the neurobiological mechanisms of morphine "analgesia" have focused on systems linking the brainstem and spinal cord. The revelance of these systems to pain control has been suggested by intracerebral electrical stimulation (Guilbaud *et al.*, 1973; Liebeskind *et al.*,1973; Mayer and Price, 1976) and has been confirmed by intracerebral application of opiate agonists and antagonists (Bennett and Mayer, 1976;

Yaksh, 1979). Other mechanisms of pain management by morphine have been proposed; for example, emotional reactions or attention to pain may be disrupted, thereby reducing the "suffering" that often accompanies it.

The caudate nucleus is replete with opiate receptors (Finley *et al.*, 1981; Lewis *et al.*, 1981) and is connected reciprocally with the granular frontal cortex, which has been shown to participate in the direction of attention and the interpretation of pain (Barber, 1959; Freeman and Watts, 1948). Furthermore, stimulation of the caudate nucleus affects conduction through the multisynaptic reticulothalamic system that has been implicated as integral to evocation of the motivational-affective accompaniments of pain sensations (Melzack and Casey, 1968). Accordingly, we have characterized the effects of direct electrical stimulation of the caudate nucleus on pain reactivity in monkeys (Fig. 9; Lineberry and Vierck, 1975). Unilateral caudate stimulation does not alter the proportion of trials on which the monkeys escape electrical stimulation of the contralateral leg at intensities spanning the pain sensitivity range. However, the vigor of escape responses is reduced reliably, for each of the electrocutaneous stimulation intensities, when the caudate stimulus precedes the leg stimulus by 25–200 msec. This period corresponds precisely to the duration of inhibition within the reticulothalamic projection system following caudate stimulation (Feltz *et al.*, 1967; Lineberry and Siegel, 1971).

Because the caudate nucleus contributes to the regulation of motor actions (Kitsikis and Rougeul, 1968; Kornhuber, 1971), the effect of operant response vigor may represent a direct motoric effect rather then sensory modulation. However, when the temporal relationships between caudate stimulation and operant responses are observed, there is no correlation with the attenuation of response vigor. Altering the interval between caudate and leg stimulation by 25 msec can make the difference between no effect and maximal attenuation of pain reactivity, but the interval between caudate stimulation and the response is not relevant to response vigor. Thus, precise regulation of the timing and duration of peripheral and central stimulation that follows from the use of electrical stimulation permits control procedures that are not feasible with other techniques (such as peripheral thermal, or central pharmacological stimulation). Independent tests of the positive or negative reinforcement value of caudate stimulation do not correlate with the effect on pain reactivity. That is, the animals do not press a lever to produce or escape caudate stimulation trains at intensities that reduce the vigor of escape from leg stimulation. These results could support the hypothesis that the caudate nucleus is involved in regulating the degree of emotional reactivity to painful stimuli without affecting recognition of the stimuli as aversive. On the other hand, the activating or alerting effects of pain could be attenuated, independent of changes in emotional quality or "tone."

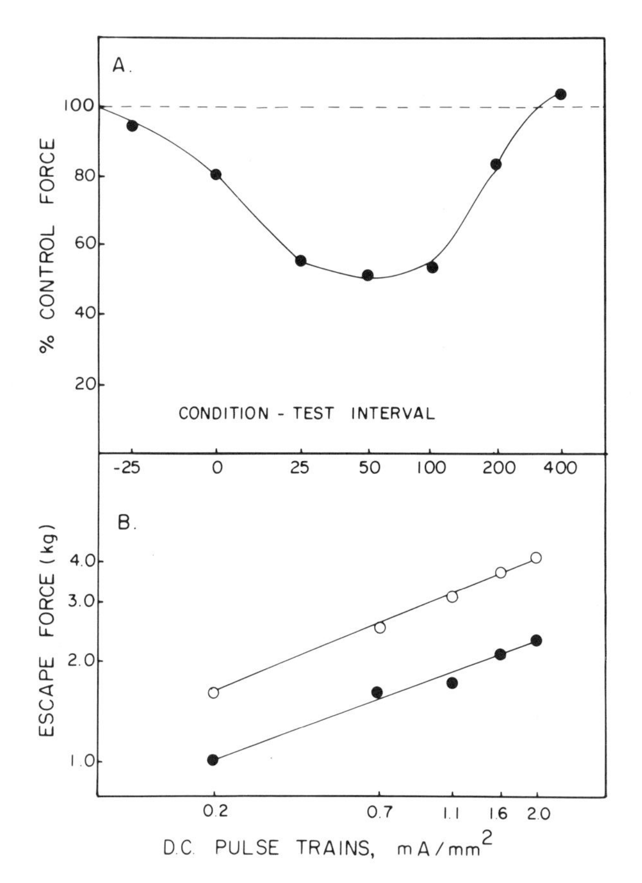

FIG. 9. Data averaged from three *M. speciosa* monkeys stimulated electrically in the contralateral caudate nucleus at different intervals preceding, during, or following electrocutaneous stimulation of one leg. Panel A displays the percentage reduction of operant escape force to high-intensity leg stimulation (31 or 40 mA) as a function of the condition–test (C–T) interval. Positive C–T intervals indicate that 50-msec trains of brain stimulation preceded 50-msec trains of leg stimulation. Escape force was significantly reduced when caudate stimulation preceded leg stimulation by 25 to 200 msec. Panel B combines data obtained with C–T intervals of 25, 50, and 100 msec and shows escape force as a function of the intensity of leg stimulation. Response force was reduced at all intensities of electrocutaneous stimulation, producing similar slopes without brain stimulation (open circles) and with brain stimulation (closed circles). These animals responded consistently to low-intensity stimulation of the leg (4 mA)—possibly because the intensities were randomly ordered, and a large proportion of the trials presented intensities within the human pain sensitivity range.

Either way, the possibility that systemic opiate "analgesics" operate in part via modulation by the caudate nucleus is strengthened. The therapeutic potential of caudate stimulation has not been determined; there may be side effects of caudate excitation (e.g., production of amnesia or kindling of synchronous activity) that make it undesirable.

III. Effects of Systemic Morphine on Pain Reactivity

A. Behavioral Measurement of Morphine "Analgesia" in Laboratory Animals

Although hundreds of years of experience with opiates were required to discover their usefulness in controlling pain, morphine is now considered the standard for systemic pharmacological analgesia (Goodman and Gilman, 1975). Anaglesic potency is often measured as the percent of morphine's effect on a behavioral or physiological measure that bears some relationship to pain. Of necessity, some assay procedures for pain sensitivity must be simplistic, permitting efficient screening of drugs and nervous system structures that are related to pain. Quick and easy procedures, such as the tail-flick and hot-plate measures, have permitted an explosion of knowledge concerning opiates and their mechanisms and sites of action in the nervous system (Sherman and Liebeskind, 1980; Yaksh, 1981; Yaksh and Rudy, 1978). Unfortunately, opiate effects on pain cannot be determined by these methods. The standard algesiometric techniques for laboratory animals (*a*) represent threshold measures for sensations that usually are not painful, (*b*) reflect a behavioral suppression by morphine that is not specific for pain reactions, and (*c*) are relatively insensitive to systemic morphine.

In the hot-plate test, the animal (a rodent) is placed such that the glabrous skin of all four feet is in contact with a floor preheated to 50–55°C. Latencies to the first observable response (e.g., paw lick) range from 6 to 10 sec (Cicero, 1974; Samanin and Bernasconi, 1972; Yaksh *et al.*, 1977). If a human observer contacts a 50°C metal plate with the glabrous skin of a hand or foot, he or she will observe reflex withdrawal within 100 msec of stimulus onset. Operant withdrawal will come into play within 200 msec. Hence, at the outset, we know that thermal sensitivity of rodent feet is substantially different from our own. Even if we grant the assumption that skin temperature very slowly approaches levels sensed as noxious by rodents standing on a 55°C plate, it is likely that the animals will begin to increase heat dissipation by licking the paws when the feet become warm—that is, before they become painfully hot. Similarly, in the tail-flick test, radiant heat to the tail gradually increases skin temperature (latencies range from 3 to 6 sec; Buxbaum *et al.*, 1973; Proudfit and Anderson, 1975; Yaksh *et al.*,

1977), and the animals can be expected to avoid painful levels of stimulation by withdrawing the tail when it becomes warm (Jackson, 1952a). The operant technique involving titration of escape responses is subject to the same flaw. The animals can maintain stimulus intensities below painful levels by setting the criterion for escape well below the pain detection threshold. The lowest reported thresholds approach detection thresholds for nonnoxious tingle, and the highest values are below human pain thresholds or monkey escape thresholds on paradigms with random ordering of intensities spanning the pain sensitivity range. These observations indicate that the most popular assay systems for analgesia (*a*) utilize stimuli that are potentially painful but are maintained at non-painful levels, and (*b*) employ responses that are not affected uniquely by noxious stimuli or by putative analgesic drugs. To control for nonspecific depression of sensorimotor responsivity, it is necessary to show that opiates reduce responses specifically related to presentation of painful stimuli.

To evaluate systemic morphine as an analgesic for monkeys, our pain reactivity measurements have been expanded to monitor three clases of behaviors: (*a*) pain-terminating operants—the percentage, latency, and force of shock escape responses, (*b*) pain-induced reflexes, and (*c*) intertrial behaviors—the frequency of body movements, vocalizations, and unrewarded bar pulls. The frequency of each intertrial behavior increases only slightly as a function of pain intensity, but the baseline frequency could be relatively high in the context of pain testing. That is, the frequency of intertrial behaviors could reflect situational anxiety. The relative sensitivities of the different categories of behavior to systemic intramuscular injections of morphine are shown in Fig. 10 as the average dosage producing statistically significant depression on the component measures in each animal. Consistent with the view that morphine's primary action is to reduce the activation or anxiety that accompanies chronic pain (or recurrent pain, in the present model), only the intertrial behaviors were affected at dosages comparable to the standard therapeutic dosage for humans (Cooper and Vierck, 1982).

Too often, the strategy for investigating mechanisms of morphine analgesia involves selection of *a* behavior (usually tail-flick or hot-plate, paw-lick latencies or liminal escape thresholds) and *a* dosage that depresses that behavior. Other treatments are then added to morphine, and interactions are interpreted in terms of *the* effect of morphine on pain. This approach has led to the following typical dosages of systemic morphine: 5–10 mg/kg in rats or mice, 3–6 mg/kg in rabbits, and 2–12 mg/kg in monkeys. Certainly, there are differences in sensitivity of individual animals, specific behaviors, and different species to morphine; for example, the minimal effective dosages for respiratory depression are quite disparate among species

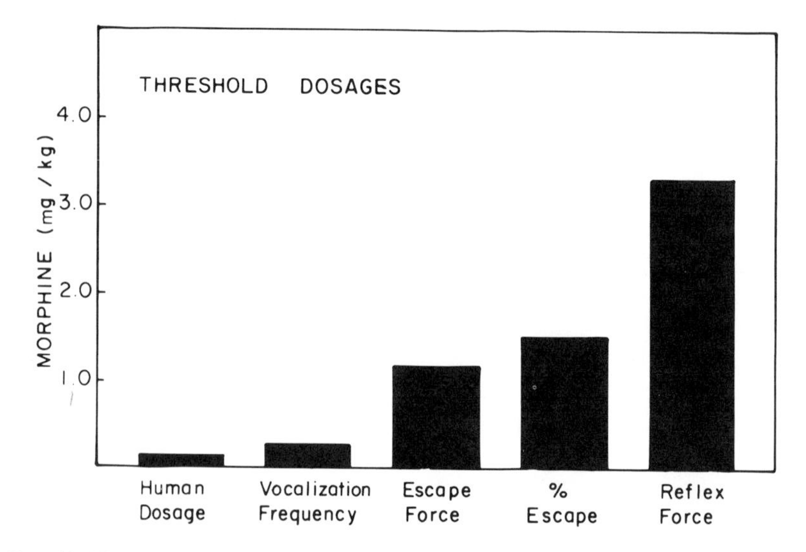

FIG. 10. Threshold dosages for the production of statistically significant depression of the listed behavioral categories in three *M. speciosa* monkeys tested on the escape paradigm. The typical human therapeutic dose of morphine is given for comparison. The data from different electrocutaneous stimulation intensities are combined for all measures. The measure most sensitive to systemic morphine is the frequency of intertrial vocalizations.

(Jackson, 1952a). Before accepting large dosages as specific for modulation of pain, it must be shown, within each species, that the animals are not experiencing a more generalized behavioral suppression. The data presented in Fig. 10 indicate that an analgesic dosage commonly employed for monkeys (4 mg/kg) is six times the dosage required for attenuation of adjunctive (intertrial) behaviors in a pain context and four times the drug level that depresses the vigor of operant pain reactions. In order to minimize the potentially confounding, nonspecific affects of morphine, its hypalgesic properties should be evaluated at the lowest effective dosages.

It should be noted that the systemic dosages of morphine required to produce reflex suppression in monkeys in our paradigm are comparable to those used to suppress reflexive reactions in rats (Grossman *et al.*, 1973). The measured responses in most paradigms are likely to be reflexive on the first exposures of a given animal to the stimulus, before avoidance strategies are learned (e.g., on tasks such as the tail-flick and hot-plate procedures). Many studies of morphine have used naive animals responding to novel stimuli and likely to react reflexively. For anesthetic-analgesics, the point of reflex suppression is utilized as an endpoint of generalized behavioral suppression, and our data suggest that nociceptive reflexes are relatively insensitive to morphine as well.

B. Effects of Morphine on Stimulus Detection

In view of the wide distribution of opiate receptors in the peripheral nervous system and CNS, it is to be expected that morphine will produce effects other than modulation of pain (Finley *et al.,* 1981; Lewis *et al.,* 1981). In terms of sensory receptivity, opiate receptors are not restricted to pain-related pathways but are also prevalent in cortical and subcortical portions of the visual, olfactory, and auditory–vestibular systems. Hence, an animal receiving morphine could be less responsive to environmental cues directing adaptive responses (including those to pain), or the animal could be "distracted" by disruptions of sensory input (e.g., vertigo). Similarly, opiate actions on CNS regions implicated in the control of motor activity, attention, memory, reward, and emotionality (e.g., the caudate nucleus, the hippocampus, the amygdaloid nuclei, and portions of the reticular formation) would be expected to influence behaviors outside contexts of pain. Even the systems of descending control over spinal nociceptive transmission that are activated by morphine and thought to contribute to modulation of pain are suspect as generalized modulators. The periaqueductal gray, raphe nuclei, locus coeruleus, and nucleus reticularis gigantocellularis have ascending as well as descending projections, and the descending terminations are not restricted to the superficial laminae of the dorsal horn (Basbaum *et al.,* 1976; Basbaum *et al.,* 1978; Hamilton, 1973; Karoum *et al.,* 1980; Pin *et al.,* 1968; Saavedra *et al.,* 1976; Sakuma and Pfaff, 1980).

In order to evaluate the relative morphine sensitivity of pain reactivity vs. general behavioral proficiency on comparable tasks, we have employed several approaches. Because it is likely that titrated thresholds for escape responses represent avoidance responses to nonnoxious stimuli, in anticipation of truly aversive events, and because there is controversy concerning the selective inhibition by morphine of pain vs. touch conduction through the dorsal horn of the spinal cord (Dykstra, 1980; Grilly and Genovese, 1979; Hernandez and Appel, 1979; Wikler *et al.,* 1945), we have trained two monkeys to produce absolute thresholds (RLs) for touch detection (Fig. 11; Cooper and Vierck, 1982). Morphine significantly elevated touch RLs when administered at a dosage of 0.5 mg/kg; a further increase was observed at 1.0 mg/kg. Touch thresholds are at least as sensitive to morphine as any of the behaviors recorded in sessions involving pain. Similarly, shock detection paradigms in rats reveal performance deficits following dosages of morphine below those commonly used with the tail-flick or hot-plate procedures (Poling *et al.,* 1978). These results complicate interpretation of elevations of titrated escape thresholds by systemic morphine (Weiss and Laties, 1964). The threshold current densities reported for the titrated escape procedure are closer to shock detection thresholds (approximately 0.002 mA/mm^2) than to

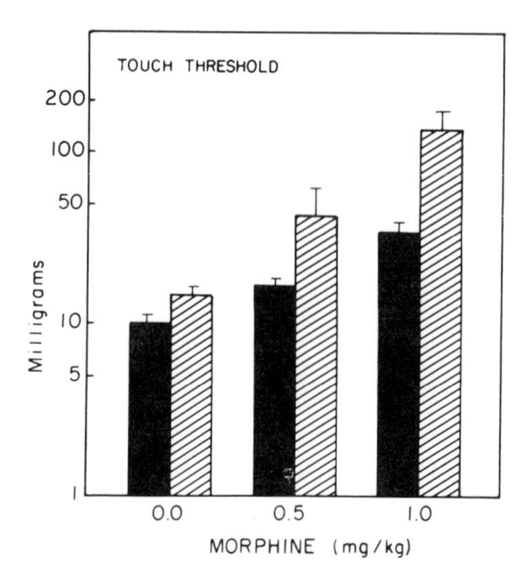

FIG. 11. Touch thresholds of two *M. speciosa* monkeys under control conditions (vehicle injections) and following the lowest dosages (0.5 or 1.0 mg/kg) that produce significant depression of behaviors in a pain context. Thresholds were obtained by the method of limits, using calibrated nylon monofilaments. Bars representing touch detection thresholds are shaded differently for each animal.

pain thresholds (approximately 0.2 mA/mm^2). Either systemic morphine inhibits CNS transmissions of touch as effectively as pain, or the elevation of touch RLs represents a deterioration of performance not related to direct sensory modulation. The latter possibility is supported by signal detection analysis of the capacity to discriminate among mildly painful shock levels (Dykstra, 1980; Grilly and Genovese, 1979; Hernandez and Appel, 1979; Lineberry and Kulics, 1978). Systemic morphine (0.5 mg/kg) affects response bias but not discriminability (d'). In our own experience, morphine (0.11–0.15 mg/kg) elevated touch detection thresholds in the absence of a warning cue, but not when the trials were signaled by an auditory stimulus. We felt that the difficulty on the unsignaled task was related to an attentional deficit.

C. Effects of Morphine on Responsivity to Nonnoxious Stimuli

In order to assess baseline levels and sensitivity to morphine of the nonreflexive behaviors incorporated in the pain reactivity paradigm, five monkeys have been trained to pull the Lindsley manipulandum for food reinforcement in response to a tone presented at 60-sec intervals. Thus, it is possible to compare operant vigor and the frequency of intertrial behaviors on similar schedules of responses signaled by aversive vs. nonaversive stimuli. A rigorous comparison of baseline response vigor and frequency depends on switching animals from the pain-motivated to the food-motivated tasks (and vice versa). However, the effects of different dosages of systemic morphine on behaviors in the two situations can be appreciated by plotting the percentage reduction from control levels obtained following injections of the morphine vehicle (saline). Inspection of Fig. 12 reveals a surprising concordance of general trends for most measures on the two tasks (except operant force) at dosages below those typically used in subhuman primate models of pain (see also McKearney, 1980). It is important to point out that the behavioral suppression in the food-reinforced task (and the touch RL task) occurred at dosages that did not reduce the amount of food consumed in independent tests. That is, the behavioral attenuation at low dosages cannot be ascribed to the lack of appetite that occurs at higher dosages of morphine. Thus, it should not be assumed that pain-modulating systems of the CNS are the most highly sensitive to systemic morphine. It appears that any systemic dose affecting pain reactivity also produces other forms of behavioral suppression. This must be taken into account in research concerned with morphine hypalgesia (Cooper and Vierck, 1982).

It is possible that the nonspecific effects of morphine plateau at low dosages, whereas a true hypalgesic effect increases at higher dosages, which would suggest the use of high dosages therapeutically. There is an increasing effect of morphine for monkeys on all pain reactivity measures up to 4 mg/kg (Cooper and Vierck, 1982). Unfortunately, we cannot evaluate the nonspecific effects easily at the higher dosages, because the monkeys will not work for food or water. This could reflect a general effect of morphine on reinforcement processes since intracranial reinforcement values are also altered by intermediate dosages (Esposito and Kornetsky, 1978; Jackler *et al.*, 1979). Secondary reinforcers (such as anxiety or fear reduction) could be affected by morphine as well (Davis, 1979). Simple observation of the animals in their communal enclosures and in the close interactions involved in daily handling indicate the following: (*a*) Low dosages below 2 mg/kg, produce visible pallor, presumably from peripheral vasoconstriction. Otherwise, the animals appear normal. (*b*) At 2mg/kg and above, the monkeys appear to be disoriented spatially, and glassy-eyed facial expressions are common. They seem normally coordinated and stable when climbing, walking, or running, but they do not reliably follow the correct route when walking (on a leash) to the experimental room and chamber. These observations indicate that high morphine dosages do not preferentially inhibit pain. This point is made clearly by demonstrations of pronounced motor effects, including catatonia, at very high dosages of morphine (Tang and Schoenfeld, 1978; DeRyck *et al.*, 1980).

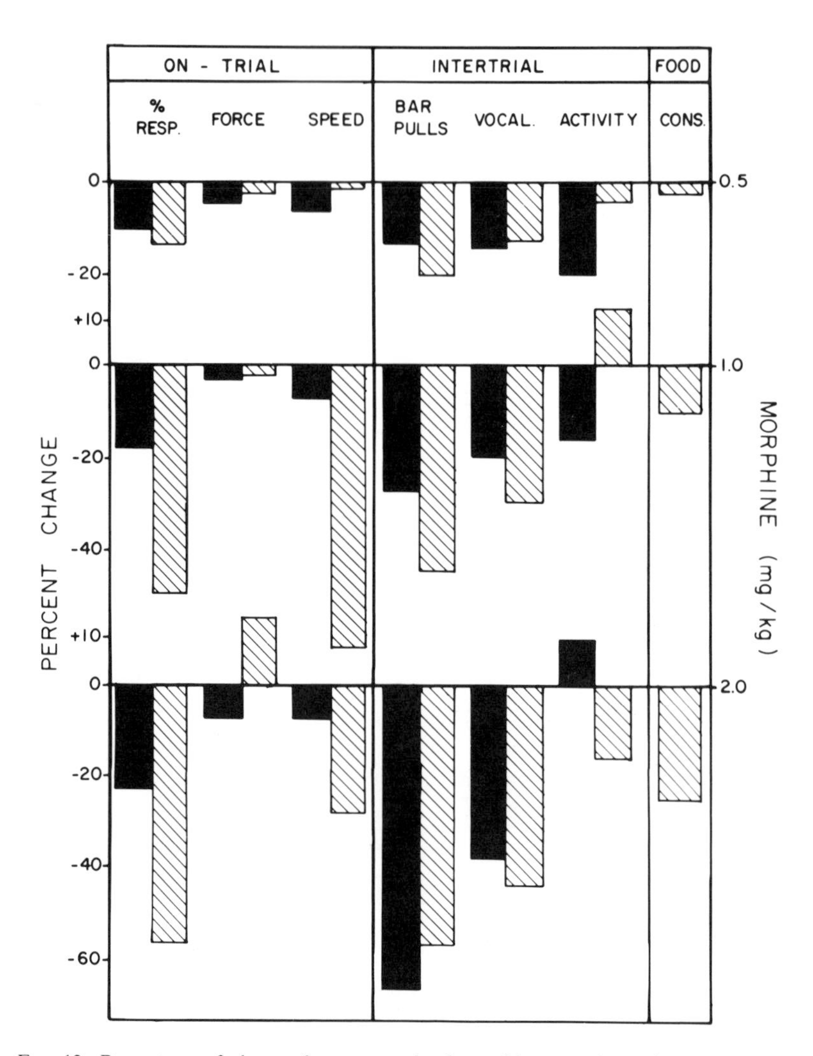

FIG. 12. Percentage of change from control values of log-transformed operant measures dependent on the morphine dosage and the task. Shaded bars represent performance on the pain reactivity paradigm by three *M. speciosa* monkeys. Dosage-dependent depression of pain reactivity occurs over 0.5, 1.0, and 2.0 mg/kg. Lined bars represent the same measures on a task involving bar pulls for food reinforcement during presentation of an auditory signal (five *M. speciosa* monkeys). Again, most of the operant response measures are decreased progressively over the range of 0.5 to 2.0 mg/kg. The percentage reductions by morphine of all measures except force are similar for the two tasks or greater on the food reinforcement paradigm. Operant force did not show statistically significant depression at any dosage on the food task. Significant reductions of force were obtained at 1 and 2 mg/kg on the escape task. The significant effects on behaviors associated with the food-motivated task are not accounted for by a loss of appetite, as indicated by the right column. The amount of food consumed was affected appreciably only at the highest dosage, causing three monkeys to cease responding. Response rates of the remaining monkeys were not affected.

One of the behavioral measures most sensitive to morphine in pain and no-pain contexts is the frequency of intertrial vocalizations (Cooper and Vierck, 1982). Vocalization threshold has been shown in rats to be sensitive to morphine as well; significant depression can be obtained at a dosage of 2 mg/kg (Paalzow, 1979). If one is interested in comparing the relative potency of opiate-related compounds, it is advisable to utilize a behavioral assay that is highly sensitive to morphine, and vocalization frequency or threshold seems preferable to the tail-flick and hot-plate techniques. However, it should be recognized that none of these are pure indicants of analgesia.

D. Human Psychophysical Evaluation of Morphine's Effects on Pain

The effects of morphine on food-motivated behaviors demonstrate influences other than control of aversion to pain but do not rule out the presence of true hypalgesia on the pain reactivity task. Also, putative anxiety reduction by morphine would not necessarily affect performance in the pain context alone (see Panksepp *et al.,* 1978). Food-deprived monkeys are highly aroused, alert, impatient, and manipulative in the testing situation; the positively rewarded task does not represent a control-at-rest. To deal with these issues, it is useful to rely upon human observers. Accordingly three of us (C.V., B.C., and O.F.) have taken 10 mg of morphine (0.11–0.15 mg/kg) an hour before pain testing on several paradigms and occasions. We have performed on the shock-escape paradigm (control data shown in Fig. 2) and have rated the stimulus intensities by free magnitude estimation and by applying verbal descriptors. On the latter procedures, the stimulus duration was set at 3 sec so that we could experience the effects of morphine on ongoing pain. On trials involving a single train of stimulation (Fig. 1), evaluative processes occur *post hoc;* that is, a remembered trace of the stimulus is evaluated. However, the 3-sec stimuli elicit cognitive and emotional reactions as the stimulus continues. The 3-sec trial durations reduced our pain sensitivity range for DC trains (50-msec duration at 4 Hz) to 7–21 mA, as determined by the method of limits. In addition, 3-sec thermal stimuli, within a range of 44.7–50.0°C, were interposed in random sequence with shock trials. Within this range, the discharge of thermal nociceptors increases with temperature, whereas the activity of warm receptors decreases (Franzen and Torebjork, 1981; Georgepoulos, 1977). Heat was applied to the shaved medial calf via a Peltier device, set to increase in temperature at a rate of 2.5°C/sec. These sessions are proving quite informative to us, and several important conclusions are clear.

We have observed little or no effect of morphine on the objectified intensity of elicited pain sensations through much of the pain sensitivity range (Cooper *et al.*, 1982). This finding confirms and extends observations by numerous laboratories that morphine has little effect on pain thresholds in humans (e.g., Beecher, 1957). Since both morphine and frontal lobotomy have been reported to reduce "suffering" or fear without affecting the pain sensations (Barber, 1959; Beecher, 1957; Hill *et al.*, 1952), we were curious to appreciate whether our emotional reactivity was blunted. On control trials at the highest intensities (21 mA and 50°C) at 3-sec durations, frequently there is agitation. It is difficult to avoid body movement or isometiric tension, vocalization, and grimacing. There is a "wow" feeling that is not present at lower intensities. This reaction does not always attend the highest intensities. Our introspective accounts indicate no effect of the morphine on the frequency or quality of these experiences.

Clearly identified emotional reactions occur most often in naive subjects and early in experimental sessions for experienced subjects. The lack of an effect of morphine on the affective component of pain reactions has been confirmed by delivering morphine to subjects when anxiety is maximal, during their first full session with random presentation of intensities established in a single preliminary session, administered a week earlier and using ascending series by the method of limits. Relative to a second, control session with the random series, anxiety and emotional reactivity are affected little, if at all, by morphine for these subjects at a time when emotional reactions are most prominent (Cooper *et al.*, 1982). Observation of the subjects, on the other hand, gives the impression of blunted affect; the subjects' reactions are not animated after they have received morphine.

The management of pain by morphine is *in part* illusory, in that pain-related behaviors are suppressed. We found it difficult to generate any behavior, and without noticeable alteration of mentation, it was difficult to talk; that is, vocalization required increased effort—not to form the sounds, but to converse. This is representative of a general behavioral suppression, meaning a tendency to withdraw and to avoid stimulation and activity. Thus, morphine promotes inactivity, rest, and inattention, and this behavioral profile should be conducive to pain tolerance by minimizing positive feedback interactions of pain, arousal, and tension. In this sense, management of pain by morphine would be effective by indirectly reducing progressive exaggeration of reactions to continuous pain. These effects could give the appearance of a direct effect of morphine on anxiety (particularly in the occasional patient who experiences euphoria), but clearly more general influences on behavioral reactivity are exerted. In our experience, following a therapeutic dosage of morphine, normal energy levels and attentiveness did not return the day after morphine administration. If this effect is additive with repeated dosages, the ability of a patient to cope with environmental events can be compromised undesirably.

The principal goal of our studies of morphine has been to provide a foundation for elucidating the neural mechanisms of morphine's effect on pain. We have been surprised to learn that strong pain can be unaffected by systemic morphine in physiological dosages. It follows that all forms of pain transmission through the dorsal horn are not inhibited by a therapeutic dosage of systemic morphine on the central gray–reticulospinal projection system or by activating spinal opiate receptors (Sherman and Liebeskind, 1980; Yaksh, 1981; Yaksh and Rudy, 1978).

E. Comparison of Morphine's Effects on Fast and Slow Pain Sensations

An objection to the investigation of morphine's effects on acute elicited pain is based on conjecture that the drug selectively depresses chronic pains of endogenous origin (Beecher, 1957) or tonic pain consequent to tissue damage (Dennis and Melzack, 1979) or ischemia (Smith *et al.,* 1966). Similarly, it has been suggested that morphine is especially effective in reducing temporal summation of synaptic neural activity (Yaksh, 1981), which could preferentially attenuate convergent interactions of tonically active nociceptors (Chung and Wurster, 1978; Collins and Randt, 1965; Price *et al.,* 1978). Of importance to these notions is the physiology of dorsal horn cells receiving nociceptive inputs. These cells are given to repetitive discharge at low frequencies for long durations (Kenshalo *et al.,* 1979; Mendell and Wall, 1965), and they project from (or are modulated by) the superficial laminae of the spinal cord, containing (*a*) the highly convergent substantia gelatinosa–Lissauer's tract system, (*b*) terminals of descending and intrinsic inhibitory systems, and (*c*) opiate receptors (Duggan *et al.,* 1977; Fields *et al.,* 1980; Hokfelt *et al.,* 1977; Kumazawa and Perl, 1978; LaMotte *et al.,* 1976; Light and Perl, 1977; Oliveras *et al.,*1977). Both A-delta and C-fiber nociceptors synapse on projection neurons with cell bodies or dendrites in the superficial laminae (I and II), but systemic morphine may exert a more powerful influence on unmyelinated nociceptor inputs (Jurna and Heinz, 1979; Le Bars *et al.,* 1979b). To evaluate this possibility, it is necessary to determine whether our electrical stimulation elicits activity in C-nociceptors. We have been careful to elicit strong suprathreshold pain intensities that should activate unmyelinated fibers, but it could be important to direct the subjects' attention to the different components of elicited pain. The duration of the sensations elicited by strong stimulation should correspond to the well-established time course of first and second pain (Price *et al.,* 1977; Zotterman, 1939).

The time course of changes in pain intensity following shock has been determined by instructing human subjects to adjust the distance between their right thumb and forefinger in proportion to the relative magnitude of pain as it varies following single trains of stimulation. This procedure has been used successfully for relating the magnitude and time course of pain to the peripheral neural discharge elicited by tooth pulp stimulation in dental patients (Ahlqvist *et al.*, 1982). The arms of a potentiometer are attached to the thumb and forefinger; variations in finger span alter the voltage dropped across the potentiometer. The highest intensities of stimulation elicit a second pain sensation with a time course that is easily followed by finger movements. With our parameters of stimulation, the AC stimulus provokes the clearest wave of second pain, suggesting that C-fiber activity is evoked more readily by AC than by DC intensities that evoke comparable first pain intensities (1.3 mA/mm^2 AC and 2.1 mA/mm^2 DC).

The second pain sensation to a single 50-msec train of AC shock is observed as a distinct wave of pain that begins on the gradually decrementing first pain sensation. Second pain latencies are approximately 0.9 sec with stimulation of the lateral calf; the peak occurs at 1.25 sec, and the sensation is complete 1.87 sec following stimulus onset. At the hip the onset is not distinguishable from the declining A-delta sensation, but a peak latency of 0.625 sec and an offset of 1.1 sec suggest a mean conduction velocity of 0.78 m/sec. We have employed magnitude estimation and a direct matching procedure for comparing the relative magnitudes of first and second pain sensations. For 1.3 mA/mm^2 AC shock, the second pain magnitude is approximately one-fourth of the first pain sensation. Second pain is absent at 0.3 mA/mm^2, very weak at 0.5–0.7 mA/mm^2 and weak at 1.3 mA/mm^2.

Having rated the time course and relative magnitudes of first and second pain sensations relating to activity in A-delta and C-fibers, respectively, we have repeated these psychophysical rating procedures starting 1 hour following administration of 10 mg of morphine. The result is clear and obvious to the observers. Second pain sensations are absent or barely detectable following the strongest shock (1.3 mA/mm^2; Cooper *et al.*, 1982). Conditional upon verification in naive observers, this is clear behavioral evidence for a selective effect of morphine on C-fiber input. Some observers must be naive with respect to the possibility that morphine would affect second pain selectively, but they must also be trained to identify second pain. In our initial psychophysical studies, we attended to the peak intensity properties, which are dominated by the first pain sensations. The rapid onset and startling nature of first pain minimized the saliency of second pain sensations. We have noted similar contrast effects on first pain sensations between successive trials.

Our monkey paradigm in its present form is primarily a model of reactivity to A-delta pain, because the operant escape and reflex responses occur prior to the onset of second pain (within 0.5 sec, as estimated for the monkeys). Thus, our monkey and human psychophysics confirm that A-delta input is not attenuated significantly at dosages of systemic morphine comparable to those used in a clinical context (Jurna and Heinz, 1979; LeBars *et al.*, 1979a,b). On the other hand, pain sensations presented by synchronous activation of C-fibers are markedly diminished by human therapeutic dosages of morphine. It appears that experimental pain can be relevant to clinical pain if both A-delta and C-fiber sensations are evaluated. That is, the distinction between chronic and phasically elicited pain sensations may not be fundamental to the actions of morphine. This reinforces the feasibility of humane models of clinical pain, without the induction of chronic pain. The morphine-sensitive, directly elicited, C-fiber pain sensation is brief and is milder than a preceding, more compelling A-delta pain sensation that is quite tolerable.

IV. Summary Comments

An animal model of pain reactivity has been reviewed in terms of its ability to reflect and contribute to an understanding of phenomena known to be associated with human pain sensitivity. The model employs brief, acute, recurrent pain and notes a variety of immediate and delayed reactions to these fleeting stimuli. It is unconscionable to induce chronic pain in experimental animals for the direct investigation of pain control, but a major question concerns whether any nonchronic model of pain is capable of elucidating neural mechanisms of clinical pain. One approach has been to produce sensory deafferentation (Sweet, 1981) and to assume that the resulting self-mutilation (*a*) results from nonpainful paresthesias that (*b*) result from activity in the pain pathways and (*c*) obey the same principles of regulation as pain. Unfortunately, the occurrence of autotomy is quite variable; the nature of the sensory experiences is not amenable to direct verification; deafferentation eliminates the opportunity for sensory stimulation of the affected region; the animals are difficult to care for; the putative paresthesias could result from abnormal states of CNS activity (Anderson *et al.*, 1971; Loeser and Ward, 1967) that are not present in many pain conditions; and autotomy can be produced by interruption of the spinothalamic tracts (Levitt and Levitt, 1981), indicating that it may not depend upon activity in the pain pathways. Although the study of sensory restriction or other methods of producing chronic, abnormal central discharge (Anderson *et al.*, 1971) is interesting in its own right, the potential for elucidating fundamental mechanisms of pain coding and control is limited with these techniques. Thus, it is important to determine whether humane paradigms of acute pain can serve as models of pain coding and control that generalize to a variety of chronic pain conditions. Although it is unlikely that acute and chronic pain sensations would be affected identically by all manipulations, just as spontaneous and driven CNS activity do not always covary in responsivity to morphine (Hosford and Haigler, 1980), it is expected that correspondence would be the rule, rather than the exception. For example, visceral and muscular nociceptors that give rise to chronic pain in response to tonic distention or contraction are convergent with cutaneous nociceptors onto cells of origin of the spinothalamic tracts (Foreman *et al.*,1977, 1981).

Essential features of an animal model of pain are: (*a*) the stimuli excite nociceptors and elicit pain that is tolerable but yet spans much of the pain sensitivity range; (*b*) nonreflexive responses are related quantitatively to the intensity of pain and are indicative of the presence of pain; and (*c*) the measures of pain reactivity are responsive to treatments known to modify pain sensitivity in humans. In order to define the pain sensitivity range for stimuli that do not traumatize the tissue, we have compared nonhuman and human primate performance on tasks permitting escape from focal electrical stimulation of the skin. The appearance of an escape response appears to differentiate painful from nonpainful stimuli, as indicated by the correspondence of escape thresholds for the monkeys and human pain thresholds defined by verbal descriptors. The vigor of a well-ingrained aversive reaction to brief trains of stimulation increases with shock intensity over a range of pain intensities described by human observers as weak to strong. The growth of escape force or speed with pain intensity is comparable in monkey subjects and humans instructed to escape rapidly. The magnitude of relfex withdrawal increases substantially with stimulus intensity in the nonpainful range (from stimulus detection to pain detection thresholds). Reflex force is related to shock intensity within the pain sensitivity range, but the slope of the function for painful stimuli is very low relative to nonpainful intensities. The frequency of adjunctive intertrial behaviors appears to reflect generalized arousal and is not obviously related to the presence of pain or its intensity. Thus, of the three categories of behavior monitored, the direct operant reactions to pain most reliably and sensitively reflect the occurrence and magnitude of pain (Cooper and Vierck, 1982).

Interruption of the principal spinal pathways for conduction and modulation of pain produces distinct changes in pain reactivity, as revealed by the probability and vigor of aversive reactions. The operant aversive reactions of monkeys reliably quantitate effects on acute pain that parallel in magnitude and time course the effects of chordotomy on chronic pain in humans. Ventral lesions of the spinal cord can produce substantial and enduring decreases in all measures, reducing the likelihood of aversive reactions and decreasing the vigor of responses that do occur with the strong stimuli. When the lesion interrupts the lateral and ventral fibers within the contralateral ventral quadrant, pain detection thresholds are elevated, and sensitivity to suprathreshold stimuli is blunted to a great extent. After 6 or more months of postoperative testing, there is some recovery of pain reactivity, but substantial deficits can be maintained for longer than a year. In contrast, inclusion of both ventral columns in the lesion produces a less severe deficit that can disappear over months of postoperative testing. A lesion of both ventral columns appears to counteract partially the effects of chordotomy on pain sensitivity. The role of the ventral spinothalamic tract (Giesler *et al.*, 1981a; Kerr, 1975) in transmission of impulses interpreted as painful is questioned by this finding. The pathway responsible for the release of hypalgesia is an open question. The pathway released by chordotomy and ventral column section (i.e., the pathway(s) mediating the recovery) is located in the ipsilateral anterolateral column, as suggested by the large and enduring deficit that follows ventral hemisection of the spinal cord. The pathways essential for transmission of pain appear to reside in the ventral half of the spinal cord and to include (*a*) the contralateral spinothalamic tract, and (*b*) the bilateral spinoreticular pathways.

The vigor of escape reactions is also affected predictably by lesions of the cord that interrupt systems that modulate transmission of nociceptive input to the dorsal horn (Crutcher and Bingham, 1978; Vierck *et al.*, 1971). Ipsilateral interruption of Lissauer's tract (and the dorsal column) attenuates the intensity of pain reactions, and section of the ipsilateral posterolateral or anterolateral columns produces hyperreactivity (increased response vigor). The dorsal lesions do not affect response probability, suggesting that the identification of stimuli as aversive is not altered. This could result from modulation of the effectiveness of a proportion of the convergent inputs to spinothalamic projection cells, or it is possible that the dorsal pathways selectively modulate the deeper (laminae IV–VI) touch and pain convergent cells (Le Bars *et al.*, 1979a,b), but both nociceptor-specific and "wide dynamic range" cells gradate their rates of discharge in proportion to stimulus intensity within the pain sensitivity range (Kenshalo *et al.*, 1979). Hence, the lamina I cells could signal pain intensity as well as pain detection. If the modulation is selective for a given population of spinal cells, then the attenuated growth of pain reactions could result from diminished convergent interactions at supraspinal loci.

As with chronic pain in humans, the probability, latency, and force of aversive reactions of monkeys to elicited pain are attenuated by systemic morphine in a dosage-dependent manner. On the surface, this result appears to reflect the hypalgesic properties of morphine. Some of the operant measures are affected by morphine at dosage levels used with human pain patients and at dosages well below levels required to elevate liminal escape thresholds or to attenuate the magnitude of reflex withdrawal. However, it is necessary to show that the latency and intensity of nonaversive reactions are not affected. When monkeys are tested on a positively reinforced task, the latency of operant responses to an auditory stimulus is increased at the same dosages (0.5 and 1.0 mg/kg) and in comparable proportions to the elevations in latency of the same motor response to aversive stimuli. The sensitivity of response latency to relatively low dosages of morphine in the absence of pain is a serious source of confounding, since most contemporary algesiometric methods rely upon latency measures of one kind or another (i.e., latency to move the tail, raise the paw, or withdraw the paw).

Although the force of operant responses that escape shock or produce food are both diminished by low dosages of morphine, there are differences in the reliability of these effects on the two tasks. Significant effects are obtained on the shock paradigm at 1.0 mg/kg, but positively rewarded responses are not significantly diminished in force at dosages that leave some of the animals responsive and motivated for food (2 mg/kg and below; Cooper and Vierck, 1982). This comparison reemphasizes the difficulty in separating hypalgesic from other effects of morphine, but it also suggests that response force is the best operant measure for detecting hypalgesia for first pain (A-delta pain). This conclusion is supported by previous demonstrations of the resistance of muscular power to morphine (see Yaksh and Reddy, 1981). The dosage of morphine required to decrease significantly the monkeys' escape force (approximately eight times the human therapeutic dosage) is consistent with neurophysiological observations that large dosages are required to reduce activity in spinal cord cells elicited by A-delta fibers. Responses to C-nociceptor input are diminished at lower dosages (Jurna and Heinz, 1979; Le Bars *et al.*, 1979a,b).

The effects of morphine on motor performance appear to have less to do with influences on the final common pathway than with the initiation or generation of behavior. For example, the frequency of "spontaneous" behaviors (i.e., behaviors without obvious eliciting stimuli) is markedly reduced by morphine. The decrease in intertrial adjunctive behaviors occurs at the lowest threshold dosages of all behaviors tested in our paradigm, and this effect seems representative of a general depression of arousal and attention by systemic morphine.

In the search for effective means of pain control, it is important to establish the selectivity of each manipulation for effects on pain sensations and reactions. If systemic morphine at safe dosages acts on arousal and attention, then we should not invoke inhibition of pain transmission at the primary spinal synapse as the mechanism of morphine's influences on pain reactions. We must elucidate the contribution of structures such as the caudate nucleus, which contains opiate receptors in abundance, inhibits activity in the reticular activating system, and attenuates pain reactions when stimulated. Although morphine does activate systems of descending inhibitory control over nociceptive input, it should be recognized that typical concentrations of morphine in CNS tissue, when applied locally (e.g., intracerebrally or intrathecally), are 2000–20,000 times the estimated concentration of the drug in CNS tissue when administered systemically (Liu and Wang, 1981). Furthermore, intracerebral activation of structures with diverse outputs can be excepted to exert a variety of effects. For example, injection of morphine into the midbrain central gray inhibits conduction through the midbrain reticular formation (Mohrland and Gebhart, 1980), and therefore could influence arousal, in addition to affecting sensory conduction at spinal levels. Direct application of opiates in high concentrations to a CNS region rich in opiate receptors can serve to analyze the functions of a given system, but this tells us little about the systemic effects of opiates, which act at much lower concentrations on many systems with differential sensitivities and actions (Dafny *et al.,* 1978, 1980). Systemic morphine can enhance or reverse the effects of inhibitory systems of control over pain transmission (Fitzgerald and Woolf, 1980; LeBars *et al.,* 1981). In either case, it is important to recognize that animals may not be experiencing hypalgesia for all varieties of pain in response to the drug.

A low range of systemic dosages of morphine (less than 0.2 mg/kg in nontolerant humans or 0.5 mg/kg in monkeys) produces little or no direct inhibition of the first pain sensation that is experienced during electrocutaneous stimulation. However, our preliminary evidence from human subjects strongly indicates that the second pain response, attributable to unmyelinated, C-fiber activity, is powerfully attenuated by systemic morphine. This result corroborates the findings of physiological studies of dorsal horn neurons (Jurna and Heinz, 1979; LeBars *et al.,* 1979a,b) and is consistent with the efficacious use of morphine for a variety of clinical pain conditions. A recent evaluation of postsurgical pain following self-administration of an opiate (Meperidine) has shown that the patients take enough of the drug to attenuate but not eliminate pain (Franzen *et al.,* 1982). The dosage of Meperidine varied considerably among patients but was inversely related to preoperative levels of beta-endorphin in the cerebrospinal fluid. A weighted sum of the exogenous and endogenous opiates produced approximately equal levels of comfort for these patients. If systemic morphine quiets a patient, promoting inactivity and inattention, and if it also blocks input from unmyelinated nociceptors, its usefulness for control of pain is readily understood. The sparing of A-delta pain accounts for reports that pain is not eliminated in patients or experimental subjects following the administration of nonanesthetic dosages (Jackson, 1952b; Javert and Hardy 1951). In certain cases, it can be regarded as advantageous that some pain sensitivity remains, giving the patient needed feedback concerning activities that could be injurious. The blunting of C-fiber-mediated pain may often be the most crucial goal of pain therapy, because of the ubiquitous distribution of

C-nociceptors in visceral and other deep tissues and because of a propensity for prolonged, repetitive discharge to all forms of noxious stimulation (mechanical, thermal, and chemical; Bessou and Perl, 1969). Thus, an important distinguishing feature of many clinical pain conditions (vs. most experimental pain sensations) may be the involvement of and attention to C-fiber nociceptor activity. The distinction between chronic and acute pain may depend fundamentally upon the relative saliency of sensations dependent on C- and A-delta fibers, respectively. That is, experimental treatments that are effective in blunting directly elicited C-fiber activity are expected to be effective in controlling chronic pain.

Because this chapter has focused on experimental methods of algesiometry, a comment is offered about the use of morphine as the standard for comparison of potential pain medications. Clearly, it is improper to state analgesic potency in terms of the percentage of systemic effect of morphine on a single behavioral task that is highly sensitive to general behavioral suppression. Furthermore, morphine is not an analgesic in the strict sense of the term; that is, nonanesthetic dosages do not eliminate pain. Just as clinical pain can be manifest in many specific forms, it is desirable to have an arsenal of tailor-made pain treatments. Certainly, it can be imagined that an ideal analgesic might not produce dysphoria, behavioral suppression, withdrawal, tolerance, and addiction, and it may be important in some cases to suppress A-delta pain rather than, or in addition to, C-fiber nociception. Therefore, putative pain modulators should be evaluated with respect to a number of characteristics relating to primary inhibition and secondary management of different pain sources.

Acknowledgments

Research support to the authors that funded the collection of data included in the chapter has come from Public Health Service grants NS 07261, NS 14899, NS 06835, NS 06347, NS 07166, and MH 15737. The research involved animals maintained in animal-care facilities fully accredited by the American Association for Accreditation of Laboratory Animal Care. The technical assistance of Jean Kaufman, Ruth Rand, Steve Borabeck, Mike Young, and Larry Osterman is gratefully acknowledged.

References

Ahlqvist, M., Edwall, L., Franzen, O., and Haegerstrom, G. (1982). Perception of pulpal pain as a function of intradental nerve activity. Submitted.

Anderson, L. S., Black, R. G., Abraham, J., and Ward, A. A., Jr. (1971) Neuronal hyperactivity in experimental trigeminal deafferentation. *Journal of Neurosurgery* **35**, 444.

Anderson, S. D., Basbaum, A. I., and Fields, H. I. (1977). Response of medullary raphe neurons to peripheral stimulation and to systemic opiates. *Brain Research* **123**, 363–368.
Andrell, P. O. (1954). Cutaneous pain elicited in man by thermal radiation: Dependence of the threshold intensity of stimulation time, skin temperature and analgesics. *Acta Pharmacologica Toxicologica* **10**, 30–37.
Applebaum, A. E., Beall, J. E., Foreman, R. D., and Willis, W. D. (1975). Organization and receptive fields of primate spinothalamic tract neurons. *Journal of Neurophysiology* **38**, 572–586.
Badia, R., Culbertson, S., and Harsh, J. (1973). Choice of longer or stronger signalled shock over shorter or weaker unsignalled shock. *Journal of the Experimental Analysis of Behavior* **19**, 25–32.
Barber, T. X. (1959). Toward a theory of pain: Relief of chronic pain by prefrontal leucotomy, opiates, placebos, and hypnosis. *Psychological Bulletin* **56**, 430–460.
Basbaum, A. I., Clanton, C. H., and Fields, H. I. (1976). Ascending projections of nucleus gigantocellularis and nucleus raphe magnus in the cat: An autoradiographic study. *Anatomical Record* **184**, 354.
Basbaum, A. I., Marley, N. J. E., O'Keefe, J., and Clanton, C. H. (1977). Reversal of morphine and stimulus-produced analgesia by subtotal spinal cord lesions. *Pain* **3**, 43–56.
Basbaum, A. I., Clanton, C. H., and Fields, H. I. (1978). Three bulbospinal pathways from the rostral medulla of the cat: An autoradiographic study of pain modulation systems. *Journal of Comparative Neurology* **178**, 209–224.
Beecher, H. K. (1957). The measurement of pain: Prototype for the quantitative study of subjective responses. *Pharmacological Review* **9**, 59–209.
Belcher, G. (1977). Correlation between effects of brainstem stimulation and effects of serotonin and noradrenaline on nonnociceptive and nociceptive spinal neurons. *British Journal of Pharmacology* **61**, 149–150.
Bennett, G. J., and Mayer, D. J. (1976). Effects of microinjected narcotic analgesics into the periaqueductal gray (PAG) in the response of rat spinal cord dorsal horn interneurons. *Proceedings of the Society of Neuroscience* **2**, 928.
Bernstein, M. E., and Bernstein, J. J. (1973). Regeneration of axons and synaptic complex formation rostral to the site of hemisection in the spinal cord of the monkey. *International Journal of Neuroscience* **5**, 15–26.
Bessou, P., and Perl, E. R. (1969). Response of cutaneous sensory units with unmyelinated fibers to noxious stimuli. *Journal of Neurophysiology* **32**, 1025–1042.
Brown, A. G. (1981). "Organization in the Spinal Cord. The Anatomy and Physiology of Indentified Neurons." Springer-Verlag, Berlin and New York.
Buxbaum, D. M., Yarbrough, G. G., and Carter, M. E. (1973). Biogenic amines and narcotic effects. I. Modification of morphine-induced analgesia and motor activity after alteration of cerebral amine levels. *Journal of Pharmacology and Experimental Therapeutics* **185**, 317–327.
Carlsson, A., Falck, B., Fuxe, K., and Hillarp, N.-A. (1964). Cellular localization of monoamines in the spinal cord. *Acta Physiologica Scandinavica* **60**, 112–119.
Casey, K. L. (1969). Spinal pathways, and size of cutaneous fibers influencing unit activity in the medial medullary reticular formation. *Experimental Neurology* **25**, 35–55.
Casey, K. L., Hall, B. R., and Morrow, T. J. (1981). Effect of spinal cord lesions on responses of cats to thermal pulses. *Pain (Supplement)* **1**, 130.
Christensen, B. N., and Perl, E. R. (1970). Spinal neurons specifically excited by noxious or thermal stimuli: Marginal zone of the dorsal horn. *Journal of Neurophysiology* **33**, 293–307.
Chung, J. M., and Wurster, R. D. (1978). Neurophysiological evidence for spatial summation in the CNS from unmyelinated afferent fibers. *Brain Research* **153**, 596–601.

Cicero, T. J. (1974). Effects of α-adrenergic blocking agents on narcotic induced analgesia. *Archives Internationales de Pharmacodynamie* **208**, 5–13.

Collins, W. F. and Randt, L. T. (1956). An electrophysiological study of small myelinated axons in anterolateral column in cat. *Journal of Neurophysiology* **19**, 438–445.

Cooper, B. Y., and Vierck, C. J., Jr. (1980). A comparison of operant and reflexive measures of morphine analgesia. *Society for Neuroscience Abstracts* **6**, 430.

Cooper, B. Y., and Vierck, C. J., Jr. (1982). Response system properties in the measurement of pain and hypalgesia in M. speciosa I: Pain and morphine hypalgesia. Submitted.

Cooper, B. Y., Vierck, C. J., Jr., and Franzen, O. (1982). Morphine diminishes C-fiber but not A-delta mediated pain sensations in humans. Submitted.

Crutcher, K. A., and Bingham, W. G., Jr. (1978). Descending monoaminergic pathways in the primate spinal cord. *American Journal of Anatomy* **153**, 159–164.

Dafny, N., Brown, M., Burks, T. F., and Rigor B. M. (1978). Patterns of unit responses to incremental doses of morphine in central gray, reticular formation, medial thalamus, caudate nucleus, hypothalamus, septum, and hippocampus in unanesthetized rats. *Neuropharmacology* **18**, 489–495

Dafny, N., Marchand, J., McClung, R., Salamy, J., Sands, S. Wachtendorf, H., and Burks, T. F. (1980). Effects of morphine on sensory-evoked responses recorded from central gray, reticular formation, thalamus, hypothalamus, limbic system, basal ganglia, dorsal raphe, locus coeruleus, and pineal body. *Journal of Neuroscience* **5**, 399–412.

Dahlström, A., and Fuxe, K. (1965). Evidence for the existence of monoamine neurons in the central nervous system. II. Experimentally induced changes in the intraneuronal amine levels of bulbospinal neuron systems. *Acta Physiologica Scandinavica* **52**, (Suppl. 247), 1-36.

D'Amour, F. E., and Smith, D. (1941). A method for determining loss of pain sensation. Journal of Pharmacology and Experimental Therapeutics **72**, 74–79.

Davis, M. (1979). Morphine and naloxone: Effects on conditioned fear as measured with the potentiated startle paradigm. *European Journal of Pharmacology* **54**, 341–347.

Dennis, S. G., and Melzack, R. (1979). Comparison of phasic and tonic pain in animals. *Advances in Pain Research and Therapy* **3**, 747–760.

Denny-Brown, D. (1979). The enigma of crossed sensory loss with cord hemisection. *Advances in Pain Research and Therapy* **3**, 889–895.

DeRyck, M., Schallert, T., and Teitelbaum, P. (1980). Morphine versus haloperidol catalepsy in the rat: A behavioral analysis of postural support mechanisms. *Brain Research* **201**, 143–172.

Dickenson, A. H., Oliveras, J.-L., and Besson, J.-M. (1979). Role of the nucleus raphe magnus in opiate analgesia as studied by the microinjection technique in the rat. *Brain Research* **170**, 95–111.

Duggan, A. N., Hall, J. G., and Headley, P. M. (1977). Suppression of transmission of nociceptive impulses by morphine: Selective effects of morphine administered in the region of the substantia gelatinosa. *British Journal of Pharmacology* **62**, 65–76.

Dykstra, L. A. (1980). Discrimination of electric shock: Effects of some opioid and nonopioid drugs. *Journal of Pharmacology and Experimental Therapeutics* **213**, 234–240.

Eddy, N. B., and Leimbach, D. (1953). Synthetic analgesics II. Dithienylbutenyl and dithienylbutyl amines. *Journal of Pharmacology and Experimental Therapeutics* **107**, 388–393.

Esposito, R. U., and Kornetsky, C. (1978). Opioids and rewarding brain stimulation. *Neuroscience and Biobehavioral Reviews* **2**, 115–122.

Feltz, P., Krauthamer, G., and Albe-Fessard, D. (1967). Neurons of the medial diencephalon. I. Somatosensory responses and caudate inhibition. *Journal of Neurophysiology* **30**, 585–80.

Fields, H. I., Wagner, G. M., and Anderson, S. D. (1975). Some properties of spinal neurons projecting to the medial brain-stem reticular formation. *Experimental Neurology* **47,** 118–134.

Fields, H. I., Emson, P. C., Gilbert, R. F. T., and Iverson, L. L. (1980). Multiple opiate receptor sites on primary afferent fibers. *Nature (London)* **284,** 351–353.

Finley, J. C. W., Maderdrut, J. L., and Petrusz, P. (1981). The immunocytochemical localization of enkephalin in the central nervous system of the rat. *Journal of Comparative Neurology* **198,** 541–565.

Fitzgerald, M., and Woolf, C. J. (1980). The stereospecific effect of naloxone on rat dorsal horn neurons: Inhibition in superficial laminae and excitation in deeper laminae. *Pain* **9,** 293–306.

Foreman, R. D., Schmidt, R. F., and Willis, W. D. (1977). Convergence of muscle and cutaneous input onto primate spinal thalamic tract neurons. *Brain Research* **124,** 555–560.

Foreman, R. D., Hancock, M. B., and Willis, W. D. (1981). Responses of spinothalamic tract cells in the thoracic spinal cord of the monkey to cutaneous and visceral inputs. *Pain* **11,** 149-162.

Franzen, O., and Lindblom, U. (1976). Tactile intensity functions in patients with sutured peripheral nerve. *In* "Sensory Functions of the Skin in Primates" (Y. Zotterman, ed.), pp. 113–118. Pergamon, Oxford.

Franzen, O., and Torebjork, E. H. (1981). The relative contribution of warm and nociceptive fibres to the sensations of warmth, heat and pain. *Electroencephalography and Clinical Neurophysiology* **52,** 34.

Franzen, O., Tamsen, A., and Terenius, L. (1982). The capability of the endorphin system to modulate pain in surgical patients as reflected in their postoperative demand for analgesics. *Scandinavian Meeting on Physiology and Behavior, Stockholm.*

Freeman, W., and Watts, J. W. (1948). Pain mechanisms and the frontal lobes: A study of prefrontal lobotomy for intractable pain. *Annals of Internal Medicine* **28,** 747–754.

Gelfand, S. (1964). The relationship of experimental pain tolerance to pain threshold. *Canad. J. Psychol.,* **18,** 38–42.

Georgoupulos, A. P. (1977). Stimulus-response relations in high-threshold mechanothermal fibers innervating primate glabrous skin. *Brain Research* **128,** 547–552.

Gibson, R. H. (1968). Elecrical stimulation of pain and touch. *In* "The Skin Senses" (D. R. Kenshalo, ed.), pp. 223–261. Thomas, Springfield, Illinois.

Giesler, G. J., Apiel, H. R., and Willis, W. D. (1981a). Organization of spinothalamic tract axons within the rat spinal cord. *Journal of Comparative Neurology* **195,** 243–252.

Giesler, G. J., Jr., Yezierski, R. P., Gebhart, K. D., and Willis, W. D. (1981b). Spinothalamic tract neurons that project to medial and/or lateral thalamic nuclei: Evidence for a physiologically novel population of spinal cord neurons. *Journal of Neurophysiology* **46,** 1235–1308.

Goldberger, M. E., and Murray, M. (1978). Recovery of movement and axonal sprouting may obey some of the same laws. *In* "Neuronal Plasticity" (C. Cotman, ed.), pp. 73–96. Raven, New York.

Goodman, L. S., and Gilman, A. (1975). "The Pharmacological Basis of Therapeutics," p. 256. Macmillan, New York.

Gould, K. G., Warner, H., and Martin, D. E. (1978)). Rectal probe electroejaculation of primates. *Journal of Medical Primatology* **7,** 213–222.

Greenspan, J. D. (1980). Effects of skin compressibility upon psychophysical functions of tactile intensity: A comparison of force and depth of skin indentation as stimulus dimensions. Doctoral dissertation, Florida State University.

Grilly, D. M., and Genovese, R. F. (1979). Assessment of shock discrimination in rats with signal detection theory. *Perception and Psychophysics* **25,** 466–472.

Grossman, W., Jurna, I., Nell, T., and Theres, C. (1973). The dependence of the anti-nocioceptive effects of morphine and other analgesic agents on spinal motor activity after central monamine depletion. *European Journal of Pharmacology* **24,** 69–77.

Guilbaud, G., Besson, J. M., Oliveras, J. L., and Liebeskind, J. C. (1973). Suppression by LSD of the inhibitory effect excited by dorsal raphe stimulation on certain spinal cord interneurons in the cat. *Brain Research* **61,** 417–422.

Hallin, R. G., and Torebjork, H. E. (1976). Studies on cutaneous A and C fiber afferents, skin nerve blocks and perception. *Wenner-Gren International Symposium Series* **27,** 137–148.

Hamilton, B. L. (1973). Projections of the nuclei of the periaqueductal gray matter in the cat. *Journal of Comparative Neurology* **152,** 45–58.

Hardy, J. D., Wolff, H. G., and Goodell, H. (1952). " Pain Sensations and Reactions." Williams & Wilkins, Baltimore, Maryland.

Hayes, R. L., Price, D. D., and Dubner, R. (1979). Behavioral and physiological studies of sensory coding and modulation of trigeminal nociceptive input. *Advances in Pain Research and Therapy* **3,** 219–243.

Headley, P. M., Duggan, A. W., and Griersmith, B. T. (1978). Selective reduction by noradrenalin and 5-hydroxytryptamine of nociceptive responses of cat dorsal horn neurons. *Brain Research* **195,** 185–189.

Hendry, D. P. (1969). Concluding commentary. *In* "Conditioned Reinforcement" (D. P. Hendry, ed.). Dorsey, Homewood, Illinois.

Hernandez, L. L., and Appel, J. B. (1979). Analysis of some perceptual affects of morphine, chlorpromazine and LSD. *Psychopharmacology* **60,** 466–472.

Hill, H. E., Kornetsky, C. H., Flanary, H. G., and Wikler, A. (1952a). Effects of anxiety and morphine on discrimination of intensity of painful stimuli. *Journal of Clinical Investigation* **31,** 473–480.

Hill, H. E., Kornetsky, C. H., Flanary, H. G., and Wikler, A. (1952b). Studies on anxiety associated with anticipation of pain. I. Effects of morphine. *Archives of Neurology and Psychiatry* **67,** 612–619.

Hodge, C. J., Apkarian, A. V., Stevens, R., Vogilsang, G., and Wisnicki, H. J. (1981). Locus coeruleus modulation of dorsal horn unit responses to cutaneous stimulation. *Brain Research* **204,**415–420.

Hokfelt, T., Elde, R., Johanssen, O., Terenius, L., and Stein, L. (1977). The distribution of enkephalin immunoreactive cell bodies in the rat CNS. *Neuroscience Letters* **5,** 25–31.

Hosford, D. A., and Haigler, H. J. (1980). Morphine and methionine-enkephalin: Different effects on spontaneous and evoked neuronal firing in the mesencephalic reticular formation of the rat. *Journal of Pharmacology and Experimental Therapeutics* **213,** 355–363.

Hutchinson, R. R. (1977). By-products of aversive control. *In* "Handbook of Operant Behavior" (W. K. Honig and J. E. R. Staddon, eds.), pp. 415–431. Prentice-Hall, New York.

Hyndman, O. R. (1942). Lissauer's tract section. A contribution to chordotomy for the relief of pain. *Journal of the International College of Surgeons* **5,** 394–400.

Jackler, F., Steiner, S. S., Bodnar, R. J., Achermann, R. F., Nelson, W. T., and Ellman, S. J. (1979). Morphine and intracranial self-stimulation in the hypothalamus and dorsal brainstem: Differential effects of dose, time and site. *International Journal of Neuroscience* **9,** 21–35.

Jackson, H. (1952a). The evaluation of analgesic potency of drugs using thermal stimulation in the rat. *British Journal of Pharmacology* **7,** 196–203.

Jackson, H. (1952b). The effect of analgesic drugs on the sensation of thermal pain in man. *British Journal of Pharmacology* **7,** 204–214.

Javert, C. T., and Hardy, J. D. (1951). Influence of analgesics on pain intensity during labor (with a note on natural childbirth). *Anesthesiology* **12,** 189–215.

Jurna, I. (1980). Effect of stimulation in the periaqueductal grey matter on activity in ascending axons of the rat spinal cord: Selective inhibition of activity evoked by afferent A and C fibre stimulation and failure of naloxone to reduce inhibition. *Brain Research* **196,** 33–42.

Jurna, I., and Heinz, G. (1979). Differential effects of morphine and opioid analgesics on A and C fibre-evoked activity in ascending axons of the cat spinal cord. *Brain Research* **171,** 573–576.

Karoum, F., Commissiong, J. W., Neff, N. H., and Wyatt, R. J. (1980). Biochemical evidence for uncrossed and crossed locus coeruleus projections to the spinal cord. *Brain Research* **196,** 237–241.

Kelleher, R. T., and Morse, W. H. (1968). Schedules using noxious stimuli. III. Responding maintained with response-produced electric shocks. *Journal of Experimental Analysis of Behavior* **11,** 819–838.

Kenshalo, D. R., Jr., Leonard, R. B., Chung, J. M., and Willis, W. D. (1979). Responses of primate spinothalamic neurons to graded and to repeated noxious heat stimuli. *Journal of Neurophysiology* **42,** 1370–1389.

Kerr, F. W. L. (1975). The ventral spinothalamic tract and other ascending systems of the ventral funiculus of the spinal cord. *Journal of Comparative Neurology* **159,** 335–356.

Kitsikis, A., and Rougeul, A. (1968). The effect of caudate stimulation on conditioned motor behavior in monkeys. *Physiology and Behavior* **3,** 831–837.

Knibestol, M., and Vallbo, A. B. (1980). Intensity of sensation related to activity of slowly adapting mechanoreceptive units in the human hand. *Journal of Physiology (London)* **300,** 251–267.

Kornhuber, H. H. (1971). Motor function of cerebellum and basal ganglia: The cerebellocortical saccadic (Ballistic) clock, the cerebello-nuclear hold regulator, and the basal ganglia ramp (voluntary speed movement) generator. *Kybernetik* **8,** 157–162.

Kruger, L., and Kenton, B. (1973). Quantitative neural and psychophysical data for cutaneous mechanoreceptor function. *Brain Research* **49,** 1–24.

Kumazawa, T., and Perl, E. R. (1977). Primate cutaneous units with unmyelinated (C) afferent fibers. *Journal of Neurophysiology* **40,** 1325–1338.

Kumazawa, T., and Perl, E. R. (1978). Excitation of marginal and substantia gelatinosa neurons in the primate spinal cord: Indications of their place in dorsal horn functional organization. *Journal of Comparative Neurology* **177,** 417–434.

Kuru, M. (1949). "Sensory Paths in the Spinal Cord and Brain Stem of Man," pp. 675–709. Sogensya, Tokoyo.

LaMotte, R. H., and Campbell, J. N. (1978). Comparison of responses of warm and nociceptive C-fiber afferents in monkey with human judgement of thermal pain. *Journal of Neurophysiology* **41,** 509–528.

LaMotte, C., Pert, C. B., and Snyder, S. H. (1976). Opiate receptor binding in primate spinal cord: Distribution and changes after dorsal root section. *Brain Research* **112,** 407–412.

Le Bars, D., Guilbaud, G., Jurna, I., and Besson, J. M. (1976). Differential effects of morphine on responses of dorsal horn lamina V type cells elicited by A and C fibre stimulation in the spinal cat. *Brain Research* **115,** 518–524.

Le Bars, D., Dickenson, A. H., and Besson, J. M. (1979a). Diffuse noxious inhibitory controls (DNIC). II. Lack of effect on non-convergent neurons, supraspinal involvement and theoretical implications. *Pain* **6,** 305–327.

Le Bars, D., Rivot, J. P., Guilbaud, G., Menetrey, D., and Besson, J. M. (1979b). The depressive effect of morphine on the C-fibre response of dorsal horn neurons in the spinal rat pretreated or not by PCPA. *Brain Research* **176,** 337–353.

Le Bars, D., Chitour, D., Kraus, E., Clot, A. M., Dickenson, A. H., and Besson, J. M. (1981). The effect of systemic morphine upon diffuse noxious inhibitory controls (DNIC) in the rat: Evidence for a lifting of certain descending inhibitory controls of dorsal horn convergent neurons. *Brain Research* **215,** 257–274.

Levine, J. D., Murphy, D. T., Seidenwurm, D., Cortez, A., and Fields, H. I. (1980). A study of the quantal (all-or-none) change in reflex latency produced by opiate analgesics. *Brain Research* **201**, 129–141.

Levitt, M., and Levitt, J. H. (1981). The deafferentation syndrome in monkeys: Dysesthesias of spinal origin. *Pain* **10**, 129–147.

Lewis, M. E., Mischken, M., Bragin, E., Brown, R. N., Pert, C. B., and Pert, A. (1981). Opiate receptor gradients in monkey cerebral cortex: Correspondence with sensory processing hierarchies. *Science* **211**, 1166–1169.

Liebeskind, J. C., Guilbaud, G., Besson, J. M., and Oliveras, J. L. (1973). Analgesia from electrical stimulation of the periaqueductal gray matter of the cat: Behavioral observations and inhibitory effects on spinal cord interneurons. *Brain Research* **50**, 441–446.

Light, A. R., and Perl, E. R. (1977). Differential termination of large-diameter and small-diameter primary afferent fibers in the spinal dorsal gray matter as indicated by labeling with horseradish peroxidase. *Neuroscience Letters* **6**, 59–63.

Lineberry, C. G., and Kulics, A. T. (1978). The effects of diazepam, morphine and lidocaine on nociception in Rhesus monkeys: A signal detection analysis. *Journal of Pharmacology and Experimental Therapeutics* **205**, 302–310.

Lineberry, C. G., and Siegel, J. (1971). EEG synchronization, behavioral inhibition, and mesencephalic unit effects produced by stimulation of orbital cortex, basal forebrain and caudate nucleus. *Brain Research* **34**, 143–161.

Lineberry, C. G., and Vierck, C. J., Jr. (1975). Attenuation of pain reactivity by caudate nucleus stimulation in monkeys. *Brain Research* **95**, 110–134.

Liu, S., and Wang, R. I. H. (1981). Increased sensitivity of the central nervous system to morphine analgesia by amitryptyline in naive and morphine-tolerant rats. *Biochemical Pharmacology* **30**, 2103–2109.

Loeser, J. D., and Ward, A. A., Jr. (1967). Some effects of deafferentation on neurons of the cat spinal cord. *Archives of Neurology* **17**, 629–636.

McKearney, J. W. (1980). Fixed ratio schedules of food presentation and stimulus shock termination: Effects of *d*-amphetamine, morphine and clozapine. *Psychopharmacology* **70**, 35–39.

Malagodi, E. F., Gardner, M. L., Ward, S. E., and Magyar, R. L. (1981). Responding maintained under intermittent schedules of electric-shock presentation: "Safety" or schedule effects. *Journal of Experimental Analysis of Behavior* **36**, 171–190.

Marks, L. E. (1974). "Sensory Processes: The New Psychophysics." Academic Press, New York.

Mayer, D. J., and Price, D. D. (1976). Central nervous system mechanisms of analgesia. *Pain* **2**, 361–376.

Melzack, R., and Casey, K. L. (1968). Sensory motivational and central control determinants of pain. *In* "The Skin Senses" (D. R. Kenshalo, ed.), pp. 423–429. Thomas, Springfield, Illinois.

Melzack, R., and Wall, P. D. (1965). Pain mechanisms: A new theory, *Science* **150**, 971–979.

Mendell, L. M., and Wall, P. D. (1965). Responses of single dorsal cord cells to peripheral cutaneous unmyelinated fibers. *Nature (London)* **206**, 97–99.

Mohrland, J. S., and Gebhart, G. F. (1980). Effects of focal electrical stimulation and morphine microinjection in the periaqueductal gray of the rat mesencephalon on neuronal activity in the medullary reticular formation. *Brain Research* **201**, 23–37.

Nathan, P. W., and Smith, M. C. (1979). Clinico-anatomical correlation in anterolateral chordotomy. "Advances in Pain Research and Therapy" pp. 921–926.

Noordenbos, W., and Wall, P. D. (1976). Diverse sensory functions with an almost totally divided spinal cord. A case of spinal cord transection with preservation of part of one anterolateral quadrant. *Pain* **2**, 185–196.

Nygren, L.-G., and Olson, L. (1977). A new major protection from locus coeruleus: The main source of noradrenergic nerve terminals in the ventral and dorsal columns of the spinal cord. *Brain Research* **132,** 87–93.
Oliveras, J. L., Bourgoin, S., Hery, F., Besson, J. M., and Hamon, M. (1977). The topographical distribution of serotonergic terminals in the spinal cord of the cat: Biochemical mapping by the combined use of microdissection and microassay techniques. *Brain Research* **138,** 393–406.
Paalzow, G. (1979). Naloxone antagonizes theophylline-induced potentiation of morphine inhibition of a nocioceptive reaction in rats. *Psychopharmacology* **62,** 235–239.
Panksepp, J., Herman, B. H., Vilberg, T., Bishop, P., and DeEskinazi, F. G. (1978). Endogenous opioids and social behavior. *Neuroscience and Biobehavioral Reviews* **4,** 373–487.
Perl, B. R., Kumazawa, T., Lynn, B., and Kenins, P. (1976). Sensitization of high threshold receptors with unmyelinated (C) afferent fibers. *Progress in Brain Research* **43,** 263–277.
Pert, C. B., Kuhar, M., and Snyder, S. (1975). Autoradiographic localization of the opiate receptor in rat brain. *Life Sciences* **16,** 1849–1853.
Pin, C., Jones, B., and Jouvet, M. (1968). Topographie des neurones monaminergiques du tronc cerebral du chat: etuck par histoflorescence. *Comptes Rendus des Seances de la Societe de Biologie* **162,** 2136–2141.
Poling, A., Simmons, M. A., and Appel, J. B. (1978). Morphine and shock detection: Effects of shock intensity. *Psychopharmacology Communications* **2,** 333–336.
Price, N. J., and Fibiger, H. C. (1975). Ascending catecholamine systems and morphine alagesia. *Brain Research* **99,** 189–193.
Price, D. D., Hu, J. W., Dubner, R., and Gracely, R. H. (1977). Peripheral suppression of first pain and central summation of second pain evoked by noxious heat pulses. *Pain* **3,** 57–68.
Price, D. D., Hayes, R. L., Ruda, N., and Dubner, R. (1978). Spatial and temporal transformations of input to spinothalamic tract neurons and their relation to somatic sensations. *Journal of Neurohysiology* **41,** 933–947.
Proudfit, H. K., and Anderson, E. G. (1975). Morphine analgesia: Blockade by raphe magnus lesions. *Brain Research* **98,** 612–618.
Ritz, L. A., Greenspan, J. D., and Vierck, C. J., Jr. (1981). Behavioral tests of the effects of anterolateral chordotomy in primates. *Pain* **1,** (Suppl.), 289.
Saavedra, J. M., Grobecker, H., and Zivin, J. (1976). Catecholamines in the raphe nuclei of the rat. *Brain Research* **114,** 339–345.
Sakuma, Y., and Pfaff, D. W. (1980). Cells of origin of medullary projections in central gray of rat mesencephalon. *Journal of Neurophysiology* **44,** 1002–1011.
Samanin, R., and Bernasconi, S. (1972). Effect of intraventricularly injected 6-OH-dopamine or midbrain raphe lesions on morphine analgesia in rats. *Psyhcopharmacologia* **25,** 175–182.
Satoh, K., Tokyama, M., Yamamoto, K., Sakumoto, T., and Shimizu, N. (1971). Noradrenaline innervation of the spinal cord. Studies by horseradish peroxidase method combined with monoamine oxidase staining. *Experimental Brain Research* **30,** 175–186.
Sherman, J. E., and Liebeskind, J. C. (1980). An endorphinergic, centrifugal substrate of pain modulation: Recent findings, current concepts, and complexities. *Pain* 191–204.
Smith, G. M., Egbert, L. D., Markowitz, R. A., Mosteller, F., and Beecher, H. K. (1966). An experimental pain method sensitive to morphine in man: The submaximum effort tourniquet technique. *Journal of Pharmacology and Experimental Therapeutics* **154,** 324–332.
Stebbins, W. C. (1970). Studies of hearing and hearing loss in the monkey. *In* "Animal Psychophysics" (W. C. Stebbins, ed.), Prentice-Hall, New York.
Sweet, W. H. (1981). Animal models of chronic pain: Their possible validation from human experience with posterior rhizotomy and congenital analgesia. *Pain* **10,** 275–296.

Tang, A. H., and Schoenfeld, M. J. (1978). Comparison of subcutaneous and spinal subarachnoid injections of morphine and naloxone on analgesic tests in the rat. *European Journal of Pharmacology* **52**, 215–223.

Tedford, W. H., Warren, D. E., and Flynn, W. E. (1977). Alteration of shock aversion thresholds during the menstrual cycle. *Perception and Psychophysics* **21**, 193–196.

Tenen, S. S. (1968). Antagonism of the analgesic effect of morphine and other drugs by *p*-chlorophenylalanine, a serotonin depletor. *Psychopharmacologia* **12**, 278–285.

Torebjork, H. E., and Hallin, R. G. (1976). Skin receptors supplied by unmyelinated (C) fibers in man. *Werner-Gren Center International Symposium Series* **27**, 475–485.

Trevino, D. L., and Carstens, E. (1975). Confirmation of the location of spinothalamic neurons in the cat and monkey by the retrograde transport of horseradish peroxidase. *Brain Research* **98**, 177–182.

Tursky, B. (1974). Physical, physiological, and psychological factors that affect pain reaction to electric shock. *Psychophysiology* **11**, 95–112.

Vierck, C. J., Jr. (1982). Plasticity of somatic sensations and motor capabilities following lesions of the dorsal spinal columns in monkey. *In* "Changing Concepts of the Nervous System" (A. R. Morrison and P. L. Strick, eds.). Academic Press, New York.

Vierck, C. J., Jr., and Cooper, B. Y. (1980). Contextual determinants of pain reactions. *Brain and Behavioral Sciences* **3**, 314–315.

Vierck, C. J., Jr., and Luck, M. M. (1979). Loss and recovery of reactivity to noxious stimuli in monkeys with primary spinothalamic cordotomies, followed by secondary and tertiary lesions of other cord sectors. *Brain* **102**, 233–248.

Vierck, C. J., Jr., Hamilton, D. M., and Thornby, J. I. (1971). Pain reactivity of monkeys after lesions to the dorsal and lateral columns of the spinal cord. *Experimental Brain Research* **13**, 140–158.

Vierck, C. J., Jr., Franzen, O., and Cooper, B. Y. (1980). Evaluation of electrocutaneous pain: (1) comparison of operant reactions of humans and monkeys and (2) magnitude estimation and verbal description by the human subjects. *Neuroscience Abstracts* **6**, 430.

Voris, H. C. (1957). Variations in the spinothalamic tract in man. *Journal of Neurosurgery* **14**, 55–60.

Vrensen, G., and Nunes Cardozo, J. (1981). Changes in size and shape of synaptic connections after visual training: An ultrastructural approach. *Brain Research* **218**, 79–97.

Warren, R. M. (1981). Measurement of sensory intensity. *Behavioral Brain Science* **4**, 175–225.

Weaver, T. A., and Walker, A. E. (1941). Topical arrangement within the spinothalamic tract of the monkey. *Archives of Neurology and Psychiatry (Chicago)* **46**, 877–883.

Weiss, B., and Laties, V. G. (1961). Changes in pain tolerance and other behavior produced by salicylates. *Journal of Pharmacology and Experimental Therapeutics* **131**, 120–129.

Weiss, B., and Laties, V. G. (1963). Characteristics of aversive thresholds measured by a titration schedule. *Journal of Experimental Analysis of Behavior* **6**, 563–572.

Weiss, B., and Laties, V. G. (1964). Analgesic effects in monkey of morphine, nalorphine, and a benzomorphan narcotic antagonist. *Journal of Pharmacology and Experimental Therapeutics* **143**, 169–173.

Westlund, R. N., and Coulter, J. D. (1980). Descending projections of the locus coeruleus and subcoeruleus/medial parabrachial nuclei in monkey: Axonal transport studies and dopamine-B-hydroxylase immunocytochemistry. *Brain Research Review* **2**, 235–264.

White, J. C., and Sweet, W. H. (1969). "Pain and the Neurosurgeon: A Forty Year Experience." Thomas, Springfield, Illinois.

Wikler, A., Goodell, H., and Wolff, H. G. (1945). The effects of analgesic agents on sensations other than pain. *Journal of Pharmacology and Experimental Therapeutics* **83**, 294–299.

Willis, W. D. (1979). Supraspinal control of ascending pathways. *Progress in Brain Research* **50,** 163–174.

Woolfe, G., and MacDonald, A. D. (1944). The evaluation of the analgesic action of pothidine hydrochloride (Demerol). *Journal of Pharmacology and Experimental Therapeutics* **80,** 300–307.

Yaksh, T. L. (1978). Analgetic actions of the intrathecal opiates in cat and primate. *Brain Research* **153,** 205–210.

Yaksh, T. L. (1979). Direct evidence that spinal serotonin and noradrenaline terminals mediate the spinal antinociceptive effects of morphine in the periaqueductal gray. *Brain Research* **160,** 180–185.

Yaksh, T. L. (1981). Spinal opiate analgesia: Characteristics and principles of action. *Pain* **11,** 293–346.

Yaksh, T. L., and Reddy, S. V. R. (1981). Studies in the primate on the analgetic effects associated with intrathecal actions of opiates, alpha-adrenergic agonists and baclofen: Their pharmacology in the primate. *Anesthesiology* **54,** 451–467.

Yaksh, T. L., and Rudy, T. A. (1977). A dose ratio comparison of the interaction between morphine and cyclazocine with naloxone in rhesus monkeys on the shock titration task. *European Journal of Pharmacology* **46,** 83–92.

Yaksh, T. L., and Rudy, T. A. (1978). Narcotic analgetics: CNS sites and mechanisms of action as revealed by intracerebral injection techniques. *Pain* **4,** 299–360.

Yaksh, T. L., Plant, R. L., and Rudy, T. A. (1977). Studies in the antagonism by raphe lesions of the antinocioceptive action of systemic morphine. *European Journal of Pharmacology* **41,** 399–408.

Zivin, J. A., Reid, J. L., Saavveedra, J. M., and Kopin, I. J. (1975). Quantitative localization of biogenic amines in the spinal cord. *Brain Research* **99,** 293–301.

Zotterman, Y. (1939). Touch, pain and tickling: An electrophysiological investigation on cutaneous sensory nerves. *Journal of Physiology (London)* **95,** 1–28.

PROGRESS IN PSYCHOBIOLOGY AND PHYSIOLOGICAL PSYCHOLOGY, VOL. 10

The Engram Found? Initial Localization of the Memory Trace for a Basic Form of Associative Learning

Richard F. Thompson
In collaboration with David A. McCormick, David G. Lavond, Gregory A. Clark, Ronald E. Kettner, and Michael D. Mauk
Department of Psychology
Stanford University
Stanford, California

I. Introduction

In this chapter the focus is on conceptual issues in the search for the "engram"—the neuronal substrate of learning and memory in the brain. The nature of the engram has proved to be among the most baffling questions in science. At present, analysis of brain mechanisms of learning and memory involves problems that are both empirical and conceptual. In order to analyze mechanisms of information storage and retrieval, it is first necessary to identify and localize the brain systems, structures, and regions that are critically involved. With a very few exceptions, such information has

ISBN 0-12-542110-9

not yet been obtained. It seems necessary to know where such processes occur before they can be analyzed.

There are conceptual issues attendant upon any particular experimental approach to brain mechanisms of learning and memory. Most workers would agree that learning is not a unitary phenomenon. There is much less agreement on how many kinds of learning exist and whether they reflect one, two, or several types of basic processes. In terms of underlying brain processes, this issue can be dealt with empirically. When it has been demonstrated that a brain process is critically involved in a given learning paradigm, this process can be examined in other paradigms. The same approach can be used to answer objections that a given brain process might be limited to one particular response system or one species. For the most part, this issue of generality has not been resolved in studies of brain substrates of learning, making general conclusions and comparisons across laboratories difficult. We feel that it is essential to explore the degree of generality of brain substrates of learning.

Another conceptual issue has to do, in part, with techniques in the study of brain substrates of learning. A worker using one kind of technique, i.e., lesion-behavior or chemistry-behavior, is sometimes prone to argue that another technique provides only correlational evidence, whereas his or her approach is more causal. This argument has often been used against electrophysiological approaches. In fact, all techniques and approaches to brain-behavior relations are equally "correlational" or "causal"—the relation between the locus and extent of the lesion and the effect on behavior, the relation between the type and amount of drug given and the effect on behavior, the relation between the behavioral change and the brain level of neurotransmitter, the relation between the behavioral change and electrophysiological activity, and so on. The most sensible way of dealing with this issue seems to be to develop convergent and predictive evidence using a variety of techniques and approaches. Various approaches have particular advantages; electrophysiological recording is at present the most convenient noninvasive method for surveying the activity of brain systems in relation to learning. Lesions provide at least suggestive evidence about possible functions, drug and neurotransmitter studies and microanatomical approaches provide evidence regarding putative mechanisms, and so on.

Even within the confines of a given approach, it is possible to go beyond simple observation of a correlation. In the case of a correlation between an electrophysiological process in a brain structure and behavioral learning, one can manipulate variables that influence either the electrophysiological process or behavioral learning and determine the effect on the other. If in all cases manipulations that systematically influence one have the same effect on the other, there is a strongly predictive relationship. It does not mean that one directly causes the other, but it does mean that the two are causally linked.

II. Model Systems Approach

In recent years, the "model system" approach to analysis of the neuronal substrates of learning and memory has been valuable and productive. The basic concept is to utilize a preparation showing a clear form of learning or behavioral plasticity in which neuronal analysis is possible. Habituation has proved to be a particularly good example. It exhibits similar behavioral properties and, to the extent that it has been analyzed, similar neuronal mechanisms have been found to exist in a range of animals from molluscs to mammals (Castellucci and Kandel, 1976; Thompson and Glanzman, 1976).

Each approach and model preparation has particular advantages. Molluscan preparations (e.g., Walter *et al.,* 1981, Davis and Gillette, 1978) appear particularly useful in terms of the feasibility of cellular analysis. Classical leg flexion conditioning of the acute spinal cat (Patterson, 1976; Patterson *et al.,* 1973; Durkovic, 1975) appears to offer similar potential advantages. The difficulties of cellular analysis of learning in the intact mammal are formidable. However, they provide potential models for a basic understanding of information processing and learning in higher animals and ultimately in humans. In behavioral terms, it is clear that higher vertebrates have developed increasing capacities for learning and have made use of these capacities in adaptive behavior. It seems that the evolution of the mammalian brain has resulted in systems specially adapted for information processing, learning, and memory.

A. Rabbit NM/eyelid paradigm

We have adopted a particularly clear-cut and robust form of learning in the intact mammal as a model system: classical conditioning of the rabbit nictitating membrane (NM) response, first developed for behavioral analysis of learning by Gormezano (see the chapter by Gormenzano *et al.,* in this volume and Gormezano *et al.,* 1962). This simple form of learning is extremely well characterized behaviorally, thanks largely to the extensive studies of Gormezano and his associates, and seems particularly well suited for neurobiological analysis (see Thompson *et al.,* 1973, 1976). Eyelid conditioning exhibits the same basic laws of learning in a wide range of mammalian species, including humans, and is prototypic of classical conditioning of striated muscle responses.

A word is in order about the nature of the conditioned response (CR). Investigators typically record either extension of the NM, which is a largely passive consequence of eyeball retraction (Cegavske *et al.,* 1976), or closure of the external eyelid. However, with standard procedures for NM conditioning, both become conditioned simultaneously and synchronously, together with some degree of contraction of the periorbital facial musculature. We will discuss the motor control in more detail below. The major components are NM extension (eyeball retraction) and eyelid closure. In recent work, we have measured and/or observed both. When we refer to the CR below, we mean both the NM and eyelid. All effects reported here occur equivalently for both. This fact maps very nicely into the large animal and human behavioral literature on eyelid conditioning.

Several laboratories have adopted the model systems approach to analysis of associative learning in the intact vertebrate. Cohen and associates use classical conditioning of the heart rate in the pigeon (see Cohen, 1980); Woody uses classical conditioning of the very short latency click-evoked "alpha" eye blink response with a glabellar tap unconditioned stimulus (UCS) in the cat (see Brons and Woody, 1980); Gabriel uses instrumental avoidance learning in the rabbit (see Gabriel *et al.,* 1980); and Weinberger (1980) uses classical conditioning of the pupillary response in the paralyzed cat. Olds and associates (e.g., 1972) and Segal (Segal and Olds, 1973) have used a combined classical and instrumental task in the rat with food reward.

In the discussion that follows, we will use classical conditioning of striated muscle responses (particularly the rabbit eyelid and NM responses) as the basic paradigm. In this paradigm, the essential condition for associative learning involves effective pairing of the conditioned stimulus (CS) and UCS. The essential condition for associative learning in all paradigms, including instrumental learning, involves some form of concatenation among stimuli, responses, and reinforcement—some processes of pairing analogous to the pairing of the CS and the UCS. In referring to learning, we will generally use classical conditioning as the prototype, but we assume that the reader will grant the generalization to other instances of at least simpler forms of learning as well. In all cases, the critical requirement is some degree of contiguity. Taste aversion learning appears to stand at one extreme on the contiguity continuum, but even here there are temporal limits.

III. Localization of the Memory Trace

The first issue that must be addressed in the search for the engram is the identification and localization of neuronal structures and systems that appear to be involved in learning. We approached this question using electrophysiological recording of neural unit activity as the initial method of identification. More detail will be given later. It is sufficient to note here that in terms of engagement of neuronal activity during learning, at least the following structures are involved: regions of the brainstem and midbrain, the cerebellum, the hippocampus and related structures, and portions of the neocortex. Fortunately, a number of other structures do not appear to be involved, e.g., basal ganglia and most nuclei of the amygdala.

It seems a reasonable assumption that the various brain structures and systems that, judged from their electrophysiological activity, do become involved in learning and memory retrieval. In particular, higher brain regions appear, under normal circumstances, do play such roles. The conditioned response is selectively and reversibly abolished by spreading depression of the contralateral motor cortex (Papsdorf *et al.,* 1965)—a clear effect on memory retrieval. On the other hand, the conditioned response cannot be learned if training is given only during periods of penicillin-induced hippocampal seizures (Thompson *et al.,* 1980). Yet the conditioned response can be learned in the absence of the neocortex (Oakley and Russell, 1972) or hippocampus (Solomon and Moore, 1975). All these data hold for the standard-delay conditioned response (in which the UCS overlaps the termination of the CS.) In fact, higher brain structures assume essential roles if more demands are placed on the learning and memory systems. Thus, animals with prior bilateral ablation of the hippocampus are unable to learn a trace CR, in which a period of no stimulation intervenes between CS offset and UCS onset (Weisz *et al.,* 1980). The same is true for a number of other phenomena of learning, e.g., latent inhibition, blocking, and discrimination reversal (see Solomon, 1980).

A. Hippocampus

The hippocampus is of particular interest. Even in the short-delay paradigm, activity of pyramidal neurons always grows rapidly over training to form a temporal model of the behavioral conditioned response (see Fig. 1). Examples of conditioned increases in the activity of identified pyramidal neurons (identified by antidromic stimulation and/or collision techniques) from the dorsal hippocampus are shown in Fig. 2. These neurons develop a very clear model of the behavioral response, with correlations between the pattern of unit increase and the behavioral NM response as high as 0.90. This model of the behavioral response generated by pyramidal neurons is not present in the first few trials of training, develops rapidly, initially in the UCS period and then in the CS period as the learned behavioral response develops, and grows considerably in amplitude. The initial growth in unit activity in the UCS period is the earliest sign of learning over the trials of training that we have seen in the brain. Note that the increased unit activity models the entire behavioral response, both in the learned CS and the UCS

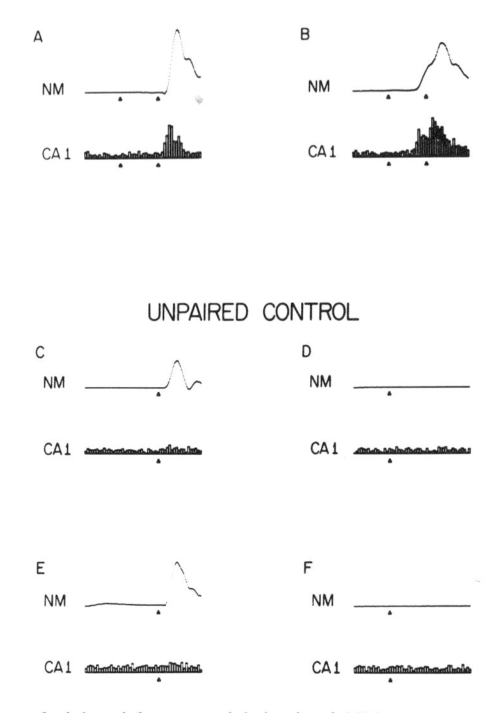

FIG. 1. Examples of eight-trial averaged behavioral NM responses and associated multiple-unit histograms of hippocampal activity for a conditioning (A, B) and a control (C–F) animal at the beginning and end of short delay training. Upper trace: Average NM response for one block of eight trials. Lower trace: Hippocampal unit poststimulus histogram (15-msec time bins) for one block of eight trials. (A) First block of eight paired conditioning trials, day 1. (B) Last block of eight paired conditioning trials, day 1, after conditioning has occurred. (C) First block of eight unpaired UCS–alone trials, day 1. (D) Last block of eight unpaired UCS-alone trials, day 2. (E) First block of eight unparied Cs-alone trials, day 1. (F) Last block of eight unpaired CS-alone trials, day 2. The trace duration is 750 msec, the first cursor is tone onset, and the second cursor is air puff onset. (From Berger and Thompson, 1978a.)

periods (the latter probably reflects both learned and reflexive behavioral components). This learning-induced increase in pyramidal neuron activity does not develop in unpaired control animals.

We have characterized the learning-induced hippocampal unit response over a wide range of conditions, including acquisition and extinction (Berger and Thompson, 1978a, b, 1981), variation of the CS–UCS interval (Hoehler and Thompson, 1980), temporal alternation (Hoehler and Thompson, 1979), and, in another learning paradigm, leg flexion conditioning (Thomp-

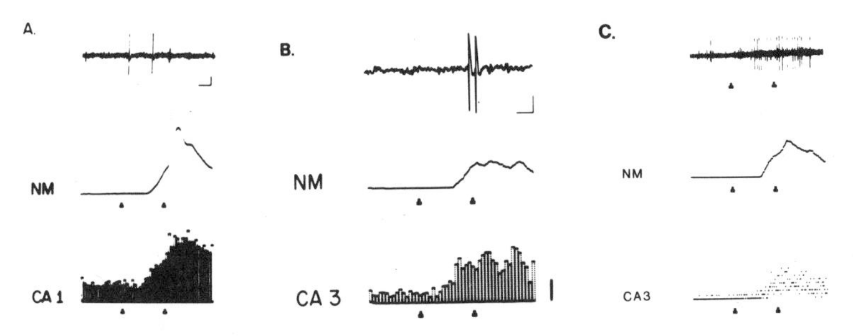

FIG. 2. Examples of learning-induced responses of identified pyramidal neurons in trained animals. Upper traces show individual raw unit records (A and B, 100-msec duration; C, one full trial of 750-msec duration). Middle traces show averaged NM responses, and lower traces show histograms of pyramidal neurons for the same blocks of trials, in all cases for at least 50 trials. Unit histogram bin widths are 15 msec in A and B and 3 msec in C. (From Berger and Thompson, 1978b, and unpublished observations.)

son *et al.,* 1980). We have reviewed this work in recent chapters and need not repeat it here (e.g., Thompson *et al.,* 1980; Berger *et al.,* 1980). In brief, over a wide range of conditions that impair or alter acquisition, maintenance, or extinction of the learned response, *the learning-induced increase in hippocampal unit activity invariably precedes and accurately predicts subsequent behavioral learning performance.* The hippocampal response has all the properties of a direct measure of the inferred processes of learning and memory in the brain. In terms of mechanisms, the neuronal plasticity is exhibited by identified pyramidal neurons of fields CA3–CA1 but not, in general, by other types of hippocampal neurons, and has many formal similarities to the process of long-term potentiation (LTP) (Swanson *et al.,* 1982).

B. Lower Brain Systems

Rabbits can learn the standard delay NM extension CR following ablation of all brain tissue above the level of the thalamus (Enser, 1976), and cats with high decerebration can learn the delay conditioned eye blink response (Norman *et al.,* 1977). Several possible inferences can be made from these results. One possibility is that no brain structures above the level of the midbrain are normally involved at all in the learning of the CR. This seems clearly to be wrong, as noted above. The other extreme is that midbrain-brainstem systems are not normally involved at all in learning the CR but can be made to do so. This may in fact be the case for spinal conditioning. Classical conditioning of the hindlimb flexion reflex can be established in an acute spinal animal, but such plasticity at the spinal level may not occur when an intact animal learns a leg flexion response (Patterson, 1976). The intermediate inference is that both midbrain-brainstem and higher brain regions are normally involved. We have adopted this as a working hypothesis.

If a number of brain systems are normally involved in learning this simple CR, is there some essential circuitry? It seems necessary to distinguish between brain structures and systems that are required for the execution of the CR and those that form the neuronal plasticity—the associative links—that is the essential neuronal substrate of the learned response. Some portion of the primary auditory system is necessary to convey the information that the tone CS is occurring. However, several lines of evidence to be discussed below argue strongly that the primary auditory system is not the locus of the essential neuronal plasticity. By the same token, motorneurons in certain cranial nerve nuclei are necessary for the normal performance of the CR. Again, several lines of evidence argue strongly that they are not the locus of neuronal plasticity. The same is true for the reflex pathways that generate the unconditioned response (UCR).

The question remains: What is the circuitry that codes the essential neuronal plasticity of learning and memory for the CR? Either there is one locus or system, or there is not. If not, there is a depressingly large number of possibilities, the most commonly held being that the engram is distributed widely and diffusely in the brain (e.g., John, 1967). However, if a discrete lesion in the midbrain-brainstem can selectively abolish the CR, and it is not simply a sensory or motor impairment, then it appears that there is a localized midbrain-brainstem circuit that is the substrate for the essential neuronal plasticity for the standard delay CR. This might be termed the "primary engram" for the delay CR. If so, it becomes extremely important to identify and characterize this circuitry. It will provide a basic model for the analysis of the neuronal-synaptic processes that underlie learning and memory. We think we may have found this circuit; very recent evidence from our laboratory suggests that it is in the cerebellum. We will expand on this below.

This is not to say that higher brain structures do not normally play important roles and, in fact, develop substantial learning-induced neuronal plasticity. Indeed, the hippocampus does so. It seems important to analyze the mechanisms of learning-induced neuronal plasticity wherever such plasticity can be shown to occur in the brain. This analysis will provide information both about the putative mechanisms underlying learning-induced neuronal plasticity and about the roles of brain structures exhibiting such plasticity in learning and memory.

Perhaps the minimum requirement for the demonstration that learning-induced plasticity has occurred in neurons of a given brain region is that the neurons show altered output to constant input, or at the very least an output that does not simply relay the input but changes relative to it. A further requirement for associative learning is that the change in neuronal activity occurs under conditions that yield associative learning, and only under these conditions. For classical conditioning, this would be effective paired CS and UCS trials, and for instrumental learning an analogous effective occurrence of stimulus, response, and reinforcement contingencies. This requirement would exclude nonassociative aspects of neuronal plasticity induced by training, such as habituation and sensitization.

C. The Hebb synapse

Identification of neurons that contain "learning synapses"—processes of synaptic plasticity that code various aspects of learning and memory phenomena—is a major goal of studies on brain substrates of learning and memory. At our current level of understanding, it seems most likely that this plasticity occurs at synapses. Hebb (1949) proposed what is perhaps the simplest type of synaptic plasticity; it has come to be termed the "Hebb synapse". In brief, it is assumed that under special circumstances of use, as in learning, certain synapses, usually taken to be excitatory, develop persisting and eventually permanent increases in excitability. Hebb argued that the fundamental event was synaptic use associated with the firing of the postsynaptic neuron. In simple learning terms, this means that if synapses from the CS pathway act on neurons that are being fired by the UCS pathway neurons, then plasticity will develop at the conditioned stimulus synapses. The Hebb synapse is a form of use-induced plasticity (see also Eccles, 1957; Stent, 1973).

Actually, in terms of current knowledge of synaptic processes, there is no need to require firing of the postsynaptic neurons to establish plasticity. Transmitter interactions could occur presynaptically, in the synaptic space, postsynaptically, and intracellularly, as in interaction effects on a "second messenger" system. What does appear to be necessary for the Hebb synapse —for synaptic plasticity that codes learning—is some degree of convergent synaptic action. In the case of simple conditioning, synapses from the CS and UCS pathways must at some point(s) act together on the same neurons, and similarly for stimulus (and/or response) events in more complex learning. The Hebb synapse would only require repeated convergent synaptic input; firing of the postsynaptic cell is not necessary.

Milner (1957) elaborated Hebb's notion and emphasized the importance of reinforcement in establishing synaptic plasticity. There is something special about the kinds of converging influences that can establish plasticity, and perhaps something special about the kinds of neurons and/or structures in the brain that code plasticity. Contiguous activation of the same spinal motoneurons by stimulation of group IA and group II afferents does not establish long-lasting plasticity. The minimal condition then becomes appropriate convergent, repetitive synaptic actions. This might be termed the "memory synapse," or, more properly, the "memory neuron." These are the neurons and circuits that code learning and memory in the brain. They can be defined operationally, and so identified, as neurons whose output changes relative to input under conditions of associative learning.

Another important requirement of memory neurons is that the learning-induced plasticity they exhibit must obey the basic laws of learning. In classical conditioning of striated muscle responses, these basic laws include at least the following: (*a*) the process of plasticity must develop initially at the time of onset of the UCS and move forward in time with training; (*b*) the development of plasticity must be under very powerful control by the CS–UCS interval, in terms of both amplitude and pattern of activity, and must show maximum learning with an interval of about 200–300 msec but not with intervals of 50 msec or less. There are also laws of learning dealing with such matters as stimulus generalization, discrimination and reversal, and extinction. The learning-induced plasticity of pyramidal neurons in fields CA1–CA3 of the hippocampus obeys these laws very well, as we have noted elsewhere (Thompson *et al.,* 1980).

D. The lesion approach

Many workers still place their greatest faith in the lesion approach to localization of the engram (Mishkin, 1978). Certainly, if a specific brain lesion causes selective and permanent abolition of a learned response in a given learning task, it is strong presumptive evidence that the region, structure, or pathway plays an essential role in memory. However, as noted above, this might involve necessary sensory pathways or motor nuclei. If the CS is auditory, bilateral ablation of the cochlear nuclei will abolish the learned response. Similarly, destruction of the motor neurons necessary for performance of the task will abolish the learned response. However, if these possibilities can be excluded, then the lesion may be presumed to have destroyed a significant part of the circuitry containing the essential neuronal plasticity for the learned response.

The lesion technique is considerably less helpful with negative results. The absence of a lesion deficit in no way implies that the structure so damaged or destroyed is not normally involved in learning. Assume that three partially separate systems in the brain all code the engram. Destruction of any one or even two might have no effect on the learned response. Just such a situation was found by Cohen (1980) in terms of the necessary visual pathways for the CS in classical conditioning of the heart rate response in the pigeon. Any one of these separate visual pathways can support the response. It remains an article of faith, but at this point in time a fairly reasonable one, that if two or more neuronal systems can each function to code the learned response, then destruction of all of them will eliminate the learned response. Again, the lesion approach *per se* will not necessarily tell us how these systems function in learning and memory. Electrophysiological recording of neuronal activity is at present the only technique that can provide such information.

In sum, for the standard delay CR there are three extreme possibilities: (*a*) the engram is widely and diffusely distributed in the brain; (*b*) there are two or more systems in the brain, each of which codes the engram; or (*c*) there is one essential circuitry, probably in the midbrain-brainstem, and higher brain structures play very important modulatory roles but are not essential. At present, we favor the third alternative. Certain brain structures always play important roles in learning. "Memory" neurons exist and always code learning in the hippocampus. When more demands are made on the memory system, as in trace conditioning and other paradigms (see Solomon, 1980; Weisz *et al.*, 1980), then the hippocampal system, and perhaps other higher structures as well, become essential.

IV. Analysis of Brain Substrates of the Learned NM/Eyelid Response

All studies that manipulate biological and/or behavioral variables and examine the consequences for either neural or behavioral outcomes are basically correlational, as noted above. In general, more weight is placed on the absence of a correlation than on its presence—so-called strong inference. It is much easier to rule out possibilities than rule them in. In the sections that immediately follow, we present evidence that rules out certain possibilities for the neuronal substrates of the engram, at least for the standard delay conditioned NM and eyelid resonse, with varying degress of confidence. We begin with the CS channel, the auditory system.

A. The CS channel—the auditory system

In studies involving simple learning paradigms in which an acoustic CS has been used, training-related changes in unit activity have been reported at virtually all levels of the auditory system in at least some studies: cochlear nucleus (Oleson *et al.*, 1975), inferior colliculus (Disterhoft and Stuart, 1976), medial geniculate body (Buchwald *et al.*, 1966; Disterhoft and Stuart, 1977; Ryugo and Weinberger, 1978; Gabriel *et al.*, 1975); auditory cortex (Disterhoft and Stuart, 1976; Kitzes *et al.*, 1978), and association cortex (Woody *et al.*, 1976; Disterhoft *et al.*, 1981). Negative results were also reported in several of these studies for certain areas, including the inferior colliculus, medial geniculate body, and auditory cortex. In our own earlier work on the rabbit NM response, we did not see consistent changes over training in auditory unit activity in the cochlear nucleus and inferior colliculus (Lonsbury-Martin *et al.,* 1976). In most of these studies, the exact locations of recording electrodes were not specified. Weinberger and associates (Ryugo and Weinberger, 1978; Weinberger, 1980) found training-induced changes in the medial but not the ventral division of the medial geniculate body. Similarly, Gabriel *et al.* (1975) found such changes more medially than ventrally. Note that the negative result occurs in the "mainline" auditory specific portion of the medial geniculate body, the ventral division.

The observation that tone–CS-evoked activity of units in an auditory relay nucleus shows an increase as a result of training *per se* is simply a statement of a correlation, with its attendant problems of interpretation. Olds attempted to deal with the problem by specifying that the increase must be the shortest latency event within a trial in order to be a critical aspect of the neuronal substrate of learning (Olds *et al.,* 1972). Gabriel (1976) pointed out that a change in "bias"—the influence of another structure or system on the auditory relay nuclei—could result in short latency increases. Such a bias increase need not play an essential role in learning. It might, for example, reflect a process of conditioned "arousal" which itself might not be a necessary part of the neuronal changes that form the essential substrate of the behavioral learning. We suggested that any neuronal changes that form the essential substrate for learning must develop earlier than (or certainly no later than) the appearance of behavioral signs of learning over the trials of training (Thompson *et al.,* 1976). However, we did not argue that this is a sufficient condition, only a necessary one. In any event, studies that report increases in unit activity in auditory structures with training do not necessarily find any clear relationship between such change in neural activity and the development of behavioral learning over the trials of training.

In extensive recent studies, we have examined neuronal unit activity over the course of initial training of the rabbit NM response to an acoustic CS (Kettner and Thompson, 1982) in the anteroventral cochlear nucleus and the central nucleus of the inferior colliculus. There were absolutely no changes in background or CS-evoked levels of neuronal activity for any recording in either structure over the course of training.

These data are strongly negative but are still at the level of simple correlation, in this case the absence of a correlation. A much more powerful test of the possible role of the auditory relay nuclei in learning would be to manipulate the dependent behavioral variable—the occurrence of the learned NM response—while holding the independent variable—the accoustic stimulus—constant. We have developed just such a paradigm-signal detection (Kettner *et al.,* 1980). In brief, the animal is trained, overtrained, and taken to threshold using a staircase procedure so that the animal responds 50% of the time to the same intensity acoustic CS. A white noise CS is used to avoid problems related to tonotopic representation. At a constant CS threshold, a 25% reinforcement schedule is used, with data collected only on the 75% of white noise-alone trials. The behavioral NM response at the threshold is extremely reliable and well behaved. It is in fact dichotomous, being clearly present on detection trials and completely absent on nondetection trials.

1. Signal Detection

Learning and memory processes are fundamental to signal detection. In order to indicate behaviorally the detection of a threshold-level stimulus, the organism must make use of a learned response. When an organism is detecting a constant-intensity acoustic stimulus at threshold, the learned response is activated on 50% of the trials. The neuronal circuitry that plays an essential role in this memory retrieval must be activated on behavioral detection trials and either not activated or not sufficiently activated on nondetection trials. Consequently, any neuronal regions or systems in the brain that do show dichotomous, or at least differential, activation by detected and nondetected stimuli are candidate substrates for the learning-memory circuitry (note the hippocampal detection response in Fig. 3). The only alternative is that such structures are a part of the motor system generating the learned behavioral response.

Conversely, neurons and circuits activated identically by detected and nondetected stimuli are not a part of the neuronal substrate of the learning-memory circuitry. We have now completed an extensive analysis of the anteroventral cochlear nucleus, the central nucleus of the inferior colliculus, and the ventral division of the medial geniculate body, using multiple-unit recording, and a single-unit analysis of the central nucleus of the inferior colliculus (87 cells). The central nucleus of the inferior colliculus is particularly important because it is an obligatory relay nucleus for all fibers of the primary auditory system ascending from the brainstem. The results are completely consistent and clear (see Fig. 3). For every recording electrode in every structure, there is a substantial white noise-evoked unit response at threshold that is *identical* on detection and nondetection trials. In our judgment, this provides very strong evidence that the principal relay nuclei of the auditory system are not a part of the neuronal plasticity that codes learning.

This result cannot be accounted for by assuming that the animals are not performing at the behavioral threshold. Our animals were very well trained,

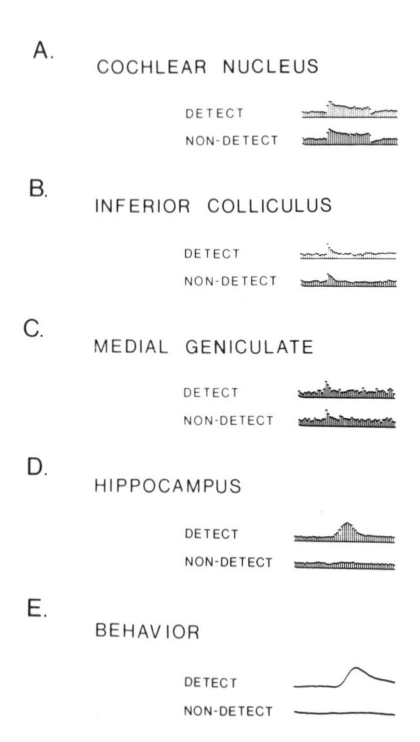

FIG. 3. Camparison of multiunit responses from auditory relay nuclei (and the hippocampus) during detection vs. nondetection trials at an absolute auditory threshold for a white noise stimulus. In all cases, the acoustic stimulus intensity is constant and identical on both detect and nondetect trials. A–D: average poststimulus histograms (15-msec time bins) created by averaging 200–300 trials (obtained from several testing sessions) for the cochlear nucleus (A), inferior colliculus (B), medial geniculate (C), and hippocampus (D) on detection (upper histogram) vs. nondetection (lower histogram) trials. (E) Average NM response for detection (upper trace) vs. nondetection (lower trace) trials. Note that the behavioral response and the hippocampal response are both dichotomous, being clearly present on detection trials and completely absent on nondetection trials. Responses from the auditory relay nuclei, in marked contrast, are clearly present and identical on detect and nondetect trials. (From Thompson *et al.*, 1980.)

and each showed an extremely reliable threshold (average standard deviation of no more than 2.4 dB). Our best animals had lower thresholds than do humans who are detecting a similar white noise stimulus. Furthermore, although there were, of course, individual differences between animals in threshold value, for every animal the threshold of evoked neural unit response in the auditory nuclei was at least 10 dB lower than the behavioral threshold. The constancy of the evoked unit response in the auditory nuclei indicates that stimulus control in our situation is excellent and that threshold detection behavior cannot be accounted for by systematic fluctuations in stimulus intensity or intrinsic noise. In signal detection terms, the decision to respond is not made in the primary auditory relay nuclei.

In sum, the primary auditory relay nuclei from the cochlear nucleus through the medial geniculate body are not a part of the engram—the neuronal plasticity that codes learning and memory. On the other hand, they obviously must transmit the information that the acoustic CS is occurring. Preliminary data indicate that animals with bilateral ablation of the inferior colliculi still show the learned response. Consequently, it appears that CS information is transmitted from the auditory system to other brain structures and systems below the level of the inferior colliculus.

B. The unconditioned reflex response pathways

The afferent limb of the reflex pathway for the NM response is limited to fibers of the trigeminal nerve. The efferent limb involves several cranial nerve nuclei. The primary response that produces NM extension is retraction of the eyeball (Cegavske *et al.,* 1976). A major muscle action producing this response is contraction of the retractor bulbus, which in rabbit is innervated by motoneurons of the abducens and accessory abducens nuclei (Gray et al., 1981). However, it appears that most of the extrinsic eye muscles may contract synchronously with the retractor bulbus (Berthier and Moore, 1980). In addition, the external eyelid (which is normally held open in NM conditioning) extends, under the control of motoneurons in the seventh nucleus. Finally, there is a variable degree of contraction of facial muscles in the vicinity of the eye. In sum, the total response is a coordinated defense of the eye involving primarily eyeball retraction (NM extension) and eyelid closure, with some contraction of periorbital facial musculature (see McCormick *et al.,* 1982a).

Simultaneous recordings from one NM and both eyelids during conditioning of the left eye show essentially perfect correlations in both amplitude and latency of the conditioned responses as they develop over the course of training (see Fig. 4). Other evidence indicates that the relevant motor nuclei (left accessory/abducens, left seventh, and right seventh) are not tightly coupled (McCormick *et al.,* 1982a). If the essential neuronal plasticity develops at the cranial motor nuclei, it must do so independently at each nucleus. If this is the case, it is very difficult to imagine how the several motor nuclei could generate perfectly correlated conditioned responses. Consequently, there must be a common central system at some point that acts synchronously on all the cranial motor nuclei engaged in the generation of the conditioned response.

Perhaps the simplest common central system is some component of the reflex pathways. If experimental manipulations could be developed that

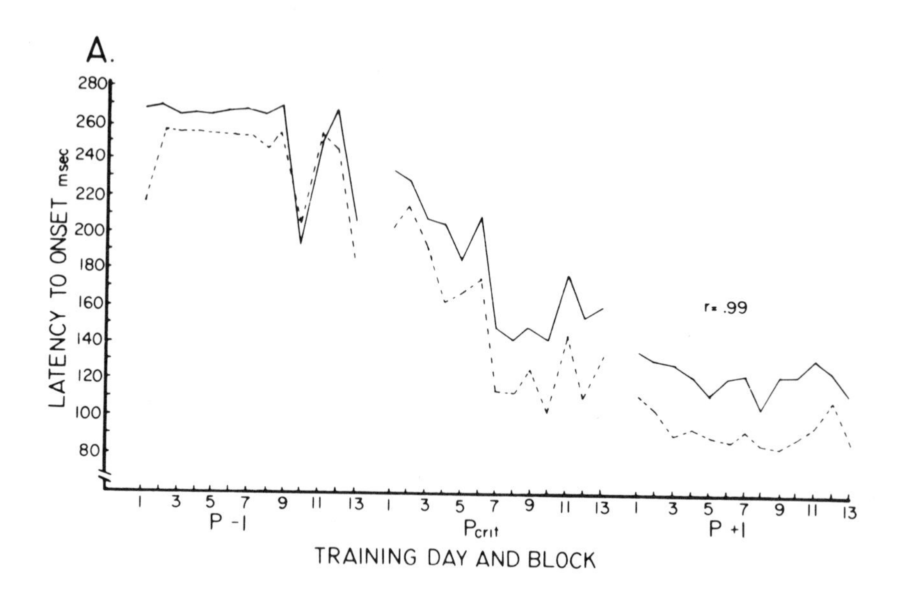

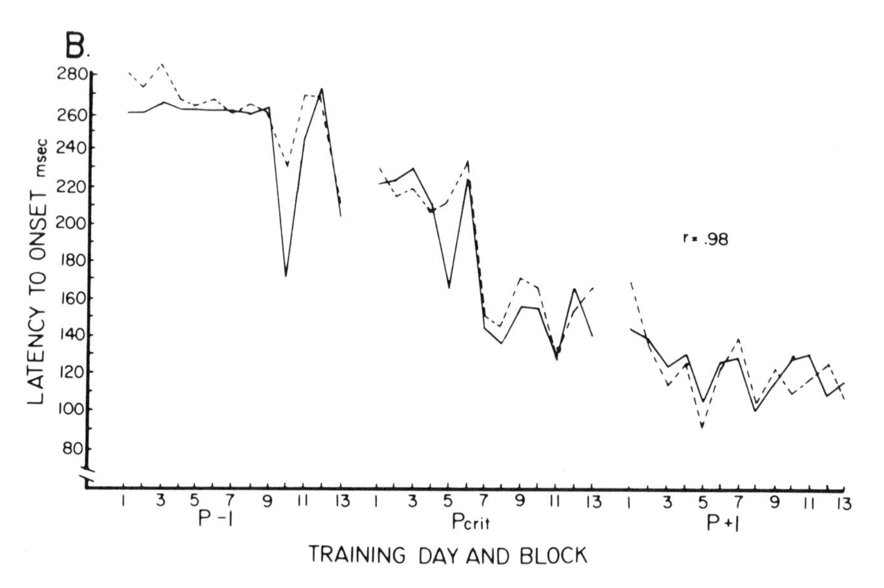

FIG. 4. Latency to onset of the behavioral responses from the onset of the tone in milliseconds over the course of training averaged in eight-trial blocks. (A) represents the latencies found for the left eyelid (dashed line) and left NM (solid line) of all eight animals. (B) represents the latencies for the right eyelid (dashed line) and left NM (solid line) for the six animals which showed bilateral conditioning. Pcrit is the day on which the animals reached criterion performance of eight conditioned responses on any nine consecutive trials. P − 1 is the training day prior to Pcrit, and P + 1 is the training day after Pcrit. (From McCormick *et al.*, 1982a.)

could independently vary the CR and the UCR, they would provide very strong evidence that the unconditioned reflex pathways—trigeminal afferents, interneurons, motoneurons—are not a critical part of the essential neuronal plasticity coding the learned response. Recently, we succeeded in doing this for the conditioned response using morphine (Mauk *et al.*, 1981). In brief, animals are trained to the criterion (eight CRs in nine successive trials), given two nine-trial blocks of additional training, injected with morphine (5 or 10 mg/kg IV), run for five blocks, and then injected with naloxone (0.1 mg/kg). The results are striking (see Fig. 5). There is an immediate and complete abolition of the CR, but no effect at all on the UCR. In unpaired control animals, morphine has no effect at all on the UCR, the reflex response to a corneal air puff. This provides strong evidence against essential participation of the unconditioned reflex response pathways in the engram.

The highly specific naloxone-reversible action of morphine on the CR appears to provide a powerful tool for the study of the learning circuitry in the brain. It must somehow inactivate some portion of the essential neuronal plasticity coding the learned response. Any brain structure of system showing learning-induced neuronal plasticity that is strongly and reversibly influenced by morphine becomes a candidate for the engram. One possibility is that conditioned aversiveness is an essential part of the engram in eyelid conditioning—an aversive component of the corneal air puff becomes conditioned to the tone CS—a form of conditioned fear. If such is the case, then morphine might act on this aspect of the associative network. A large body of literature suggests that both morphine and the endogneous opioids act

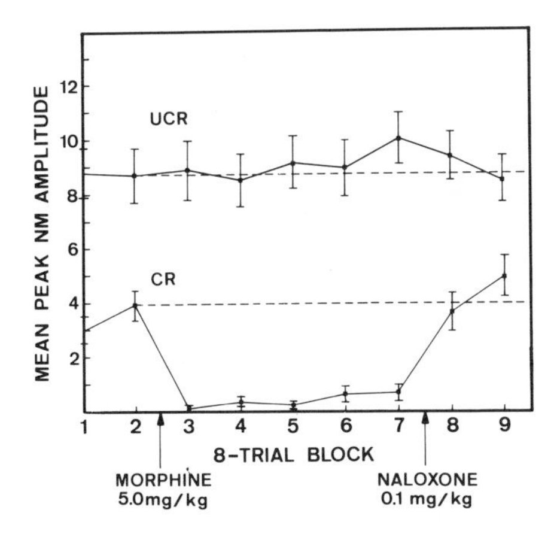

FIG. 5. Effects of morphine and naloxone on behavioral performance of the learned (CR) and reflex (UCR) components of the NM response in animals ($N = 13$) previously trained to criterion plus two eight-trial blocks. Dotted lines represent the mean premorphine baseline. (From Mauk *et al.*, 1981.)

more on learned fear or anxiety than on pain *per se* (see e.g., Jaffe and Martin, 1980; Martinez *et al.,* 1981; Wikler, 1958).

C. The "alpha response" pathway

The relatively long latency of the standard NM/eyelid CR—typically, at least 80 msec (see Fig. 4)—and the similarly long CS–UCS interval necessary for learning have implications for the brain systems and pathways that underlie learning. For an auditory CS, there is a relatively direct pathway from the auditory system to the cranial motor nuclei, particularly the seventh nucleus, as indicated by the short latency of the startle or alpha response to a loud or sudden sound. Woody reports a latency of about 20 msec for the alpha eyelid response in the cat to a click stimulus (Woody and Brozek, 1969). Woody's learning paradigm, incidentally, is an interesting model of associative plasticity: Pairing a click and a glabellar tap leads to an increase in the alpha response that does not occur with unpaired stimulus presentations. The properties of this very short latency eyelid response are quite different from those of the standard eyelid (and NM) conditioned response. In any event, if the essential neuronal plasticity coding the standard delay learned NM/eyelid response develops within the alpha response pathway, the learned response would have a latency of about 20 msec. This is much too short. Consequently, the alpha response is not the locus of the engram.

V. The Cerebellum—Locus of the Memory Trace?

In the course of our signal detection studies, we obtained recordings from 10 electrode placements in the ipsilateral cerebellar cortex just dorsal to the cochlear nucleus (Kettner, 1981). All these recordings showed a clear and striking dichotomous response—a substantial increase in unit firing on detection trials that closely modeled the behavioral detection response and an absence of such a response on nondetection trials (see Fig. 6). Interestingly, there was typically a short latency noise-onset evoked auditory response that was identical on both detection and nondetection trials.

As noted above, any brain structure that exhibits a dichotomous or differential response on detection and nondetection trials is a candidate for the decision-memory system, or it is part of the motor system generating the behavioral response. At the level of the motor nuclei, the neuronal response always closely models the behavioral response, whether learned or reflex, and would of course show a dichotomous response on detection vs. nondetection trials (see Fig. 7). The cerebellum is commonly viewed as a

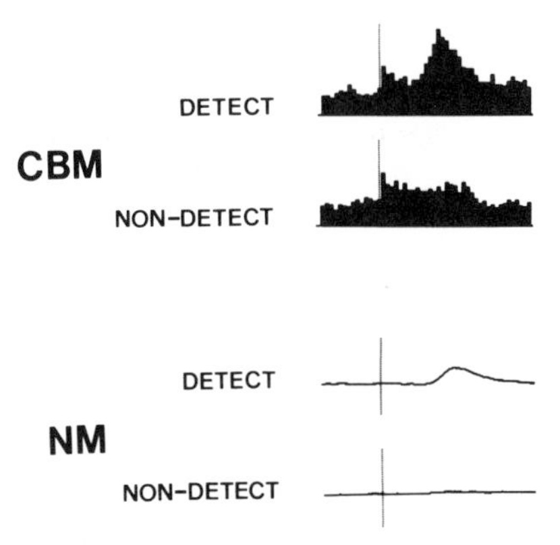

FIG. 6. Histograms of neuronal activity recorded from the cerebellar cortex dorsal to the cochlear nucleus on detection (above) and nondetection (below) trials to an identical threshold-level white noise stimulus, as in Fig. 3. Note the identical short latency stimulus onset-evoked response on both and the later "decision-memory" response that occurs only on detection trials. Behavioral NM detection and nondetection responses summed over the same trials are shown below. The vertical line indicates white noise onset. (From Kettner, 1981.)

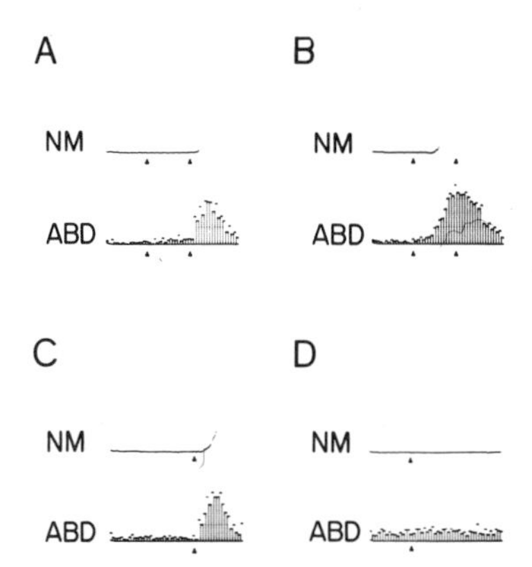

FIG. 7. Examples of eight-trial averaged behavioral NM responses and associated multiple-unit histograms of abducens nucleus activity (15-msec time bins) for a conditioning animal at the beginning and end of training (A, B) and a control animal for the air puff UCS (C) and the tone CS (D). The early cursor indicates tone onset, and the late cursor indicates airpuff onset. The total trace length equals 750 msec. Note the close correspondence between the histogram of unit activity and the behavioral NM response in all cases. (From Cegavske *et al.*, 1979.)

motor structure and might be considered a part of the neuronal system generating the behavioral response in the detection paradigm. However, the neuronal detection response in the cerebellum precedes the behavioral detection response by about 50 msec (see Fig. 6), too long a time period even to participate in the reflex response. (With the conditions of our studies, the mean onset latency of the reflex eyelid response is 7.3 msec and NM is 22.4 msec.)

A. The brainstem map

Over the past 3 years, we have been completing an extensive and detailed mapping of the midbrain-brainstem, recording neuronal activity in already trained animals (McCormick *et al.*, 1982b). For this purpose, we developed a chronic micromanipulator system that permits mapping of unit activity in a substantial number of neural loci per animal. Data from the mapping study will not be given here in any detail, except to indicate that learning-related increases in unit activity—increases that form a temporal model in a trial of the learned behavioral response—were prominent in certain regions of the cerebellum, both in the cortex and in deep nuclei, certain regions of the pontine nuclei, the red nucleus, the inferior olive, and the motor cortex. Such unit activity is also seen in certain regions of the reticular formation, in the deeper laminae of the superior colliculus, and, of course, in the cranial motor nuclei engaged in the generation of the behavioral response—portions of the third, fifth, sixth, accessory sixth, and seventh nuclei.

B. Learning-related neuronal activity in the cerbellum

The results to date of the mapping study point to substantial engagement of the cerebellar system in the generation of the CR. An example of a multiunit recording from the medial portion of the dentate nucleus ipsilateral to the eye being trained (left) is shown in Fig. 8. This represents an eight-trial average of paired trials with a standard 85-dB tone CS. In comparing this response with the detection response of Fig. 6, it should be noted that the detection response is to a threshold-level acoustic CS (white noise) on trials in which no UCS is given. Note that in Fig. 8 there are evoked responses to stimulus onsets and an increase in unit activity that models the behavioral CR but shows no clear model of the reflex response.

Current studies in which we have recorded the neuronal unit activity from the deep cerebellar nuclei (dentate nucleus) over the course of training have at times revealed a striking pattern of learning-related growth in activity. In the example shown in Fig. 9, the animal did not learn on day 1 of training.

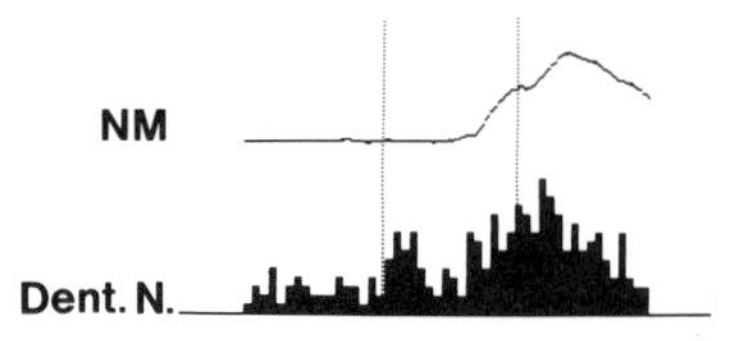

FIG. 8. Example of multiunit activity recorded from the dentate nucleus of the ipsilateral cerebellum (Dent. N.) and the corresponding NM response in a well-trained animal (average of eight paired trials). The vertical dashes indicate tone and air puff onsets. Note the stimulus onset-evoked unit activity and a model of the learned behavioral NM response.

Unit activity showed evoked responses to tone and air puff onsets but no response in association with the reflex NM response, in marked contrast to unit recordings from the cranial motor nuclei. On day 2 (Fig. 9), the animal began showing CRs, and the unit activity in the dentate nucleus developed a model of the CR. On day 3 (Fig. 9), the learned behavioral response and the cerebellar model of the learned response were well developed, but there was still no clear model of the reflex behavioral response. A neuronal model of the *learned* behavioral response appeared to develop *de novo* in the cerebellum. (Note the contrast between this response and the learning-induced response in the hippocampus that models the entire behavioral response; see Fig. 1.)

C. LESION STUDIES OF THE CEREBELLUM

Two lesion experiments were done to determine if the lateral cerebellum is essential for retention of the standard delay conditioning of the NM and eyelid responses: extensive ablations and localized electrolytic destruction (McCormick *et al.,* 1981, 1982c). In both studies, animals were first trained

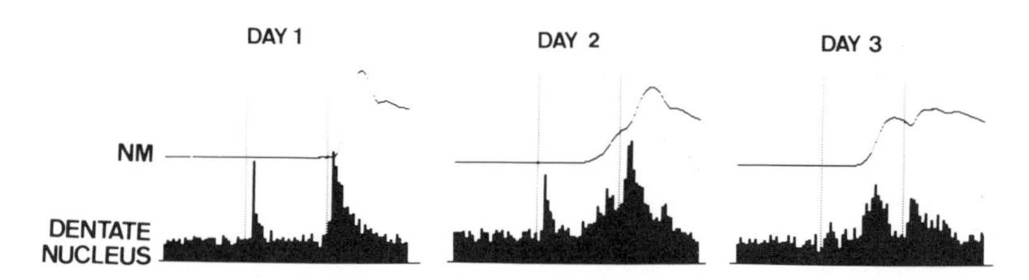

FIG. 9. Growth of unit activity (multiunit record) in the dentate nucleus of the left (ipsilateral) cerebellum over the course of learning. Each record (NM above and unit histogram below) is the average for the entire day's training session. On day 1 the animal showed no learned responses, and the units showed only stimulus onset-evoked responses. On day 2 the animal began to learn, and a model of the learned NM response developed. On day 3 the learned NM response was well developed, as was the neuronal model in the cerebellum, but there does not appear to be a neuronal model of the reflex NM response.

to a criterion of eight CRs in any nine consecutive trials, given a full day of overtraining, then subjected to lesions, allowed to recover (24 hours for the electrolytic lesion and 7 days for the ablation), and given at least 4 full days of retraining. All animals in both studies initially learned the response in less than 2 days of training.

Ipsilateral (left) ablation of the lateral cerebellum (six animals) completely and permanently abolished the CR (see Fig. 10). However, the ablation had no effect at all on the amplitude of the UR reflex. Three of these animals were then shifted to training of the other (right) eye and learned the response very rapidly, with significant savings over the original learning. They were then shifted back to training of the left eye and again showed no learned response. All ablations included the left paramedian and ansiform lobes and the most lateral aspects of the left pyramis, median lobe, and anterior lobe, together with damage to the left dentate and interpositus nuclei.

The localized lesion study involved nine animals with stereotaxically

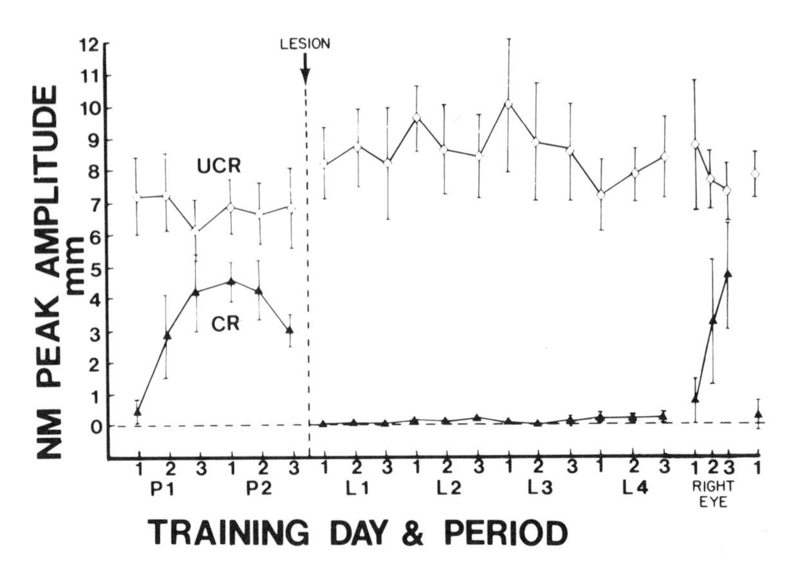

FIG. 10. Effects of ablation of the left lateral cerebellum on the learned NM (and eyelid) response (six animals). Solid triangles, amplitude of the CR; open diamonds, amplitude of the UCR. All training was to the left eye (ipsilateral to the lesion) except where labeled "right eye." The cerebellar lesion completely and permanently abolished the CR of the ipsilateral eye but had no effect on the UCR. P1 and P2 indicate initial learning on the 2 days prior to the lesion. L1–L4 indicate the 4 days of postoperative training to the left eye. The right eye was then trained (in three animals) and learned rapidly. The left eye was again trained and showed no learning. Numbers on the abscissa indicate 40-trial blocks, except for "right eye," which are 24-trial blocks. (From McCormick *et al.*, 1982c.)

placed electrolytic lesions in the deep cerebellar nuclei. Four of these animals showed complete or nearly complete abolition of the CR, with no effect on the UCR. All four animals had substantial damage to the left dentate and interpositus nuclei and associated fibers. Three of the remaining five animals showed no memory deficits, and their lesions did not involve any damage to the deep nuclei. Two animals with partial deficits incurred some damage to the deep nuclei. In still another study, now in progress, animals were first given unilateral ablation of the lateral cerebellum, then trained for 4 days with the ipsilateral eye, then shifted to the contralateral eye, and finally trained again on the ipsilateral eye. Five animals have been run to date. None showed any signs of CRs in the 4 days of initial training with the ipsilateral eye. They then learned with the contralateral eye in the same number of trials as do normal naive animals, and again did not show CRs when shifted back to the original eye.

Finally, in other current work (Lavond *et al.*, 1981), we have found that pontine reticular lesions that encroach upon the ipsilateral superior cerebellar pendduncle also selectively abolish the learned response (see Fig. 11). The superior cerebellar peduncle is, of course, the major pathway containing efferents from the cerebellum. Moore and associates (Desmond *et al.*, 1981) have independently reported similar behavioral effects resulting from ipsilateral lesions in the pontine brainstem. Although it is not yet entirely clear what structures or pathways in the pons are critical in Moore's studies, it is very possible that the superior cerebellar peduncle is critically involved.

The results of our lesion studies demonstrate that the lateral cerebellum ipsilateral to the eye being trained is essential for the learned eyelid and NM responses. The fact that the UCR was completely unaffected indicates that the deficit is not due to motor impairment, i.e., an inability to perform the response. Indeed, three of the animals with severe memory deficits as the result of electrolytic lesions showed no detectable motor symptoms. The fact that the eye opposite the lesion learned easily rules out possible nonspecific lesion effects.

We suggest that an essential part of the memory trace for classical conditioning of the eyelid and NM responses is localized to the ipsilateral lateral cerebellum. The learned response is abolished completely, selectively, and permanently. The possible ways this could occur include damage to the memory trace or to essential afferent or efferent pathways. Since the lesions were limited to the cerebellum, the classical pathways subserving the auditory CS and the somatic sensory UCS are not involved. The fact that the training-induced increase in neuronal activity in the cerebellum may precede the behavioral response by a substantial period of time (50 msec or more) seems to argue against the possibility that the cerebellum is merely efferent

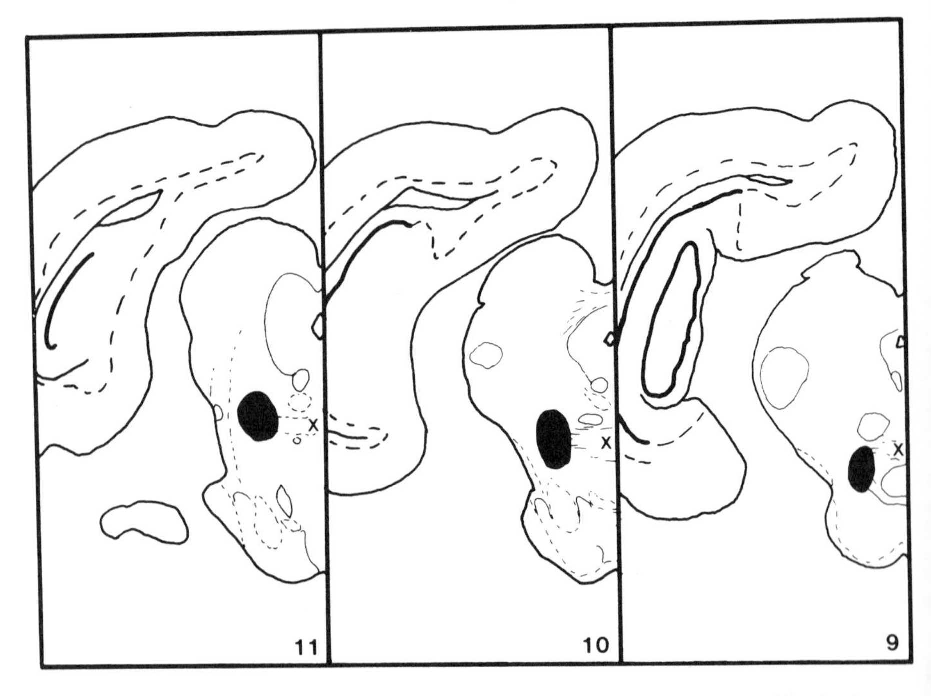

FIG. 11. Example of an electrolytic lesion in the ipsilateral (left) brainstem-midbrain that abolishes the learned NM response completely and selectively but has no effect on the reflex NM response. This lesion is at the lateral margin of the decussations of the superior cerebellar peduncle (denoted by X). (From Lavond *et al.*, 1981.)

from the memory trace. This time period, interestingly, is close to the minimum onset latency for CRs in a well-trained animal and is also close to the minimum CS–UCS interval that can support the development of learning in this preparation.

D. Role of the cerebellum in learning and memory

The cerebellum has been suggested as a possible locus for the coding of learned motor responses (Eccles *et al.*, 1967). Indeed, Marr's theory of the cerebellum (1969), and those of Albus (1971) and Ito (1970), constitute one of the more compelling treatments of putative neuronal substrates of learning. Cerebellar lesions have been reported to impair a variety of skilled movements in animals (Brooks, 1979). Our results indicate further that cerebellar damage can selectively abolish simple learned responses. Since there is no reason to suppose that the cerebellum has any special role in such movements as NM extension and eyelid closure, we argue that the present finding may hold for all simple learned responses involving discrete, striated muscle movements, at least with an aversive UCS.

VI. Two Processes of Learning in the Brain?

Behavioral analyses of aversive learning suggest that it may occur as two processes or phases, the first involving classical conditioning of a central state, e.g., "conditioned fear," and the second concerned with learned performance of discrete, adaptive motor responses (Brush, 1971; Mowrer, 1947; Prokasy, 1972; Rescorla and Solomon, 1967). The first process presumably involves brainstem-hypothalamic mechanisms and hormonal actions, and the second would involve whatever mechanisms underlie the learning of the specific adaptive motor responses, in this case the NM and eyelid responses.

In this context, it seems reasonable to suggest that the selective morphine depression of the CR might be due to an action on the conditioned-fear aspect of learning in the NM/eyelid paradigm, as noted above. Studies in which both the NM/eyelid and heart rate are recorded during conditioning (using a periorbital shock rather than a corneal air puff UCS) show that conditioned slowing of the heart rate develops in a few trials and then fades away as the discrete NM/eyelid response is learned (Powell *et al.*, 1974). Conditioned heart rate slowing seems a very good candidate for an autonomic expression of an initial process of conditioned fear. As the animal "masters" the situation and learns to make the discrete, adaptive NM/eyelid response, conditioned fear decreases. Interestingly, in current work we have found that the learned NM/eyelid response becomes relatively impervious to the action of morphine if animals are given overtraining. The time course of susceptibility of the CR to morphine depression seems to parallel the time course of conditioned heart rate slowing.

Given our results described above, it seems a very reasonable possibility that learning of the discrete, adaptive motor response (NM/eyelid) occurs in the cerebellum. Perhaps the most prominent feature of the learned response is its precise timing. The CR is under very strong control by the CS–UCS interval in terms of onset latency and temporal morphology, and is always timed to be at a maximum at the time when the onset of the UCR occurs. The cerebellum is very well designed to provide such precise timing (see, e.g., Eccles *et al.*, 1967). As the discrete motor response becomes well learned in the cerebellum, it becomes "functionally autonomous"; conditioned fear is no longer necessary. Although many aspects of these arguments are speculative at present, they are testable and seem to fit well within the general framework of behavioral views of aversive learning.

Our results to date on the cerebellum suggests strongly that the memory trace for the learned eyelid/NM response may be localized to the cerebellum. Electrophysiological recording will permit delineation of the regions and circuits involved. This, in turn, will permit analysis of the neuronal/synaptic mechanisms of the memory trace for a basic form of associative learning.

Acknowledgment

Supported by a research grant from the National Science Foundation, BNS 81-06648, and the Virginia Day Robbins Fund. We thank Jann Lincoln for histology and Peggy E. Guyer, David T. Holmes, John Madden IV, Christina E. Rising, and John T. Warren for assistance.

References

Albus, J. S. (1971). A theory of cerebellar function. *Mathematical Bioscience* **10,** 25–61.

Berger, T. W., and Thompson, R. F. (1978a). Neuronal plasticity in the limbic system during classical conditioning of the rabbit nictitating membrane response. I. The hippocampus. *Brain Research, 145*(2), 323–346.

Berger, T. W., and Thompson, R. F. (1978b). Identification of pyramidal cells as the critical elements in hippocampal neuronal plasticity during learning. *Proceedings of the National Academy of Sciences of the U.S.A.* **75**(3), 1572–1576.

Berger, T. W., and Thompson, R. F. (1981). Hippocampal cellular plasticity during extinction of classically conditioned nicitating membrane behavior. *Behavioral Brain Research* **4,** 63–76.

Berger, T. W., Clark, G. A., and Thompson, R. F. (1980). Learning-dependent neuronal responses recorded from limbic system brain structures during classical conditioning. *Physiological Psychology* **8**(2), 155–167.

Berthier, N. E., and Moore, J. W. (1980). Role of extraocular muscles in the rabbit *(Oryctolagus cuniculus)* nictitating membrane response. *Physiology and Behavior* **2,** 931–937.

Brons, J. F., and Woody, C. D. (1980). Long term changes in excitability of cortical neurons after Pavlovian conditioning and extinction. *Journal of Neurophysiology* **44**(3), 605–615.

Brooks, V. B. (1979). Control of intended limb movement by the lateral and intermediate cerebellum. *In* "Integration in the Nervous System" (H. Asghuma and W. J. Wilson, eds.). Igaku-Shoin, Tokyo.

Brush, F. R., ed. (1971) "Aversive Conditioning and Learning." Academic Press, New York.

Buchwald, J. S., Halas, E. S., and Schramm, S. (1966). Changes in cortical and subcortical unit activity during behavioral conditioning. *Physiology and Behavior* **1,** 11–22.

Castellucci, V., and Kandel, E. R. (1976). An invertebrate system for the cellular study of habituation and sensitization. *In* Habituation: Perspectives From Child Development, Animal Behavior and Neurophysiology," (T. J. Tighe and R. N. Leaton, eds.). Wiley, New York.

Cegavske, C. F., Thompson, R. F., Patterson, M. M., and Gormezano, I. (1976). Mechanisms of efferent neuronal control of the reflex nictitating membrane response in the rabbit. *Journal of Comparative and Physiological Psychology* **90,** 411–423.

Cegavske, C. F., Patterson, M. M., and Thompson, R. F. (1979). Neuronal unit activity in the abducent nucleus during classical conditioning of the nictitating membrane response in the rabbit. *Oryctolagus cyniculus. Journal of Comparative and Physiological Psychology,* **93,** 595–609.

Cohen, D. H. (1980). The functional neuroanatomy of a conditioned response. *In* "Neural Mechanisms of Goal-Directed Behavior and Learning" (R. F. Thompson, L. H. Hicks, and V. B. Shvyrkov, eds.) Academic Press, New York.

Davis, W. J., and Gillette, R. (1978). Neural correlate of behavioral plasticity in command Neurons of *Pleurobranchaea. Science* **199,** 801–804.

Desmond, J. E., Berthier, N. E., and Moore, J. W. (1981). Brain stem elements essential for the classically conditioned nictitating response of rabbit. *Abstracts, Society of Neuroscience* **7**(214.16), 650.

Disterhoft, J. F., and Stuart, D. K. (1976). Trial sequence of changed unit activity on auditory system of alert rat during conditioned response acquisition and extinction. *Journal of Neurophysiology* **39,** 266–281.

Disterhoft, J. F., and Stuart, D. K. (1977). Differentiated short latency response increases after conditioning in inferior colliculus neurons of alert rat. *Brain Research* **130,** 315–333.

Disterhoft, J. F., Shipley, M. T., and Kraus, N. (1981). Analyzing the rabbit NM conditioned reflex arc. *Asilomar Conference, October 25–27.*

Durkovic, R. G. (1975). Classical conditioning, sensitization, and habituation of the flexion reflex of the spinal cat. *Physiology and Behavior* **14,** 297–304.

Eccles, J. C. (1957). "The Physiology of Nerve Cells." Johns Hopkins Press, Baltimore, Maryland.

Eccles, J. C., Ito, M., and Szentagothai, J. (1967). "The Cerebellum as a Neuronal Machine." Springer-Verlag, Berlin and New York.

Enser, D. (1976). Ph.D. Thesis, University of Iowa.

Gabriel, M. (1976). Short-latency discriminative unit response: Engram or bias? *Physiological Psychology* **4**(3), 275–280.

Gabriel, M., Saltwick, S. E., and Miller, J. D. (1975). Conditioning and reversal of short-latency multiple-unit responses in the rabbit medial geniculate nucleus. *Science* **189,** 1108–1109.

Gabriel, M., Miller, J. D., and Saltwick, S. E. (1976). Multiple-unit activity of the rabbit medial geniculate nucleus in conditioning, extinction and reversal. *Physiological Psychology* **4,** 124–134.

Gabriel, M., Foster, K., and Orona, E. (1980). Unit activity in cingulate cortex and anteroventral thalamus during acquisition and overtraining of discriminative avoidance behavior in rabbits. *In* "Neural Mechanisms of Goal-Directed Behavior and Learning" (R.F. Thompson L. H. Hicks, and V. B. Shvyrkov, eds.). Academic Prèss, New York.

Gormezano, I., Schneiderman, N., Deaux, E., and Fentues I. (1962). Nictitating membrane: Classical conditioning and extinction in the albino rabbit. *Science* **138,** 33–34.

Gray, T. S., McMaster, S. E., Harvey, J. A., and Gormezano, I. (1981). Localization of retractor bulbi motoneurons in the rabbit. *Brain Research* **226,** 93–106.

Hebb, D. O. (1949). "The Organization of Behavior." Wiley, New York.

Hoehler, F. K., and Thompson, R. F. (1979). The effect of temporal single-alternation of learned increases in hippocampal unit activity in classical conditioning of the rabbit nictitating membrane response. *Physiological Psychology* **7,** 345–351.

Hoehler, F. K., and Thompson, R. F. (1980). Effect of the interstimulus (CS–UCS) interval on hippocampal unit activity during classical conditioning of the nictitating membrane response of the rabbit, *Oryctolagus cuniculus. Journal of Comparative and Physiological Psychology* **94,** 201–215.

Ito, M. (1970). Neurophysiological aspects of the cerebellar motor control system. *International Journal of Neurology* **7,** 162–176.

Jaffe, J. H., and Martin, W. R. (1980). *In* "The Pharmacological Basis of Therapeutics" (A. G. Gilman, L. S. Goodman, and A. Gilman, eds.) Macmillan, New York.

John, E. R. (1967). "Mechanisms of Memory. Academic Press, New York.

Kettner, R. N. (1981). Ph.D. Thesis, University of California, Irvine.
Kettner, R. N., and Thompson, R. F. (1982). Auditory signal detection and decision processes in the nervous system. *Journal of Comparative and Physiological Psychology,* **96,** 328–331.
Kettner, R. N., Shannon, R. V., Nguyen, T. M., and Thompson, R. F. (1980). Simultaneous behavioral and neural (cochler nucleus) measurement during signal detection in the rabbit. *Perception and Psychophysics* **28**(6), 504–513.
Kitzes, L. M., Farley, G. R., and Starr A. (1978). Modulation of auditory cortex unit activity during the performance of a conditioned response. *Experimental Neurology* **62,** 678–697.
Lavond, D. G., McCormick, D. A., Clark, G. A., Holmes, D. T., and Thompson, R. F. (1981). Effects of ipsilateral rostral pontine reticular lesions on retention of classically conditioned nictitating membrane and eyelid response. *Physiological Psychology,* **9,** 335–339.
Lonsbury-Martin, B. L., Martin, G. K., Schwartz, S. M., and Thompson, R. F. (1976). Neural correlates of auditory plasticity during classical conditioning in the rabbit. *Journal of the Acoustical Society of America* **60,** S82.
McCormick, D. A., Lavond, D. G., Clark, G. A., Kettner, R. E., Rising, C. E., and Thompson, R. F. (1981). The engram found? Role of the cerebellum in classical conditioning of nictitating membrane and eyelid response. *Bulletin of the Psychonomic Society* **18,** 103–105.
McCormick, D. A., Lavond, D. G., and Thompson, R. F. (1982a). Concomitant Classical conditioning of the rabbit nictitating membrane and eyelid responses: correlations and implications. *Physiology and Behavior,* **28,** 769–775.
McCormick, D. A., Lavond, D. G., and Thompson, R. F. (1982b). Neuronal activity in the cerebellum and related structures during the performance of the classically conditioned nictitating membrane/eyelid responses. In preparation.
McCormick, D. A., Clark, G. A., Lavond, D. G., and Thompson, R. F. (1982c). Initial Localization of the Memory Trace for a Basic Form of Learning. *Proceedings of the National Academy of the Science of the U.S.A.,* **79,** 2731–2735.
Marr, D. (1969). A theory of cerebellar cortex. *Journal of Physiology (London)* **202,** 437–470.
Martinez, J. L., Jr., Jensen, R. A., Messing, R. B., Rigter, H., and McGaugh, J. L. (1981). "Endogenous Peptides and Learning And Memory Processes." Academic Press, New York.
Mauk, M. D., Warren, J. T., and Thompson, R. F. (1981). Selective naloxone-reversible morphine depression of learned behavioral and hippocampal responses. *Science,* **216,** 434–436.
Milner, P. M. (1957). The cell assembly: Mark II. *Psychological Review* **64,** 242–252.
Mishkin, M. (1978). Memory in monkeys severely impaired by combined but not by separate removal of amygdala and hippocampus. *Nature (London)* **273,** 297–298.
Mowrer, O. H. (1947). On the dual nature of learning—a re-interpretation of "conditioning" and "problem-solving." *Harvard Educational Review* **17,** 102–148.
Norman, R. J., Buchwald, J. S., and Villablanca, J. R. (1977). Classical conditioning with auditory discrimination of the eye blink in decerebrate cats. *Science* **196,** 551–553.
Oakley, D. A., and Russell, I. S. (1972). Neocortical lesions and Pavlovian conditioning *Physiology and Behavior* **8,** 915–926.
Olds, J., Disterhoft, J. F., Segal, M., Kornblith, C. L., and Hirsch, R. (1972). Learning centers of rat brain mapped by measuring latencies of conditioned unit responses. *Journal of Neurophysiology* **35,** 202–219.
Oleson, T. D., Ashe, J. H., and Weinberger, N. M. (1975). Modification of auditory and somatosensory system activity during pupillary conditioning in the paralyzed cat. *Journal of Neurophysiology* **38,** 1114–1139.
Papsdorf, J. D., Longman, D., and Gormezano, I. (1965). Spreading depression: Effects of applying KCl to the dura of the rabbit on the conditioned nictitating membrane response. *Psychonomic Science* **2,** 125–126.
Patterson, M. M. (1976). Mechanisms of classical conditioning and fixation in spinal mammals.

In "Advances in Psychobiology" (A. H. Riesen and R. F. Thompson, eds.), Vol. 3. Wiley, New York.

Patterson, M. M., Cegavske, C. F., and Thompson, R. F. (1973). Effects of a classical conditioning paradigm on hindlimb flexor nerve response in immobilized spinal cat. *Journal of Comparative and Physiological Psychology* **84,** 88–97.

Powell, D. A., Lipkin, M., and Milligan, W. L. (1974). Concomitant changes in classically conditioned heart rate and corneoretinal potential discrimination in the rabbit *(Oryctolagus cuniculus). Learning and Motivation* **5,** 532–547.

Prokasy, W. F. (1972). Developments with the two-phase model applied to human eyelid conditioning. *In "Classical conditioning II: Current Research and Theory"* (A. H. Black and W. F. Prokasy, eds.) Appleton, New York.

Rescorla, R. A., and Solomon, R. L. (1967). Relationships Between Pavlovian conditioning and instrumental learning. *Psychological Review* **74,** 151–182.

Ryugo, D. K., and Weinberger, N. M. (1978). Differential plasticity of morphologically distinct neuron populations in the medial geniculate body of the cat during classical conditioning. *Behavioral Biology* **22,** 275–301.

Segal, M., and Olds, J. (1973). The activity of units in the hippocampal circuit to the rat during classical conditioning. *Journal of Comparative and Physiological Psychology* **82,** 195–204.

Solomon, P. R. (1980). A time and place for everything? Temporal processing views of hippocampal function with special reference to attention. *Phsyiological Psychology* **8**(2), 254–261.

Solomon, P. R., and Moore, J. W. (1975). Latent inhibition and stimulus generalization of the classically conditioned nictitating membrane response in rabbits *(Oryctolagus cuniculus)* following dorsal hippocampal ablations. *Journal of Comparative and Physiological Psychology* **89,** 1192–1203.

Stent, G. S. (1973). A physiological mechanisms for Hebb's postulate of learning. *Proceedings of the National Academy of Sciences of the U.S.A.* **70,** 997–1001.

Swanson, L. W., Teyler, T. J., and Thompson, R. F. (1982). Mechanisms and functional implications of hippocampal LTP. *Neurosciences Research Program Bulletin* (in press).

Thompson, R. F., and Glanzman, D. S. (1976). Neural and behavioral mechanisms of habituation and sensitization. *In* "Habituation: Perspectives From Child Development, Animal Behavior, and Neurophysiology" (T. J. Tighe and R. N. Leaton, eds.). Erlbaum, Hillsdale, New Jersey.

Thompson, R. F., Cegavske, C., and Patterson, M. M. (1973). Efferent control of the classically conditioned nictitating membrane response in the rabbit. *The Psychonomic Society Program Abstracts* pp. 15–16.

Thompson, R. F., Berger, T. W., Cegavske, C. F., Patterson, M. M., Roemer, R. A., Teyler, T. J., and Young, R. A. (1976). The search for the engram. *American Psychologist* **31,** 209–227.

Thompson, R. F., Berger, T. W., Berry, S. D., Hoehler, F. K., Kettner, R. E., and Weisz, D. J. (1980). Hippocampal substrate of classical conditioning. *Physiological Psychology* **8**(2), 262–279.

Walters, E. T., Carew, T. J., and Kandel, E. R. (1981). Associative learning in *Aplysia:* Evidence for conditioned fear in an invertebrate. *Science* **211,** 504–506.

Weinberger, N. M. (1980). Neurophysiological studies of learning in association with the pupillary dilation conditioned reflex. *In* "Neural Mechanisms of Goal-Directed Behavior and Learning" (R. F. Thompson, L. H. Hicks, and V. B. Shvyrkov, eds.). Academic Press, New York.

Weisz, D. J., Solomon, P. R., and Thompson, R. F. (1980). The hippocampus appears necessary for trace conditioning. *Bulletin of the Psychonomic Society Abstracts* **193,** 244.

Wikler, A. (1958). Mechanisms of action of opiates and opiate antagonists: A review of their mechanisms of action in relation to clinical problems. Public Health Monograph No. 52, U.S. Govt. Printing Office, Washington, D.C.

Woody, C. D., and Brozek, G. (1969). Changes in evoked responses from facial nucleus of cat with conditioning and extinction of an eye blink. *Journal of Neurophysiology* **32,** 717–726.

Woody, C. D., Knispel, J. D., Crow, T. J., and Black-Cleworth, P. A. (1976). Activity and excitability to electrical current of cortical auditory receptive neurons of awake cats as affected by stimulus association. *Journal of Neurophysiology* **39**(5), 1045–1061.

PROGRESS IN PSYCHOBIOLOGY AND PHYSIOLOGICAL PSYCHOLOGY, VOL. 10

Twenty Years of Classical Conditioning Research with the Rabbit

I. Gormezano
The University of Iowa
Iowa City, Iowa

E. James Kehoe
University of New South Wales
Kensington, New South Wales, Australia

Beverly S. Marshall
The University of Iowa
Iowa City, Iowa

ISBN 0-12-542110-9

I. Introduction

The present chapter is intended to reveiw the behavioral methods and findings of classical conditioning with the rabbit, particularly with the rabbit nictitating membrane response (NMR) preparation. A companion piece by Thompson *et al.,* reviewing the burgeoning body of neurobiological research using the NMR preparation, may be found in the chapter by Thompson *et al.* in this volume. Although research findings with the rabbit preparations may be regarded as a set of biopsychological phenomena which stand by themselves, the significance of these phenomena is derived not only from the quality of the data but also from their relevance to long-standing questions regarding the nature of learned behavior. In a historical context, classical conditioning with the rabbit can be viewed from at least three perspectives: as laboratory models of associative learning (Gormezano, 1972; Gormezano and Kehoe, 1981); as laboratory models of behavioral adaptation (Gormezano, 1965; Gormezano and Coleman, 1973); and as sources of axioms for theories regarding the mediation of extended sequences of goal-directed activity (Gormezano and Kehoe, 1975, 1982). Accordingly, the present chapter will attempt to place classical conditioning with rabbit preparations in its broader experimental and theoretical contexts.

II. Historical and Methodological Background

A. Classical Conditioning and Associationism

In psychological research and theory, classical conditioning has frequently occupied the cleft between complex behavior and its neural substrate. Pavlov (1927) himself saw his conditioned reflex method as a tool for revealing the functional properties of higher neural processes and, more broadly, for the study of neural mechanisms governing the behavioral adaptation of an individual animal to the exigencies of its environment. However, Pavlov made only modest attempts to coordinate his extensive behavioral observations with an empirical investigation of neural processes. In the context of behavior theory, Bekhterev (1913), Pavlov's more psychologically oriented contemporary, was the first to propose classical conditioning as a prototypical example of association by contiguity. One of the earliest and still most useful statements in the American literature regarding the relationship of classical conditioning to associative learning was articulated by Lashley (1916, pp. 459–460). In particular, he saw classical conditioning as possessing several methodological advantages over the then prevailing trial-and-error procedures:

> Conditions may be so arranged that only two stimuli, and presumably, one reaction are involved . . ., but its greatest usefulness should be for studies of the temporal relation between the primary and associated stimulus necessary for the formation of the association.
>
> The fact that a single reaction is involved is an advantage. The associated reaction either does, or does not, occur and there is no question of the elimination of errors or simplification of reaction.

Thus, Lashley noted that the classical conditioning method permits the investigator precision in the control of stimuli and in the measurement of responses to delineate clearly the effects of important associative variables.

The recognition of the methodological advantages of classical conditioning led initially to an extravagant use of conditioning concepts as identical to associative doctrine and as mechanisms of learning (Frank, 1923; cf. Gormezano and Kehoe, 1981; Holt, 1931; Smith and Guthrie, 1921; Watson, 1925; Wilson, 1924). The speculative use of classical conditioning ended with the appearance of detailed descriptions of Pavlov's (1927, 1928) work and experimental reports in the United States which revealed the complexities of classical conditioning (e.g., Cason, 1922; Hilgard, 1931). Despite the more sober view regarding the role of classical conditioning in psychology, there has continued to be a strong identification of "conditioning" and "contiguity," which fails to do justice to either the complexities of the empirical phenomena or the sophistication of philosophical associationism (Hilgard, 1937; Robinson, 1932).

Few associative theories in philosophy or psychology have specified the contiguity between events as the single sufficient condition for the establishment of a new association. Little thought on the matter is required to conclude that not every pair of sensations, ideas, or events which occur together are necessarily later recalled together. In philosophical associationism, the Law of Frequency acknowledged that a single repetition of a pair of events is not sufficient to establish an association. Furthermore, lists of Secondary Laws of Association specified as determinants of association such factors as the intensity of the events and the number of other associations involving members of the pair (Brown, 1820/1977; pp. 199–214). In addition, the philosophical associationists devoted a large portion of their writings to a consideration of principles for describing the organization of pairwise associations into unified perceptions and coherent streams of memories. Similar constraints on the effectiveness of contiguity and organizing principles for multiple associations may be found in virtually every associationistic learning theory (cf. Gormezano and Kehoe, 1981).

Empirically, investigations of classical conditioning and, for that matter, most other learning paradigms have revealed counterparts to the philosophical Law of Frequency and the other Secondary Laws. Moreover, it has become clear that previous theoretical constraints on a contiguity principle were insufficient to account for associative learning in two types of complex situations. First, research with compound stimuli has produced an accumulation of evidence that a conditioned response (CR) acquisition to one conditioned stimulus (CS) as a result of otherwise effective CS–unconditioned stimulus (US) pairings may be impaired in lawful ways by the presence of other CSs during training; these findings have been collectively known as "stimulus selection" or "selective association" phenomena (Gormezano and Kehoe, 1981; Rudy and Wagner, 1975). Second, research in which a CS and a US are intermixed but not always paired has revealed that the level of conditioning may vary as a function of the overall "correlation" or "contingency" between the CS and the US (Prokasy, 1965; Rescorla, 1967, 1972). Consequently, the trend of theorizing has been toward formulations which retain an axiomatic contiguity principle but assume that additional processes of competition between stimuli and/or inhibition are intimately involved in the formation of associations (Mackintosh, 1975; Rescorla, 1972; Rescorla and Wagner, 1972). Finally, a more fundamental challenge to a blind application of the Law of Contiguity has existed since the first systematic studies of classical conditioning in the United States, which revealed that CR acquisition failed to occur when the CS and US were truly contiguous, i.e., simultaneous, but did occur when there was some degree of asynchrony between the two stimuli (Bernstein, 1934). Together, these theoretical and empirical considerations militate against the comfortable but simpleminded identification of the empirical laws of classical conditioning with the doctrines of philosophical associationism (Hilgard, 1937).

B. Definition of Associative Learning

Athough the identification of classical conditioning with the Law of Contiguity is inaccurate, the use of associative doctrine has nonetheless provided a useful guide to the basic methodology, research, and theory of classical conditioning in Western laboratories. What, then, is considered an instance of associative learning? Whereas a broad but still objective definition of "learning" states that a change in behavior must be a result of "experience" and must be relatively permanent (Kimble, 1961; Mpitsos *et al.*, 1978), the associative doctrine provides the additional stipulation that the experience consists of a temporal conjunction of two events. As Lashley (1916) noted, it is the full experimental control of the temporal conjunction between the intended CS and the US–unconditioned response (UR) which makes classical conditioning preparations attractive vehicles for the study of associative learning.

The above definitional concerns seem clear until one realizes that the behavioral changes denoted as learning, not to mention associative learning, must be distinguished from the continuous stream of behavior that characterizes even the most passive laboratory species. Consequently, considerable controversy and ambiguity have arisen in the identification of specific instances of learning and memory phenomena, posing a serious problem for a neurobiology of these phenomena. Put simply, it is rather difficult to identify the neural processes underlying a set of behavioral laws if there is no agreement as to which laws fall into the set. The adoption of standardized "model" preparations provides one means to finesse the lack of precise criteria for specific instances of learning and memory (Moore, 1979; Mpitsos *et al.,* 1978; Thompson *et al.,* 1972). The use of model preparations focuses neurobiological research on preparations for which the behavioral methods and laws are relatively well delineated, thus leaving the neurobiological researcher free to discover the underlying neural processes with confidence that the behavioral phenomena are robust. Furthermore, a focus on specific behavioral preparations and on delineation of their particular underlying processes appears to encourage empirical confirmation of any perceived commonality (or difference) in process between examples of learning, thus avoiding unwarranted generalizations (or distinctions) merely on the basis of common (or different) labels.

C. Control Methodology

From a behavioral viewpoint, the associative nature of a given preparation has come to be determined not only by the use of contiguous occurrence of the CS and US but also by a set of control operations intended to estimate the contribution of other possible processes to the observed response. If behavior in a classical conditioning preparation were governed strictly by an associative process, then the single observation of the designated target response to a CS after CS–US pairings would be sufficient to indicate the establishment of a CR. Not surprisingly, this ideal case has never been achieved, for not all responses observed in connection with a CS result uniquely from prior CS–US pairings. At a minimum, all response systems show some level of baseline activity, often raised by US presentations, which will produce an accidental coincidence of the CS and target responses. Moreover, the likelihood of a response to the CS may be systematically affected by (*a*) alpha responses, which are URs to the CS in the same effector system as the target response, and (*b*) "pseudo-conditioned" and "sensitized" responses, which can be established on the basis of prior US-alone presentations. Where nonassociative processes are operating, any specific response following a CS cannot in principle be ascribed to an associative process. Accordingly, to ascertain the establishment of CRs, it has been conventional to assess the contribution of the nonassociative processes to the likelihood of responses by a variety of control procedures, entailing US-alone, CS-alone, and unpaired presentations of the CS and US (Gormezano and Kehoe, 1975).

D. Origin of the Rabbit Preparations

The rabbit preparations were initially developed by the senior author and his associates to remedy long-term deficiencies and difficulties in the study of classical conditioning. Despite the potential of classical conditioning for revealing the functional properties of higher neural processes, and despite its axiomatic status in behavior theories, there was a paucity of research in Western laboratories with preparations suitable for fulfilling both physiological and theoretical roles. In part, the relative neglect of research in classical conditioning can be attributed to the early speculative use of the term "classical conditioning" (e.g., Watson, 1925), which created the illusion that its laws had been fully specified by Pavlov (Gormezano and Kehoe, 1975, p. 145). This is not to say that there was no research in classical conditioning. Over the decades, a number of response systems were explored in humans and infrahumans for use in classical conditioning procedures (Hilgard and Marquis, 1940; Kimble, 1961), but in these concerted attempts methodological difficulties were encountered. In human eyeblink conditioning, extensive methodological work had removed many of the measurement difficulties, but the data still displayed considerable variability, and the human preparation was clearly unusable for physiological interventions. More importantly, despite the physicalistic and deterministic nature of conditioning theory stretching back to Pavlov (1927, pp. 3–5) and Bekhterev (1913), data from humans were perpetually subjected to interpretation in terms of "volitional" processes (Gormezano, 1965; Hilgard and Marquis, 1940, pp. 255–258; Peak, 1933a,; Theios, 1972; Wolfle, 1932). In both humans and animals, the other major conditioning preparations suffered from substantial intrusions by responding not attributable to associative processes. For example, in salivary and generalized stimulus-response (GSR) conditioning, the contribution of one or more of the aforementioned factors made response frequency and latency relatively insensitive indices of the effects of CS–US presentations (Gormezano, 1966; Stewart *et al.,* 1961). Consequently, to focus attention on the objective determinants of conditioning and to provide the robust data necessary to address both physiological and theoretical questions, we sought a more suitable animal preparation.

1. Conditioning of the Eyelid, Nictitating Membrane, and Eyeball Retraction Responses

In our initial experiments (Deaux and Gormezano, 1963; Gormezano *et al.,* 1962; Schneiderman *et al.,* 1962), it was found that rabbits, if properly restrained, remained passive even during strong stimulation, thus minimizing the problem of struggling and competing behavior that frequently attends the prolonged restraint of other nonhuman species (Gormezano, 1966). As shown in Fig. 1, each rabbit was restrained in a Plexiglas box, and either the rabbit's eyelid closure (Schneiderman *et al.,* 1962), eyeball retraction (Deaux and Gormezano, 1963), or nictitating membrane extension (Gormezano *et al.,* 1962) was monitored by a displacement transducer (rotary potentiometer) whose electrical signal was amplified and recorded by an ink-writing oscillograph. The CS was a 600-msec tone, and the US was a 100-msec puff of air delivered to the dorsal region of the right cornea at a CS–US interval of 500 msec. (Subsequently, the air puff US continued to be used in conjunction with electrophysiological recordings or stimulation, but

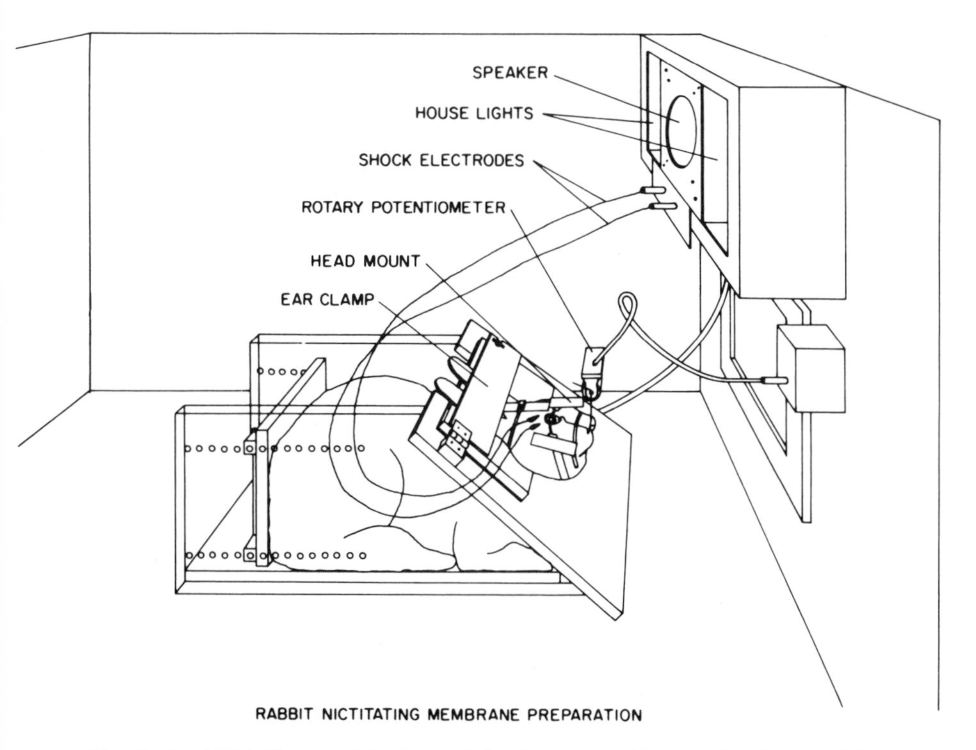

FIG. 1. A rabbit in the restraining box with headset arranged for recording from the NMR.

the majority of behavioral studies have used a US consisting of a 60-Hz electric shock administered to the paraorbital region.)

In all three response systems, initial experiments indicated that CR acquisition proceeded in a smooth fashion, with orderly changes in response frequency, latency, and amplitude. Control conditions indicated that contributions by other sources of responding were negligible. Panels A, B, and C of Fig. 2 show the results of the initial experiments with the eyelid, eyeball retraction, and nictitating membrane responses, respectively. The data are plotted as a function of trial blocks for adaptation, acquisition, and extinction. During adaptation, the rabbits were placed in the conditioning apparatus for a period equal to the length of the subsequent training sessions, but no presentations of either the CS or US occurred. A measure of the base rate of responding was obtained by scoring responses during the 500-msec periods in which the CS would later be presented. Inspection of the figure reveals that the mean likelihood of a "spontaneous" response was less than 3%. During acquisition training, the performance of CS-alone, US-alone, and unpaired control groups never exceeded 6% on any day, a level not appreciably higher than the base rate. In marked contrast, the paired CS–US experimental group showed a progressive increase in CR frequency across days to an asymptote which, for example, reached 95% CRs in the NMR preparation. With further investigations, we have been able to delineate conditioning parameters which reliably produce rapid NMR acquisition to asymptotic levels near 100% CRs within a single session of 200–300 CS–US trials (e.g., Gormezano and Coleman, 1975). [The rabbit's retractor bulbi muscle governs eyeball retraction, and the force of this mechanical action also produces a passive extension of the nictitating membrane (Gray *et al.*, 1981). However, because of its relative ease of measurement and other methodological virtues (cf. Gormezano, 1966), we have primarily employed the NMR preparation.)]

2. *Jaw Movement Response (JMR) Conditioning*

As a companion to the above conditioning preparations, which are based on aversive USs, the JMR preparation was developed to provide an appetitive conditioning procedure based on a US consisting of the delivery of water to the oral cavity (Smith *et al.*, 1966). As can be seen in panel A of Fig. 3, the restraint and recording apparatus are largely the same as those of the NMR preparation. However, for delivery of water under pressure to the oral cavity, each experimental chamber was equipped with a solenoid-operated liquid delivery system which terminates in a blunted hypodermic needle inserted into a polyethylene cannula permanently implanted in each rabbit's

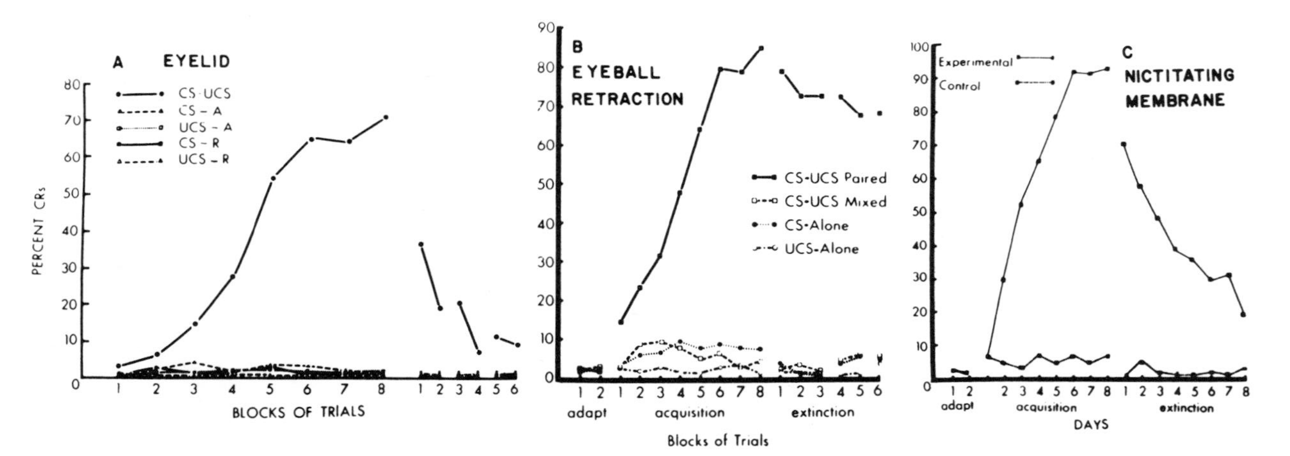

FIG. 2. (A) Mean percentage of eyelid responses plotted in 82-trial blocks during acquisition and 41-trial blocks during extinction (Schneiderman, Fuentes, & Gormezano, 1962); (B) mean percentage of eyeball retraction responses plotted in 70-trial blocks for adaptation, acquisition, and extinction (Deaux and Gormezano, 1963); (C) mean percentage of NMRs plotted in 70-trial blocks for adaptation, acquisition, and extinction. (Gormezano *et al.*, 1962.)

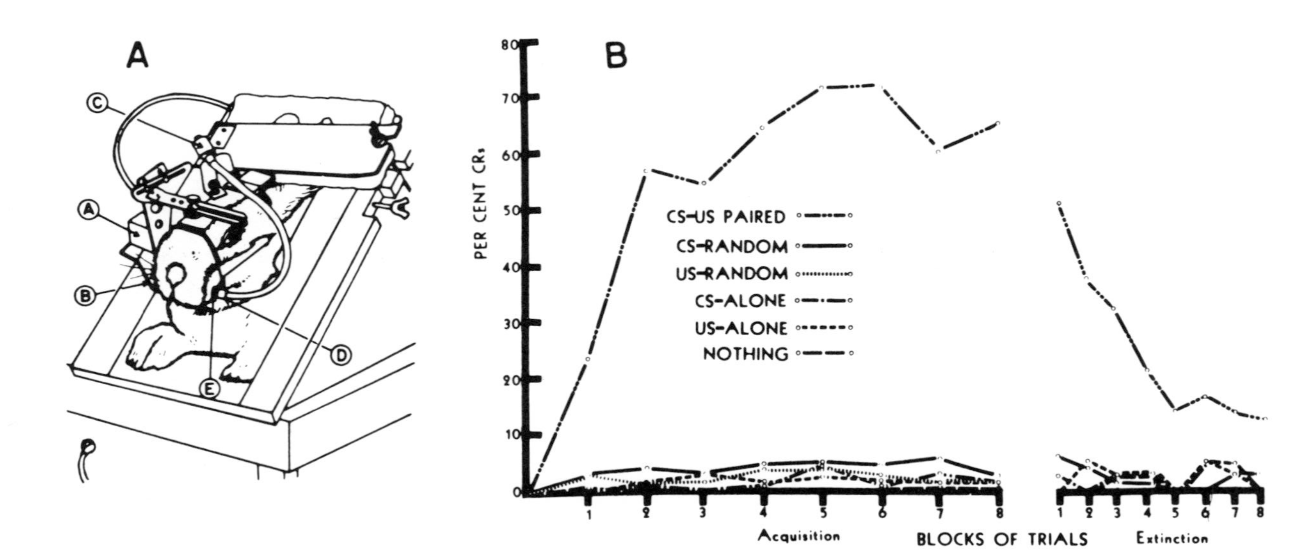

FIG. 3. The left side shows a restrained rabbit prepared for recording the JMR: (A) photo cell transducer, (B) piano-wire armature, (C) luer-lock connector; (D) blunted hypodermic needle, and (E) polyethylene cannula. The right side shows the mean percentage JMR for acquisition (40-trial blocks) and extinction (10-trial blocks).

right cheek. The rabbits were maintained on a restricted water intake to ensure reliable unconditioned JMRs.

Panel B of Fig. 3 shows the results of the initial investigation of JMR conditioning by Smith *et al.* (1966). Whereas the CS–US paired condition produced systematic increases in the JMR percentage, there was a low incidence of spontaneous responses, alpha responses, and pseudo-CRs, thus permitting an assessment of conditioning in terms of response frequency, latency, and amplitude parallel to those in the NMR preparation. Subsequent investigations (Mitchell and Gormezano, 1970; Sheafor, 1975; Sheafor and Gormezano, 1972) have revealed that there can be systematic increases in the frequency of responding attributable to pseudoconditioning. However, the frequency and amplitude of pseudo-CRs are substantially lower than those obtained for CRs with paired CS–US procedures.

3. *Heart Rate Conditioning*

Since the NMR as well as the JMR preparations are based on skeletal musculature, Schneiderman *et al.*, (1966) developed a preparation for conditioning the heart rate. In the original demonstration, the rabbits were held in the standard Plexiglas restrainer, the CS was a 2500-msec, 72-dB, 1000-Hz tone, and the US was a 500-msec, 1.5 mA, 60-Hz shock delivered to the pinna of the subject's right ear. Both the UR and the CR were a deceleration in the heart rate. Since the procedure produced few overt struggling responses, the rabbit heart rate response was relatively uncomplicated by gross body movement. Figure 4 shows the performance levels across days obtained from separate groups of rabbits trained with CS–US paired trials, unpaired CS and US presentations, CS-alone presentations, and US-alone presentations. Inspection of the figure reveals that animals in the paired group showed acquisition of a decelerative CR as measured on CS test trials presented after 0, 9, 18, 27, 36, and 45 training trials. In contrast, the control groups showed no systematic changes in heart rate to the CS. Subsequently, Schneiderman and his associates (Brickman and Schneiderman, 1977; Sampson *et al.*, 1974; Schneiderman, 1970, 1972) pursued an extensive program of behavioral, neurophysiological, and neurochemical investigations using the rabbit heart rate conditioning preparation.

E. Relation of Rabbit Preparations to Other "Pavlovian" Procedures

During the 1950s and 1960s, research in animal learning frequently entailed free-operant procedures, in which the role of the instrumental contingency (i.e., the response–reinforcer relation) was of most interest and, con-

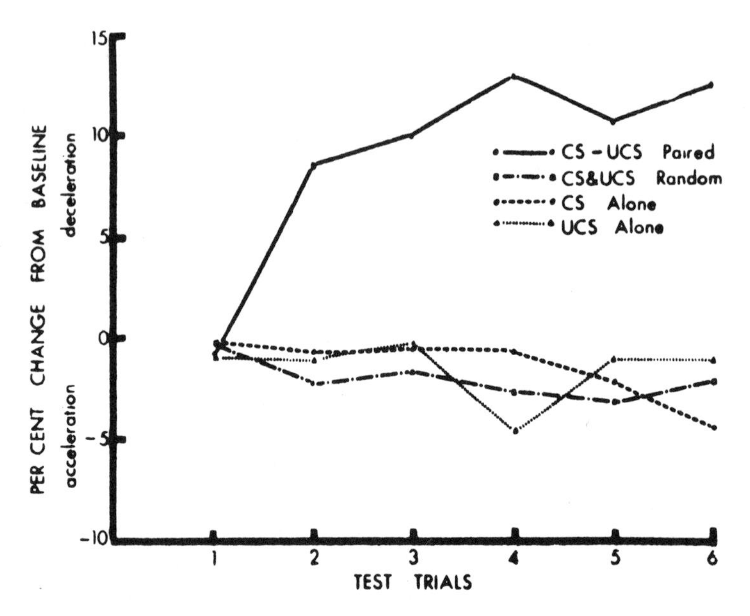

FIG. 4. The mean percentage change from baseline of the 30 beats subsequent to CS onset on each test trial for groups receiving CS-alone adaptation trials. (Schneiderman *et al.*, 1966.)

versely, in which the role of the stimulus antecedents was obscured. The 1970s witnessed a shift in research interests to the stimulus anetecedents of behavior under the headings of "stimulus–reinforcer relations," "cue-to-consequence associations" and "Pavlovian conditioning." However, the resurgent interest in stimulus antecedents suffers from the historic identification of classical conditioning and association. Consequently, events that only a few years ago would have been labeled as "discriminative stimuli," "warning signals," or "cues" are now designated as CSs. By itself, the use of Pavlov's nomenclature is harmless and even useful for acknowledging the associative character of otherwise disparate learning procedures. However, the widespread use of Pavlov's terminology has been accompanied by a belief in a unitary, central associative process for which the overt behavior has become the mere index (e.g., Pearce and Hall, 1980). In summary, the zeitgeist has moved from a radical behaviorism, which minimizes the importance of stimulus antecedents, to an equally radical associationism, which minimizes the importance of the overt behavior. Neither zeitgeist does justice to the interesting complexities of learned behavior and its stimulus antecedents. Under the impact of the identification of associative learning with classical conditioning, the term "classical conditioning" has been extended gradually to include at least four distinct associative paradigms: (*a*) CS–CR, (*b*) CS–instrumental response (IR), (*c*) instrumental approach procedures, and (*d*) "autoshaping." All these procedures administer or purport to administer the CS and US in a response-independent fashion, but they may be distinguished by the nature of the target behavior.

1. CS–CR Paradigms

All the rabbit preparations fall into the class of CS–CR procedures, in which the CR refers to a response to the CS that appears in any effector system in which a UR is evoked by the US; the CR and UR, however, need *not* be *identical* (Gormezano and Kehoe, 1975). Thus, the CS–CR procedures are the traditional procedures which have also been described as "respondent learning" (cf. Skinner, 1937, 1938) or "learning by homogeneous reinforcement" (Hilgard and Marquis, 1940, pp. 75; 98–100). Through the US–UR, the experimenter has independent control over the occurrence of the target response system as well as the key stimulus events. With the degree of experimental control available in the CS–CR procedures, they have continued to provide the analytical power, recognized by Lashley (1916), for discovering the precise conditions for the acquisition of responding to both associative and nonassociative variables.

2. CS–IR Paradigms

The class of CS–IR paradigms includes, most notably, the conditioned suppression procedure, as well as other "transfer of control" or "classical-instrumental transfer" procedures (Gormezano and Moore, 1969; Overmier and Lawry, 1979; Rescorla and Solomon, 1967). In CS–IR procedures, the stimulus pairings of classical conditioning are carried out, but without any measurement of a CR in the sense that we have used it above. Then, in the test phase, the CS is presented during ongoing instrumental responding, and the CS's facilitory or disruptive effect on instrumental behavior is measured. The CS–IR paradigms were originally developed with the recognition that any instrumental learning experiment inherently contains the elements of a classical conditioning procedure (e.g., Hilgard, 1937; Hull, 1930, 1931, 1934; Mowrer, 1947, 1960). Specifically, the reinforcer is also an US for a constellation of USs, and the reinforcer always occurs in the context of antedating stimuli, one or more of which could become a CS. A variety of "CR-mediational" theories have evolved which assume not only that CRs are acquired in a collateral fashion during instrumental conditioning but also that the stimulus consequences of these hypothetical CRs serve as reinforcers, motivators, and/or cues for instrumental behavior (e.g., Amsel, 1958; Gormezano and Kehoe, 1975, 1981; Hull, 1930, 1931, 1934; Konorski, 1967; Logan and Wagner, 1965; Mowrer, 1947, 1960; Overmier and Lawry, 1979).

In testing CR-mediational theories, the CS–IR paradigms provide an elegant means for manipulating the classical conditioning parameters, and presumably the strength of the covert CRs, without becoming entangled in the complexities of identifying which of the many candidates represents an actual mediating CR. In fact, the CS–IR paradigms have revealed that interactions between the hypothetical CRs and the overt IRs are a good deal more complex than a unidirectional CR–IR interaction. Most notably, it appears that the covert CRs acquired during the explicit classical phase interact with other covert CRs, which are presumably acquired in a collateral fashion during initial instrumental training (Scavio, 1972; Trapold and Overmier, 1972). The apparent CR–CR–IR interactions have received substantial attention in recent theories predicated on the general assumption that conditioned appetitive and aversive motivational states summate in an algebraic fashion to affect overt instrumental behavior (Dickinson and Pearce, 1977; Konorski, 1967; Miller, 1963; Rescorla and Solomon, 1967). In addition to CR–IR and CR–CR interactions, there appear to be recursive influences of the IR on one or more of the CRs (IR–CR interactions), which have been indicated by findings that the outcome of classical-instrumental procedures can be altered dramatically by (*a*) the instrumental contingency schedule (e.g., Blackman, 1968; Overmier and Schwartzkopf, 1974), (*b*) the order of classical and instrumental training (e.g., Overmier and Seligman, 1967; Seligman and Maier, 1967), and (*c*) alterations in the effects of parameters of classical conditioning when it is administered in conjunction with instrumental training (e.g., Brackbill and Overmier, 1979; Scobie, 1972).

3. *Instrumental Approach Behavior*

Some instrumental procedures which entail the observation of an approach to food have been designated as "Pavlovian" because an explicit cue (CS) is presented and a hopper of food (grain or pellets), designated the US, is made available at a fixed time following the onset of the cue (e.g., Holland, 1977; Holland and Rescorla, 1975; Longo *et al.*, 1964). This procedure is identical to instrumental runway or maze procedures, particularly the goal box segment in which the food source is seen by the subject. As in the goal box, some approach behavior is necessary and, by definition, instrumental to actual receipt of the reinforcing agent/US. By confusing the availability and the presumed sight of food with receipt of the food (food in the mouth), the approach activity, usually measured grossly by stabilimetric devices, following availability of the food but before its receipt has been mistakenly identified as a UR. Although the development of anticipatory activity to the cue prior to food availability is undeniably associative, it is also undeniably an instrumental conditioning procedure with features distinct from those of CS–CR conditioning. For studying basic associative processes, the usefulness of the instrumental approach procedures in examining such key variables as the interval between the intended cue and receipt of the reinforcer is limited by uncontrolled variation in the instrumental approach behavior cued by the sight of food.

4. Autoshaping

Autoshaping may tap basic associative processes in the same way as the CS–CR paradigms, but with one important and interesting exception: The acquired response is heterogeneous rather than homogeneous with respect to the US–UR. In the best examples, autoshaping consists typically of response-independent presentation of a lighted manipulandum (e.g., a lighted key) as a CS and proximal presentation of the US (e.g., water in the mouth), with the target response being contact with the manipulandum (e.g., key pecking). Where care has been taken to administer the US without requiring an IR, the acquired key-pecking response does not appear in the constellation of URs (Lucas *et al.,* 1979; Wasserman, 1973; Woodruff and Williams, 1976). The acquisition of a response in an effector system not affected by the US would qualify autoshaping as a new associative learning procedure arising from the stimulus presentations of the older CS–CR procedures, but with a response having the interesting property of stimulus antecedents which are to some degree separate from the US. As yet, the mechanism by which the responses, which are neither URs to the US nor instrumental to the reinforcer, are mobilized remains mysterious (cf. Woodruff and Williams, 1976).

5. A Comment

Although all the foregoing paradigms have an associative character, the class of behaviors conventionally used in each of them affects their suitability for investigations of not only basic associative processes but also the underlying neural substrate. In the CS–CR procedures, the class of behaviors studied has been an anatomically defined set of movements or secretions mediated by a relatively small group of muscles and/or glands. Consequently, the CS–CR procedures have allowed for the potential identification of neural final common pathway(s) for behavior. Moreover, since it is known in advance that responding in the target effector system will be elicited by the US, it has been possible to study the motor pathways of the responses prior to or in the absence of the conditioning trials. This situation permits the observation of changes in the activity of those pathways from the start of conditioning (cf. Thompson, 1976). In the other associative paradigms, it is much more difficult to identify the final common pathways for the target behavior or to observe changes in them brought about by training, since the target response is usually outcome-defined (e.g., pressing the bar). A definition of a behavior in terms of its effects on the environment allows a wide variety of different body movements to yield the required outcome. Although an outcome definition may have utilitarian advantages and may approximate the way behavior is described in ordinary speech, the allowable variation makes it difficult, if not impossible, to identify clearly a final common pathway for the movements that make up the behavior. Moreover, since there is usually no known US for the target behaviors, their pathway cannot be identified outside the learning situation. This is not to say that instrumental conditioning or autoshaping cannot be done with discrete movements or secretions (anatomically defined behaviors), only that it has been rare and largely confined to instrumental avoidance procedures, e.g., leg flexion avoidance (Brogden, 1939; Wahlsten and Cole, 1972).

III. Mechanisms of Association and Reinforcement

Although associative doctrine has guided research with classical conditioning, early investigations revealed that the empirical laws of classical conditioning depart in important ways from a simple Law of Contiguity. In brief, it has been found that CR acquisition can reliably occur when the CS and US are temporally separated. This fundamental challenge to the Law of Contiguity was originally raised by Pavlov's discovery of "trace conditioning." A second challenge to a contiguity principle has been the observation that strict simultaneity between a CS and US yields little or no responding, while asynchronous presentation of the CS and US produces the most reliable CR acquisition (Bernstein, 1934; Kimble, 1947; McAllister, 1953). In addition to the problems of trace conditioning and stimulus asynchrony, the topographic characteristics of the behavioral CR have placed a burden on the conversion of associative doctrine to a scientific theory. Specifically, it has long been recognized that the form of the CR differs in many respects from that of the UR (e.g., Hilgard, 1936a,b). Most noticeably, the CR is initiated in advance of the US, rather than coinciding with the time of US application. Accordingly, this section will discuss the characteristics of trace conditioning, CS–US asynchrony, and CR topography in the rabbit NMR preparation, and what they have revealed regarding the fundamental mechanisms of associative learning.

A. Trace Conditioning and Stimulus Asynchrony

In trace conditioning, Pavlov (1927, p. 40) found that CR acquisition occurs even though the offset of the CS antedates that of the US, leaving an "empty" interval between them. Furthermore, when the CR occurs, it is usually initiated in the interval after CS offset. Thus, there is no form of simultaneity between the CS and the US–UR, or between the CS and the CR. For Pavlov, the phenomenon of trace conditioning raised the awful specter of unsubstantial "psychic" causes underlying the apparent action at a distance. To bridge the gap between the CS and CR, Pavlov (1927) proposed that the CS event left a "trace," i.e., a perseverative representation in the central nervous system, and that the portion of the trace immediately antedating the CR was the effective instigator of the response. In addition to trace conditioning, as mentioned above, some degree of asynchrony rather than simultaneity between the CS and US appears to be necessary for CR acquisition to occur. Specifically, systematic manipulations of the CS–US interstimulus interval (ISI) in CS–CR paradigms have typically yielded concave ("inverted U")-shaped functions between CR frequency and ISI. At ISIs of zero or near-zero, responding to the CS is negligible; slightly longer ISIs produce dramatically higher levels of responding; and at even longer ISIs, a "contiguity gradient" appears in that the level of responding progressively diminishes across ISIs (cf. Gormezano and Moore, 1969, p. 136; Hall, 1976, pp. 111–115).

A joint demonstration of trace conditioning and stimulus asynchrony, using the rabbit NMR preparation, was conducted by Smith *et al.*, (1969). Specifically, the ISI manipulation included seven experimental groups ($n = 12$) receiving paired CS–US presentations at ISI values of 800, 400, 200, 100, 50, 0, and −50 msec. In addition, a control group received unpaired presentations of CS-alone and US-alone. The CS was a 50-msec, 92-dB, 1000-Hz tone, and the US was a 50-msec, 4-mA, 60-Hz shock. With the brief CS, the ISI values longer than 50 msec constituted a trace-conditioning procedure. For each of eight acquisition sessions, the experimental groups received 80 paired CS–US trials, and the control group received 80 CS-alone and 80 US-alone trials. Furthermore, all groups received 21 CS-alone test trials daily with a fixed observation interval of 1 sec. Following acquisition, all subjects received one extinction session of 100 CS-alone trials.

Figure 5 presents the mean percentage of NMRs for all groups in daily blocks of 21 test trials in acquisition and blocks of 20 trials in extinction. The figure indicates that there was little evidence of pseudo-conditioning (Group C). Despite the large number of conditioning trials (640), there was no evidence of CR acquisition at the backward (−50 msec), simultaneous (0 msec), and shortest forward (50 msec) intervals. In contrast, Groups 100, 200, 400, and 800 showed clear increases in percentage CRs and substantial responding in extinction. The Smith *et al.*, (1969) experiment is only one of an extensive series of rabbit NMR studies in which we have documented the effects of the CS–US interval (Gormezano, 1972; Kehoe, 1976, 1979; Kehoe *et al.*, 1981a; Schneiderman and Gormezano, 1964; Schneiderman, 1966;

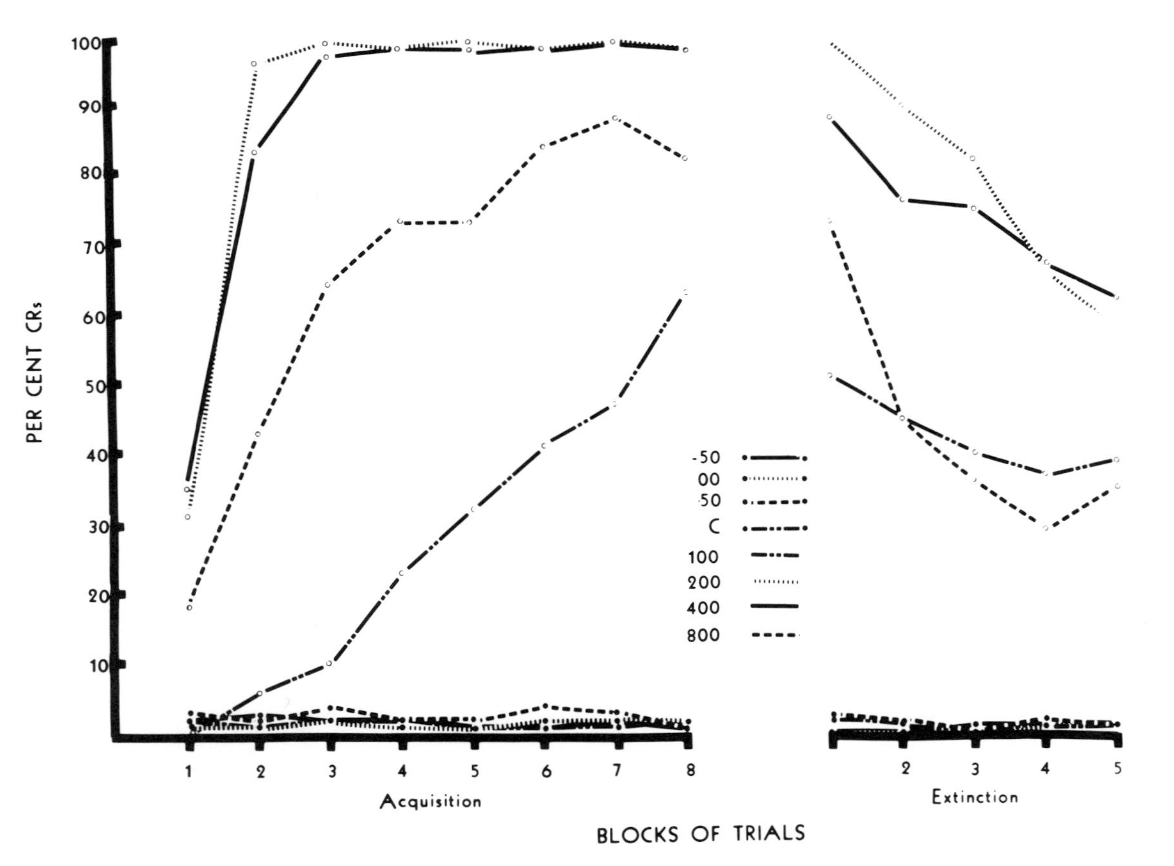

FIG. 5. The percentage of NMRs of all groups in blocks of 21 test trials (days) for acquisition and in blocks of 20 trials for extinction. (Smith *et al.*, 1969.)

Smith, 1968). Similar functions have also been obtained in delay conditioning, in which the CS duration fills the entire CS–US interval. Figure 6 summarizes the results of both the trace- and delay-conditioning studies by showing the mean CR percentage over all days of training. Inspection of Fig. 6 clearly reveals that a concave function describes the relation between ISI and CR frequency with a variety of additional conditioning parameters (e.g., US intensity).

In brief, the above NMR studies show that a CS–US interval of zero produces no CR acquisition but, as the CS–US interval approaches values between 200 and 400 msec, CR acquisition becomes increasingly rapid and reaches progressively higher asymptotic levels. However, CS–US intervals longer than 400 msec produce progressively lower rates and levels of acquisition. From inspection of the acquisition curves, some of which are shown in Fig. 5, it appears that the rate of CR acquisition is more sensitive to variations in the ISI than are asymptotic levels (Kehoe, 1976, 1979; Smith, 1968). For example, an 800-msec CS–US interval which produces only a modest

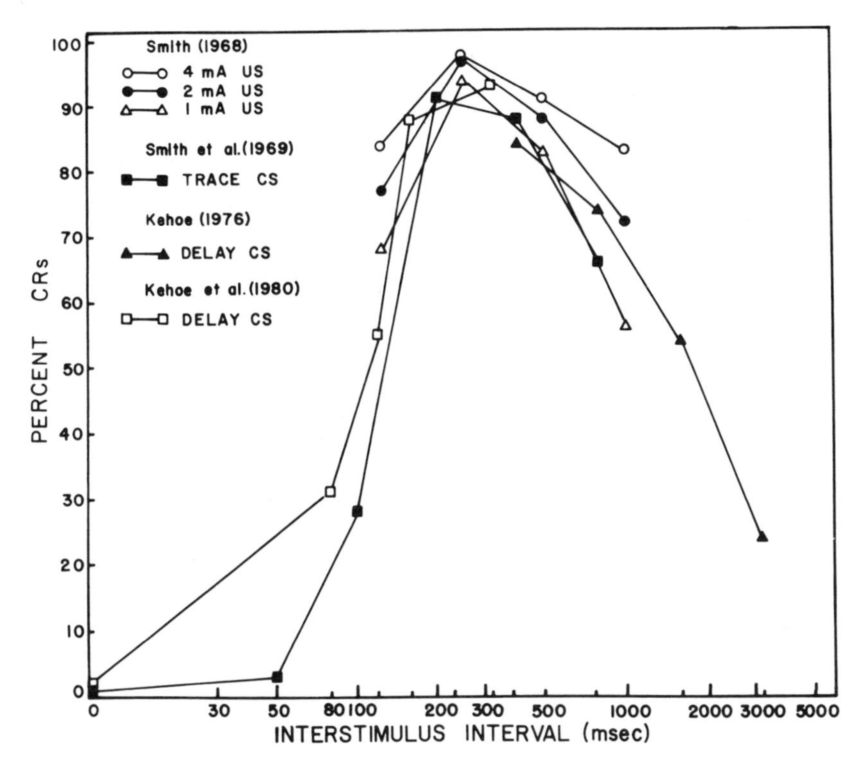

FIG. 6. The percentage of NMRs in acquisition as a function of the ISI in both trace and delay conditioning procedures.

rate of CR acquisition nevertheless, will ultimately produce asymptotic levels of responding near 100% CRs (Kehoe, 1976, 1979). However, longer CS–US intervals do produce asymptotic levels which are progressively less than 100% CRs (Schneiderman, 1966; Smith, 1968).

B. The Anticipatory Response

The most ubiquitous, and thus almost unnoticed, feature of CR acquisition is the anticipatory nature of the CR. In instrumental as well as classical conditioning, the acquired behavior has been observed to move forward in time to stimuli antedating the reinforcing event. Although the classical conditioning paradigm is regarded as providing an ideal vehicle for demonstrating the occurrence of anticipatory responses, detailed measurement of their quantitative characteristics has often been made difficult by the occurrence of baseline responses, alpha responses, and pseudo-conditioned responses. However, since contributions from these nonassociative sources are negligible in the rabbit NMR preparation, it has been possible to observe clearly the emergence of anticipatory CRs. In the NMR preparation, examination of CR latency data reveals that the first CRs are initiated just before the US, but then CR initiation rapidly shifts to progressively earlier portions of the CS–US interval. At asymptote, the frequency distribution of CR onset latencies is centered at about the midpoint of the CS–US interval, but with an increasing positive skew for longer CS–US intervals. For example, Fig. 7 shows the frequency histogram of latencies for the first CR (left panel) and the last CR (right panel) of 120 rabbits, all of which were trained with a 400-msec ISI. Unless one is willing to credit animals and humans with precognizance, the anticipatory response must be tied to an interaction between the prior training history and some aspect of the stimulus conditions immediately antedating the observed response. For deducing the systematic decrease in CR latency which constitutes a primary quantitative feature of the anticipatory CR, trace accounts, as will be detailed below, have provided insight into the processes governing the emergence of the anticipatory CR (Gormezano, 1972; cf. Hull, 1943, 1952).

C. CS Trace Hypotheses

Attempts to account for stimulus asynchrony and trace conditioning originated with Pavlov's (1927, pp. 39–40) proposal that the CS event leaves a perseverative trace in the central nervous system. Subsequent accounts have followed Pavlov's lead by postulating hypothetical stimuli which bridge the gap between the nominal CS and the US–UR (Anderson, 1959; Gormezano, 1972; Guthrie, 1930, 1933, 1935; Hull, 1937, 1943, 1952).

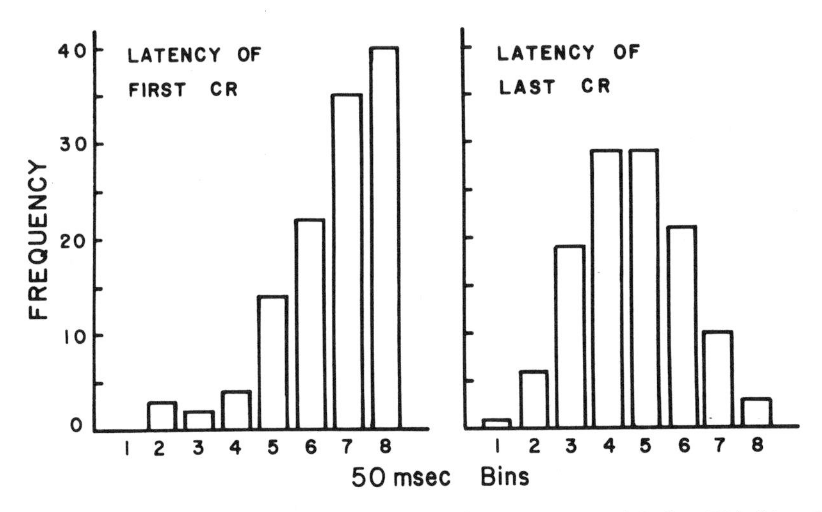

FIG. 7. Frequency histograms for onset latency of the first CR and the last CR in bins of 50 msec for a 400-msec ISI (n = 120).

Futhermore, all trace hypotheses have maintained that an association is formed through the strictly simultaneous occurrence of the effective CS (i.e., a portion of the trace) with the US–UR. Although the trace accounts manage to retain the Law of Contiguity, they do so at the cost of postulating hypothetical stimuli which are not identical in their time course to the objective CS. Nevertheless, in research with the rabbit conditioning preparations, the trace hypothesis has served as a heuristic guide in generating a considerable body of data, which, in turn, has provided indirect but converging evidence for some form of trace (Gormezano, 1972; Gormezano and Kehoe, 1981).

Recent CS trace accounts postulate that CS onset initiates a molar stimulus trace which rises in intensity to a maximum some time after CS onset and then gradually decays back to a null value (Gormezano, 1972; Hull, 1943). Associative strength is presumed to accrue at the point of contiguity between the CS trace and US–UR initiation, and the increment in associative strength on each trial is presumed to be a direct function of the intensity of the CS trace at the point of contiguity with the US–UR. Thus, the largest increments in associative strength would result from training with those forward CS–US intervals for which the CS trace is at a high or maximum intensity at the time of the US–UR. At shorter or longer CS–US intervals, the CS trace is too weak (or altogether absent) to be able to produce appreciable increments in associative strength. Consequently, the form of the empirical ISI–CR frequency function is postulated to reflect the variation in the intensity of the CS trace over time. To explain the occurrence of anticipatory CRs, trace formulations assume that anticipatory CRs result from generalization along the intensity dimension from the point of CS trace and US–UR contiguity to earlier portions of the trace (Gormezano, 1972; Hull, 1943, 1952). Moreover, as associative strength at the point of contiguity increases, generalization would be expected to extend further along the intensity dimension and, accordingly, the CS trace. Thus, the CS trace hypothesis correctly predicts that the first CRs occur near the US, after which the mean CR latency decreases toward the onset of the CS (Gormezano *et al.,* 1962; Schneiderman, 1966; Schneiderman and Gormezano, 1964; Smith, 1968; Smith *et al.,* 1969).

1. The CS Trace as a Behavioral Construct

Although the concept of the stimulus trace has carried sensory and neurophysiological connotations, the form and characteristics of the trace are actually behavioral constructs defined in a given preparation under a given set of conditions (Gormezano, 1972; Gormezano and Kehoe, 1981). A case-by-case behavioral anchoring of the trace has been necessary since the divergence in ISI–CR frequency functions dashed early hopes that their form would be invariant over species and response systems (cf. Gormezano and Moore, 1969, pp. 135–138; Hall, 1976, p. 110). For example in the rabbit preparations, the ISI–CR frequency functions for the JMR and heart rate systems are substantially broader and may even have different optimal values than the function for the NMR preparation (Gormezano, 1972; Schneiderman, 1972). Since these divergences in ISI effects occur in the same species, it is clear that the neural counterparts of the CS trace construct lie only partly in the sensory system. For example, divergences in the ISI–CR frequency functions across response systems may arise, in part, from unavoidable differences in the definition of a single response occurrence. In the NMR preparation, the response is, in fact, a discrete, uniphasic behavior which occurs against a "quiet" background of low spontaneous responding and negligible contributions from nonassociative sources. In contrast, the JMR is a prolonged, multiphasic behavior which is affected to some degree by nonassociative processes (Gormezano, 1972, p. 169). In even greater contrast, the heart rate response is actually a specified change in a tonic, multiphasic behavior.

2. Converging Evidence for the CS Trace

a. CR Peak Latency. Although CR acquistion is characterized by the progressively earlier inititation of the target response, the CR should not be construed as a fixed pattern that is triggered by the CS. Instead, examination of CR topography reveals orderly but diverse changes throughout acquisition. Whereas CR onset latency decreases, the maximal response amplitude, the CR peak, tends to be located around the time of US–UR occurrence (Coleman and Gormezano, 1971; Gormezano, 1972; Millenson *et al.*, 1977; Smith, 1968). For example, Fig. 8 shows the mean CR topographies obtained on CS-alone test trials by Smith (1968) for a factorial combination of four different ISI values (125, 250, 500, and 1000 msec) and three US intensities (1, 2, and 4 mA). Examination of Fig. 8 reveals that, across all conditions, the temporal peak of otherwise diverse-looking CRs is centered on the point at which the US occurred on reinforced trials.

In further support of the trace hypotheses, the location of the CR peak follows the point of CS trace–US contiguity quite closely. When the CS–US interval was altered, Coleman and Gormezano (1971) found that the CR peak at the original temporal locus of the US disappeared, and a peak appeared at the new temporal locus of the US. Similarly, when CS–US pairings were conducted with two randomly mixed ISI values, the CR topography showed two distinct peaks located at the points at which the US occurred. Millenson *et al.* (1977) varied the proportion of two ISIs (200 and 700 msec) across five groups, which were designated in terms of their proportion of 200-msec ISI trials. Three mixed ISI groups, labeled P7/8, P1/2, and P1/8 received, respectively, seven-eights, one-half and one-eighth of 90 daily paired trials at the 200-msec ISIs and their remaining paired trials at the 700-msec ISI. Each mixed ISI group also received five 200-msec and five 700-msec CS-alone test trials. In addition, there were two fixed ISI groups. One, labeled 200F, received all its trials at the 200-msec ISI, and the other group labeled 700F, received all its trials at the 700-msec ISI. Figure 9 presents mean CR topographies for each group on days 3 and 10 under each test trial CS duration. Under the 700-msec CS duration (right panel), two of the mixed ISI groups, P7/8 and P1/2, developed pronounced double peaks located around the 200- and 700-msec points after CS onset. The other mixed ISI group, P1/8, showed only a slight "shoulder" at approximately 200 msec after CS onset and a distinct peak at around 700 msec after CS onset. Under the 200-msec test CS duration (left panel), peaks appeared at 200 msec but not 700 msec. The absence of the later peak on 200-msec test trials suggests that response performance is modulated, moment by moment, by the ongoing characteristics of the CS.

At a minimum, the placement of CR peaks around the temporal locus of the US may be regarded as evidence of a timing mechanism which precisely controls the response topography and could be based on a CS trace (Gormezano, 1972; Patterson, 1970). A stronger interpretation, which accounts for the precise characteristics of the CR topography for the NMR, contends that the momentary CR amplitude is a direct function of general-

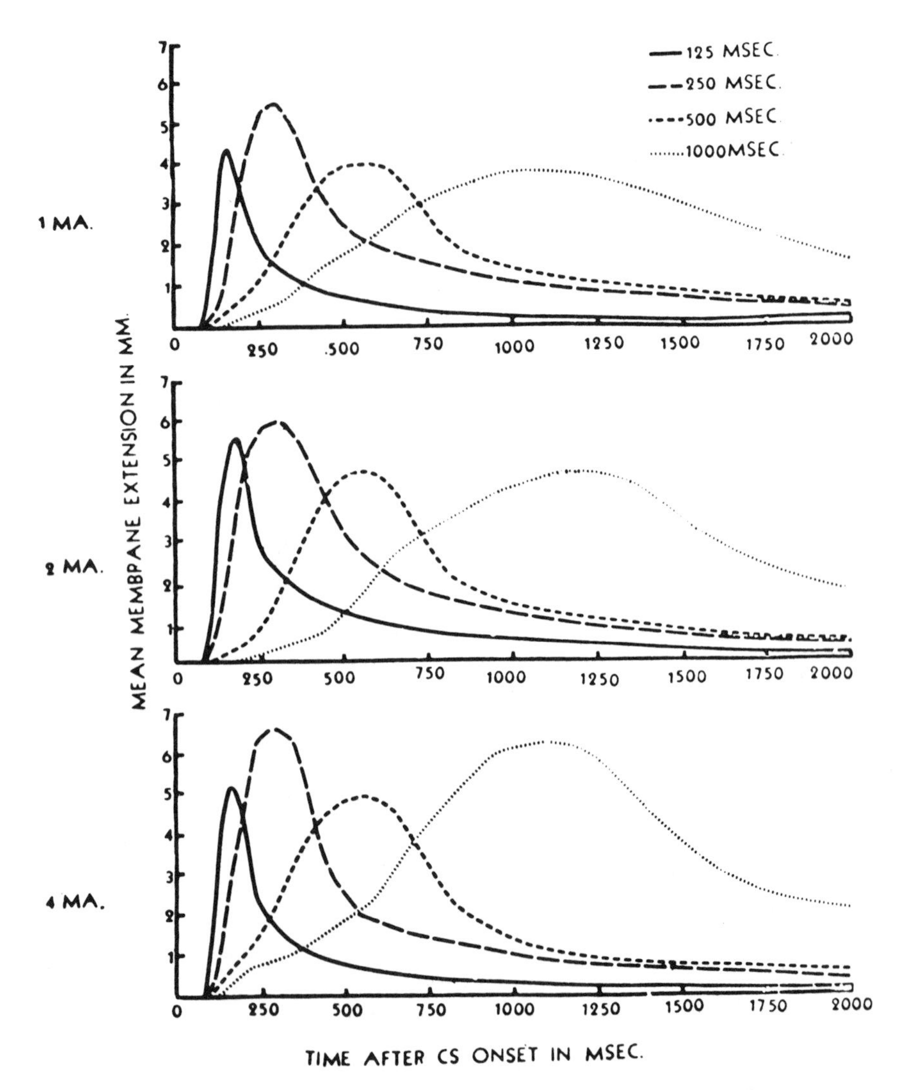

FIG. 8. The mean topography of NMRs based on five test trials on day 10. The mean membrane extension in millimeters as a function of time after CS onset in milliseconds is presented for groups receiving US intensities of 1 mA (top panel), 2 mA (middle panel), and 4 mA (bottom panel), with the ISI as the parameter. (Smith, 1968.)

ized associative strength at the corresponding point on the CS trace. Accordingly, the CR's maximal amplitude would be at the point(s) of maximal associative strength, which for CS trace accounts occur at the point(s) of contiguity between the CS trace and the US–UR (Gormezano and Kehoe, 1981).

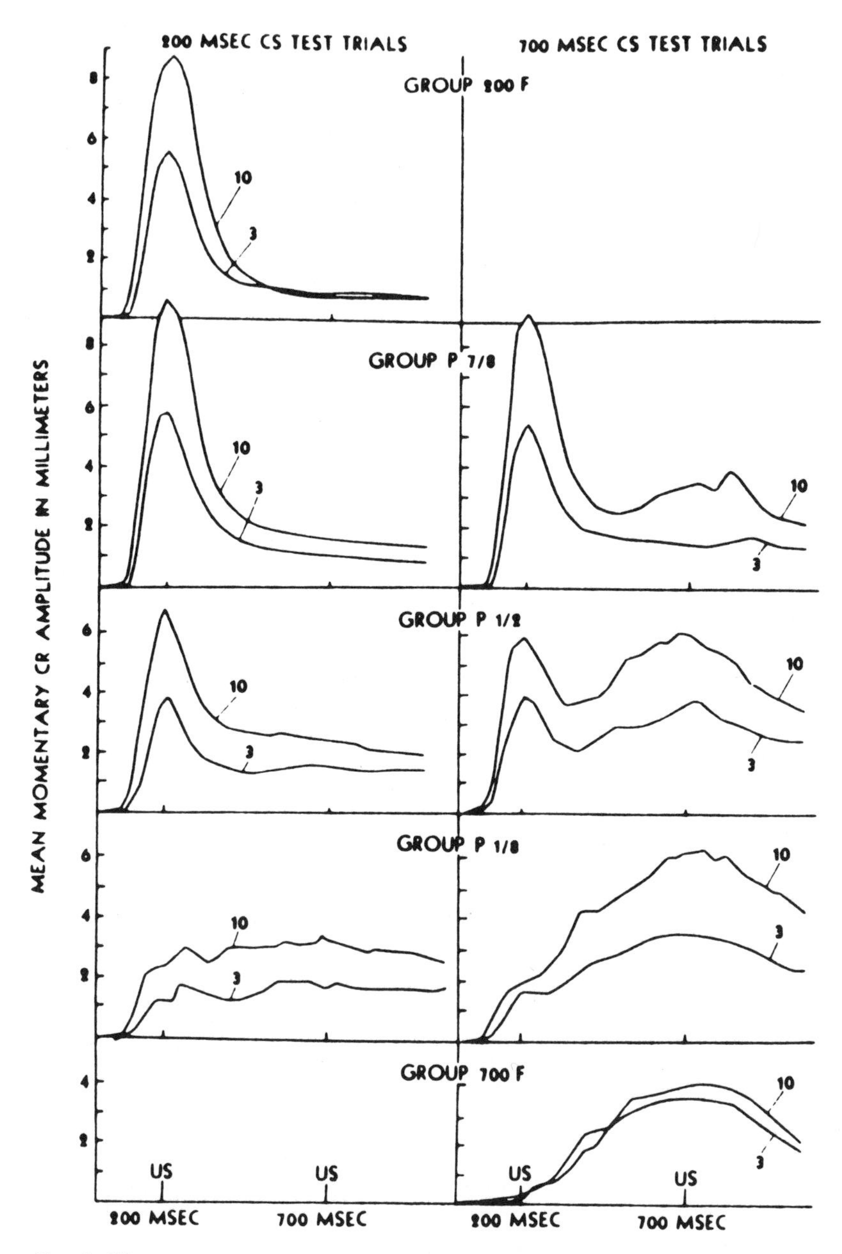

FIG. 9. The mean topography of NMRs based on five test trials on days 3 and 10 for 200-and 700-msec tests CS durations. The mean membrane extension in millimeters is presented as a function of CS onset in milliseconds. (Millenson *et al.*, 1977.)

b. Properties of the CS. The initial attempts to manipulate the CS trace were guided by Hull's conceptual appeal to the rate of neural firings as the physical basis for the intensity of the neural trace. Accordingly, a series of experiments were conducted using manipulations of the CS that might be expected to affect the frequency of neural firings. For instance, through activation of on–off fibers, intermittent stimuli should generate a greater number of neural firings contiguous with the UR to produce more effective conditioning. By the same token, the offset of a stimulus should, by itself, produce a brief train of neural firings and, hence, a weaker trace relative to the onset of a delay CS. In agreement with the expectations from Hull's formulation, a pulsed-tone CS produced faster CR acquistion than a constant CS, and the offset of a tonal stimulus present during the intertrial interval (ITI) produced slower conditioning than the same tone in a delay conditioning procedure (Gormezano, 1972, pp. 156–158; cf. Liu and Moore, 1969). Similarly, trace conditioning, in which the CS is brief, produces slower CR acquisition than delay conditioning (Schneiderman, 1966). In further agreement with Hull's trace hypothesis, CR acquisition in the NMR preparation is a direct function of the intensity of a tone CS over the range 65–86 dB (Gormezano, 1972, pp. 157–159; Scavio and Gormezano, 1974).

c. Intracranial Stimulation. Patterson (1970) has been able to manipulate the time course of the trace by using electrical stimulation of the rabbit's inferior colliculus as a CS. Such a stimulus, which bypasses a portion of the afferent system, should reduce the initial recruitment time of the CS trace and, thereby, foreshorten the minimal ISI necessary for conditioning. In fact, Patterson (1970) obtained a substantial level of responding at an ISI of 50 msec, a value which yielded no evidence of conditioning when a tone CS was used by Smith *et al.* (1969). Patterson's findings cannot be attributed to a greater dynamogenic effect of the intracranial CS relative to the tone CS used by Smith *et al.* (1969) because, at an ISI of 400 msec, the intensity of Patterson's intracranial CS was one that had been empirically demonstrated to support a lower level of responding than the tone CS.

d. ISI–UR Amplitude Functions. An even more promising means of behaviorally anchoring the form of the trace may be found in the ISI–UR amplitude ("CS excitability") function for reflex modification in the NMR preparation (Ison and Leonard, 1971; Thompson, 1976). In the ISI–UR amplitude modification procedure, animals are presented with threshold-intensity USs preceded by a tone or light CS at various ISIs. The total number of CS–US trials is restricted to preclude the appearance of CRs which would obscure the URs. In general, it has been found that the UR amplitude varies as a function of the ISI, and in terms of the CS trace hypothesis, the effects of the CS on the UR can be construed as reflecting the inherent dynamogenic effects of CS trace intensity at the time of UR occurrence. Figure 10 shows, as a function of the ISI, the mean change in UR amplitude from the baseline UR amplitude to the US-alone. Inspection of the figure indicates that the form of the ISI–UR amplitude generally agrees with the concave ISI–CR frequency functions (cf. Smith *et al.*, 1969). In particular, the ISIs of 0 and 50 msec failed to augment UR amplitude. On the other hand, ISIs of 100–800 msec produced progressively larger URs, and longer ISIs produced a progressive decline in the amplitude of augmentation. In comparison to ISI–CR frequency functions, the maximum ISI–UR amplitude function is displaced toward the value of 800 msec, which produces only a modest rate of CR acquisition (cf. Kehoe, 1976, 1979; Smith *et al.*, 1969). However, Thompson (1976) has obtained an ISI–UR amplitude function which more closely duplicates the ISI–CR frequency functions for the NMR preparation. In view of the parallels between ISI effects on CR acquisition and UR amplitude, it is possible to anchor the trace independently of conditioning and to predict truly the ISI–CR frequency function.

D. Contingency Formulations and the "Truly Random" Control

Since the inception of our research with rabbit preparations, unpaired presentations of the CS and US have been used to obtain a joint estimate of nonassociative contributions to responding (Schneiderman *et al.*, 1962). The unpaired procedure evolved from earlier independent assessments of nonassociative contributors based on CS-alone (e.g., Hilgard, 1931) and US-alone procedures (e.g., Grant, 1943). Guided by contiguity principles, the

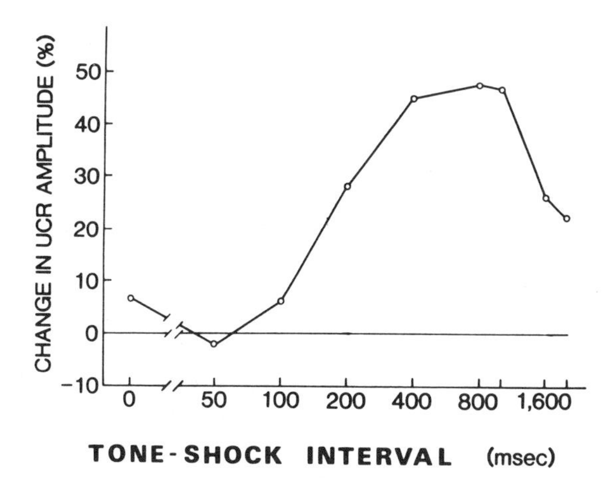

Fig. 10. The mean percentage change in UCR amplitude as a function of the tone–shock interval.

unpaired procedure entailed the randomized sequencing of the CS and US and long intervals between stimulus events to minimize the operation of any CS–US contiguity effects. In the late 1960s, contiguity-based associative theory and its control methodology came into question when several theorists considered the possibility that associative learning could be reconceptualized in molar terms, in which the statistical relation between the CS and US is the fundamental determinant of response acquisition (cf. Gormezano and Kehoe, 1981; Prokasy, 1965; Rachlin, 1976, pp. 80–86, 190–192; Rescorla, 1967). Most notably, Rescorla (1967) proposed a contingency hypothesis which focused on the degree to which the CS "predicts" or carries "information" about the US, as specified in terms of the relative frequency or probability of US occurrence in the presence and absence of the CS. Furthermore, the contingency hypothesis assumed that there are symmetric excitatory and inhibitory associative contributions to responding to the CS arising from CS and US presentations. Specifically, if the probability of a US is greater in the presence of the CS than in its absence, a "positive contingency" would prevail and "exictatory" associative effects would accrue to the CS. Conversely, "inhibitory" associative effects would presumably accrue if the probability of a US were higher in the absence of the CS than in its presence, thus yielding a "negative contingency." Accordingly, an unpaired control condition, in which there is a perfect negative contingency, was expected to be inhibitory in its consequences. To provide an associatively neutral condition in which to assess inhibitory as well as excitatory conditioning, Rescorla (1967) proposed the "truly random control," which was variously specified in terms of independent programming of the CS and US (p. 74) or, more precisely, in terms of equal probabilities of US occurrence in the presence and absence of the CS (p. 76).

As a first step in discussing the contingency–contiguity controversy, it must be recognized that all descriptions of interstimulus relationships, whether CS–US contingency or contiguity, are conventional shorthand notations which draw attention to theoretically important features of the sequence of events to which the animal is exposed. A classical conditioning procedure, taken by itself without theoretical preconceptions, consists of predetermined stimulus presentations and certain types of response measurements (cf. Gormezano and Kehoe, 1975; Hilgard, 1937). On the stimulus side, any session of classical conditioning can be comprehensively described by the duration of events and the intervals between successive events, as is typically done in connection with the actual programming of control apparatus. The occurrences of each type of event, i.e., CS and US, can be described separately with respect to a common reference point at the start of the session. As a concrete example, the separate event-marker lines for the CS and US traced on a polygraph chart constitute a complete record of events presented to an organism under study. Any relationship of contingency or pairing can be seen to be an abstraction of this record.

Although both CS–US pairing and contingency describe features of the sequence of stimulus durations and ISIs in a classical conditioning session, the precise specification of pairing/unpairing or the value of a contingency for a given preparation cannot be arrived at through *a priori* arguments; it relies on extensive empirical knowledge as well as the record of events. At a minimum, the distinction between pairing and unpairing of a CS and an US relies on a delineation of the empirical effects of CS–US interval manipulations. Although contingency hypotheses are couched in terms of the statistical relations between the CS and the US, the operational implementation of the truly random control must acknowledge CS–US interval effects to identify what constitutes the effective presence or absence of the CS at the time of US occurrence.

In the contiguity–contingency controversy, one important set of facts concerning the unpaired control has been continually obscured: In many CS–CR preparations, the unpaired procedure frequently produces substantial levels of responding to the CS, which hardly implies the acquisition of an inhibitory potential. In fact, it was the responding produced by the CS-alone and US-alone procedures which led to the development of the unpaired control as a means for estimating the cumulative contribution of nonassociative but excitatory processes (Gormezano and Kehoe, 1975). Whereas (as detailed previously) the NMR preparation displays no evidence of nonassociative contributions, the JMR preparation can show substantial levels of nonassociative responding (Mitchell and Gormezano, 1970; Sheafor, 1975; Sheafor and Gormezano, 1972). For example, Sheafor and Gormezano (1972) manipulated the magnitude of the water US across the values of 1, 5, and 20 cc and examined its effect on the JMR in paired and unpaired conditions. In the paired condition, the CS–US interval was 500 msec, whereas in the unpaired condition, the CS and US were each presented once per day in random order, with a minimum interval of 4 min between them. Figure 11 shows the percentage measures of JMRs during the CS and a pre-CS period as a function of 5-day blocks (one trial per day) in both acquisition and extinction. For all three US magnitudes, the level of responding to the CS was higher in the paired than in the unpaired condition. Nevertheless, responding in the unpaired condition was appreciable and was positively related to US magnitude. Moreover, the excitatory effects of the unpaired procedure persisted into extinction, in which all presentations of the US were suspended. Throughout training, baseline responding during the pre-CS period remained at a low level, thus controlling for any general "arousal" produced by US presentations. In brief, the unpaired procedure in the JMR preparation, as well as other CS–CR preparations (e.g., human eye blink),

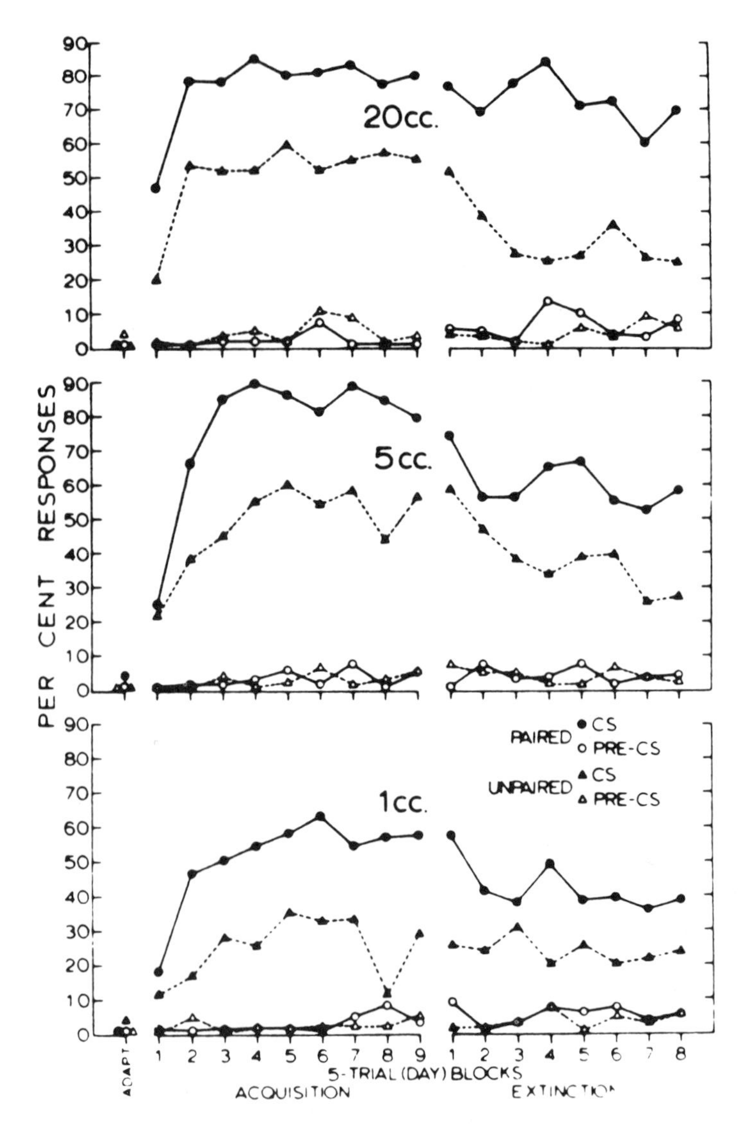

FIG. 11. Percentage of JMRs during CS and pre-CS periods as a function of five-trial (day) blocks in acquisition and extinction. (Sheafor and Gormezano, 1972.)

has hardly had the suppressive effect that the contingency formulation would lead one to expect. In the case of these preparations, the use of a truly random control, which allows chance pairings of the CS and US, would produce even higher levels of responding to the CS, which would largely mask the consequences of the systematic CS–US pairings in the paired condition.

Of course, a committed contingency theorist could reverse the argument and contend that the excitatory nonassociative processes mask the inhibitory associative processes in the unpaired condition. If the unpaired procedure does have an inhibitory effect, it should be readily apparent in the NMR preparation, in which the unpaired procedure yields only baseline levels of responding. Accordingly, Holmes (1971), as part of a larger set of experiments, compared the effects of four "control" conditions—no stimulation, explicitly unpaired, truly random and US-alone—on subsequent CR acquisition under paired CS–US training in which the CS–US interval was 250 msec. In the truly random condition, the CS and US were programmed independently of one another, such that the likelihood of a chance conjunction of the CS and US within a 4-sec time unit was 0.004. In the CR acquisition transfer test, it was found that the no-stimulation group showed a significantly higher level of responding (51%) than the unpaired (19%), truly random (22%), and US-alone (23%) groups, which failed to differ significantly from one another. Since the US-alone group showed a level of performance similar to that of the unpaired and truly random groups, it may be concluded that the difference between the no-stimulation group and the remaining groups arises from the US presentations in the first stage and not from any associative consequences of the contingency between the CS and US presentations. Subsequently, the decremental effect of US-alone presentations has been confirmed in the rabbit NMR preparation (Mis and Moore, 1973) and subjected to scrutiny in other CS–CR and CS–IR procedures (Randich and LoLordo, 1979). A variety of associative and nonassociative accounts of the decremental effects of prior US exposure have been considered, but this set has not included the contingency formulations (cf. Randich and LoLordo, 1979).

In summary, it appears that the associative methodology embodied in the unpaired control is entirely appropriate for assessing the contributions to responding made by excitatory nonassociataive processes. Where the contiguity-based associative methodology has indicated negligible nonassociative contributions, as in the NMR, there is no evidence of acquired inhibitory effects arising from a negative contingency between the CS and the US. However, this is not to say that there are no processes for the acquisition of inhibitory potential. In fact evidence for the acquisition of inhibitory potential to the CS has been obtained in the NMR using Pavlov's (1927) conditioned inhibition paradigm. In the paradigm, one CS—CS(A)—is paired with the US when by itself but not when compounded with a second CS—CS (X). As a result, CS (X) acquires the ability to inhibit responding to otherwise excitatory stimuli (Marchant *et al.*, 1972). In Pavlov's view, the acquisition of inhibition was dependent upon the prior acquisition of excitatory strength through CS–US pairings. Thus, whereas the dimension of excitatory and inhibitory strength is perfectly symmetric, the acquisition processes are asymmetric. As formalized by Rescorla and Wagner (1972), the acquisition of excitatory strength is achieved through CS–US contiguity, but the acquisition of inhibitory strength by a stimulus can take place only when there is extinction of the excitatory strength of a concurrent stimulus.

E. Bidirectional and Backward Conditioning

1. *Bidirectional Conditioning*

Although the most robust conditioning occurs with forward CS–US presentations, there has been a persistent interest in the use and effects of backward US–CS presentations. Beritov (1924) and, subsequently, Pavlov (1932) and his successors in the Soviet Union (e.g., Asratian, 1952, 1966) have regarded backward procedures as a means for investigating the bidirectional nature of associative connections between two stimuli (see Gormezano and Tait, 1976; Razran, 1971; Tait, 1974). Specifically, the bidirectional conditioning hypothesis is based upon a neural model which assumes that bidirectional (forward and backward) connections are formed in both classical and instrumental conditioning situations. In classical conditioning, it is assumed that during the traditional pairings of the CS and US, discrete cortical areas are activated and two independent connections are formed. One connection, a forward connection, is presumed to traverse a pathway from the cortical representation of the CS to that of the US, whereas a backward connection is assumed to run from the US "center" to the CS "center." At the behavioral level, subsequent to the formation of the connections the presentation of either stimulus is expected to elicit the response corresponding to the other stimulus. In theory, bidirectional conditioning is presumed to occur under all pairing operations and, hence, with the pairing of two CSs (i.e., sensory preconditioning), a US followed by a CS (i.e., backward conditioning), and two USs. However, because of its greater analytical power, the paradigm involving the pairing of two USs is commonly employed by the more active Russian investigators in their studies of bidirectional conditioning. In the US_1–US_2 pairing operation, two responses, UR_1 and UR_2, can be readily observed; accordingly, the paradigm permits concurrent examination of the development of both forward and backward conditioning (connections). Forward conditioning is revealed by the anticipatory occurrence of "UR_2" (forward CR) to US_1 (forward CS), whereas backward conditioning is shown by the occurrence of "UR_1" (backward CR) on test trial presentations of US_2 alone (backward CS). Consequently, the paradigm of pairing two USs has the methodological virtue of permitting the behavioral assessment of the purported formation of both forward and backward connections within the subjects.

To determine whether bidirectional conditioning occurs in the US_1-US_2 paradigm, two rabbit investigations have been conducted involving an oral injection of a water US paired with either a corneal air puff (Gormezano and Tait, 1976) or a paraorbital shock US (Tait, 1974). Thus, it was possible to measure both the JMR and the NMR. The order of stimulus pairings was counterbalanced, and evidence for forward and backward associative learning was assessed against the performance of groups receiving unpaired presentations of the two USs. When water–air puff and air puff–water pairings were used, forward conditioning was clearly obtained, but the responding to the backward stimulus (US_2-UR_1) did not differ from the level obtained in the unpaired controls (Gormezano and Tait, 1976). When shock–water pairings were used, some indication of NMR backward conditioning was obtained: In water test trials, NMRs showed (*a*) a smaller number of trials to the first NMR CR relative to the unpaired group and (*b*) an initial but temporary increase in the percentage of responses over the consistently low level shown by the unpaired group. With water–shock pairings, it was not possible to make a clear determination of forward JMR conditioning because shock reliably evoked a small unconditioned JMR. However, some indication of backward conditioning of the JMR to shock was detected: The frequency of responses and their amplitude showed small but significant increases in the shock–water group but not in the unpaired group. Consequently, the safest assessment of the empirical status of the bidirectional conditioning hypothesis is that under the US_1-US_2 paradigm, if backward associations exist, their behavioral manifestations are much weaker and more difficult to detect than associations based on forward stimulus pairings.

2. *Backward Conditioning*

In the tradition of Western associationism, the backward pairing procedure has been used to test a variety of conflicting conceptions regarding the nature of associative connections. Thus, under backward US–CS pairings, some contiguity theories predict excitatory associative effects symmetric with those obtained with forward CS–US pairings (Guthrie, 1933; Jones, 1962), whereas stimulus trace theories have predicted no associative effects (Gormezano, 1972; Hull, 1943, 1952), and contingency theories have predicted the acquisition of an inhibitory effect resulting from the long US-free interval which follows the CS (Prokasy, 1965; Rescorla, 1967; Wagner and Rescorla, 1972). Evidence for incremental effects of backward pairings has been obtained in studies with the human galvanic skin response (Champion, 1962; Champion and Jones, 1961; Jones, 1961; Trapold *et al.*, 1964; Zeiner and Grings, 1968). However, the susceptibility of the GSR to augmentation by nonassociative processes (Gormezano, 1966; Stewart *et al.*, 1961; Venables and Martin, 1967) severely lessens the confidence that can be placed in the data. In animal studies using classical–instrumental (CS–IR) paradigms, in which the consequences of stimulus pairings are measured by the facilitory or disruptive effects of presenting the nominal CS during instrumental (operant) responding, the results of backward pairings have yielded both excitatory (Heth and Rescorla, 1973; Matsumiya, 1960; Mowrer and Aiken, 1954) and inhibitory effects (see Kamin, 1963, for criticism of Singh's study; Moscovitch and LoLordo, 1968; Siegal and Domjan, 1971, Experiment 1; Singh, 1959).

In research with the rabbit NMR preparation, the results have largely indicated that backward presentations of a shock US and a tone CS produce no consistent effects (Holmes, 1971; Smith *et al.*, 1969). In these investigations, a variety of procedures have been used to detect excitatory and inhibitory effects of backward pairings. Specifically, Smith *et al.'s* (1969) investigation of the ISI–CR frequency function included one group in which the 50-msec US immediately preceded the onset of a 50-msec tone CS. Test trials and extinction with CS-alone presentations yielded a mean level of responding of less than 2%. Subsequently, Holmes (1971) examined two different classical conditioning transfer procedures. In the first paradigm, Stage I consisted of backward pairings or control treatments and Stage II of transfer testing with forward pairings with a 250-msec ISI. Transfer testing revealed that four different backward US–CS intervals (50, 500, 5000, and 10,000 msec) produced a lower rate of CR acquisition than a group which had received no stimulus presentations during Stage I. However, the apparent retardation did not differ from that of other control groups which received unpaired stimulus presentations, truly random stimulus presentations, or US-alone presentations. Evidence obtained with a rabbit eye blink preparation (Siegal and Domjan, 1971) suggests that a greater number of backward pairings (495) may produce a retardation relative to a truly random control. However, since Siegal and Domjan's truly random control contained several forward CS–US pairings, an excitatory contribution from these pairings may have produced the difference between the backward group and the truly random group (cf. Ayres *et al.*, 1975).

Whereas transfer from backward to forward pairings has yielded ambiguous results, Holmes found that transfer from forward to backward pairings has yielded evidence that backward pairings slowed extinction of the CR established during forward pairings. In Stage I, all groups received training with forward CS–US pairings such that all group means exceeded 95% CRs. In Stage II, different groups received either backward pairings at US–CS intervals of 50, 500, 5000, or 10,000 msec, explicitly unpaired stimulus presentations, truly random stimulus presentations, or CS-alone presentations (i.e., extinction). It was found that the groups receiving 50 and 500 msec backward US–CS presentations showed a higher level of responding than all the other groups. On the one hand, the relatively high levels of responding in the backward groups may indicate that backward pairings have a weak excitatory effect capable of maintaining an already established forward connection. On the other hand, Holmes noted that the presentation of the US prior to the CS at the 50- and 500-msec intervals may "mask" (perceptually obscure) the CS, thus protecting the CS from extinction.

F. Mechanisms of Reinforcement

Despite the persistent identification of classical conditioning with association through contiguity (Robinson, 1932), the mechanism of reinforcement for the CR remains a subject of continued debate (Coleman and Gormezano, 1979; Gormezano and Kehoe, 1975, pp. 166–172; Kimmel and Burns, 1975). Empirically, the US–UR complex is responsible for the acquisition and maintenance of a CR. In fact, it was Pavlov (1927, p. 49) who coined the term "reinforcement" to designate the crucial role of the unconditioned reflex in conditioning. However, the mechanism by which the US–UR provides a reinforcing state of affairs remains unclear. The two principal theoretical accounts have been contiguity and effect formulations. In contiguity accounts (e.g., Estes, 1959; Guthrie, 1930, 1952; Sheffield, 1965), the role of the US is presumed to ensure the occurrence of the UR in an appropriate temporal relationship to the CS, whereas effect theories hold that the US must also have motivational consequences. Effect theorists have made numerous proposals regarding the character of the motivational consequences arising from the US. These proposals may be divided into two broad classes based on whether CR acquisition is determined (*a*) by the presumed motivational properties of US occurrence *per se* or (*b*) through CR-produced modification of the sensory consequences of the US.

1. The Law of Contiguity and Thorndike's Law of Effect

Contiguity accounts and US effect accounts differ only in regard to whether any motivational consequences of the US are necessary to CR acquisition and maintenance. In its most elementary form, a contiguity account argues that the necessary and sufficient condition for a CS–CR association is the co-occurrence of the designated stimulus and response (UR). In this basic contiguity formulation, the US simply provides the means for the experimenter to evoke the target response (UR) in the presence of the CS. Likewise, the Law of Effect as originally formulated by Thorndike

(1913) is first and foremost a principle of association through stimulus-response contiguity. The relevant portion of the law states, "Of the several responses made to the same situation, those which are accompanied or closely followed by satisfaction to the animal will, other things being equal, be more firmly connected with the situation so that, when it recurs, they will be more likely to recur" (p. 4). Thus, Thorndike's Law of Effect focused on the "connection" (association) between "situations" (stimuli) and "responses" in exactly the same manner as the Law of Contiguity. The distinguishing mark of Thorndike's Law of Effect is that it required the contiguity of three events—situation, response, and satisfier—for the formation of an association. Nevertheless, the only members of the association were the situation and the response; satisfaction served as a necessary catalyst to the formation of the association without itself being a member. Although the Law of Effect was formulated in connection with what has since been recognized as instrumental conditioning, it should be clear that, like the Law of Contiguity, it does not restrict the means by which contiguity of events occurs. Thus, the Law of Effect can and has been applied without modification to classical conditioning (e.g., Hull, 1943). Under this law as applied to classical conditioning, the US serves as the source of both the response and the necessary motivational satisfaction. With the response–motivation contiguity assured by the US, the pairing of the CS with the US–UR is all that is experimentally necessary to establish a CS–CR association. Thorndike's Law of Effect has been adopted by a number of theorists, who have differed primarily over the nature of the motivational catalyst provided by the US (e.g., Hull, 1943; Konorski, 1967; Miller, 1963; Mowrer, 1960; Spence, 1956). Using the basic contiguity and effect formulations as guides, an extensive series of experiments has been conducted with the NMR preparation to delineate the characteristics of the US which govern conditioning.

Frequent attempts have been made to distinguish between contiguity and effect hypotheses by discovering a stimulus which reliably evokes a UR but does not ostensibly have motivational consequences (Loucks, 1935; Loucks and Gantt, 1938; Young, 1958). Under such circumstances, contiguity theory predicts that CR acquisition would occur, whereas effect theory predicts that it would not (Brogden, 1962; Kimble, 1961, p. 214). However, there are no conventional criteria for identifying motivational properties of a sitmulus independent of a learning situation. Historically, Thorndike objectively tied the hedonistic satisfying and annoying qualities of an event to the approach or evasive behavior evoked by the event in question (Hilgard, 1948). Unfortunately, all too often it appears that identification of an event's motivational properties relies on an anthropomorphic reconstruction of the subjective pleasure or pain produced by the event. Although ambiguities in the definition of "motivation" make it difficult to reject an effect account of any instance of learning, it is possible to doubt the sufficiency of S–R contiguity any time that a US–UR constellation fails to produce conditioning. In the rabbit NMR preparation, some characteristics of the US beyond its response-evoking capacity appears to be required to produce CR acquisition. Specifically, CR acquisition has been routinely obtained with both paraorbital shock and corneal air puff USs, but not with a strong light which reliably evoked a UR (Bruner, 1963). Specifically, Bruner (1963) compared the effectiveness of a modest air puff US (an 80-mm puff of compressed nitrogen) and a light US (a 200-watt incandescent lamp). Across 700 CS–US trials, the air puff US produced an asymptotic level of approximately 80% CRs, whereas the light US produced no increase over the base rate of 2% responses. Clearly, these results suggest that S–R contiguity is insufficient to produce CR acquisition. Conversely, these results yield tentative support for an effect formulation, although the motivational property possessed by an air puff and not an intense light remains to be identified.

Using both contiguity and effect formulations as heuristic guides, we have gone on to examine the effects produced by the manipulation of the intensity and duration of a paraorbital shock US on CR acquisition. According to contiguity hypotheses, anything which increases the "vigor" (e.g., amplitude and duration) of the UR will increase the likelihood of the target response. Whereas contiguity theory is clear in its predictions regarding US parameters, effect formulations differ dramatically in their expectations regarding US variables. Thus, according to Hull's "drive-reduction" version of Thorndike's Law of Effect, the onset of an aversive US induces a "drive" state, as well as evoking the target response. However, reinforcement of the S–R association does not occur until drive is reduced by the offset of the US. Hence, increases in US intensity would increase the drive level and, accordingly, the magnitude of drive reduction at the time of offset. However, increases in US duration would delay the time of drive reduction, thus reducing its contiguity with the CS and UR. Consequently, increases in US duration would be expected to have an inverse effect on the rate of CR acquisition (Miller, 1963, pp. 73–75; Mowrer, 1951, 1960). In summary, contiguity and drive-reduction formulations largely agree in their predictions regarding US intensity while differing with respect to US duration. However, virtually complete convergence between contiguity and effect formulations can be obtained with those effect formulations which maintain that reinforcement of an S–R association occurs at the point of "drive induction," i.e., US onset (Mowrer, 1960).

Empirically, investigations which manipulated US intensity and duration have yielded results which have largely supported contiguity/drive-induction rather than drive-reduction formulations. Specifically, US intensity has a strong positive effect on the rate of CR acquisition in the NMR preparation

(Ashton *et al.,* 1969; A. Smith, 1966; M. Smith, 1968). As shown in Fig. 6, Smith (1968) found that a 50-msec shock US at intensities of 1, 2, and 4 mA produced progressively higher overall levels of responding, with the largest effects appearing at the longer ISIs. As required by contiguity formulations, recent examinations of the shock–NMR unconditioned reflex reveal that there is a positive effect of US intensity on UR vigor as indexed by UR magnitude, a measure which averages together the amplitude of observed responses and zeros for instances in which a UR failed to occur. For the 1-, 2-, and 4-mA values used by Smith (1968), the mean UR magnitudes are approximately 3.0, 6.0, and 8.5 mm of nictitating membrane extension.

In further agreement with contiguity/drive-induction hypotheses, the rate of CR acquisition is a positive function of the US duration (Asthon *et al.,* 1969; Tait *et al.,* 1981). In a differential conditioning procedure, Ashton *et al.* (1969) compared the effects of a 50- and a 350-msec US duration. They found that the 350-msec US duration increased the mean level of responding to CS+ by approximately 10 percentage points while having no differential effect on the low level of responding to CS–. The difference between US durations was obtained across US intensity values of 0.5, 2.0, and 4.0 mA. Similarly, Tait *et al.* (1981, Experiment 1) found that the mean number of trials before the first CR for US durations of 50, 1500, and 6000 msec was 99, 67, and 52, respectively. (The lower the number of trials, the faster the rate of CR acquisition.) Although the 6000-msec US duration produced the most rapid initial CR acquisition, it also produced pronounced decrements in responding within each session. These within-session decrements, together with the prolonged UR produced by the long US, suggested that a "fatigue-like" performance factor may have had a deleterious effect on CR performance. Subsequently, Tait *et al.* (1981, Experiment 4) equated groups for total US exposure by using US-alone presentations interpolated between CS–US pairings. Thus, a group receiving a 50-msec US on paired trials was administered a 6000-msec US during the intertrial interval. When the potential contribution of performance factors was controlled, the rate of CR acquisition, as indexed by the percentage CR measure, was a positive function of the US duration. As an alternative to controlling the contribution of performance factors, Tait *et al.* (1981, Experiment 5) conducted training using only one trial per daily session. Presumably, the 24-hour interval between successive trials would be sufficient to permit the total dissipation of any energizing or fatigue effect of the prior US presentation. Again, the CR percentage measure was a positive function of US duration.

2. Instrumental Interpretations

In its most general form, the instrumental "law of effect" hypothesis contends that a CR is acquired because it is capable of so affecting the stimulus consequences of the US that execution of a CR is "rewarding" relative to a failure to make a CR. Specifically, CR–US overlap is presumed to attenuate the noxiousness of an aversive US or to enhance the "attractiveness" of the appetitive US. Thus, a hypothetical instrumental contingency is postulated to be embedded intrinsically in classical conditioning procedures. Historically, the instrumental interpretation of classical conditioning can be traced to a strong but nonlogical identification of the Law of Effect with instrumental conditioning procedures as laboratory models of adaptive behavior (see Coleman and Gormezano, 1979; Gormezano and Coleman, 1973; Gormezano and Kehoe, 1975, pp. 168–172; Hull, 1929; Schlosberg, 1937; Skinner, 1938).

a. Laboratory Models of Adaptation. Pavlov viewed the conditioned reflex as the basic unit by which an animal's behavior would be adjusted to correspond to the exigencies of its particular environment (Pavlov, 1927, pp. 15–17, 395; see Coleman and Gormezano, 1979). In Pavlov's conception of behavioral adaptation, conditioning mechanisms are fixed in any individual member of a species and are adaptive only in the sense that they, being physically based on the nervous system, are the product of the Darwinian laws of variation and natural selection. Thus, through evolution, conditioning mechansims are adaptive insofar as they have contributed to the survival of the species. However, conditioning mechanisms do not ensure that an individual member of a species will necessarily behave in the most appropriate manner in a particular situation. Conceiveably, conditioning mechanisms could operate to produce self-destruction of an individual if unusual circumstances arose. In summary, mechanisms of conditioning do not guarantee that behavioral adjustment will occur in all cases, only in enough cases to ensure survival of the species. In Pavlov's concept of adaptation, the primary principle of individual adjustment is that of "signalization," whereby stimuli antedating biologically significant events come to evoke anticipatory responses in the organism in preparation for those events (Donahoe and Wessells, 1980, pp. 17–20.).

The instrumental interpretation of classical conditioning arises from a concept of adaptation which stresses the individual's "success" in each situation (Schlosberg, 1937), an approach which is most clearly exemplified in Skinner's (1937, 1938) views of instrumental conditioning. The Pavlovian model emphasizes stimulus determinants of behavior, whereas Skinner has emphasized the consequences of an animal's acts as the determinants of subsequent behavior. The individual animal is viewed as both a provider and an evader of biologically significant events which are most suitable in each particular situation. In stressing the relation between a behavioral act and its subsequent consequences, Skinner reformulated the effect principle in terms of the experimentally arranged instrumental contingency between the target response and an empirically reinforcing event. In a similar fashion, Schlosberg's (1937) criterion for the application of the Law of Effect was the instrumental nature of a response. Consequently, effect principles in general became identified with instrumental procedures, even though Thorndike's (and Hull's) Law of Effect does not refer to the experimental procedure by which a stimulus, response, and reinforcer are brought together. In this historical context, instrumental interpretations of classical conditioning can be seen as an attempt to assimilate classical conditioning in a situation-specific model of adaptation.

Schlosberg (1937) offered what appears to be the first instrumental effect interpretation of classical conditioning, although it was couched as a methodological device for determining whether experiments carried out ostensibly by classical conditioning had, in fact, administered the US in a manner independently of the CR. A CR found to modify the reception of the US would be said to reflect not only the laws of Pavlovian conditioning but also the Law of Effect, tied as it was to instrumental conditioning. By an imaginative reconstruction of the possible consequences of a CR for receipt of the US, Schlosberg reasoned that, for example, the eyelid CR may avoid the air puff, the knee jerk CR may decrease the stimulating value of the tap on the tendon, and the salivary CR may enhance the stimulating value of a dry meat powder US. Thus, Scholsberg's interpretation of conditioned reflex preparations hypothesized an intrinsic causal relationship between the CR and its presumed situationally adaptive outcome by which the sensory consequences of the US are altered. These alterations were alleged by Schlosberg to act as "intrinsic reinforcers" for the CR. However, this allegation was not supported by any experimental demonstration that increases in CR strength depend on CR modification of the US, nor were operations provided for determining when CRs did, in fact, modify the sensory properties of the US.

b. Research Strategies. Because criteria for determining the presence of CR modification of the US and its presumed reinforcing consequences wait upon operational specification, no procedure has been proposed for deciding unequivocally the legitimacy of an instrumental interpretation in any particular classical conditioning preparation. However, various reconstructions of the situationally adaptive consequences of CRs have been readily produced by such theories. Nevertheless, as yet, no procedure exists which simultaneously permits the manipulation of CR–US overlap and adherence to classical conditioning's procedural requirement that the US be delivered independently of the CR. Hence, an intrinsic CR–US overlap reinforcement contingency cannot be give a procedural specification similar to that of an extrinsic experimenter-arranged instrumental contingency. Given the lack of such a procedural specification, two research strategies have been pursued to assess the plausibility of instrumental interpretations of classical conditioning.

Response-Contingent Alterations of US Intensity. First, attempts have been made to determine the reinforcing effects of CR-produced US attenuation in aversive conditioning through the use of explicit response-contingent alterations in US intensity, thus making completely extrinsic the presumed relation between the CR and its effects upon US sensory consequences. Although the introduction of such a contingency would designate the paradigm as one of instrumental conditioning, it would not constitute a confounding of the procedural and theoretical distinctions under consideration, since such a procedure would bring under experimental control what has been the speculative source of reinforcement in classical conditioning by instrumental "law of effect" accounts. Accordingly, Coleman (1975), using the NMR preparation, examined the effects of CR-contingent decrements in the amperage of a shock US. The standard US was a constant-current 100-msec, 5-mA, 60-Hz shock delivered to the paraorbital region, and the CS was a 500-msec tone. There were four groups of subjects, all of which received the 5-mA shock if a CR did not occur on a trial. The subjects in Groups 5-0, 5-1, and 5-3 received the 5-mA US if no CR occurred, but when a CR did occur, they received a reduction in the US intensity to the values of 0, 1.7, and 3.3 mA, respectively. The subjects in Group 5-5 received the same 5-mA US whether a CR occurred or not and, accordingly, served as a conventional classical conditioning group. A plot of the frequency of CRs on 6 days of training is presented in Fig. 12. It is apparent from examination of the figure that except for Group 5-0, the separation among groups is not large. However, there was a significant increasing linear trend across the overall mean percentage of CRs for Groups 5-0, 5-1, 5-3, and 5-5. In a second experiment, Coleman (1975) used three groups, each exposed to a standard shock of 3 mA when no CR occurred. On CR trials for one group, there was an increase in the US to 5 mA (Group 3-5), for another the shock was maintained at 3 mA (Group 3-3), and for the third group the US was reduced to 1 mA (Group 3-1). In agreement with the results of the first experiment, the level of performance across the three groups was ordered with respect to the shock–US intensity with the mean percentage of CRs for Groups 3-1, 3-3, and 3-5 being 71%, 80%, and 85%, respectively.

The observation in both experiments that percentage CRs decreased with a contingent decrease in US intensity is inconsistent with expectations from an instrumental interpretation of classical conditioning. Instrumental effect hypotheses contend that reduction by the CR of the noxious sensory consequences of the US is a source of response-contingent reinforcement in classical conditioning. The observed decrease in percentage CRs with CR-contingent reductions in shock intensity is, thus, in a direction opposite to that expected from the instrumental effect hypotheses. Minimally, Coleman's findings indicate that a *reduction* in the physical intensity of the US was not a reinforcing state of affairs.

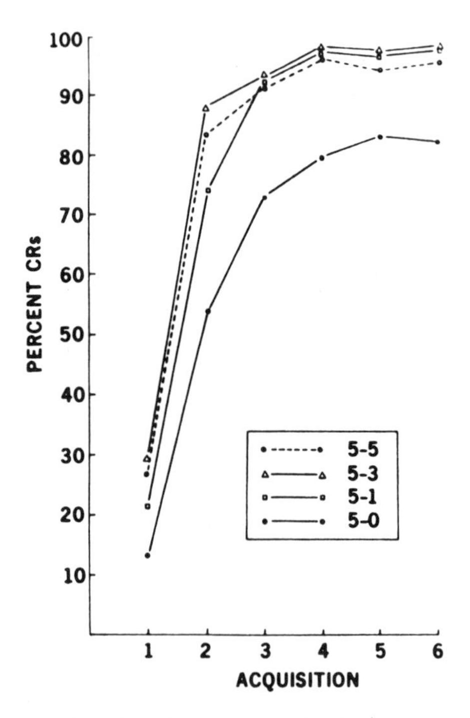

FIG. 12. Percentage NMRs to the CS plotted in blocks of 80 trials for each day of acquisition (Gormezano and Coleman, 1973).

An instrumental-effect theorist could argue that reinforcement arises solely from the intrinsic CR–US overlap, as opposed to an experimenter-imposed contingency. However, in Coleman's (1975) findings, the substantial level of CR acquisition seen in Group 5-0 provides contradictory evidence, since in that group there was never CR–US overlap, the postulated source of reinforcement. In a similar fashion, Gormezano and Coleman (1973) found that acquisition of a JMR to a stable asymptote of 60% CRs would occur even when there was a CR-contingent omission of the water US, again precluding CR–US overlap. Moreover, from the perspective of an instrumental-effect hypothesis, the acquisition of a CR under the omission schedule is highly maladaptive in the situational sense, for it produces a reduction in the frequency of reward. However, from the perspective of the Thorndike/Hull Law of Effect, CR acquisition under an omission procedure is not the least surprising. Specifically, reinforcement of the CS–JMR association occurs on the CS–US–UR trials, whereas the CS–CR trials (without the US) have extinctive effects equivalent to those of a CS-alone presentation on a partial reinforcement schedule.

Response shaping by CR–US overlap. The second major tactic for assessing instrumental-effect hypotheses has grown out of the "response-shaping" formulations of the basic instrumental interpretation of CR acquisition (Boneau, 1958; Kimmel, 1965; Kimmel and Burns, 1975; Prokasy, 1965). Through the operation of a CR–US overlap reinforcement mechanism, CRs with quantitatively different topographical features are regarded by response-shaping formulations as constituting separate response classes. Moreover, through the operation of a response-correlated reinforcement mechanism (cf. Logan, 1956), each class is assumed to be differentially reinforced in proportion to the degree of CR–US overlap that it produces. Accordingly, there have been persistent examinations of CR topography in search of features which tend to coincide with the point of US occurrence and, thus, could be regarded as indicants of the operations of a CR–US overlap reinforcement mechanism. For the rabbit NMR preparation, the temporal characteristics of the CR peak amplitude correspond, in a descriptive sense, to the desired properties of an index of a response class subject to a CR–US overlap reinforcement mechanism. Specifically, the peak of the NM CR tends to coincide with the temporal loci of the US under fixed ISIs (Smith, 1968), shifted ISIs (Coleman and Gormezano, 1971), and mixed ISIs (Millenson *et al.,* 1977).

Although response-shaping formulations have been useful in directing attention to CR topography, they possess no means for predicting which CR measures will reflect the presumed operation of the response-correlated reinforcement mechanism. In the absence of a precise definition of a CR–US overlap indicant, response-shaping theorists have had to rely on *post hoc* determinations of the correspondence between expectations of their formulation and any given CR measure. Thus, the tenability of response-shaping formulations is vulnerable to any arbitrary measure which fails to be correlated with the time of the US. Most notably, in the rabbit NMR preparation, the initiation of the CR, as measured by CR latency, decreases systematically away from the US toward CS onset, rather than assuming some relatively fixed position near US onset. In an attempt to account for decreases in CR latency, Martin and Levey (1969, p. 93) have asserted that CR latency decreases "in the service of changes in amplitude which adjust the response more closely to the UCS/UCR complex." Thus, they are maintaining that CR latency is only indirectly subject to differential reinforcement through CR–US overlap. However, Martin and Levey (1969) do not specify the functional relationship between CR latency and any indirect indicant of CR–US overlap, nor how CR latency would change as a function of independent variable manipulations. More generally, Martin and Levey's account and any other account which maintains that a CR measure is, for example, a secondary consequence of the directly reinforced CR (e.g., muscular tensing) still provides no means for predicting whether a given CR feature in a given experimental situation would be a direct indicant of CR overlap or would be serving in an ancillary capacity.

IV. Manipulations with Multiple CSs

Although the thrust of research with the NMR preparation has been directed at questions concerning the fundamental variables of classical conditioning and associative learning (e.g., CS–US interval, CS duration, CS intensity), a wide variety of experiments have been conducted to address wider issues of attention, perception, and expectancy. Empirically, these experiments have entailed the paradigms of discrimination, generalization, and compound conditioning, in which the contrast and blending of multiple CSs have been found to exert a powerful influence on behavior.

A. Discrimination and Generalization

The study of generalization and discrimination has provided an objective basis for the delineation of the sensory/psychophysical capabilities of nonverbal animals (Pavlov, 1927, p. 111). Moreover, it has long been recognized that the transfer of responding which characterizes stimulus generalization is crucial to the adaptive economy of the animal, because environmental situations never recur in nature without changes. By the same token, the selective responding which characterizes discrimination learning represents a corrective to any excesses produced by the generalization process (Hilgard and Marquis, 1940, pp. 176–177).

In the rabbit NMR preparation, extensive studies of discrimination and generalization along the dimension of tone frequency have been carried out by Moore and his associates (Ashton *et al.,* 1969; Chisholm *et al.,* 1969; Hupka, *et al.,* 1969; Liu and Moore, 1969; Moore, 1972; O'Malley *et al.,* 1969). Studies with tone intensity have been conducted by Moore (1972) and Scavio and Gormezano (1974). In addition to studies with single sensory dimensions, conditional discriminations and patterning procedures have been used as means for investigating the perceptual processes by which animals integrate stimuli from multiple dimensions and/or modalities (Blough, 1972; Chase and Heinemann, 1972; Kehoe and Gormezano, 1980; Pavlov, 1927, p. 144; Saavedra, 1975; Wickens, 1954, 1959, 1973). "Patterning" entails the differential reinforcement of a compound and its components. In positive patterning, reinforced presentations of, say, a tone–light compound (TL+) are intermixed with unreinforced presentations of the separate components (T- and L-), whereas in negative patterning, unreinforced compound presentations (TL-) are mixed with reinforced component presentations (T+ and L+). "Conditional discriminations" entail differential reinforcement of different compounds which share at least one component.

An example of a conditional discrimination in the NMR preparation has been demonstrated recently by Marshall *et al.* (1980). In their experiment, rabbits were exposed to two serial compounds consisting of a tone–light sequence and a noise–light series. One compound was always paired with the US (A-X+) and the other compound was presented alone (B-X-). The particular assignment of tone–light and noise–light serial compounds to the A-X+ and B-X- conditions was counterbalanced across subjects. Rabbits were assigned to six groups (n = 12) which resulted from the orthogonal combination of three durations of the first stimulus (400, 600, and 800 msec) and two durations of the second stimulus (100 and 400 msec). The ISI between the first and second CS was fixed at 900 msec, and the ISI between the second CS and the US was fixed at 400 msec. Each of 20 daily sessions included 30 A-X+ trials and 30 B-X-trials, plus two nonreinforced test trials of A-X, A, B, and X.

The rabbits showed clear evidence of differential responding to the compounds as a whole. Across all groups, responding to A-X+ reached mean levels above 90%, whereas performance to B-X- reached a considerably lower level, averaging about 50%. In addition, the use of the serial compound procedure permitted examination of responding to the individual elements of the compound as well as the compound as a whole. Of most interest, responding to the common light element X showed differentiation depending on whether it was preceded by A, B, or nothing at all. Figure 13 shows the percent CRs to X on A-X+, B-X-, and X-alone test trials across 10 2-day blocks. The performance curves represent the average of all six groups. Inspection of the figure reveals that responding to X when preceded by A, which signaled an impending US, showed systematic increases to a mean level of 54% at the termination of the experiment, but when preceded by the nonreinforced B, responding to X reached a mean level of only 33% CRs midway through training and then began to show some declines. This differential responding to X demonstrated that responding to one stimulus can be made conditional on another or, in the case of the serial compound, on the aftereffects of another stimulus. Moreover, responding to X was even lower when presented by itself, which suggests that there was some degree of stimulus generalization between the aftereffects of the tone and noise used as the A and B stimuli. The apparent confusability between the aftereffects of A and B has permitted us to employ differential conditioning with serial compounds to examine not only the perceptual integration of complex stimuli but also to assess the psychophysical and memorial properties of stimulus traces.

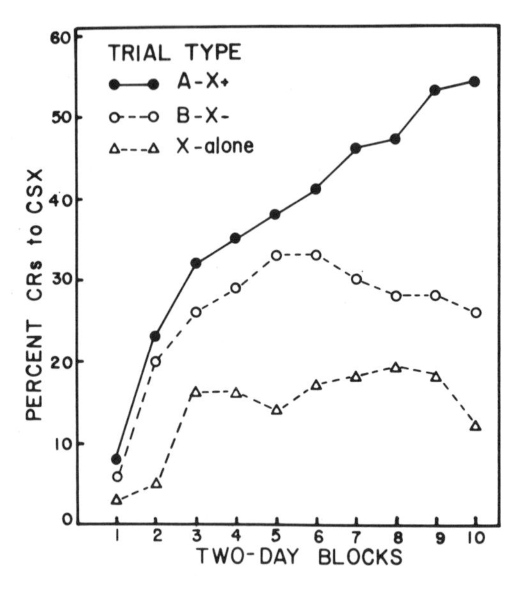

FIG. 13. Percentage NMRs to CSX (the second stimulus) on A–X+, B–X-, and X-alone trials plotted as a function of two-day blocks of trials. (Marshall *et al.,* 1980.)

B. Compound Stimulus Conditioning

Any animal in even the most sterile environment is faced with a continual and multifaceted stream of stimulus events. To discover the laws governing behavioral adjustments to the exigencies of an environment, Pavlov (1927, pp. 110–113) and subsequent investigators used compounds of separable stimuli as a laboratory model for the array of innocuous events which antedate a biologically significant stimulus (e.g., Hull, 1943; Kehoe and Gormezano, 1980; Razran, 1965, 1971; Wickens, 1954, 1959, 1965). More recently, investigations of NMR using relatively simple compounds of tone and light stimuli have revealed that an astonishing variety of processes affect CR acquisition in an environment of even modest complexity (Gibbs, 1979; Gormezano and Kehoe, 1981, 1982; Kehoe *et al.,* 1979, 1981b).

In any compound stimulus-conditioning procedure, it is possible to examine not only the integration of the stimuli which make up a compound but also the interactions among stimuli. Logically, there are two types of interactions: negative interactions, in which CR acquisition is impaired by training to a compound stimulus, and positive interactions, in which CR acquisition of the target CR is facilitated by compound stimulus training. The study of negative interactions has been motivated by the repeated recognition that not every pair of contiguous events appears to become associated (Brown, 1820/1977; pp. 199–214; Gormezano and Kehoe, 1981; Kamin, 1968, 1969; Lashley,

1929, 1942; Rudy and Wagner, 1975). This apparent selectivity in the formation of associations has been investigated under the headings of "stimulus selection" "selective attention" and "compound-to-component generalization" (Dickinson and Mackintosh, 1978; Kamin, 1969; Kehoe, 1979; Mackintosh, 1975; Riley and Leith, 1976, Rudy and Wagner, 1975, pp. 270–272; Wickens, 1959, 1965). The study of positive interactions has been conducted with compounds containing the serial presentation of stimuli (CS1–CS2). Serial compounds have produced CR acquisition to CSs long antedating a US, i.e., CSs located beyond the bounds of CS–US contiguity as empirically described by the ISI–CR frequency function (Gibbs, 1979; Gormezano and Kehoe, 1981, 1982; Kehoe *et al.*, 1979). The positive interaction obtained in serial compounds has provided an empirical basis for those behavior theories which contend that covert CRs and their stimulus consequences mediate temporally extended instrumental behavior (e.g., maze learning, operant chains), in which complex sequences of behavior are initiated to stimuli which are temporally remote from the goal object (Hull, 1930, 1931, 1934; Konorski, 1948, 1967; Logan and Wagner, 1965; Mowrer, 1947, 1960). More generally, the concept of mediating CRs has been considered a behaviorally anchored analog to the mentalistic notion of "expectancies" as instigators of action based on past experience. Accordingly, the investigation of CR acquisition in serial compounds can be regarded as providing an objective counterpart to the principles governing the acquisition of expectancies.

1. Stimulus Selection

a. Basic Phenomena. The design for detecting interactions has usually entailed fixing the training parameters for one target stimulus (X) while varying the parameters of another stimulus (A) in a compound. The level of responding to X observed on individual test trials outside the compound is then compared to the level of responding observed with corresponding groups trained with only X (Kehoe, 1979; Wickens, 1965). Using this general tactic, it has been found possible to impair CR acquisition to an otherwise effective X stimulus through manipulations of (*a*) the schedule of prior CS–US pairings, (*b*) the CS–US interval of A, and (*c*) the relative intensity of A.

The capacity of prior CSA–US training to impair CR acquisiton to CSX during subsequent AX training has been labeled "blocking" (Kamin, 1968, 1969). The first demonstrations of blocking with the rabbit NMR preparation were conducted by Marchant and Moore (1973). Three experiments all contained two essential groups. The main group (A-AX) received CSA–US pairings until the level of responding reached 80–90% CRs. During the same stage, the second group (sit-AX) was exposed to handling and restraint in the experimental chambers but was not exposed to either the CS or the US. Then, both groups received reinforced compound training with simultaneous presentations of A and X followed by the US. Finally, testing with X in extinction revealed a low level of responding to X in the A-AX group as compared to the sit-AX group. Since both groups had an equal number of AX training trials, the low level of responding to X in the A-AX group could not be solely attributed to any deleterious effect of compound training and/or generalization decrement arising from tests with CSX outside the compound.

Marchant and Moore (1973) went on to show that the blocking effect depended on prior training with CSA, for training of CSA following AX compound training (AX-A) yielded a high level of responding to CSX during final extinction testing. Furthermore, the blocking of CR acquisition to CSX depended on the compounding of A with X, because separate and successive training to CSA and CSX (A-X) yielded a high level of responding to CSX approaching that of a group which received only CSX–US training (sit-X). Additional investigations by Kehoe *et al.* (1981b) and Schreurs and Gormezano (1980) have described further details of the parameters of blocking.

Stimulus selection among serial stimuli (Egger and Miller, 1962; Wickens, 1959, 1965, 1973) has been obtained in the NMR preparation (Kehoe, 1979; Kehoe *et al.*, 1979). Specifically, CR acquisition to a CS relatively contiguous to the US may be impaired by a preceding stimulus which has a more remote temporal relation to the US. In the work of Kehoe *et al.* (1979, Experiment 1), the serial compound consisted of two components: CS1, a 400-msec 1000-Hz tone, and CS2, a 400-msec 20-Hz flashing houselight. In Experiment 1, the CS2–US interval was held constant at an efficacious interval of 350-msec, and the CS1–US interval was manipulated across the values of 750, 1250, 1750, and 2750 msec, respectively. Training was conducted for 16 days, each day consisting of 60 CS1–CS2–US trials interspersed with two test trials each of CS1, CS2, and CS1–CS2. Figure 14 depicts the mean percentage of CRs to CS1 and CS2 across blocks of four test trials. For expository purposes, the four groups are labeled in terms of the modality of CS1 (tone), the trace interval between CS1 offset and CS2 onset (0, .5, 1, and 2 sec), and the modality of CS2 (light). Thus, the groups were labeled T-O-L, T-.5-L, T-1-L, and T-2-L, respectively. Examination of the right-hand panel shows that, despite the constant 350-msec CS2–US interval, the rate of acquisition and the terminal level of CRs to CS2 were an inverse function of the CS1–US (and CS1–CS2) interval. In particular, Group T-O-L, which had the shortest CS1–US interval, showed slow CR acquisition to an asymptote of around 40% CRs. In a subsequent experiment, Kehoe *et al.* (1979, Experiment 2) replicated the low level of responding to

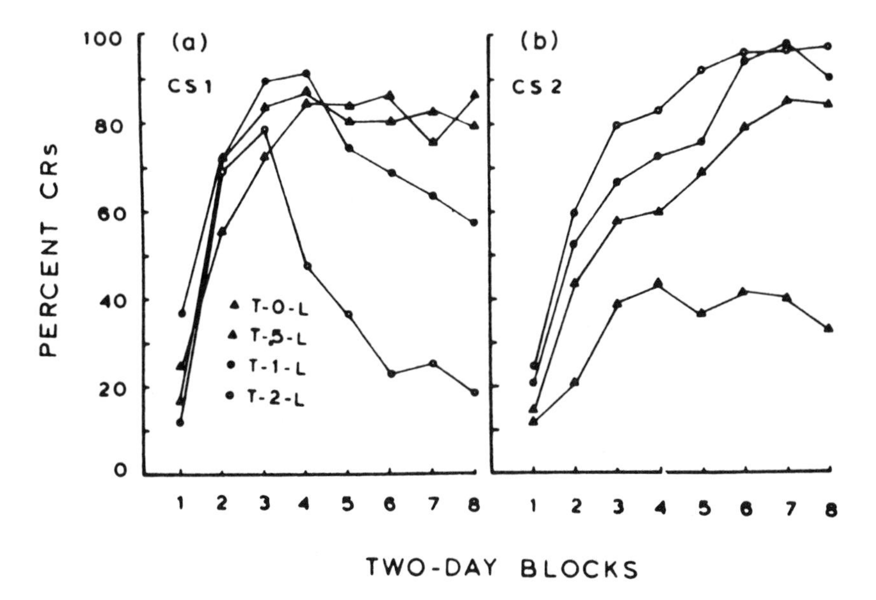

FIG. 14. Percentage NMRs on CS1 and CS2 test trials plotted as a function of two-day blocks. Groups T-0-L, T-.5-L, T-1-L, and T-2-L are labeled in terms of the first component of the serial compound; the tone (T), the trace interval expressed in seconds (0, 0.5, 1, or 2), and the modality of the second component, light (L). (Kehoe *et al.*, 1979.)

CS2 in Group T-O-L and confirmed that it was significantly lower than the asymptote of 100% CRs obtained when the same CS was trained by itself at the 350-msec CS–US interval.

Examination of the left-hand panel of Fig. 14 indicates that despite the rather large differences in the CS1–US interval across groups, the acquisition of CRs to CS1 was at first rapid and uniform across groups. Moreover, all groups attained at least 80% CRs before the groups trained under the longer CS1–US intervals (Groups T-1-L and T-2-L) showed pronounced declines in performance. Later experiments confirmed that the high levels of responding to CS1 in the serial compound represented a substantial augmentation of CR acquisition relative to groups trained with a single CS at the same CS–US interval (Kehoe *et al.*, 1979, Experiments 2 and 3). A more detailed discussion of the augmentation of CRs to CS1 in a serial compound will be discussed below in the section on "Associative Transfer." In summary, the results of Kehoe *et al.* (1979) revealed a large impairment in CR acquisition to CS2 when the CS1–US interval (and thus the CS1–CS2 interval) was short. When the CS1–US interval was long, CR acquisition to CS2 was normal, but surprisingly, CR acquisition to CS1 was markedly facilitated.

The original demonstration of a stimulus selection phenomenon was conducted by Pavlov (1927, p. 141) under the label of "overshadowing." Overshadowing is said to occur when the rate and level of CR acquisition to CSX are reduced through compound training with another relatively intense CSA (Kamin, 1969; Mackintosh, 1976). Kehoe (1981) has recently demonstrated overshadowing in the NMR preparation by using a visual CS (a 20-Hz flashing houselight) as X and varying the intensity of a tone CS as A in independent groups over values of 85, 89, and 93 db. During reinforced training with the compound, light-alone and tone-alone test trials were interspersed among the compound trials. In addition, single-stimulus control groups were trained with either the light or one of the tone intensity values. Overshadowing was demonstrated in that responding to the light in the groups trained with compounds containing the 89 and 93 db tones was significantly lower than the level of responding shown by the control group trained with only light. Across 6 days of training, the light-control group showed a mean level of 79% CRs, whereas the 85, 89, and 93-db compound groups showed mean levels of 82%, 47%, and 34% CRs, respectively, to the light. In the NMR preparation, overshadowing appeared to be unilateral in that the level of responding to the tone in all three compound groups was uniformly high and failed to differ from the levels obtained in the tone control groups. Specifically, the 85, 89, and 93-db compound groups displayed mean levels of 78%, 83%, and 85% CRs to the tone, whereas the corresponding tone control groups showed mean levels of 79%, 87%, and 75% CRs, respectively, to the tone.

b. Stimulus Selection Theory. The most well-developed accounts of stimulus selection phenomena include "attentional" theory (e.g., Mackintosh, 1975; Sutherland and Mackintosh, 1971) and "modified continuity" theory (Rescorla and Wagner, 1972). Although these two theories differ in many respects,their accounts of "selective association" have two common assumptions: (*a*) CS–US contiguity is necessary, i.e., the laws of conditioning obtained with a single CS and US are applicable at all times; and (*b*) selective effects in compound conditioning result from competition between the concurrent CSs for attention or associative strength. Mackintosh (1975) has dispensed with the assumption that there is a strictly limited capacity for attention at any one time. Nevertheless, he has retained the proposition that there is a tradeoff in the degree of attention accruing to concurrent stimuli as a function of their relative associative strengths (Kehoe *et al.,* 1981b). Thus, blocking, serial stimulus selection, and overshadowing can all be explained by noting that CR acquisition to CSX suffers because of a competitive advantage which accrues to CSA through prior training, temporal primacy in a serial compound, and greater "saliency," respectively. Support for the competitional hypotheses has recently been obtained by Kehoe *et al.* (1981b), who found that blocking was still obtained even when CSX was more contiguous to the US (ISI = 400 msec) than CSA (ISI = 800 msec), thus providing further evidence that the ordinary associative consequences of CS–US contiguity can be highly attenuated by processes of attention or competition for associative strength.

Although competitional theories appear to describe the major mechanism underlying stimulus selection phenomena, Kehoe (1979) has found some evidence that a "recognition failure" or, more technically, a generalization decrement does operate to lower the level of responding to CSX. A generalization decrement hypothesis contends that associative strength acquired to a stimulus within the context of a compound fails to transfer completely to testing situations with a single CS outside the context of the compound (Borgealt *et al.*, 1972; Rescorla, 1972; Wickens, 1959, 1965, 1973). In support of a generalization decrement hypothesis, Kehoe (1979) found that responding to CS2 inside a serial compound attained higher levels than responding to the same CS2 outside the compound.

2. *Associative Transfer*

Kehoe *et al.* (1979) found that a serial compound (CS1–CS2–US) in which the CS2–US interval was 350 msec would substantially augment responding to a CS1 even when the CS1–US interval fell outside the bounds of the NMR contiguity gradient for a single CS–US pair. Specifically, at a CS1–US interval of 2750 msec (see Group T-2-L in Fig. 14), responding to CS1 increased over the course of 6 days, or 360 reinforced compound trials, to a mean level of 80% before a gradual decline began to appear. Furthermore Kehoe *et al.* (1979, Experiment 3) found a similar pattern of acquisition followed by a decline at CS1–US intervals ranging over the values of 4750, 8750, and 18,750 msec, where the CS2–US interval remained at 350 msec. Thus, even when CS1 was located at CS1–US intervals, much longer than values which produce even slight evidence of acquisition of nictitating membrane CRs, a relatively simple tone–light compound promoted the acquisition of CRs to distal CSs. The initial acquisition of CRs to CS1 provided evidence for theories which assume that classical conditioning can be extended over a prolonged series of stimuli to produce CRs which mediate sequences of overt instrumental behaviors (see Gormezano and Kehoe, 1981, 1982; Rescorla, 1977). The ultimate decline in responding to CS1 may reflect the development of an inhibitory potential based on a discrimination between CS1 and CS2 similar to that postulated by Pavlov (1927, pp. 103–104) to account for the phenomenon of "inhibition of delay" seen with extended CS duration.

To identify the mechanisms which promote the acquisition of CRs to CS1 in a serial compound, our research has focused on three interstimulus relations in a serial compound: CS1–CS2, CS1–US, and CS2–US. A consideration of the interstimulus relations reveals that there are five broad classes of mechanims which could contribute in a cumulative fashion to CR acquisition to CS1. Moreover, each class of mechanism can be tied to a specific combination of the interstimulus relations. The possible mechanisms and their requisite interstimulus relations are as follows:

a. Direct Conditioning of CS1. Direct conditioning of CS1 requires only CS1–US pairings and can be varied through manipulation of the CS1–US interval. Kehoe *et al.* (1979, Experiments 2 and 3) found that, in comparisons between serial compounds and corresponding CS1–US controls, facilitation of CR acquisition to CS1 by the serial compound was observable at CS1–US intervals of 1600 msec and longer, CS1–US intervals which by themselves failed to produce high levels of responding. Conversely, shorter CS1–US intervals (e.g., 750 msec) were themselves able to produce sufficiently high levels of responding to CS1 to mask or prevent the contribution of any other process operating in the serial compound.

b. Stimulus generalization. Stimulus generalization requires only CS2–US pairings, plus sporadic test presentations of CS1 to observe generalized responses. In our research, the contribution of stimulus generalization has been deliberately minimized by the use of a CS1 and CS2 which are from different sensory modalities (e.g., tone and light). Where assessments have been made, some cross-modal generalization has been observed in that the mean level of responding reaches values between 15% and 25% CRs, which exceed initial baseline values of less than 5% responses (e.g., Kehoe *et al.,* 1979, Experiment 2).

c. General Transfer. General transfer is distinct from stimulus generalization and requires both CS1–US and CS2–US pairings. A general transfer mechanism can be conceptualized as a learning-to-learn process analogous to that found in discrimination learning, in which acquisition of an "easy" discrimination facilitates acquisition of a "hard" discrimination (e.g., Pavlov, 1927, pp. 121–122; Seraganian, 1979). Similarly, CR acquisition to CS2, with its short CS–US interval, could facilitate CR acquisition to CS1, with its longer, otherwise ineffective CS–US interval. In acutal practice, the use of intermixed CS1–US and CS2–US pairings provides a joint estimate of direct conditioning of CS1, stimulus generalization, and any general transfer from CS2 to CS1. With such "uncoupled" CS1–US and CS2–US training, the levels of responding to CS1 have reached only 20–40% CRs, which fall below the levels of 60–80% CRs to CS1 obtained in comparable serial compounds (Gibbs, 1979; Gormezano and Kehoe, 1982, Experiment 6; Kehoe *et al.,* 1979, Experiment 3).

d. Associative Transfer. Associative transfer relies on the CS1–CS2 and CS2–US pairings in a serial compound. Hypotheses about associative transfer are based on the phenomena of second-order conditioning (Frey *et al.,* 1971; Rescorla, 1973, p. 145; 1977) and sensory preconditioning

(Wickens, 1959, 1965, 1973), both of which involve procedurally separate CS1–CS2 and CS2–US pairings. Recently, it has been possible to obtain direct demonstrations of associative transfer by conducting training with separate but intermixed CS1–CS2 and CS2–US trials (Gormezano and Kehoe, 1981, 1982). Most notably, CR acquisition to CS1 was an inverse function of the CS1–CS2 interval, which parallels the "contiguity gradient" obtained with CS–US interval manipulations in the rabbit NMR preparation. Specifically, two investigations of the CS1–CS2 interval were carried out by Gibbs *et al.* (1979) and Kehoe *et al.* (1981b). Each day of training consisted of 30 CS1–CS2 trials interspersed with 30 CS2–US trials (CS2–US interval = 400 msec). In Gibbs *et al.*, separate groups received training at CS1–CS2 intervals of 400, 1400, 2400, 4400, and 8400 msec, whereas Kehoe *et al.* used CS1–CS2 intervals of 400, 800, and 2400 msec. To control for cross-modal generalization from CS2 to CS1 and any nonassociative contributions from the US, both studies contained an unpaired group, which received 30 unpaired presentations of CS1 and CS2 interspersed among 30 CS2–US pairings. Figure 15 shows the mean percentage CRs to CS1 as a

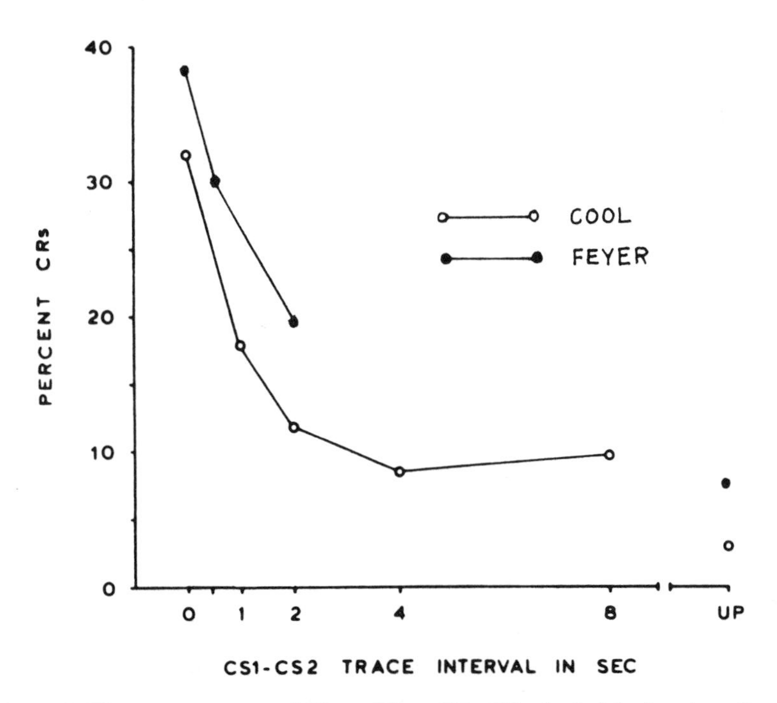

FIG. 15. The mean percentage of CRs to CS1 on CS1–CS2 paired trials plotted as a function of the CS1–CS2 trace interval. The function collected by Cool is extracted from Gibbs *et al.*, (1979), and the function collected by Feyer is extracted from Kehoe *et al.*, (1981a).

function of the CS1–CS2 interval, which is designated by the "trace interval" between the offset of CS1 (400-msec duration) and the onset of CS2. Inspection of Fig. 15 reveals that responding to CS1 was highest at the zero trace interval (400-msec CS1–CS2 interval) and rapidly declined as the CS1–CS2 trace interval increased up to 2 sec. However, even for intervals of 2 sec and longer, Gibbs *et al.* found that the level of responding to CS1 was relatively stable at a point higher than that of the unpaired control.

The relatively steep gradient obtained with manipulation of the CS1–CS2 interval does not match the high level of performance obtained across CS1–CS2 intervals in reinforced serial compounds, in which initial CR acquisition to CS1 was uniformly rapid over a wide range of CS1–CS2 intervals. Although inspection of Fig. 15 indicates that there was some associative transfer to CS1 even at the longest CS1–CS2 intervals, the absolute level of responding to CS1 was low and did not approach the maximum levels of responding to CS1 in serial compounds with comparable CS1–CS2 intervals (cf. Kehoe *et al.*, 1979).

e. Serial Stimulus Mediation. Serial stimulus mediation relies on the integrity of the entire CS1–CS2–US sequence which composes a reinforced serial compound. Such a process would not entail associative transfer from CS2 to CS1. Instead, CS2 may be thought to bridge the long CS1–US interval, effectively foreshortening it. However, at present, the hypothesis of serial stimulus mediation represents a logical possibility which can gain support only indirectly by the elimination of other possibilities.

Our experimental separation of the interstimulus event pairs in serial compound conditioning has revealed that (*a*) the processes of direct conditioning, stimulus generalization, and general transfer, as estimated jointly by the use of uncoupled CS1–US and CS2–US training, can account for a portion of the CR acquisition to CS1 in a serial compound, and (*b*) associative transfer, as estimated by the use of intermixed CS1–CS2 and CS2–US trials, can produce reliable CR acquisition to CS1, but the absolute levels at the longer CS1–CS2 intervals would appear lower than required to account for the high levels of responding to CS1 in serial compounds at comparable CS1–CS2 intervals. Consequently, we are examining three plausible alternative hypotheses regarding the sources of responding to CS1 in a serial compound: (*a*) the estimates of associative transfer are too low, perhaps due to inhibitory factors arising from the unreinforced CS1–CS2 presentations (cf. Herendeen and Anderson, 1968; Holland and Rescorla, 1975); (*b*) a process of serial stimulus mediation operates in a reinforced serial compound (cf. Gormezano and Kehoe, 1982); or (*c*) the possible contributors combine in a synergistic rather than an independent fashion, i.e., the percentage CR measure is not linearly related to associative strength (Overmier, 1980; cf. Kehoe and Gormezano, 1980).

V. Selected Topics

A. Partial Reinforcement

In both instrumental and classical conditioning, partial reinforcement procedures and their effects have a long history of research and sophisticated theory. In brief, a partial reinforcement procedure is one in which only a portion of the responses or CSs are followed by the reinforcer or US, respectively. Thus, partial reinforcement procedures fill the broad range of possibilities between extinction, in which presentation of the reinforcer is entirely suspended, and continual reinforcement, in which the reinforcer is presented following every response or CS. Moreover, from a global perspective, partial reinforcement has been regarded as one means for modeling the presumed unreliability and the intermittent nature of event sequences in the natural environment.

Across a wide variety of instrumental conditioning paradigms, partial reinforcement as compared to continual reinforcement produces (*a*) slower initial acquisition, (*b*) asymptotic levels that are as high (or higher), and (*c*) more prolonged responding during subsequent extinction, i.e., a partial reinforcement extinction effect (PREE). However, the results of partial reinforcement with classical conditioning paradigms have been less consistent: In human eye blink conditioning, partial reinforcement has a relatively permanent detrimental effect on both the rate and the asymptotic level of CR acquisition (e.g., Froseth and Grant, 1961; Ross, 1959; Schurr and Runquist, 1973; Spence and Trapold, 1961) but does produce a PREE (Grant and Schipper, 1952; Hartman and Grant, 1960; Perry and Moore, 1965). On the other hand, investigations of rabbit eye blink (Thomas and Wagner, 1964) and NMR (Gormezano and Coleman, 1975) conditioning have failed to reveal either a difference in the asymptotes or extinction performance under partial and continual reinforcement conditions. Failures to obtain a PREE have also been noted in other classical conditioning preparations (e.g., Gonzalez *et al.*, 1961, 1962; Longo *et al.*, 1962; Vardaris and Fitzgerald, 1969).

In terms of understanding basic associative processes, the PREE has presented a paradox. A fundamental assumption of virtually all learning theories has been that each instance of reinforcement produces an increment in associative strength, even if a law of diminishing returns is true. If extinction performance is taken as a measure of overall associative strength, then the level of responding should be a direct function of the number of prior reinforcements. In support of these assumptions, early investigations with instrumental bar press procedures (Perin, 1942) manipulated the number of consecutive reinforced responses prior to extinction, where all responses were reinforced, and found that the number of responses in extinction was directly related to the number of reinforced responses in acquisition. Accordingly, for a given number of trials during acquisition training, reinforcer presentation in all of them would be expected to produce the fastest acquisition and the highest level of performance during extinction. Although partial reinforcement does slow the rate of acquisition, its augmentation of responding in extinction is contrary to the expectations of the early theories. Accordingly, the determination of the effects of partial reinforcement on extinction of the conditioned NMR has implications regarding whether the NMR preparation should be viewed as a model for the associative processes postulated by the early learning theories or, alternatively, whether the NMR preparation is sensitive to the additional processes which have been postulated to account for the PREE (e.g., Capaldi, 1966).

In light of the systematic importance of partial reinforcement phenomena, a number of investigations using partial reinforcement have been conducted with the rabbit NMR preparation to determine its correspondence to other classical and instrumental preparations (Gibbs *et al.,* 1978; Gormezano and Coleman, 1975; Latham, 1971). In brief, partial reinforcement schedules have been found to have a deleterious effect on the rate of CR acquisition, but only schedules in which 25% or less of the CS presentations are paired with the US produce deficits in the asymptotic level of responding (Latham, 1971). Furthermore, if the training is started under a 100% reinforcement schedule and then reduced to a lower frequency of reinforcement, it is possible to reduce the frequency of reinforcement to 5% before any deficits in the likelihood of responding appear (Gibbs *et al.,* 1978). However, some deficits in CR amplitude do appear with schedules of less than 50% (Gibbs, 1976). Moreover, a PREE has been obtained when the schedule of reinforcement is shifted from 100% to 50% or 25% prior to extinction (Gibbs, 1976; Gibbs *et al.,* 1978, Experiment 1).

In acquisition, the CS-alone trials are not neutral but have a general decremental effect. Specifically, comparisons between continual and partial reinforcement conditions after an equal number of CS–US trials reveal that responding in the continual reinforcement condition is higher than in the partial reinforcement condition (Gormezano and Coleman, 1975). However, any local extinctive effects of CS-alone trials have proved difficult to detect; examination of the CR likelihood after sequences of one, two, and three nonreinforced trials have failed to reveal a reduction as compared to CR likelihood after a reinforced trial (Gibbs *et al.,* 1978; Gormezano and Coleman, 1975).

The accounts of the PREE most applicable to the NMR preparation are those in the tradition of Sheffield's (1949) "stimulus aftereffects" hypothesis and Capaldi's (1966) "sequential" theory. These accounts contend that the effective CS consists of a compound of the nominal CS and hypothetical stimulus elements from the previous trial. Presumably, the US–UR occurrence on reinforced trials (R) gives rise to stimulus elements distinct from those arising from nonreinforced trials (N), which consist solely of CS-alone presentations. Consequently, animals trained under a continual reinforcement procedure have acquired CRs to the compound CS + R. Thus, when exposed to extinction, the level of responding would undergo a generalization decrement attributable to the change in stimulus conditions produced by the elimination of US presentations and, accordingly, US aftereffects (R). By the same token, animals trained under partial reinforcement would acquire CRs to two compounds: (*a*) CS + R and, more importantly, (*b*) CS + N. Consequently, in extinction after partial reinforcement, responding would undergo less of a decrement, since the prevailing stimulus conditions arising from the successive CS-alone presentations would resemble the compound CS + N.

Although a stimulus aftereffects/sequential account of the PREE in the NMR preparation appears plausible, it has been difficult to obtain converging evidence for the distinctive stimuli arising from reinforced and nonreinforced trials in the NMR preparation. In instrumental conditioning research, one important line of evidence has been the demonstration of "single-alternation" behavior which occurs when reinforced and nonreinforced trials are presented in a strictly alternating fashion. If the stimulus aftereffects of each trial are salient stimuli on the following trial, the aftereffects N and R would serve as CS+ and CS−, respectively. Thus, on reinforced trials, the response to N would be strengthened, whereas on nonreinforced trials, a response to R would never be strengthened. To date, the only instance of single-alternation behavior in the NMR preparation has been obtained by Hoehler and Leonard (1973). Their work required special conditions of high US intensities, a short (10-sec) intertrial interval after reinforced trials, and a longer (60-sec) intertrial interval after nonreinforced trials, conditions quite unlike those in which the PREE has been obtained. Although single-alternation behavior is difficult to demonstrate in the NMR preparation, this does not indicate a general insensitivity by the rabbit to the stimulus consequences of previous trials, for reliable single-alternation behavior has been obtained in the JMR preparation using a water US (Poulos *et al.*, 1971).

B. Extinction and Inhibition

The associationistic tradition has tended to focus interest on the effects of CS–US pairings on observable CR acquisition. However, conditioning phenomena themselves are not confined to changes in behavior arising from the contiguity of two stimulus events. In fact, Pavlov devoted a considerable portion of his research effort to inhibitory phenomena, which are characterized by the suppression of responding arising, in part, from the presentation of a CS by itself. More recently, inhibitory phenomena have again attracted considerable interest as revealing processes which serve to govern the potentially runaway, excitatory effects of CS–US pairings (cf. Rescorla, 1967, 1969, 1975; Boakes and Halliday,1972).

The most familiar inhibitory phenomenon is extinction. The operations of extinction entail the presentation of the CS by itself after prior CR acquisition training with CS–US pairings. The behavioral extinctive outcome entails the decline in the frequency and/or amplitude of CRs over successive CS presentations. Quite frequently, the extinction procedure is used essentially as a lengthy series of test trials for assessing the excitatory associative consequences of prior CS–US pairings. Furthermore, it is tempting to attribute behavioral extinction to unlearning of the association formed during acquisition training. Although the extinction procedure is an undeniably useful test procedure, there are substantial data to indicate that extinction has interesting characteristics of its own and cannot be simply construed as an unlearning process.

In the rabbit NMR and JMR preparations, extinction is characterized by declines in CR frequency within a session, but between extinction sessions there is frequently a pronounced increase in the level of responding (i.e., "spontaneous recovery"). Although both the NMR and JMR preparations display systematic extinction, the process is quite prolonged, contrary to the prevailing mystique that CRs are generally labile and readily eliminated by extinction (cf. Kimble, 1961). A variety of both associative and performance accounts have been used to explain extinction (Estes, 1955; Hull, 1943), but in any case, the empirical phenomenon of spontaneous recovery indicates that a substantial fraction of the extinctive decrement does not reflect a corresponding unlearning. A more telling blow to an unlearning hypothesis of extinction is the results of successive acquisition and extinction procedures. According to the unlearning hypothesis, the associative connection should be broken by extinction and the animal should be effectively returned to the naive state with respect to the particular association. However, CS–US pairings after extinction produce faster CR acquisition than the original CS–US pairings. Moreover, alternation of acquisition and extinction sessions produces progressively faster increases and decreases in CR frequency (Smith and Gormezano, 1965). At a minimum, both acquisition and extinction are equally subject to substantial savings.

A more well-developed area of research and theory is connected with the phenomenon of conditioned inhibition (Marchant *et al.*, 1972; Marchant and Moore, 1974). The essential feature of Pavlov's conditioned inhibition paradigm entailed reinforced presentations of one CS (CSA–US) which were interspersed with unreinforced presentations of CSA compounded with another CS (CSA + CSX). With sufficient training, the animal comes to respond to CSA but not to the compound stimulus. Presumably, the loss in responding to the compound represents the algebraic sum of the demonstrated excitatory capacity of CSA and a hypothetical negative inhibitory capacity acquired to CSX. As defining operations for the inhibitory capacity of CSX, Pavlov (1927) and, more recently, Rescorla (1969) and Hearst (1972) have provided detailed criteria for demonstrating the capacity of a suspected inhibitor to suppress responding. Thus, following conditioned inhibition training, the compounding of CSX with a CR-evoking stimulus (CSB) should lower the likelihood of a CR relative to CSB alone. Rescorla (1969) points out that a successful "summation test, " although necessary, is not sufficient for establishing the inhibitory capacity of CSX. In addition, it is essential to rule out the possiblity that the suppressive effect of CSX in combination with CSB is not merely a decremental consequence related to the novelty of the test compound. As a necessary converging operation for demonstrating the inhibitory capacity of a stimulus, Rescorla proposed a "retardation test" consisting of reinforced acquisition training in which CSX is paired with the US. According to Rescorla, a CSX which is sufficiently salient to have decremental effects on CSB's CR-evoking capability, thereby producing a suppression of responding to the novel compound, should acquire excitatory properties quite rapidly. On the other hand, if CSX does possess an inhibitory capacity, overt CR acquisition should be retarded in that the negative inhibitory capacity needs to be overcome.

Moore and his associates have performed a series of experiments with the NMR preparation which have successfully demonstrated the acquistion of inhibitory properties to a CS under the most stringent criteria. The initial experiment, conducted by Marchant *et al.* (1972), obtained both suppressive summation and retardation during final CSX–US training. Subsequently, Marchant and Moore (1974) used CSX–US acquisition training to show that retardation of acquisition to CSX was a specific result of prior training in which an unreinforced compound of CSA + CSX was contrasted to reinforced CSA–US training. When the unreinforced compound (CSA + CSX) was contrasted to reinforced training of a third stimulus (CSB–US), subsequent CSX–US training showed some positive transfer relative to control groups which had not received any prior training.

The findings of Marchant and Moore (1974) were consistent with arguments that inhibition accrues to a stimulus as a consequence of nonreinforcement in the immediate presence of excitation (Pavlov, 1927; Wagner and Rescorla, 1972). Conditioned inhibition training satisfied this stipulation since nonreinforcement of CSX occurs in the presence of the excitatory

CSA. However, in Marchant and Moore's (1974) latter group, CSA, itself having never been paired with the US, could not provide the necessary excitatory component for the development of inhibition during nonreinforced AX compound presentations (Marchant and Moore, 1974).

A recently discovered phenomenon, "latent inhibition," indicates that at least some inhibitory effects can be obtained without prior excitatory conditioning. In brief, latent inhibition is said to occur when exposure to the CS alone prior to CS–US pairings hinders subsequent CR acquisition (Lubow, 1973). Thus, the defining operations for latent inhibition are those of the "retardation" test of conditioned inhibition. Latent inhibition has been demonstrated in the NMR preparation (Clarke and Hupka, 1974; Solomon *et al.,* 1974a; Solomon and Moore, 1975), with the degree of retardation appearing to be an increasing function of the number of prior CS exposures (Clarke and Hupka, 1974). After 500 CS presentations, Clarke and Hupka (1974, Experiment 2) found that the mean level of CR acquisition over the initial 3 days of CS–US acquisition training (100 trials/day) fell 40 percentage points below that of a control group which had not received prior CS presentations. However, the inhibitory effect was not permanent, since the CR level in the preexposed group rose to an asymptote equal to that of the unexposed control group.

Although CS exposures produce retardation of CR acquisition, summation testing has not indicated that CS exposure is sufficient to suppress responding to an already established CS (Solomon *et al.,* 1974a,b; Solomon and Moore, 1975). Consequently, the latent inhibition procedure does not produce a CS with the same characteristics as the conditioned inhibition procedure. Since latent inhibition does not meet the conventional criteria for an "active inhibitor," investigators of latent inhibition have interpreted it as resulting from a "loss of cue salience by way of an habituation-like process" (Solomon *et al.,* 1974a,b; cf. Moore, 1979, Moore and Stickney, 1980). However, the exact parallels between latent inhibition and conventional habituation phenomena remain to be specified.

Even though the key feature of inhibitory operations is the presentation of CSs by themselves rather than in contiguity with a US, a large number of hypotheses have attempted to place inhibitory phenomena in an associationistic framework. Among these hypotheses, S–R formulations contend that the decrement in responding during CS-alone presentations represents the replacement of the observable CS–CR association with a new excitatory association between the CS and a hypothetical response which is incompatible with the CR (Guthrie, 1930, 1959; Hull, 1943; Weinstock, 1970; Wilson and Davison, 1971). In contrast, the most naive form of S–S theory attributes the active characteristics of an inhibitor to an association between the CS and the *absence* of the US. This postulation of a CS–$\overline{\text{US}}$ association entails treating a nonevent as if it were the functional complement as well as the logical complement to the event in question. However, more advanced S–S theories have avoided postulating a functional nonevent by resurrecting Pavlov's (1927) contention that acquisition of inhibitory potential arises from a contrast between an unreinforced CS presentation and concurrent excitatory associative strength (cf. Rescorla and Wagner, 1972; Wagner and Rescorla, 1972). Thus, in the conditioned inhibition paradigm, the potential of CSX is driven into the negative range when it occurs in conjunction with the unreinforced presentation of the excitatory CSA (cf. Gormezano and Kehoe, 1981).

C. NMR–JMR Interactions

Recently, transfer between the NMR and JMR systems has been used to examine "dual-motivational" theories, which are a variety of CR-mediational theory. Most notably, dual-motivational theories assume that, during classical as well as instrumental conditioning, covert CRs (e.g., "drive" CRs) are acquired to the stimuli antedating the reinforcer. These covert CRs have motivational consequences for the overt behavior corresponding to the appetitive or aversive nature of the reinforcer. Moreover, dual-motivational theories assume that appetitive and aversive motivational states influence each other in an antagonistic fashion (Dickinson and Pearce, 1977; Gray, 1975; Konorski, 1967; Miller, 1963; Mowrer, 1960; Rescorla and Solomon, 1967). Hence, the final valence and intensity of motivation for overt behavior are assumed to be determined by the algebraic summation of opposing appetitive and aversive sources.

Dual-motivational theories were originated to account for "approach–avoidance conflicts" and were tested with instrumental runway procedures in which the goal box contained both food and shock (Brown, 1948; Miller, 1944). Subsequently, dual-motivational theories have guided extensive research using classical-instrumental transfer (CS–IR) paradigms, e.g., conditioned suppression, in which a CS paired with, say, an aversive US is presented during instrumental behavior based on an appetitive reinforcer (Estes and Skinner, 1941; Hunt and Brady, 1951; Kamin, 1965). Early formulations and tests of dual-motivational theory focused on the effects of motivational states on instrumental behavior in which the acquisition of motivational states was anchored to the empirical (or presumed) laws of overt classical conditioning (CS–CR). However, more recent formulations have contended that "central" and unobservable motivational CRs influence overt CRs as well as instrumental behavior (Dickinson and Pearce, 1977; Konorski, 1967; Rescorla and Solomon, 1967). In addition, Konorski (1967), for example, has argued that the acquisition of hypothetical central

CRs follows different quantitative laws than the acquisition of overt CRs, thus loosening empirical constraints on the acquisition of the hypothetical mediating CRs.

Whereas the original dual-motivational theories implied that CRs based on appetitive and aversive USs are independently acquired to the same CS, the more recent formulations expect interference if the same CS is paired with two USs with different motivational consequences. Accordingly, to determine whether interference occurs between acquired motivational systems, transfer from NMR conditioning based on a presumptively aversive shock US to JMR conditioning based on a presumptively appetitive water US has been examined by Scavio (1974), Bromage and Scavio (1978), and Scavio and Gormezano (1980). In the first experiments by Scavio (1974), separate groups of rabbits were given tone–shock pairings, unpairings, or exposure to the apparatus (sit-control). During the initial stage, only animals in the paired condition showed NMR conditioning. Throughout training, all groups received a restricted water ration of 90 ml of water per day. In the second stage, all groups received transfer testing with tone–water pairings suitable for JMR conditioning. Relative to unpaired and sit-control conditions, prior tone–shock pairings retarded the acquisition of jaw movement CRs. During the second stage of tone–water pairings, NMRs to the tone CS declined faster than in a CS-alone extinction procedure (Scavio, 1974, Experiment 2). Subsequently, Bromage and Scavio (1978) duplicated the negative transfer effects of tone–shock pairings to subsequent JMR conditioning under a more severe 60-ml/day deprivation regimen, but not under a less severe 120-ml/day regimen. Although Scavio (1974, Experiment 2) found that a previously acquired NMR was depressed by tone–water pairings, Scavio and Gormezano (1980) did not find that there was always negative transfer from JMR conditioning to NMR conditioning. In fact, they found that prior tone–water pairings facilitated NMR acquisition during subsequent tone–shock pairings. These findings, indicating an asymmetry between negative aversive-appetitive transfer and positive appetitive-aversive transfer, support the general notion of motivational interactions, although not the simplistic variants which postulate a uniform mutual antagonism (cf. Dickinson and Pearce, 1977).

The use of transfer designs to infer properties of alleged central conditioned motivational states has the potential risk of being confounded by the presence of peripheral response interactions. Specifically, CS–IR procedures, which presumably measure the effects of the central motivational CRs, may have been subject to interactions between peripheral instrumental responses as well as classically conditioned responses (Dickinson and Pearce, 1977; Gormezano and Kehoe, 1975; Overmier and Lawry, 1979; Trapold and Overmier, 1972). Thus, a positive or negative transfer effect may occur simply because mutually facilitory or antagonistic behaviors are elicited by the CS and/or reinforcers. On the other hand, in the studies of Bromage and Scavio (1978) and Scavio (1974), the joint occurrence of nictitating membrane and jaw movement CRs during transfer testing were found to be statistically independent events. The statistical independence of these two response systems strongly suggests that they did not mechanically conflict with one another to yield the interaction effects.

D. Pharmacological Studies

The earliest research regarding the behavioral effects of pharmacological agents was conducted by Pavlov (1927, p. 35), who examined acquisition of the overt responses produced by apomorphine to the cues arising from the antecedent injection procedure. Despite Pavlov's pioneering efforts, drug research with the CS–CR procedure has been rare compared to the numerous experiments using instrumental procedures. However, because of the experimenter's control over presentation of the CS and US and its well-developed control methodology, classical conditioning appears to have a great deal to offer for detailing the behavioral effects of drug interventions. Accordingly, we have recently begun to use the NMR preparation to delineate the mode of action of purportedly psychotropic drugs.

1. Theoretical Models of Drug Action

a. Three-Component Model. To implement a program of psychopharmacological assessment, it was necessary to adopt an interim model of the conditioning process. From our earlier discussion, it should be apparent that the current body of conditioning theory consists of a multitude of contending formulations, e.g., contiguity vs. effect vs. contingency. The didactic assertion of any one formulation would undoubtedly yield a distorted methodology for assessing drug effects. Consequently, we adopted a more general framework which could easily be put to use and could accommodate a wide variety of formulations. Specifically, we attempted to distinguish between drug effects on three hypothetical components which intervene between the observable sensory input and the behavioral output: (*a*) sensory processing of stimuli; (*b*) learning processes; and (*c*) motor functioning. Each of these processes can be readily subdivided to suit a specific formulation. For example, the sensory processing component can be construed as including everything from the functioning of sensory detectors up to more molar "trace," "attentional," or "short-term memory" processes. Similarly, the so-called associative process can be subdivided to include relatively distinct associative and incentive processes. In any event, the learning process is presumed to entail the long-term alterations produced by experiences which are connoted by the term "learning." Finally, motor functioning can include not only specific effector functioning but also nonspecific energizing factors.

b. A Note on the Learning–Performance Hypothesis. Our three-component framework is orthogonal to the long-standing but deceptive distinction between "learning" and "performance." On the one hand, the learning–performance distinction has been useful as an acknowledgment that behavior at any given moment is determined in a multiple fashion by current, relatively temporary organismic states which may mask or reveal the more permanent latent consequences of past experience. On the other hand, the learning–performance distinction has fostered the illusion that it is easy to ascertain the relatively irreversible and reversible effects of any given variable. In fact, not all behavior theories acknowledge a learning–performance distinction (cf. Brown, 1961, pp. 99; Guthrie, 1959), and those which do (e.g., Hull, 1943, 1952) also recognize that many variables can enter both the learning process, either by producing associable stimuli or through an effect process, and the performance process by altering current stimulating or motivational conditions. A case in point is the variable of CS intensity. In Hull's (1943, 1952) theory, CS intensity is a performance variable in that it has a dynamogenic effect on current behavior. However, the particular intensity of a CS is also an associative variable in that (*a*) CS intensity determines, in part, the increment in associative strength on each reinforced trial, and (*b*) the particular value of a CS used during training is a conditionable stimulus dimension and, thus, responding is subject to a generalization decrement if another value is presented. Similarly, it is possible that a given drug could have multiple temporary and permanent effects which interact with each other. It is hoped that by first delineating the component(s) processes affected by a drug, the later determination of the relatively temporary or permanent nature of the drug effects will be easier to make.

2. A Set of Converging Operations

Our current battery of procedures for assessing drug effects was developed in connection with the investigation of LSD. In brief, the strategy has been one of progressive refinement in the localization of the drug's effect.

a. Dose–Response Curve. The initial assessment of the drug's action took the form of a dose–response curve. Gimpl *et al.* (1979) trained separate groups of rabbits under doses of 0 (saline, vehicle), 1, 10, 30, 100, and 300 nmol/kg IV. Different groups received 30 tone–shock pairings intermixed with 30 light–shock trials per day for 10 days. The CS–US interval was 800 msec. The study revealed a biphasic dose–response curve in which dosages of 1–100 nmol/kg significantly enhanced CR acquisition, with the maximal enhancement occurring at 30 nmol. However, the 300-nmol/kg dose retarded initial CR acquisition relative to the vehicle control.

b. Unpaired Stimulus Presentations. In assessing the dose–response curve in paired training, a parallel set of unpaired control groups received 30 tone, 30 light, and 60 shock trials per day presented in an intermixed fashion. In the unpaired groups, the level of responding to either the tone or light CS was negligible (2–4%) across all dosage levels. Thus, the enhancing effect of LSD on CR acquisition could not be attributed to such nonassociative factors as an elevation in the base rate of responding, sensitization, or pseudoconditioning. Furthermore, since no differences were apparent between responding to the tone vs. light CS in either the paired or unpaired groups, LSD's effects were not confined to input from a particular sensory modality. Although the paired vs. unpaired comparison indicated that LSD's effects acted through the contiguity component of the learning process, further assessment was required to determine whether the action of LSD would be characterized as altering the sensory processing of the stimuli, altering the effectiveness of the presumed associative connection as such, and/or facilitating motor output.

c. US–UR Assessment. The effects of LSD on the US–UR relationship have been determined by examining the amplitude of the UR to the 3-mA shock US under the various doses (Gimpl *et al.*, 1979; Experiment 1) and by examining the amplitude and frequency of URs across US amplitudes ranging from 0.0625 to 4.0 mA (Gormezano and Harvey, 1980, Experiment 2). In the case of LSD, the drug in a dose of 30 nmol failed to alter UR amplitude or to lower the threshold for UR evocation as compared to vehicle controls. In terms of the three-component model, the examination of the US–UR function suggests that LSD did not affect sensory processing of the US or motor functioning of the UR.

d. CS Manipulations. An assessment of the effects of LSD on the sensory processing of the CS in relative isolation from the learning process was made by examining CR likelihood when CS intensity is varied after CR acquisition has occurred (Gormezano and Harvey, 1980, Experiment 3). Post acquisition manipulation of the CS intensity revealed that the 30-nmol dose raised the likelihood of a CR by approximately 10 percentage points across the range of CS intensities, thus indicating lowering of the sensory threshold for evoking a CR to a tone CS. A preacquisition assessment of CS processing has been developed by using ISI–UR amplitude functions (cf. Hoffman and Ison, 1980; Ison and Leonard, 1971; Thompson, 1976), which measure the inherent capacity of the CS to modulate the UR to a weak US (Harvey and Gormezano, 1981). If LSD facilitates CS processing, then LSD should produce augmentations in UR amplitude over control levels at all but perhaps the shortest and longest CS–US intervals. Since LSD administration augmented CR acquisition and CS intensity effects on CR performance but not on measures of the US–UR, Gormezano and Harvey (1980) concluded that LSD has effects functionally equivalent to increasing the physical intensity, or salience, of the CS. In more theoretical terms, LSD may be said to have a dynamogenic effect which (*a*) augments the increment in associative strength on each CS–US trial and (*b*) potentiates current responding. Thus, an alteration in the sensory processing of the CS ramifies into the associative process. Recently, Harvey and Gormezano (1981) have applied the same battery of procedures, plus the ISI–UR amplitude procedure, to an assessment of haloperidol and found converging evidence that it depresses CS processing. Consequently, our procedures are sensitive to both incremental and decremental effects of drugs.

e. Future Assessment. The findings with LSD and haloperidol suggest that these drugs change the effective intensity (salience) of the CS, but additional questions may be raised regarding the nature of the apparent alterations in CS processing. First, do drugs alter the time course of CS processing, i.e., the form of the CS trace? The temporal properties of CS functioning can be assessed by locating CR peaks under drugs. For example, if LSD produces an increase in the speed of CS processing, then administration of LSD after CR acquisition would be expected to produce more rapid CR recruitment and a shift in the peak of the CR to a time in advance of its usual location coinciding with the time of US occurrence (cf. Smith, 1968). Second, does an alteration in CS salience lead only to an increase or decrease in the dynamogenic effects of the CS? Or does the alteration in CS salience affect the discriminability and/or attentional value of the CS? These alternatives can be operationalized by examining differential conditioning, conditional discriminations, and/or conditioned inhibition under drugs. If, for example, LSD enhances the dynamogenic effect of the CS, conditional discriminations or conditioned inhibition, which require a suppression of overt responding, may be difficult to produce. However, if LSD refines the processing of the CS, then conditioned inhibiton might be easier to establish. Similar questions can be couched in terms of signal detection theory and tested in discrimination paradigms (cf. Suboski, 1967). Specifically, if LSD shifts the animal's bias toward responding, then there would be parallel increases in the level of responding to CS+ and CS− in a differential conditioning paradigm. If LSD increases the discriminability of two different CSs, then there would be increased responding to CS+ and decreased responding to CS−. As can be seen, the systematic employment of known conditioning phenomena provides substantial power for the systematic elucidation of the modes of drug-induced alterations in acquired behavior.

VI. Conclusion

Hopefully, we have persuaded the reader that classical conditioning, in general, and the NMR preparation, in particular, are powerful tools for the investigation of a wide range of biological and psychological questions. In particular, Pavlov's intention of using classical conditioning to study the neural pathways and processes of behavioral adaptation appears to be occurring. Frankly, it has been gratifying to see neurobehavioral investigators (e.g., Thompson, 1976) adopting the rabbit NMR preparation on the basis of its well-documented and robust parametric effects. For similar reasons, the use of the NMR preparation in psychopharmacology appears to be promising. However, the original motive for developing the rabbit preparations was the need for classical conditioning data of a quality suitable for studying associative learning processes and substantiating the associative axioms of more extensive behavior theories. By the systematic study of major parameters, especially the CS–US ISI, and the detailing of CR topography, it has been possible to reveal the empirical counterparts and anomalies of the historical Law of Contiguity. Guided by CS trace theory, these data have made possible the precise measurement of the emergence and acquisition of the anticipatory CR. In the future, we hope to manipulate the moment-to-moment characteristics of the CS (e.g., frequency and amplitude) and thereby further delineate the determinants of CR timing. With the existing body of data, it has been possible to move forward on a systematic examination of CR acquisition to compounds of tone and light CSs. In these investigations, we have been able to discover processes of associative transfer which extend the temporal bounds of conditioning beyond the empirical CS–US contiguity gradient; stimulus selection which appears to attenuate CR acquisition within the bounds of empirical CS–US contiguity; and conditional discrimination which indicate the effective combination of temporally separate CSs. Thus, even the most minimal increase in the complexity of the stimulus environment has revealed that classical conditioning with the rabbit NMR preparation can be used as a behavioral test tube for revealing the laws governing the interactions and integration of the stream of stimulus events to which an organism must adapt. It appears that we have yet to reach the limits of what can be learned from rabbit preparations about conditioning and brain functioning.

Acknowledgments

The development of the rabbit conditioning preparations and the behavioral research reported were supported primarily by grants from the National Science Foundation to I. Gormezano. The research on drug effects has been supported by NIDA grant DA01759 (I.

Gormezano, Co–PI), Grants from the Australian Research Grant Committee, and the University of New South Wales Special Studies Project to E. J. Kehoe, and NIMH Grant MH 15773 to B. S. Marshall supported their participation in the preparation of the manuscript. The critical reading of the manuscript by B. G. Schreurs is gratefully acknowledged.

References

Amsel, A. (1958). The role of frustrative nonreward in noncontinuous reward situations. *Psychological Bulletin* **55,** 102–119.

Anderson, N. H. (1959). Response emission in time with applications to eyelid conditioning. *In* "Studies in Mathematical Learning Theory" (R. R. Bush and W. K. Estes, eds.), pp. 125–134. Stanford University Press, Stanford, California.

Ashton, A. B., Bitgood, S. C., and Moore, J. W. (1969). Differential conditioning of the rabbit nictitating membrane response as a function of US shock intensity and duration. *Psychonomic Science* **15,** 127–218.

Asratian, E. A. (1952). On the physiology of temporary connections. *Proceedings of Conference of Higher Nervous Activities, 15th Moscow.*

Asratian, E. A. (1966). Instrumental conditioned reflexes. *Conditional Reflexes* **2,** 258–272.

Ayres, J. J. B., Benedict, J. O., and Witcher, E. S. (1975). Systematic manipulation of individual events in a truly random control in rats. *Journal of Comparative and Physiological Psychology* **88,** 97–103.

Bekhterev, V. M. (1913) "Objektive Psychologie oder Psychoreflexologie. Die Lehre von den Assoziationsreflexen." Teubner, Leipzig.

Beritov, I. S. (Beritoff, J. S.). (1924). On the fundamental nervous processes in the cortex of the cerebral hemispheres *Brain* **47,** 109–148; 358–376.

Bernstein, A. L. (1934). Temporal factors in the formation of conditioned eyelid reactions in human subjects. *Journal of General Psychology* **10,** 173–197.

Blackman, D. (1968). Conditioned suppression or facilitation as a function of the behavioral baseline. *Journal of Experimental Analysis of Behavior* **11,** 53–61.

Blough, D. S. (1972). Recognition by the pigeon of stimuli varying in two dimensions. *Journal of Experimental Analysis of Behavior* **18,** 345–367.

Boakes, R. A., and Halliday, M. S., eds. (1972). "Inhibition and Learning." Academic Press, New York.

Boneau, C. A. (1958). The interstimulus interval and the latency of the conditioned eyelid response. *Journal of Experimental Psychology* **56,** 464–471.

Borgealt, A. J., Donahoe, J. W., and Weinstein, A. (1972). Effects of delayed and trace components of a compound CS on conditioned suppression and heart rate. *Psychonomic Science* **26,** 13–15.

Brackbill, R. M., and Overmier, J. B. (1979). Aversive CS control of instrumental avoidance as a function of selected parameters and method of Pavlovian conditioning. *Learning and Motivation* **10,** 229–244.

Brickman, A. L., and Schneiderman, N. (1977). Classically conditioned blood pressure decreases induced by electrical stimulation of posterior lateral hypothalamus in rabbits. *Psychophysiology* **14,** 287–292.

Brogden, W. J. (1939). Sensory pre-conditioning. *Journal of Experimental Psychology* **25,** 323–332.

Brogden, W. J. (1962). Contiguous conditioning. *Journal of Experimental Psychology* **64,** 172–176.

Bromage, B., and Scavio, M. J., Jr. (1978). Effects of an aversive CS+ and CS− under deprivation upon successive classical appetitive and aversive conditioning. *Animal Learning and Behavior* **6,** 57–65.

Brown, J. S. (1948). Gradients of approach and avoidance responses and their relation to level of motivation. *Journal of Comparative and Physiological Psychology* **41,** 450–465.

Brown, J. S. (1961). "The Motivation of Behavior." McGraw-Hill, New York.

Brown, T. (1977). Sketch of a system of the philosophy of the human mind. Edinburgh, 1820. *In* "Significant Contributions to the History of Psychology, 1750–1920" (D. N. Robinson, ed.), Vol. 1. University Publications of America, Washington, D.C.

Bruner, A. (1963). Investigations of the properties of the unconditioned stimulus in classical conditioning of the nictitating membrane response in the albino rabbit. Unpublished doctoral dissertation, Indiana University.

Capaldi, E. J. (1966). Partial reinforcement: a hypothesis of sequential effects. *Psychological Review* **73,** 459–477.

Cason, H. (1922). The conditioned eyelid reaction. *Journal of Experimental Psychology* **5,** 153–196.

Champion, R. A. (1962). Stimulus-response contiguity in classical aversive conditioning. *Journal of Experimental Psychology* **64,** 35–39.

Champion, R. A., and Jones, J. E. (1961). Forward, backward, and pseudoconditioning of the GSR. *Journal of Experimental Psychology* **62,** 58–61.

Chase, S., and Heinemann, E. G. (1972). Choices based on redundant information: An analysis of two-dimensional stimulus control. *Journal of Experimental Psychology* **92,** 161–175.

Chisholm, D. C., Hupka, R. B., and Moore, J. W. (1969). Auditory differential conditioning of the rabbit nictitating membrane response. II. Effects of interstimulus interval and cue similarity. *Psychonomic Science* **15,** 125–126.

Clarke, M. E., and Hupka, R. B. (1974). The effects of stimulus duration and frequency of daily preconditioning stimulus exposures on latent inhibition in Pavlovian conditioning of the rabbit nictitating membrane response. *Bulletin of the Psychonomic Society* **4,** 225–228.

Coleman, S. R. (1975). Consequences of response-contingent change in unconditioned stimulus intensity upon the rabbit (*Oryctolagus cuniculus*) nictitating membrane response. *Journal of Comparative and Physiological Psychology* **88,** 591–595.

Coleman, S. R., and Gormezano, I. (1971). Classical conditioning of the rabbit's (*Oryctolagus cuniculus*) nictitating membrane response under symmetrical CS–US interval shifts. *Journal of Comparative and Physiological Psychology* **77,** 447–455.

Coleman, S. R., and Gormezano, I. (1979). Classical conditioning and the "law of effect": Historical and empirical assessment. *Behaviorism* **7**(2), 1–33.

Deaux, E. G., and Gormezano, I. (1963). Eyeball retraction: Classical conditioning and extinction in the albino rabbit. *Science* **141**(3581), 630–631.

Dickinson, A., and Mackintosh, N. J. (1978). Classical conditioning in animals. *Annual Review of Psychology* **29,** 587–612.

Dickinson, A., and Pearce, J. M. (1977). Inhibitory interactions between appetitive and aversive stimuli. *Psychological Bulletin* **84,** 690–711.

Donahoe, J. W., and Wessells, M. G. (1980). "Learning, Language, and Memory." Harper, New York.

Egger, D. M., and Miller, N. E. (1962). Secondary reinforcement in rats as a function of information value and reliability of the stimulus. *Journal of Experimental Psychology* **64,** 97–104.

Estes, W. K. (1955). Statistical theory of spontaneous recovery and regression. *Psychological Review* **62,** 145–154.

Estes, W. K. (1959). The statistical approach to learning theory. *In* "Psychology: A Study of a Science" (S. Koch, ed.), vol. 2, pp. 380–491. McGraw-Hill, New York.

Estes, W. K., and Skinner, B. F. (1941). Some quantitative properties of anxiety. *Journal of Experimental Psychology* **29,** 390–400.

Frank, L. K. (1923). Suggestion for a theory of learning. *Psychological Review* **30,** 145–148.

Frey, P. W., Englander, S., and Roman, A. (1971). Interstimulus interval analysis of sequential CS compounds in rabbit eyelid conditioning. *Journal of Comparative and Physiological Psychology* **77,** 439–446.

Froseth, J. Z., and Grant, D. A. (1961). Influence of intermittent reinforcement upon acquisition, extinction, and spontaneous recovery in eyelid conditioning with fixed acquisition series. *Journal of General Psychology* **64,** 225–232.

Gibbs, C. M. (1976). Effects of partial reinforcement, introduced subsequent to continuous reinforcement training, on response maintenance and resistance to extinction in classical aversive and appetitive conditioning. Unpublished master's thesis, University of Iowa.

Gibbs, C. M. (1979). Serial compound classical conditioning (CS1–CS2–UCS): Effects of CS2 intensity and pretraining on component acquisition. Unpublished doctoral dissertation, University of Iowa.

Gibbs, C. M., Latham, S. B., and Gormezano, I. (1978). Classical conditioning of the rabbit nictitating membrane response: Effects of reinforcement schedule on response maintenance and resistance to extinction. *Animal Learning and Behavior* **6,** 209–215.

Gibbs, C. M., Cool, V., and Gormezano, I. (1979). Conditioning of the rabbit's nictitating membrane response under CS–CS pairings: Interstimulus interval effects. *Annual Meeting of the Midwestern Psychological Association, 51st, Chicago, May.*

Gimpl, M. P., Gormezano, I., and Harvey, J. A. (1979). Effects of LSD on learning as measured by classical conditioning of the rabbit nictitating membrane response. *Journal of Pharmacology and Experimental Therapeutics* **208,** 330–334.

Gonzalez, R. C., Longo, N., and Bitterman, M. E. (1961). Classical conditioning in the fish: Exploratory studies of partial reinforcement. *Journal of Comparative and Physiological Psychology* **54,** 452–456.

Gonzalez, R. C., Milstein, S., and Bitterman, M. E. (1962). Classical conditioning in the fish: Further studies of partial reinforcement. *American Journal of Psychology* **75,** 421–428.

Gormezano, I. (1965). Yoked comparisons of classical and instrumental conditioning of the eyelid response; and an addendum on "voluntary responders." *In* "Classical Conditioning: A Symposium" (F. Prokasy, ed.), p. 48–70. Appleton, New York.

Gormezano, I. (1966). Classical conditioning. *In* "Experimental Methods and Instrumentation in Psychology" (J. B. Sidowski, ed.), p. 385–420. McGraw-Hill, New York.

Gormezano, I. (1972). Investigations of defense and reward conditioning in the rabbit. *In* "Classical Conditioning II: Current Research and Theory" (A. H. Black and W. F. Prokasy, eds.). Appleton, New York.

Gormezano, I., and Coleman, S. R. (1973). The law of effect and CR contingent modification of the UCS. *Conditional Reflex* **8,** 41–56.

Gormezano, I., and Coleman, S. R. (1975). Effects of partial reinforcement on conditioning, conditional probabilities, asymptotic performance, and extinction of the rabbit's nictitating membrane response. *Pavlovian Journal of Biological Sciences* **10,** 80–89.

Gormezano, I., and Harvey, J. A. (1980). Sensory and associative effects of LSD in classical conditioning of rabbit (*Oryctolagus cuniculus*) nictitating membrane response. *Journal of Comparative and Physiological Psychology* **94,** 641–649.

Gormezano, I., and Kehoe, E. J. (1975). Classical conditioning: Some methodological-conceptual issues. *In* "Handbook of Learning and Cognitive Processes" (W. K. Estes, ed.), Vol. 2, p. 143–179. Erlbaum, Hillsdale, New Jersey.

Gormezano, I., and Kehoe, E. J. (1981). Classical conditioning and the law of contiguity. *In* "Advances in Analysis of Behavior" (P. Harzem and M. D. Zeiler, eds.), Vol. 2, Predictability, Correlation, and Contiguity, p. 1–45. Wiley, New York.

Gormezano, I., and Kehoe, E. J. (1982). Stimulus selection and associative transfer in classical conditioning to serial compounds: Theory and data. *In* "Conditioning, Cognition, and Methodology: Contemporary Issues in Experimental Psychology" (J. B. Sidowski and H. Hake, eds.). Erlbaum, Hillsdale, New Jersey, in press.

Gormezano, I., and Moore, J. W. (1969). Classical conditioning. *In* "Learning: Processes" (M. H. Marx, ed.). Macmillan, New York.

Gormezano, I., and Tait, R. W. (1976). The Pavlovian analysis of instrumental conditioning. *Pavlovian Journal of Biological Sciences* **11**, 37–55.

Gormezano, I., Schneiderman, N., Deaux, E. G., and Fuentes, I. (1962). Nictitating membrane: Classical conditioning and extinction in the albino rabbit. *Science* **138**, 33–34.

Grant, D. A. (1943). Sensitization and association in eyelid conditioning. *Journal of Experimental Psychology* **32**(2), 201–212.

Grant, D. A., and Schipper, L. M. (1952). The acquisition and extinction of conditioned eyelid responses as a function of the percentage of fixed-ratio random reinforcement. *Journal of Experimental Psychology* **43**, 313–320.

Gray, J. A. (1975). "Elements of a Two-Process Theory of Learning." Academic Press, New York.

Gray, T. S., McMaster, S. E., Harvey, J. A., and Gormezano, I. (1981). Localization of retractor bulbi motoneurons in the rabbit. *Brain Research* **226**, 93–106.

Guthrie, E. R. (1930). Conditioning as a principle of learning. *Psychological Review* **37**, 412–418.

Guthrie, E. R. (1933). Association as a function of time interval. *Psychological Review* **40**, 355–367.

Guthrie, E. R. (1935). "The Psychology of Learning." Harper, New York.

Guthrie, E. R. (1952). "The Psychology of Learning" (Revised Ed.). Harper, New York.

Guthrie, E. R. (1959). Association by contiguity. *In* Psychology: A Study of a Science" (S. Koch, ed.), Vol. 2. McGraw-Hill, New York.

Hall, J. F. (1976). "Classical Conditioning and Instrumental Learning: A Contemporary Approach." Lippincott, Philadelphia, Pennsylvania.

Hartman, T. F., and Grant, D. A. (1960). Effect of intermittent reinforcement on acquisition, extinction, and spontaneous recovery of the conditioned eyelid response. *Journal of Experimental Psychology* **60**, 89–96.

Harvey, J. A., and Gormezano, I. (1981). Effects of haloperidol and pimozide on classical conditioning of the rabbit nictitating membrane response. Unpublished observations.

Hearst, E. (1972). Some persistent problems in the analysis of conditioned inhibition. *In* "Inhibition and Learning" (R. A. Boakes and M. S. Halliday, eds.). Academic Press, New York.

Herendeen, D., and Anderson, D. C. (1968). Dual effects of a second-order conditioned stimulus: Excitation and inhibition. *Psychonomic Science* **13**, 15–16.

Heth, D. C., and Rescorla, R. A. (1973). Simultaneous and backward fear conditioning in the rat. *Journal of Comparative and Physiological Psychology* **82**, 434–443.

Hilgard, E. R. (1931). Conditioned eyelid reactions to a light stimulus based on the reflex wink to sound. *Psychological Monographs* **41**(184).

Hilgard, E. R. (1936a). The nature of the conditioned response. I. The case for and against stimulus substitution. *Psychological Review* **43**, 366–385.

Hilgard, E. R. (1936b). The nature of the conditioned response. II. Alternatives to stimulus substitution. *Psychological Review* 43, 547–564.

Hilgard, E. R. (1937). The relationship between the conditioned response and conventional learning experiments. *Psychological Bulletin* **34**, 61–102.

Hilgard, E. R. (1948). "Theories of Learning." Appleton, New York.

Hilgard, E. R., and Marquis, D. G. (1940). "Conditioning and Learning." Appleton, New York.

Hoehler, F. K., and Leonard, D. W. (1973). Classical nictitating membrane conditioning in the rabbit (*Oryctolagus cuniculus*): Single alternation with differential intertrial intervals. *Journal of Comparative and Physiological Psychology* **85,** 277–288.

Hoffman, H., and Ison, J. R. (1980). Reflex modification in the domain of startle: I. Some empirical findings and their implications for how the nervous system processes sensory input. *Psychological Review* **87,** 175–189.

Holland, P. C. (1977). Conditioned stimulus as a determinant of the form of the Pavlovian conditioned response. *Journal of Experimental Psychology: Animal Behavior Processes* **3,** 77–104.

Holland, P. C., and Rescorla, R. A. (1975). Second-order conditioning with food unconditioned stimulus. *Journal of Comparative and Physiological Psychology* **88,** 459–467.

Holmes, J. D. (1971). Effects of backward pairings of the CS and US on classical conditioning of the nictitating membrane response in the rabbit. Doctoral dissertation, University of Iowa.

Holt, E. B. (1931). Animal Drive and the Learning Process. Holt, New York.

Hull, C. L. (1929). A functional interpretation of the conditioned reflex. *Psychological Review* **36,** 498–511.

Hull, C. L. (1930). Knowledge and purpose as habit mechanisms. *Psychological Review* **37,** 511–525.

Hull, C. L. (1931). Goal attraction and directing ideas conceived as habit phenomena. *Psychological Review* **38,** 487–506.

Hull, C. L. (1934). The rat's speed-of-locomotion gradient in the approach to food. *Journal of Comparative Psychology* **17,** 393–422.

Hull, C. L. (1937). Mind, mechanism, and adaptive behaviors. *Psychological Review* **44,** 1–32.

Hull, C. L. (1943). "Principles of Behavior." Appleton, New York.

Hull, C. L. (1952). "A Behavior System." Yale University Press, New Haven, Connecticut.

Hunt, H. F. and Brady, J. V. (1951). Some effects of electroconvulsive shock on conditioned emotional response (anxiety). *Journal of Comparative and Physiological Psychology* **44,** 88–98.

Hupka, R. B., Liu, S. S., and Moore, J. W. (1969). Auditory differential conditioning of the rabbit nictitating membrane response: V. Stimulus generalization as a function of the composition of CS+ and CS− on the frequency dimension. *Psychonomic Science* **15,** 129–131.

Ison, J. R., and Leonard, D. W. (1971). Effects of auditory stimuli on the amplitude of the nictitating membrane reflex of the rabbit, (Oryctolagus cuniculus), *Journal of Comparative and Physiological Psychology* **75,** 157–164.

Jones, J. E. (1961). The CS-UCS interval in conditioning short- and long-latency responses. *Journal of Experimental Psychology* **62,** 612–617.

Jones, J. E. (1962). Contiguity and reinforcement in relation to CS–UCS intervals in classical aversive conditioning. *Psychological Review* **69,** 176–186.

Kamin, L. J. (1963). Backward conditioning and the conditioned emotional response. *Journal of Comparative and Physiological Psychology* **56,** 517–519.

Kamin, L. J. (1965). Temporal and intensity characteristics of the conditioned stimulus. *In* "Classical Conditioning: A Symposium" (W. F. Prokasy, ed.), p. 118–147. Appleton, New York.

Kamin, L. J. (1968). Attention-like processes in classical conditioning. *In* "Miami Symposium on the Prediction of Behavior: Aversive Stimulation" (M. R. Jones, ed.). University of Miami Press, Miami, Florida.

Kamin, L. J. (1969). Selective association and conditioning. *In* "Fundamental Issues in Associative Learning" (N. J. Mackintosh and F. W. K. Honig, eds.). Dalhousie University Press, Halifax.

Kehoe, E. J. (1976). Effects of serial compound stimuli on stimulus selection in classical conditioning of the rabbit nictitating membrane response. Doctoral dissertation, University of Iowa.

Kehoe, E. J. (1979). The role of CS–US contiguity in classical conditioning of the rabbit's nictitating membrane response to serial stimuli. *Learning and Motivation* **10**, 23–38.

Kehoe, E. J. (1981). Stimulus selection and combination in classical conditioning with the rabbit. *In* "Classical Conditioning" (I. Gormezano, W. F. Prokasy, and R. F. Thompson, eds.). Erlbaum, Hillsdale, New Jersey, in press.

Kehoe, E. J., and Gormezano, I. (1980). Configuration and combination laws in conditioning with compound stimuli. *Psychological Bulletin* **87**, 351–378.

Kehoe, E. J., Gibbs, C. M. Garcia, E., and Gormezano, I. (1979). Associative transfer and stimulus selection in classical conditioning of the rabbit's nictitating membrane response to serial compound CSs. *Journal of Experimental Psychology: Animal Behavior Processes* **5**, 1–18.

Kehoe, E. J., Feyer, A., and Moses, J. L. (1981a). Second-order conditioning of the rabbit's nictitating membrane response as a function of the CS2–CS1 and CS1–US intervals. Unpublished observations.

Kehoe, E. J., Schreurs, B. G., and Amodei, N. (1981). Blocking acquisition of the rabbit's nicititating membrane response to serial conditioned stimuli. *Learning and Motivation* **12**, 92–108.

Kimble, G. A. (1947). Conditioning as a function of the time between conditioned and unconditioned stimuli. *Journal of Experimental Psychology* **37**, 1–15.

Kimble, G. A. (1961). "Hilgard and Marquis' Conditioning and Learning" (2nd Ed.). Appleton, New York.

Kimmel, H. D. (1965). Instrumental inhibitory factors in classical conditioning. *In* "Classical Conditioning" (W. F. Prokasy, ed.). Appleton, New York.

Kimmel, H. D., and Burns, R. A. (1975). Adaptational aspects of conditioning. *In* "Handbook of Learning and Cognitive Processes" (W. K. Estes, ed.), Vol. 2. Erlbaum, Hillsdale, New Jersey.

Konorski, J. (1948). "Conditioned Reflexes and Neuron Organization." Cambridge University Press, London and New York.

Konorski, J. (1967). "Integrative Activity of the Brain." University of Chicago Press, Chicago, Illinois.

Lashley, K. S. (1916). The human salivary reflex and its use in psychology. *Psychological Review* **23**, 446–464.

Lashley, K. S. (1929). Learning: I. Nervous-mechanisms of learning. *In* "The foundations of experimental psychology" (C. Morechison, ed.). Clark University Press, Worcester, Massachusetts.

Lashley, K. S. (1942). An examination of the "continuity theory" as applied to discriminative learning. *Journal of General Psychology* **26**, 241–265.

Latham, S. B. (1971). Effects of percentage reinforcement shifts on the classically conditioned nictitating membrane response in the rabbit. Doctoral dissertation, University of Iowa.

Liu, S. S., and Moore, J. W. (1969). Differential conditioning of the rabbit nictitating membrane response: IV. Training based on stimulus offset and the effect of intertrial tone. *Psychonomic Science* **15**, 128–129.

Logan, F. A. (1956). A micromolar approach to behavior theory. *Psychological Review* **63**, 63–73.

Logan, F. A., and Wagner, A. R. (1965). "Reward and Punishment." Allyn and Bacon, Boston, Massachusetts.

Longo, N., Milstein, S., and Bitterman, M. E. (1962). Classical conditioning in the pigeon: Exploratory studies of partial reinforcement. *Journal of Comparative and Physiological Psychology* **55**, 983–986.

Longo, N., Klempay, S., and Bitterman, M. E. (1964). Classical appetitive conditioning in the pigeon. *Psychonomic Science* **1,** 19–20.
Loucks, R. B. (1935). The experimental delimitation of neural structures essential for learning: The attempt to condition striped muscle responses with faradization of the sigmoid gyri. *Journal of Psychology* **1,** 5–44.
Loucks, R. B., and Gantt, W. H. (1938). The conditioning of striped muscle responses based upon faradic stimulations of dorsal roots and dorsal columns of the spinal cord. *Journal of Comparative Psychology* **25,** 415–426.
Lubow, R. E. (1973). Latent inhibition. *Psychological Bulletin* **79,** 398–407.
Lucas, G. A., Vodraska, A., and Wasserman, E. A. (1979). A direct fluid delivery system for the pigeon. *Journal of Experimental Analysis of Behavior* **31,** 285–288.
McAllister, W. R. (1953). Eyelid conditioning as a function of the CS–UCS interval. *Journal of Experimental Psychology* **45,** 417–422.
Mackintosh, N. J. (1975). A theory of attention: Variation in the associability of stimuli with reinforcement. *Psychological Review* **82,** 276–298.
Mackintosh, N. J. (1976). Overshadowing and stimulus intensity. *Animal Learning and Behavior* **4,** 186–192.
Marchant, H. G., III, and Moore, J. W. (1974). Below-zero conditioned inhibition of the rabbit's nictitating membrane response. *Journal of Experimental Psychology* **102,** 350–352.
Marchant, H. G., III, Mis, F. W., and Moore, J. W. (1972). Conditioned inhibition of the rabbit's nictitating membrane response. *Journal of Experimental Psychology* **95,** 408–411.
Marchant, H. G., III, and Moore, J. W. (1973). Blocking of the rabbit's conditioned nictitating membrane response in Kamin's two-stage paradigm. *Journal of Experimental Psychology* **101,** 155–158.
Marshall, B. S., Gray, T. S., and Gormezano, I. (1980). Classical differential conditioning of the rabbit's nictitating membrane response to serial compound CS's as a function of component CS duration. *Annual Meeting of the Midwestern Psychological Association, 52nd, St. Louis, May.*
Martin, I., and Levey, A. B. (1969). "The Genesis of the Classical Conditioned Response." Pergamon, Oxford.
Matsumiya, Y. (1960). The effects of US intensity and CS–US pattern on conditioned emotional response. *Japanese Psychological Research* **2,** 35–42.
Millenson, J. R., Kehoe, E. J., and Gormezano, I. (1977). Classical conditioning of the rabbit's nictitating membrane response under fixed and mixed CS–US intervals. *Learning and Motivation* **8,** 351–366.
Miller, N. E. (1944). Experimental studies of conflict. *In* "Personality and the Behavior Disorders" (J. McV. Hunt, ed.). Ronald Press, New York.
Miller, N. E. (1963). Some reflections on the law of effect produce a new alternative to drive reduction. *Nebraska Symposium on Motivation, Lincoln.*
Mis, F. W., and Moore, J. W. (1973). Effect of preacquisition UCS exposure on classical conditioning of the rabbit's nictitating membrane response. *Learning and Motivation* **4,** 108–114.
Mitchell, D. S., and Gormezano, I. (1970). Water deprivation effects in classical appetitive conditioning of the rabbit's jaw movement response. *Learning and Motivation* **1,** 199–206.
Moore, J. W. (1972). Stimulus control: Studies of auditory generalization in rabbits. *In* "Classical Conditioning II: Current Research and Theory" (A. H. Black and W. F. Prokasy, eds.). Appleton, New York.
Moore, J. W. (1979). Brain processes and conditioning. *In* "Mechanisms of Learning and Motivation: A Memorial Volume to Jerzy Konorski" (A. Dickinson and R. A. Boakes, eds.). Erlbaum, Hillsdale, New Jersey.
Moore, J. W., and Stickney, K. J. (1980). Formation of attentional-associative networks in real

time: Role of the hippocampus and implications for conditioning. *Physiological Psychology* **8,** 207–217.

Moscovitch, A., and LoLordo, V. M. (1968). Role of safety in the Pavlovian backward fear conditioning procedure. *Journal of Comparative and Physiological Psychology* **66,** 673–678.

Mowrer, O. H. (1947). On the dual nature of learning—a reinterpretation of "conditioning" and "problem solving." *Harvard Educational Review* **17,** 102–148.

Mowrer, O. H. (1951). Two-factor learning theory: Summary and comment. *Psychological Review* **58,** 350–354.

Mowrer, O. H. (1960). "Learning Theory and Behavior." Wiley, New York.

Mowrer, O. H., and Aiken, E. G. (1954). Contiguity vs. drive reduction in conditioned fear: Temporal variations in conditioned and unconditioned stimulus. *American Journal of Psychology* **67,** 26–38.

Mpitsos, C. J., Collins, S., and McClellan, A. (1978). Learning: A model system for physiological studies. *Science* **199,** 497–506.

O'Malley, P., Hupka, R. B., and Moore, J. W. (1969). Auditory differential conditioning of the rabbit nictitating membrane response. I. Effects of mixed- and separate-phase training. *Psychonomic Science* **15,** 123–124.

Overmier, J. B. (1980). Personal communication.

Overmier, J. B., and Lawry, J. A. (1979). Pavlovian conditioning and the mediation of behavior. *In* "The Psychology of Learning and Motivation" (G. Bower, ed.), Vol. 13. Academic Press, New York.

Overmier, J. B., and Schwarzkopf, K. H. (1974). Summation of food and shock based responding. *Learning and Motivation* **5,** 42–52.

Overmier, J. B., and Seligman, M. E. P. (1967). Effects of inescapable shock upon subsequent escape and avoidance responding. *Journal of Comparative and Physiological Psychology* **63,** 28–33.

Patterson, M. M. (1970). Classical conditioning of the rabbit's *(Oryctolagus cuniculus)* nictitating membrane response with fluctuating ISI and intracranial CS. *Journal of Comparative and Physiological Psychology* **72,** 193–202.

Pavlov, I. P. (1927). "Conditioned Reflexes" (translated by G. V. Anrep). Oxford University Press, London and New York.

Pavlov, I. P. (1928). "Lectures on Conditioned Reflexes" (translated by W. H. Gantt). International Publishers, New York.

Pavlov, I. P. (1932). The reply of a physiologist to psychologists. *Psychological Review* **39,** 91–127.

Peak, H. (1933a). Reflex and voluntary reactions of the eyelid. *Journal of General Psychology* **8,** 130–156.

Peak, H. (1933b). An evaluation of the concepts of reflex and voluntary action. *Psychological Review* **40,** 71–89.

Pearce, J. M., and Hall, G. (1980). A model for Pavlovian learning: Variations in the effectiveness of conditioned but not of unconditioned stimuli. *Psychological Review* **87,** 532–552.

Perin, C. T. (1942). Behavior potentiality as a joint function of the amount of training and the degree of hunger at the time of extinction. *Journal of Experimental Psychology* **30,** 93–113.

Perry, S. L., and Moore, J. W. (1965). The partial-reinforcement effect sustained through blocks of continuous reinforcement in classical eyelid conditioning. *Journal of Experimental Psychology* **69,** 158–161.

Poulos, C. X., Sheafor, P. J., and Gormezano, I. (1971). Classical appetitive conditioning of the rabbit's *(Oryctolagus cuniculus)* jaw movement response with a single-alternation schedule. *Journal of Comparative and Physiological Psychology* **75,** 231–238.

Prokasy, W. F. (1965). Classical eyelid conditioning: Experimenter operations, task demands, and response shaping. *In* "Classical Conditioning" (W. F. Prokasy, ed.). Appleton, New York.

Rachlin, H. (1976). "Behavior and Learning." Freeman, San Francisco, California.

Randich, A., and LoLordo, V. M. (1979). Associative and nonassociative theories of the UCS preexposure phenomenon: Implications for Pavlovian conditioning. *Psychological Bulletin* **86,** 523–548.

Razran, G. (1965). Empirical codification and specific theoretical implications of compound-stimulus conditioning: Perception. *In* "Classical Conditioning" (W. Prokasy, ed.). Appleton, New York.

Razran, G. (1971). "Mind in Evolution: An East-West Synthesis of Learned Behavior and Cognition." Houghton, New York.

Rescorla, R. A. (1967). Pavlovian conditioning and its proper control procedures. *Psychological Review* **74,** 71–80.

Rescorla, R. A. (1969). Pavlovian conditioned inhibition. *Psychological Bulletin* **72,** 77–94.

Rescorla, R. A. (1972). Informational variables in Pavlovian conditioning. *In* "The Psychology of Learning and Motivation" (G. Bower, ed.), Vol. 6. Academic Press, New York.

Rescorla, R. A. (1973). Second-order conditioning: Implications for theories of learning. *In* "Contemporary Approaches to Conditioning and Learning" (F. J. McGuigan and D. B. Lumsden, eds.). Winston, Washington, D.C..

Rescorla, R. A. (1975). Pavlovian excitatory and inhibitory conditioning. *In* "Handbook of Learning and Cognitive Processes." (W. K. Estes, ed.), Vol. 2. Erlbaum, Hillsdale, New Jersey.

Rescorla, R. A. (1977). Pavlovian second-order conditioning: Some implications for instrumental behavior. *In* Operant-Pavlovian Interactions (H. Davis and H. M. B. Hurwitz, eds.). Erlbaum, Hillsdale, New Jersey.

Rescorla, R. A., and Solomon, R. (1967). Two-process learning theory: Relationships between Pavlovian conditioning and instrumental learning. *Psychological Review* **74,** 151–182.

Rescorla, R. A., and Wagner, A. R. (1972). A theory of Pavlovian conditioning: Variations in the effectiveness of reinforcement and nonreinforcement. *In* "Classical Conditioning II: Current Theory and Research" (A. Black and W. F. Prokasy, eds.). Appleton, New York.

Riley, D. A., and Leith, C. R. (1976). Multidimensional psychophysics and selective attention in animals. *Psychological Bulletin* **83,** 138–160.

Robinson, E. S. (1932). "Association Theory Today." Century, New York.

Ross, L. E. (1959). The decremental effects of partial reinforcement during acquisition of the conditioned eyelid response. *Journal of Experimental Psychology* **57,** 74–82.

Rudy, J. W., and Wagner, A. R. (1975). Stimulus selection in associative learning. *In* "Handbook of Learning and Cognitive Processes" (W. K. Estes, ed.), Vol. 2. Erlbaum, Hillsdale, New Jersey.

Saavedra, M. A. (1975). Pavlovian compound conditioning in the rabbit. *Learning and Motivation,* **6,** 314–326.

Sampson, L., Francis, J., and Schneiderman, N. (1974). Selective autonomic blockades: Effects upon classical conditioning of heart rate and lever-lift suppression in rabbits. *Journal of Comparative and Physiological Psychology* **87,** 953–962.

Scavio, M. J., Jr. (1972). Classical-classical transfer: Effects of prior classical aversive conditioning upon classical appetitive conditioning. Doctoral dissertation, University of Iowa.

Scavio, M. J., Jr. (1974). Classical-classical transfer: Effects of prior aversive conditioning upon appetitive conditioning in the rabbit. *Journal of Comparative and Physiological Psychology* **86,** 107–115.

Scavio, M. J., Jr., and Gormezano, I. (1974). CS intensity effects upon rabbit nictitating membrane conditioning, extinction, and generalization. *Pavlovian Journal of Biological Sciences* **9,** 25–34.

Scavio, M. J., Jr., and Gormezano, I. (1980). Classical-classical transfer: Effects of prior appetitive conditioning upon aversive conditioning in rabbits. *Animal Learning and Behavior* **8,** 218–224.

Schlosberg, H. (1937). The relationship between success and the laws of conditioning. *Psychological Review* **44,** 379–394.

Schneiderman, N. (1966). Interstimulus interval function of the nictitating membrane response in the rabbit under delay versus trace conditioning. *Journal of Comparative and Physiological Psychology* **62,** 397–402.

Schneiderman, N. (1970). Determinants of heart rate classical conditioning. *In* "Current Issues in Animal Learning" (J. H. Reynierse, ed.). University of Nebraska Press, Lincoln, Nebraska.

Schneiderman, N. (1972). Response system divergences in aversive classical conditioning. *In* "Classical Conditioning II: Current Theory and Research" (A. H. Black and W. F. Prokasy, eds.). Appleton, New York.

Schneiderman, N., and Gormezano, I. (1964). Conditioning of the nictitating membrane of the rabbit as a function of CS–US interval. *Journal of Comparative and Physiological Psychology* **57,** 188–195.

Schneiderman, N., Fuentes, I., and Gormezano, I. (1962). Acquisition and extinction of the classically conditioned eyelid response in the albino rabbit. *Science* **136,** 650–652.

Schneiderman, N., Smith, M. C., Smith, A. C., and Gormezano, I. (1966). Heart rate classical conditioning in rabbits. *Psychonomic Science* **6,** 39–40.

Schreurs, B. G., and Gormezano, I. (1980). Classical conditioning of the rabbit's nictitating membrane response to compound and component stimuli as a function of component pretraining. *Annual Meeting of the Midwestern Psychological Association, 52nd, St. Louis.*

Schurr, B. C., and Runquist, W. N. (1973). Acquisition and extinction of the human eyelid CR as a function of the schedule of reinforcement and UCS intensity under two masked conditioning procedures. *Journal of Experimental Psychology* **101,** 398–401.

Scobie, S. R. (1972). Interaction of an aversive Pavlovian conditional stimulus with aversively and appetitively motivated operants in rats. *Journal of Comparative and Physiological Psychology* **79,** 171–188.

Seligman, M. E. P., and Maier, S. F. (1967). Failure to escape traumatic shock. *Journal of Experimental Psychology* **74,** 1–9.

Seraganian, P. (1979). Extradimensional transfer in the easy-to-hard effect. *Learning and Motivation* **10,** 39–57.

Sheafor, P. J. (1975). "Pseudoconditioned" jaw movements of the rabbit reflex associations conditioned to contextual background cues. *Journal of Experimental Psychology: Animal Behavior Process* **104,** 245–260.

Sheafor, P. J., and Gormezano, I. (1972). Conditioning the rabbit's *(Oryctolagus cuniculus)* jaw-movement response: US magnitude effects on URs, CRs, and pseudo-CRs. *Journal of Comparative and Physiological Psychology* **81,** 449–456.

Sheffield, F. D. (1965). Relation between classical conditioning and instrumental learning. *In* "Classical Conditioning" (W. F. Prokasy, ed.). Appleton, New York.

Sheffield, V. F. (1949). Extinction as a function of partial reinforcement and distribution of practice. *Journal of Experimental Psychology* **39,** 511–526.

Siegal, S., and Domjan, M. (1971). Backward conditioning as an inhibitory procedure. *Learning and Motivation* **2,** 1–11.

Singh, S. D. (1959). Conditioned emotional responses in the rat: I. Constitutional and situational determinants. *Journal of Comparative and Physiological Psychology* **52,** 574–578.

Skinner, B. F. (1937). Two types of conditioned reflex: A reply to Konorski and Miller. *Journal of General Psychology* **16,** 272–279.

Skinner, B. F. (1938). "The Behavior of Organisms: An Experimental Analysis." Appleton, New York.

Smith, A. C. (1966). The effects of locus of application and intensity of the unconditioned stimulus on conditioning of the nictitating membrane and heart rate responses in the rabbit. Doctoral dissertation, Indiana University.

Smith, M. C. (1968). CS–US interval and US intensity in classical conditioning of the rabbit's nictitating membrane response. *Journal of Comparative and Physiological Psychology* **66**, 679–687.

Smith, M. C., and Gormezano, I. (1965). Effects of alternating classical conditioning and extinction sessions on the conditioned nictitating membrane of the rabbit. *Psychonomic Science* **3**, 91–92.

Smith, M. C., Coleman, S. R., and Gormezano, I. (1969). Classical conditioning of the rabbit's nictitating membrane response at backward, simultaneous, and forward CS–US intervals. *Journal of Comparative and Physiological Psychology* **69**, 226–231.

Smith, M. C., DiLollo, V., and Gormezano, I. (1966). Conditioned jaw movement in the rabbit. *Journal of Comparative and Physiological Psychology* **62**, 479–483.

Smith, S., and Guthrie, E. R. (1921). "General Psychology in Terms of Behavior." Appleton, New York.

Solomon, P. R., and Moore, J. W. (1975). Latent inhibition and stimulus generalization of the classically conditioned nictitating membrane response in rabbits *(Oryctolagus cuniculus)* following dorsal hippocampal ablation. *Journal of Comparative and Physiological Psychology* **89**, 1192–1203.

Solomon, P. R., Brennan, G., and Moore, J. W. (1974a). Latent inhibition of the rabbit's nictitating membrane as a function of CS intensity. *Bulletin of the Psychonomic Society* **4**, 557–559.

Solomon, P. R., Lohr, A. G., and Moore, J. W. (1974b). Latent inhibition of the rabbit's nictitating membrane responses: Summation tests for active inhibition as a function of number of CS pre-exposures. *Bulletin of the Psychonomic Society* **4**, 557–559.

Spence, K. W. (1956). "Behavior Theory and Conditioning." Yale University Press, New Haven, Connecticut.

Spence, K. W., and Trapold, M. A. (1961). Performance in eyelid conditioning as a function of reinforcement schedules and changes in them. *Proceedings of the National Academy of Sciences of the U.S.A.* **47**, 1860–1868.

Stewart, M. A., Stern, J. A., Winokur, G., and Fredman, S. (1961). An analysis of GSR conditioning. *Psychological Review* **68**, 60–67.

Suboski, M. D. (1967). The analysis of classical discrimination conditioning experiments. *Psychological Bulletin* **68**, 235–242.

Sutherland, N. S., and Mackintosh, N. J. (1971). "Mechanisms of Animal Discrimination Learning." Academic Press, New York.

Tait, R. W. (1974). Assessment of the bidirectional conditioning hypothesis through the UCS_1–UCS_2 conditioning paradigm. Unpublished doctoral dissertation, University of Iowa.

Tait, R. W., Kehoe, E. J., and Gormezano, I. (1981). Effects of US duration on classical conditioning of the rabbit's nictitating membrane response. Unpublished observations.

Theios, J. (1972). Formalization of Spence's dual process model for eyelid conditioning. *In* "Classical Conditioning II: Current Theory and Research" (A. H. Black and W. F. Prokasy, eds.). Appleton, New York.

Thomas, E., and Wagner, A. R. (1964). Partial reinforcement of the classically conditioned eyelid response in the rabbit. *Journal of Comparative and Physiological Psychology* **58**, 157–158.

Thompson, R. F. (1976). The search for the engram. *American Psychologist* **31**, 209–227.

Thompson, R. F., Patterson, M. M., and Teyler, T. J. (1972). The neurophysiology of learning. *Annual Review of Psychology* **23**, 73–104.

Thorndike, E. L. (1913). "The Psychology of Learning." Columbia University Press, New York.

Trapold, M. A., and Overmier, J. B. (1972). The second learning process in instrumental conditioning. *In* "Classical Conditioning" (A. H. Black and W. F. Prokasy, eds.). Appleton, New York.

Trapold, M. A., Homzie, M., and Rutledge, E. (1964). Backward conditioning and UCR latency. *Journal of Experimental Psychology* **67**, 387–391.

Vardaris, R. M., and Fitzgerald, R. D. (1969). Effects of partial reinforcement on a classically conditioned eyeblink response in dogs. *Journal of Comparative and Physiological Psychology* **67**, 531–534.

Venables, P. H., and Martin, I. (1967). The relation of palmar sweat gland activity to level of skin potential and conductance. *Psychophysiology* **3**, 302–311.

Wagner, A. R., and Rescorla, R. A. (1972). Inhibition in Pavlovian conditioning: Application of a theory. *In* "Inhibition and Learning" (R. A. Boakes and M. S. Halliday, eds.). Academic Press, New York.

Wahlsten, D. L., and Cole, M. (1972). Classical and avoidance training of leg flexion in the dog. *In* "Classical Conditioning II: Current Research and Theory" (A. H. Black and W. F. Prokasy, eds.). Appleton, New York.

Wasserman, E. A. (1973). Pavlovian conditioning with heat reinforcement produces stimulus-directed pecking in chicks. *Science* **181**, 875–877.

Watson, J. B. (1925). "Behaviorism." Norton, New York.

Weinstock, S. (1970). Contiguity theory. *In* "Learning: Theories" (M. H. Marx ed.). Macmillan, New York.

Wickens, D. D. (1954). Stimulus-response theory as applied to perception. "Kentucky Symposium on Learning Theory and Personality." Wiley, New York.

Wickens, D. D. (1959). Conditioning to complex stimuli. *American Psychologist* **14**, 180–188.

Wickens, D. D. (1965). Compound conditioning in humans and cats. *In* "Classical Conditioning: A Symposium" (W. F. Prokasy, ed.). Appleton, New York.

Wickens, D. D. (1973). Classical conditioning, as it contributes to the analyses of some basic psychological processes. *In* "Contemporary Approaches to Conditioning and Learning" (F. J. McGuigan and D. B. Lumsden, eds.). Wiley, New York.

Wilson, G. T., and Davison, G. C. (1971). Processes of fear reduction in systematic desensitization: Animal studies. *Psychological Bulletin* **76**, 1–14.

Wilson, W. R. (1924). Selection in "trial and error". *Psychological Review* **31**, 150–160.

Wolfle, H. M. (1932). Conditioning as a function of the interval between the conditioned and original stimulus. *Journal of General Psychology* **7**, 80–103.

Woodruff, G., and Williams, D. R. (1976). The associative relation underlying autoshaping in the pigeon. *Journal of Experimental Analysis of Behavior* **26**, 1–13.

Young, F. A. (1958). Studies of pupillary conditioning. *Journal of Experimental Psychology* **55**, 97–110.

Zeiner, A., and Grings, W. W. (1968). Backward conditioning: A replication with emphasis on conceptualizations by the subject. *Journal of Experimental Psychology* **76**, 232–235.

Author Index

G

I

J

K

L

M

Q

R

S

W

Y

Subject Index